Poetic Justice

Poetic Justice

REREADING PLATO'S *REPUBLIC*

Jill Frank

The University of Chicago Press   CHICAGO & LONDON

The University of Chicago Press, Chicago 60637
The University of Chicago Press, Ltd., London
© 2018 by The University of Chicago
All rights reserved. No part of this book may be used or reproduced in any manner whatsoever without written permission, except in the case of brief quotations in critical articles and reviews. For more information, contact the University of Chicago Press, 1427 East 60th Street, Chicago, IL 60637.
Published 2018

27 26 25 24 23 22 21 20 19 18   2 3 4 5

ISBN-13: 978-0-226-51563-2 (cloth)
ISBN-13: 978-0-226-51577-9 (paper)
ISBN-13: 978-0-226-51580-9 (e-book)
DOI: 10.7208/chicago/9780226515809.001.0001

Library of Congress Cataloging-in-Publication Data

Names: Frank, Jill, author.
Title: Poetic justice : rereading Plato's Republic / Jill Frank.
Description: Chicago ; London : The University of Chicago Press, 2018. | Includes bibliographical references and index.
Identifiers: LCCN 2017025972 | ISBN 9780226515632 (cloth : alk. paper) | ISBN 9780226515779 (pbk. : alk. paper) | ISBN 9780226515809 (e-book)
Subjects: LCSH: Plato. Republic. | Reading—Philosophy. | Philosophy, Ancient.
Classification: LCC JC71.P6 F735 2018 | DDC 321/.07—dc23
LC record available at https://lccn.loc.gov/2017025972

*To the memory of Hershey (Harold) Frank and the
imagination of Alexander and Abigail*

Lucky the man who at that time was skilled in song. . . . Now that everything has been shared out and the arts possess their boundaries, so that we [poets] place last in the race, there is nowhere for [the poet] to steer his freshly-yoked chariot, though he may search everywhere.

CHOERILUS OF SAMOS' LAMENT (*SH 317*), trans. Michael Kicey

CONTENTS

Acknowledgments ix

    Prologue: Learning to Read   1

1 Reading Plato   19
    Reading, writing, fathers, and kings   21
    How Plato wrote   27
    Mimetic poetry   33
    Mirrors   34
    Representation   38
    Resistance and self-authorization   41

2 Poetry: The Measure of Truth   50
    Alienating authority, fathers again   55
    Poetry silenced   60
    Forms, knowledge, looks, simulacra   62
    Poetry's use   69
    Poetry's reason   71
    Poetry's benefit   75

3 A Life without Poetry   81
    The brothers' desire   82
    Warriors, guardians, dogs   86
    Poets, founders, gods   89
    Simple minds   92
    Obedience, domination, calculation, injustice   98
    An aischropolis   105
    Justice in and by itself   109

4	The Power of Persuasion	111
	Compulsion	115
	Deception	118
	A grammatical interlude	122
	Elenchos	123
	Persuading in the middle voice	127
	Analogy	131
	Free and beautiful discussions	135
5	*Erōs*: The Work of Desire	141
	Philosopher-kings, philosophers by nature, philosophical erotics	145
	Desiring possession	151
	Ladders, immortality, instrumentality	154
	Genesis, reproduction in difference, belonging	159
	Framing desire	163
	Erōs *and philosophy*	167
	Necessity, tyranny, and democracy	169
6	Dialectics: Making Sense of *Logos*	172
	Provocatives	176
	What do I see? or, The powers of sense perception	183
	What do I think? or, Having an opinion	189
	What do I make of it? or, Measuring, incommensurability, relationality	192
	Framing knowledge	196
	Impostures, images, truth	199
	Willing to pay attention, an attitude of soul, phronēsis	202
	A city in logos	206
	Epilogue: Poetic Justice	210
	Seeming, being, doing	215
	Judging, appearances, imagination	217
	*No harm, one man:one ar*t	221
	Political philosophy	224

Work Cited 227
Index 243

ACKNOWLEDGMENTS

When the "healthy city" is first mentioned in *Republic* 2, it appears to need only four or five men: a farmer, a builder, a weaver, and a shoemaker. With the origin of the city lying "in the fact that we are not, any of us, self-sufficient," and the introduction of the one man:one art principle, however, the city immediately swells to include carpenters, blacksmiths, skilled workers, cattlemen, shepherds, other herdsmen, importers, exporters, traders, merchants, seafarers, and laborers, and more (369b–371e), Socrates implies, to infinity. The same may be said of the one person:one art principle that has been the writing of this book, for its appearance and *logoi*—its words, arguments, and reasons—are the product of what feels like a near infinity of engagements. It can be hard to keep track of infinity, so apologies in advance to anyone I may inadvertently neglect to mention in these acknowledgments.

For helpful feedback on individual chapters, I am grateful to audiences and discussants at Cambridge, Cornell, Duke, Johns Hopkins, McGill, Northwestern, Princeton, Sarah Lawrence, Tufts, University of California, Berkeley, University of Chicago, University of Georgia, Athens, University of Michigan, University of North Carolina at Chapel Hill, University of South Carolina, University of Virginia, University of Wisconsin–Madison, and Yale, as well as at meetings of the American Political Science Association, the Association for Political Theory, the Conference for the Study of Political Thought, and the Western Political Science Association. For conversations and comments on particular chapters, my thanks go to Larissa Atkison, Andreas Avgousti, Ryan Balot, Harry Berger Jr., Ronna Bloom, Susan Buck-Morss, Joy Connolly, Susan Courtney, Michael Davis, Alex Dressler, Peter Euben, Jason Frank, Marcie

Frank, Stephen Halliwell, Don Herzog, Bonnie Honig, Rayna Kalas, Athena Kirk, Barbara Leckie, Miriam Leonard, Nina Levine, Nancy Luxon, Patchen Markell, Allen Miller, Christopher Moore, Nina Valiquette Moreau, Sheindal Muller, Jennifer Pitts, Verity Platt, Aziz Rana, Esther Richey, Diane Rubenstein, Neil Saccamano, Steve Salkever, Arlene Saxonhouse, George Shulman, Christina Tarnopolsky, and Rachel Templer. Janet Safford provided exceptionally able research assistance for the duration of this project, from near and far. For their research help, I thank Ani Chen and Jordan Jochim as well.

For incisive, productive, and probing comments on iterations of the whole manuscript, I thank Will Altman, Larry Glickman, Melissa Lane, Alex Livingston, John Lombardini, Shalini Satkunanandan, Joel Schlosser, and Doug Thompson. For the gifts of their interlocution, time, and commitment to the work of this book in whole and in parts, and repeatedly, I am immensely grateful to Gerry Mara and Mike Kicey, and to the latter, additionally, for reading Plato's *Sophist* with me and for being a consistently invaluable resource for all things Greek. I am deeply thankful for the example, enthusiasm, and encouragement of Peter Euben. Without the inspiration, generosity, and complicity of Harry Berger Jr. this book would not be. Mistakes remain my own.

I first learned how to reread from and with Esther Frank, in the company of Marcie and, later, Adam. From Hershey Frank I learned about doing no harm. Both kinds of learning continue with Esther, Marcie, and Adam, with my extended families Frank, Pask, Glickman, and Levine, with friends, colleagues, and students, and especially with Larry and Alexander and Abigail, to whose life-sustaining relationships this book is deeply indebted.

The rereading practice I deploy in the following pages also has roots in the weekly Greek Philosophy Reading Group at the University of South Carolina, Columbia, inaugurated by Allen Miller, Jan Opsomer, and Rosamond Kent Sprague, and continued by Heike Sefrin-Weis. It developed, in that context, with Heike Sefrin-Weis and, in and outside that context, in ongoing dialogue with the inspiriting and indefatigable Allen Miller. I am grateful to Mary Anne Fitzpatrick for making possible the Classics in Contemporary Perspectives Initiative at the University of South Carolina, which, from 2008 to 2014, supported a vibrant scholarly community across disciplines in the arts and sciences that, in addition to the Political Science Department, was my intellectual home. For their collegiality and congeniality at the University of South Carolina, I thank Dan Sabia and Don Fowler, and, more recently, Doug Thompson. For funding and research support as I completed this book, I thank Cornell University. For the opportunity to read the *Republic* with fresh eyes after moving to Cornell, and the provocations that produced, my thanks go to the students in my graduate seminar on Plato in fall 2014 and to participants in the 2014–15 Mellon Sawyer Seminar on Political Will. In its earliest stages, this project benefited from a sabbatical leave at the University Center for Human Values at Princeton University, under the directorship of Anthony Appiah, for which I have Steve Macedo to thank.

Thanks to John Tryneski and Rodney Powell for their ongoing interest in and patience with this project, and to Chuck Myers, Holly Smith, Marian Rogers, Kelly Finefrock-Creed, and Melinda Kennedy for shepherding it to completion. Material in chapter 3 and the epilogue overlaps and revises work appearing in "Wages of War: On Judgment in Plato's *Republic*," *Political Theory* 35 (2007): 443–67. Material in chapter 1 draws on work appearing in "Circulating Authority: Plato, Politics, and Political Theory," in *Radical Future Pasts: Untimely Political Theory*, edited by Romand Coles, Mark Reinhardt, and George Shulman (Lexington: University Press of Kentucky, 2014), 333–50. Material in the prologue appears in "How Oligarchy Breeds Tyranny," *Public Books*, 3.7.2017, http://www.publicbooks.org/how-oligarchy-breeds-tyranny/.

The cover image captures part of an installation of plaster casts displayed at Cornell University in a fall 2014 exhibit, titled *Firing the Canon*, curated and restored by Annetta Alexandridis and Verity Platt, colleagues in Art History and Classics. Seen as secondhand copies of the originals, the casts, from a Cornell collection of nineteenth-century casts of Grecian, Roman, Egyptian, and medieval pieces, were packed away in the mid-twentieth century, becoming damaged and vandalized by graffiti until their restoration for the 2014 exhibit. The cover cast in its installation at the exhibit depicts the copy as art, announcing itself as such by the graffitied "I'M ART" etched on the cast's torso. Part of that depiction appears in the excerpted photograph on this book's cover. Taken by Abigail Glickman, the full photograph presents the argument of my book at a glance: for, in my view, Plato's dialogues are best read not as copies of conversations but as representations at a third remove from the truth, as per the definition of *mimēsis* in *Republic* 10, that, like the cast, announce themselves as art by Plato's conspicuous artistry as a writer. Reading Plato as a mimetic poet cum graffiti artist is my contribution to "firing the canon."

PROLOGUE

Learning to Read

Nosce teipsum, read thyself.
THOMAS HOBBES, *Leviathan*

Some years ago, I attended an off-Broadway double bill: a performance of Aristotle's *Poetics*, followed by Plato's *Symposium*. I wasn't sure what to expect of the solo recitation of the *Poetics*, adapted from Gerald F. Else's translation and commentary, but I was looking forward to the *Symposium*. At the time, I was near the beginning of the project that was to become this book, and, already convinced of Plato's "dramatic genius," I anticipated that seeing the *Symposium* performed would enliven my appreciation of Plato's text. The "learned and endearingly loopy" "disquisition" of Aristotle's *Poetics* turned out to be illuminating and moving.[1] The performance of the *Symposium* felt flat. That may have been a function of the two productions' differing dramaturgical choices or the acting, but the more I thought about it the more I began to wonder whether there might be something about Plato's dialogues that requires that they be neither performed nor heard in real time, but read. And reread.[2]

That wonder guides this book. That Plato wrote his dialogues in the middle 300s BCE when literacy was expanding, but set them earlier, in late fifth-century BCE Athens, when performance and oral recitation were still important modes of text dissemination, and that a number of dialogues explicitly thematize the

---

1. Phrases in this paragraph are from Isherwood, "Checking in with the Glimmer Twins." I was especially excited about the success of the *Poetics* performance because of my long-standing sense that Aristotle's writings are other than conventional treatises: see my "Political Theory of Classical Greece"; and *Democracy of Distinction*.

2. On the importance of reading and rereading Plato's texts, see Halliwell, "Life-and-Death Journey of the Soul"; Gill, *Philosophos*, 12–13.

practice of learning to read, encouraged me to think more about Plato, reading, and writing.³ I was intrigued to notice two different approaches to learning to read in the dialogues. One approach, appearing in the *Statesman*, *Sophist*, and *Protagoras*, treats learning to read as a "top-down" affair, a function of being taught by an authoritative teacher. Another approach, appearing in the *Republic* and *Theaetetus*, focuses on students' experiences of letters or letter combinations, and the opinions they come to have about those letters based on their experiences.⁴

Exemplifying the authoritative teacher, the Eleatic visitor in the *Statesman* maintains that "the easiest and best way of leading, *epagein*," children to letters that they do not yet know is to "take [children] first back, *anagein*, to those cases in which they were getting these same things right" (278a), that is, to short syllables in which they are already able to distinguish individual letters well enough (277e). The next step is to set

> these [letters] beside what they're not yet recognizing. By comparing them, we demonstrate that there is the same kind of thing with similar features in both combinations, until the things that they are getting right have been shown set beside all the ones that they don't know . . . and so become models, *paradeigmata*. (278a-b)⁵

In the *Sophist*, the Eleatic maintains that to know which letters properly bond together requires being taught an art or technique—a *technē*—specifically, the

---

3. The poetry of the ancient world was typically sung, and even such lengthy texts as Herodotus' *Histories*, completed in the 420s, were typically disseminated by being performed orally: Harris, *Ancient Literacy*, 80. For the position, based on primary source material, including poetry, drama, steles, oratory, vase painting, public documents, and juridical and legal tasks distributed by sortition, that by the fourth century, if not by the late fifth century, there already existed a general readership at Athens, see Pébarthe, *Cité, démocratie et écriture*; Missiou, *Literacy and Democracy*; Svenbro, *Phrasikleia*; Harvey, "Literacy in the Athenian Democracy"; Knox, "Silent Reading in Antiquity." Allen, *Why Plato Wrote*, 5, argues that "Plato could imagine a general reader for his dialogues, and . . . developed a mode of philosophical writing that anticipated such readers even in advance of their general emergence." On when Plato wrote, see also Gerson, *From Plato to Platonism*, 78 ff.

4. Throughout this book, I use translations, modified at times, of Plato's *Republic* by Bloom; Grube, rev. Reeve, in *Plato's Complete Works*, ed. Cooper; Griffith; and Shorey; along with the Greek text and commentary by James Adam. Translations of other dialogues are from the Loeb Library and *Plato's Complete Works*.

5. For discussion, see Lane, *Method and Politics*, 66–67.

art of grammar (253a-e). In the *Protagoras*, Protagoras describes the Athenian practice of compelling, *anangkazein*, students to trace letters, written in outline by their teachers (326d), so that, having learned their letters, the students may be compelled, *anangkazein*, to read the works of good poets and to learn them by heart (325e–326a). Across this group of dialogues the vocabulary of learning to read structures the situation in terms of passive, imitative students and active, authoritative teachers: leading (*epagein/anagein*), modeling (*paradeigmata*), compelling (*anangkazein*).

The element of compulsion in Protagoras' account distinguishes it from the account offered in the *Sophist* and *Statesman*, as does the fact that Protagoras in the eponymous dialogue is describing the conduct of aristocratic education, *paideia*, in democratic Athens, whereas the Eleatic is setting forth an ideal paradigm of pedagogy based on expertise. What allows all three examples to be grouped together, nonetheless, is that they construct learning to read as a transitive act whereby authoritative teachers lead students to true beliefs about letters and words and their order, guard against the formation of false opinions, and correct (or punish) grammatical and orthographical mistakes, drawing outside the lines. Vases, jugs, and pottery fragments from the late fifth century were inscribed with alphabets, dictation exercises, and substitution tables, depicting "a keen appreciation of the function of drill as an indispensable aid to certain types of memorization."[6]

In the view of Jacques Rancière, among others, the approach to teaching by an authoritative teacher who models "mastery" was perfected by Socrates, and the exemplary authoritative teacher is Plato, the "Old Master" par excellence.[7] For his part, Rancière advocates instead for learning without "explication," which means learning without a teacher, an emancipatory practice that involves the undivided power of saying and speaking and paying attention to what one sees and says. Calling specifically for the will to learn attention without "cheating" by recourse to incapacity ("I can't"), learning without explication involves asking: "What do you see? what do you think about it? what do you make of it?"[8]

To be sure, the approach to learning opposed by Rancière and calling for an authoritative teacher and pliable students appears in the *Protagoras*, *Sophist*,

---

6. Beck, *Album of Greek Education*, 16.

7. Rancière, *Ignorant Schoolmaster*, 29, 94. On Socrates as, by contrast, the embodiment of the "ignorant schoolmaster" celebrated by Rancière, see Schlosser, *What Would Socrates Do?*, 38–39.

8. Rancière, *Ignorant Schoolmaster*, 23.

and *Statesman*. But the position that Rancière advocates for appears in Plato's dialogues as well. Indeed, learning to read is depicted precisely as learning without explication in the *Republic*, for example, when Socrates says to Glaucon: "We could do it [i.e., read] as soon as we realized that there are only a few letters, and that they keep recurring in all the words which contain them. We never dismissed them as unworthy of our attention, either in short or long words, but were keen to recognize them everywhere, in the belief that we wouldn't be able to read until we could do this" (402a-b). Desire, belief, and attention are all key to this account. In the *Theaetetus*, too, Socrates recommends that he and his interlocutor Theaetetus "examine ourselves" to see how it was "that we learned letters" (203a). Socrates prompts Theaetetus to remember his true *and* false beliefs about the letters, letter combinations, and names he first saw, drawing on his own sense perceptual and cognitive experiences (206a).

In one approach, an authoritative teacher models well-shaped letters and permissible letter combinations to students who imitate the teacher until they master the skill.[9] In the other, learners experience letters and actively reflect on these experiences to imagine the form, range, and use of the letters. The different perspectives within which these two accounts of achieving literacy operate are equally rooted in the Greek term that the dialogues use to refer to the letters that combine to make words, namely, *stoicheia*.[10] This term, which translates as "element, unit, or fundamental principle," confers "the connotation of order and system, . . . a series of entities that can be commanded, regulated."[11] Thus, a matter of command and regulation, learning to read in either approach is fundamentally a political matter.[12] That learning to read is offered as an analogy for coming to know in all five dialogues, and is presented across the dialogues as "all-important to the formation of the human soul," and that, in the *Republic*, it is offered specifically as an analogy for coming to know justice in our souls, whose smaller letters we approach by reading the large letters of city justice (368d-369a), makes learning to read a matter of ethics and philosophy as well.[13]

---

9. The authoritative teacher approach to learning to read itself divides into two: in the *Protagoras*, the teacher models true letters before determining whether the students have gotten them right, whereas in the *Statesman* this happens afterward.

10. For appearances of *stoicheion* in these dialogues, see *Republic* 402a; *Statesman* 278d; *Sophist* 252b; *Theaetetus* 201e, 202b, e, 203a, b, c, d, e, 205b, d, 206a, b.

11. This description of *stoicheia* belongs to Muller, *Lectures on the Science of Language*, 88-90, quoted in Berger, *Perils of Uglytown*, 207-8.

12. On the eighteenth-century "disciplinary" operations of learning to read, see Foucault, *Discipline and Punish*, 159.

13. The quoted phrase is from Allen, *Why Plato Wrote*, 33.

When we are taught to read by an authoritative teacher, reading is "a means of assimilating beliefs that can govern action," beliefs that are determined as true and vouchsafed by one already in possession of knowledge.[14] These beliefs are transmitted by "implantation," or by way of what Socrates, in the *Phaedrus*, refers to as a kind of "soul writing" (276a, 278a). Assuming and reinforcing an inequality based on expertise, this approach to learning to read traces, underwrites, and reinscribes the account of philosophy as authoritative knowledge often associated with the philosopher-kings of the *Republic*. It lends force as well to the authoritarian politics associated with that philosophy. Depicting learning as a practice of assimilating the true beliefs of authoritative teachers, becoming literate by implantation also habituates students to depend on their teachers for their reading, knowledge, and soul formation. On the authoritative teacher approach to learning to read, what makes Plato, in Diogenes Laertius' words, "a politician or political leader," a *politikos*, is his success at reproducing, in and for political life, the subordination depicted in his texts of the "unlearned" to the learned.[15]

The second approach to literacy learning, with its focus on the sensory and cognitive experiences of learners, offers a different story about knowledge and soul formation in Plato's dialogues. This book tells that story, along with its associated philosophy, ethics, and politics. Taking Plato to have a complex, "entangled," interventionist, and meliorist relationship with his contemporary democratic Athens, I read his dialogues, and the *Republic* in particular, not as endorsing and enforcing fixed hierarchies in knowledge and politics, but as offering instead an education in ethical and political *self*-governance.[16] From this perspective, learning to read in the mode of the *Republic* and *Theaetetus* not only functions as an agency of authorization within readers qua citizens, but also underwrites relations among citizens that are lateral and interactional, which is to say, dialogical.

---

14. Allen, *Why Plato Wrote*, 50, who shows (chaps. 2–4) how the argument about soul writing in the *Phaedrus*, there (paradoxically) about oral dialectic, may be extended to writing. I address the treatment of writing in the *Phaedrus* in chapter 1.

15. Diog. Laert. 3.23, cited by Allen, *Why Plato Wrote*, 76. For "unlearned," see Allen, 28–29; also Arendt, "Pursuit of Happiness," 115. To Allen, Plato's "comprehensive theory of language" underwrites "the conversion of his metaphysical commitments into an enacted anti-democratic politics" through a refashioning of Athenian political language (19).

16. For "entangled," see Monoson, *Plato's Democratic Entanglements*. For other political theorists who read Plato's political thought in this way and upon whose work I build, see Euben, *Corrupting Youth*; Mara, *Socrates' Discursive Democracy*; Recco, *Athens Victorious*; Saxonhouse, "Socratic Narrative"; Schlosser, *What Would Socrates Do?*; Tarnopolsky, *Prudes, Perverts, and Tyrants*; Wallach, *Platonic Political Art*.

A few more words, then, about this second approach. What might the exercise of attention, perception, evaluation, analysis, synthesis, and correction look like in a student learning to read, and how might these practices operate by analogy in coming to know? In the *Theaetetus*, as noted, Socrates says that learning to read calls for self-examination (203a). In the *Republic*, he says that it calls for looking at everything everywhere, at the greatest things, "and all their kin, and, again, their opposites, which are moving around everywhere, *kai hosa toutōn adelpha kai ta toutōn au enantia pantachou peripheromena*" (402c). Socrates says we must see the greatest things "in all the things in which they are, both themselves and their images, *en hois enestin . . . kai auta kai eikonas autōn*" (402c), "whether in short words or in long, *out' en smikrō out' en megalō*" (402a-b), and that we must develop "the sharpest sense for what's been left out and what isn't a fine product of craft or what isn't a fine product of nature, *tōn paraleipomenōn kai mē kalōs dēmiourgēthentōn ē mē kalōs phuntōn oxutat' an aisthanoito*" (401e). Calling "knowledge of both large and small letters . . . part of the same craft and discipline, *mēte en smikrois mēte en megalois . . . alla tēs autēs oiōmetha technēs einai kai meletēs*" (402c), Socrates offers a robust and demanding account of what it takes to become "a skilled reader" (402b).[17]

By binding together literacy learning and philosophy in an analogy, Socrates also offers a robust and demanding account of coming to know. Indeed, over the course of the *Republic*, once the analogy is carried over into philosophy, Glaucon, Socrates' primary interlocutor in this dialogue, notes more than once that the kind of study Socrates adumbrates will take hard work, *ergon* (511c, 530c, 531d). It also calls for play (537a, 602b). It depends, in any case, on activity on the part of learners, activity not infrequently refused by Socrates' interlocutors, including Glaucon in the *Republic* and the eponymous Theaetetus, whom some scholars take to be among the most promising interlocutors across Plato's oeuvre.[18] As we will see in chapter 6, Theaetetus does not take up Socrates' invitation to examine his own experiences of learning to read.

17. The myth of Er uses similar language regarding the ability and knowledge to "distinguish the good life from the bad" so as to be able "choose always and everywhere . . . the life which is better" (618c).

18. For Glaucon, and sometimes Adeimantus, as most promising and also as "ideal readers" of the *Republic*, see, e.g., Lear, "Allegory and Myth in Plato's *Republic*," 36. On Glaucon's philosophical promise, see Blondell, *Play of Character*, 219-20, 333; Bloom, "Interpretive Essay," in *Republic of Plato*, 411; Dobbs, "Choosing Justice," 263; Roochnik, *Beautiful City*, 56. On Theaetetus, see Zuckert, *Plato's Philosophers*, 630. For questions about Theaetetus' promise, see Stern, *Knowledge and Politics in Plato's "Theaetetus*," 206, 218-19.

Glaucon, for his part, tends to prefer not to search and discover things on his own but instead to follow Socrates' lead (427d-e, 432c, 445c, 474c, 596a). I show in chapter 1 that these refusals on the part of Socrates' audiences within the dialogues prompt a second shift of address to an audience of other learners, namely, the growing body of literate citizens of mid-fourth-century Athens who form Plato's readership, and modern and contemporary readers of Plato's dialogues as well.

So, what happens if, in an effort to become what Socrates calls skilled readers, we try to look at everything everywhere in Plato's texts?[19] In the dialogues' abundant analogies and examples, fables, allegories, parables, myths, and similes, alongside more conventionally linear styles of argumentation, we are given a multitude of letters both big and small. We see a variety of personalities and hear diverse points of view, presented in verse and prose, in images and arguments, for and against Athenian popular morality and democratic institutions, and put variously in the mouths of politicians, sophists, lawgivers, and philosophers. We see much movement, and also a great deal of play, by way of the dialogues' embedding frames and complex narrative and dialogic structures, to say nothing of the careful anachronisms that make the dialogues' dates notoriously difficult to pinpoint in time, and the fictive or semifictive characters, usually named after real-life personages. Plato's variety of style and tone, his dramatization of disagreement, the dynamism of the personalities he depicts, and, above all, the playfulness he puts to work in all of these registers open questions of authority and authorship that inform our experiences as we read his dialogues and as we learn to read by reading them.

Do the figures of philosophic authority in the dialogues (Socrates, for example; the Eleatic in the *Statesman* and *Sophist*; Diotima in the *Symposium*; the Athenian in the *Laws*) represent the philosophy of Plato? Does the great

---

19. In looking at everything everywhere in Plato's texts, I ally with scholars from diverse interpretative perspectives who attend to the relationship between form and argument in the dialogues, and also with those who are, in the words of Annas and Rowe, *New Perspectives on Plato*, ix, skeptical of "the long-accepted paradigm for interpreting Plato ... that rests on a broad division of the dialogues" into early (and Socratic), middle, and late. In looking at everything everywhere, I also ally with scholars who read across Plato's dialogues, though I do so agreeing with Gill, "Dialectic and the Dialogue Form," 146, that each dialogue "constitutes a dialectical and dramatic unit, and that philosophical interpretation needs to register this fact," which is to say that I seek from the dialogues I read together not a "Platonic doctrine" (Gill, 160) of persuasion or *erōs* but instead links that might help to explain what these practices amount to, and I do so taking seriously what Gill calls the "striking combination of an aspiration to universality and of localization" (154) in Plato's dialogues. See also McCabe, "Plato's Ways of Writing."

speech of Protagoras in his eponymous dialogue represent the philosophic position of that real-life sophist?[20] Does Socrates' impersonation of Protagoras in the *Theaetetus*? Does the speech of Lysias in the *Phaedrus* reproduce an actual speech by the real-life orator Lysias? Were the fragments of Simonides that are preserved exclusively in Plato's texts written by Plato, or are they words shaped, sung, and written by Simonides? How are we to read these representations? What is their authority? And how are we to read dialogues like the *Theaetetus* and *Symposium*, in which we are told that the dialogues' narrators couldn't remember what they heard, or fell asleep and thus didn't hear at all? Or dialogues that depict characters, such as Callicles in the *Gorgias* or Diotima in the *Symposium*, whose lives are not attested outside of Plato's texts? Or dialogues that depict actual historical characters, portrayed in ways that invite questions about what they stand for: is the *Republic*'s Thrasymachus, for example, the real-life rhetor who aspires to practice justice as the advantage of the stronger or an ambassador from Chalcedon presenting justice in this way to shame Athenian imperialists who are exercising this form of "justice" against his city?[21] What are we to make of Aristophanes or Agathon or Alcibiades in the *Symposium* or Parmenides in the dialogue by that name? The complex, apparently composite, temporalities of the dialogues also invite questions. It's not only that some dialogues, like the *Republic*, are depicted as taking place, as Debra Nails puts it, "throughout the Peloponnesian War,"[22] and so over the unlikely course of thirty years, but also that dialogues with supposedly secure dramatic dates, like the *Symposium*, offer conflicting internal evidence for their dates of composition and/or their dramatic dates.[23]

These elements of play, as well as others, make manifest that the dialogues are staged.[24] They open the possibility, noted as well by other scholars, that, contra Socrates in the *Phaedrus* (275d), Plato's writing, with its pluralities of standpoint, disposition, image, and style of argumentation, may not be static and univocal, saying the same thing over and over again, but moving, kinetic,

---

20. See, e.g., Schiller, *Plato or Protagoras?*; Farrar, *Origins of Democratic Thinking*, 47–77.

21. See White, "Thrasymachus the Diplomat."

22. Nails, *People of Plato*, 326.

23. Bury, ed., *Symposium of Plato*, sec. viii; Nussbaum, *Fragility of Goodness*, 167–70. Rutherford, "Comments on Nightingale," 253, notes that "Athenaeus remarked that 'Plato makes many blunders in violation of chronology' (5.217c)." I agree with Rutherford that Plato "has other ends in view besides historical accuracy" (253).

24. See Von Reden and Goldhill, "Plato and the Performance of Dialogue"; Puchner, *Drama of Ideas*; and Folch, *City and the Stage*.

and polyphonic.[25] These elements prompt the "spectators" of Plato's play, that is to say, Plato's readers, to look at everything everywhere in Plato's texts. We become skilled readers of these texts in the sense offered by Socrates in the *Republic* and *Theaetetus*, I argue, not by deferring to the knowledge associated with the figures of philosophical authority in the dialogues but instead by scrutinizing the authority of that knowledge, by demanding its accountability and transparency, and by refusing it when it does not satisfy our demands. When we read Plato's dialogues in the way Socrates invites his interlocutors to do in the *Republic* and *Theaetetus*, what makes Plato a *politikos*, a politician, is that his texts, by way of their complex uses of time, character, authorship, and authority, prompt readers to develop our own ethical, political, and philosophical capacities, based on our own perceptual and cognitive experiences, as engaged, if always fallible, readers.[26]

In virtue of their multiplicity and intricacy, Plato's dialogues, it might be said, display something like the "many-colored beauty, *poikilia*," Socrates attributes to the democratic constitution in *Republic* 8 (557c).[27] Like that constitution, which Socrates likens to a "bazaar" because it contains constitutions of all kinds, available for the picking by anyone who wants to order their city (557d), Plato's dialogues similarly license readings of many kinds. If the dialogues compel no one reading, then any particular reading, including the one I offer in this book, will, like the performance of the *Symposium* I saw in 2007, be partial and fallible, itself an opinion based on a given reader's experiences of the text. Hannah Arendt says that "for mortals, the important thing is to make *doxa* truthful, to see in every *doxa* truth and to speak in such a way that the truth of one's opinion reveals itself to oneself and to others."[28] This book is my attempt to bring to light the truth of my opinion that Plato's dialogues, and the *Republic* in particular, offer an education to ethical, political, and philosophical self-governance.

---

25. For writing as static, see Allen, *Why Plato Wrote*, 25; and Halperin, "Plato and the Erotics of Narrativity," 116. For Plato as polyphonic, see Euben, *Corrupting Youth*, 218–26. For the importance of movement in Plato's *Laws*, see McWilliams, *Traveling Back*, 26–32. See also Strauss, *City and Man*, 52–53.

26. In *Philosopher's Song*, 141–72, Crotty describes Plato's *Sophist* as inaugurating what he calls a "metaphysics of fallibility," which he argues appears in the *Statesman* and *Laws* but not the *Republic*. I see such a metaphysics in the *Republic*.

27. On *poikilia*, see Monoson, *Plato's Democratic Entanglements*, chap. 8; and on the potentialities of the democratic bazaar, see Mara, *Civic Conversations of Thucydides and Plato*, 189–94.

28. Arendt, "Socrates," 19.

Does not couching this book as opinion, however, by the *Republic*'s own lights, put its epistemic status immediately in question? Why write a book that, in the language of Socrates' account of opinion in *Republic* 5, may be "brighter than ignorance, *agnoia*," but is "darker than knowledge, *gnōseōs*" (478c-d)? Should this book's readers not be dissatisfied with that which "wanders" between what is "absolutely and unqualifiedly knowable" and what is "in every way unknowable" (476e-477a), what "rolls around, *kulindeitai*," in the "mid-region between that which is not and that which is in the true and absolute sense" (479d)? If the *Republic* presents opinion and its lovers, *philodoxoi* (480a), like sights and sounds and their lovers, *philotheamones* (475d), as inferior to wisdom and its lovers, *philosophoi*, what is to be gained by calling this book "opinion," which, as what "both is and is not" (478d), is uncertain, questionable, and in question?

I locate this book between infallible knowledge and always only fallible, which is to say, equally infallible ignorance, because, as we will see, the site of opinion, sights, and sounds turns out, on my reading, also to be the site of justice, the central topic of the *Republic*, which Socrates, using the same word he will use about opinion in *Republic* 5, describes, in *Republic* 4, as "rolling around, *kulindeisthai*, at our feet" (432d). I locate this book in the "middle" (479d) between knowledge and ignorance because although the *Republic* distinguishes lovers of opinion from lovers of wisdom on the ground that the latter, but not the former, are lovers of truth, Socrates also insists that lovers of sights and sounds "bear a certain likeness, *homoious*, to philosophers." They are all "spectators, *philotheamonas*," he says (475d-e). That lovers of what appears true or seems so to the eyes and ears are spectators is obvious enough. Lovers of wisdom, for their part, are spectators as *theōroi*.[29] Having regard for what may not be seen, they see that appearances, like opinions, may not tell the whole truth.

Plato's readers tend to focus largely on the differences among these lovers. I, too, am interested in their differences. I am also, however, interested in how seeing by looking affiliates them. As we have seen, in the *Republic*, Socrates describes coming to know, by analogy to learning to read, as a practice of looking at everything everywhere, at "the greatest things," "and all their kin, and, again, their opposites," and as seeing these greatest things "in the things in which they are, *both themselves and their images*" (401e, 402c, my emphasis).

---

29. On *theōria*, see Nightingale, *Spectacles of Truth*. On the etymology of *theōria* and its relation to spectatorship, see Monoson, *Plato's Democratic Entanglements*, 206, 88–110; and McWilliams, *Traveling Back*, 24–26.

Socrates thus appears to associate coming to know the greatest things with the coming to appearance of "images." I seek to show over the course of this book that the "middle" where these modes of knowing meet articulates the site of the *Republic*'s distinctively *political* philosophy.

In my view, as noted, that political philosophy is offered as and by way of an education to ethical and political self-governance. While claiming that the *Republic* is about ethical self-governance is uncontroversial—no one would deny that the *Republic* is a dialogue about how to bring about harmony and justice in one's soul—calling the *Republic* an education in political self-governance is more controversial, for there is no disputing the fact that the text is critical of the constitution associated with political self-governance, namely, democracy. As described in *Republic* 4–5, soul justice in the ideal city is foreclosed to all but the few who are capable of philosophizing (431c). In *Republic* 6, Socrates compares the *dēmos* to an unruly beast (493a-c), and, in *Republic* 8, he links the democratic constitution's "many-colored beauty" to modes of freedom and equality that orient to anarchy and, seemingly inevitably, to tyranny (557c, 564a).[30] The dialogue also portrays Athens' late fifth-century democratic authorities—poets, rhetors, and politicians—in an exceedingly unappealing light.[31] Separately and together, this evidence points not to self-governance by the *dēmos* as the pedagogic goal of the dialogue, but instead, as the "third wave" of *Republic* 5 announces, to rule by philosopher-kings over the *dēmos* (473d).

As will come to light in the following chapters, I find the dialogue's brief in favor of philosopher-kings and its case against democracy to be less obvious than they may seem. For a sense of how I proceed, consider Glaucon's announcement in *Republic* 9 that monarch and tyrant are "exact opposites, *pan tounantion*" (576d). Glaucon's conclusion stands to reason against the backdrop of the dialogue's extended contrast between the perfectly just soul of *Republic* 4–6's philosopher-king, on the one hand, who is the "best and most just character," the "happiest," "most kingly, the one who is king over himself," and, on the other, "the worst and most unjust" soul of the one who is "unhappiest" and "the greatest tyrant over himself and his city" (580c). Given this backdrop, it even makes sense to take Glaucon's verdict to be the judgment of the dialogue as a whole.

As we will see in detail over the course of this book, however, the dialogue also gives readers reasons to wonder about the overall quality of Glaucon's

---

30. On the absence of *eidē* in democracy, see Saxonhouse, "Democracy, Equality, and *Eidê*." On democratic tyranny, see Landauer, "*Idiōtēs* and the Tyrant."

31. For discussion, see Nightingale, *Genres in Dialogue*.

judgment. There are, in any case, textual grounds for wondering about the truth of what Socrates calls Glaucon's "decree" (580c). For if monarch and tyrant are, indeed, "exact opposites," then what are we to make of what Hannah Arendt has called the "fatal resemblance between Plato's philosopher-king and the Greek tyrant"?[32] Arendt does not mention what these are, but they are myriad. Socrates describes both sets of rulers as rising to power by chance (499b; 578c) and after their respective cities have been "wiped clean" (501a; 567c). Both sets of rulers are said to maintain their power through deception, force, and stealth (414b–415d, 459c–d; 565b, c, 566e, 573e–574b), with the help of auxiliaries or bodyguards, *boēthous* (420a; 566b), and in the company of both male and female friends (466c–d, 540c; 568e).[33] Both sets of rulers are prohibited from traveling abroad (420a; 579b–c). On the part of both sets of rulers, there is the potential of envy and hate (417a–b; 579c) and harm (416a–b; 569b) toward those they rule. Socrates describes both the tyrant, as noted above, and the philosopher-kings (419–421c) as unhappy. These textual parallels are too numerous and striking to ignore. They suggest that, *pace* Glaucon's strict opposition between tyrant and philosopher-king, this may be a case where opposites coincide.

To mark these resemblances is not yet to offer an argument. That will come in the chapters that follow. My point for now is that it might be expected that these resemblances would provoke Socrates' interlocutors to wonder. Given how important the happiness of the rulers of the ideal city was to Adeimantus at the beginning of *Republic* 4 (419c), why does he not return to their unhappiness in *Republic* 9 to ask after its relation to the unhappiness of tyrants? Given the anxiety both brothers repeatedly express in *Republic* 2 about the stealth and deception employed by tyrants (361a, 365c–d, 367c), it might be expected that they would wonder about these practices when Socrates associates them with the philosopher-kings in *Republic* 3 and 5. Glaucon and Adeimantus don't wonder. But readers might. And if we do, we might also ask whether Plato may have Socrates present tyrant and philosopher-king as "exact opposites"—that is, mirror images—precisely to provoke questions about their resemblances, and about Socrates' interlocutors' failure to ask these same

---

32. Arendt, "What Is Authority?," 107.

33. When the "auxiliaries" to the guardians are first introduced in *Republic* 3, Ferrari indicates, *Republic*, 107 n. 62, that "in addition to its general meaning, the term can be used to refer to mercenary troops (compare Adeimantus' complaint at 419a), as well as to a tyrant's bodyguard, which was typically composed of such mercenaries."

questions. These are possibilities of interpretation I explore in chapters 3 and 4, where I argue that they emerge from the text not "in spite of Plato" but rather, as I show in chapters 1 and 2, because of Plato, that is, as legible effects of how Plato wrote.[34]

The text of the *Republic*, as many scholars note, is set in the "shadow of the Thirty" tyrants and is concerned with, among other things, the dangers of tyranny.[35] When such a text offers a putative counterideal to the tyrant in the philosopher-king, but at the same time exhibits a range of provocative resemblances between these types, that may be an invitation to think twice about the kind of authority the dialogue vests in philosopher-kings. If, as we are told, their compelled and compelling rule is justified on the ground that they bring justice to the souls of those who are unable to do so themselves, what are we to make of the fact that those very souls remain unjust? Might it be that the *Republic* stages *failures* on the part of the philosopher-kings to meet the conditions of their own authorization in order to criticize the authority it appears to advance?[36] What if instead of advocating on behalf of that authority, the dialogue seeks rather to cultivate an awareness of the perils and fallibility of authority of *all* kinds, including that of philosophy, and of the ways in which acquiescence to authority, including philosophical authority, can, when unchecked, pass into tyranny? As we will see, the *Republic*'s brief in favor of philosopher-kings opens to these questions.

So, too, do its arguments against democracy. While, as noted, Socrates calls the *dēmos* an unruly beast in *Republic* 6, he also admonishes a contemptuous Adeimantus not to be "so hard on the many" (499d-e). Socrates links democratic freedom and equality with anarchy and tyranny in *Republic* 8, saying that it is by being "aided and abetted by the folly of the common people, *meta dēmou anoias*," that a tyrant rises to power, and that a tyrant becomes "most

---

34. I take this phrase from Adriana Cavarero, *In Spite of Plato*.

35. Ferrari, *City and Soul in Plato's "Republic,"* 11, among others, notes that the *Republic* is set in the "shadow of the Thirty."

36. In the *Republic*, the philosophical authority under scrutiny is that of the philosopher-kings. In other dialogues, under scrutiny is the philosophical authority of the Eleatic visitor (*Sophist, Statesman*), Diotima (*Symposium*), and the Athenian visitor (*Laws*). Where Socrates appears, his philosophical authority is subject to scrutiny as well. I say more about Socrates across the chapters that follow. For a valuable exploration of Socrates across Plato's dialogues, see Peterson, *Socrates and Philosophy in the Dialogues of Plato*. I address the failures of Diotima as a philosophic authority in chapter 5. On the Eleatic and Athenian visitors, see Berger, "Plato's Flying Philosopher."

tyrannical, *turannikōtatos*," when the people who "give birth, *gennōntes*," to him "submit to him willingly, *hekontes hupeikōsin*" (575c-d). Socrates is thus harshly critical of the democratic constitution, to be sure. But what if in blaming the people for the rise of tyranny, Socrates is also acknowledging the people's power to resist tyranny?[37] What would happen, say, if the people refused to willingly submit? Socrates points out that tyrants are, "throughout their life," solitary and alone, "never friends with anyone" (576a). What if Socrates says this to bring to appearance that the people have numbers on their side? Resistance is difficult if not impossible when a tyrant is already established and has force on his side. So what if Socrates puts things the way he does to open the possibility that the people can avoid "giving birth" to a tyrant and/or "aiding and abetting" his rise to power in the first place, to open the possibility that the transition from democracy to tyranny may not be as inevitable as it can sometimes seem?

Refusing to aid and abet a tyrant requires seeing through the tyrant's initial practices of stealth and deception and being unpersuaded by his lies (573e–575c). These are capacities that the democratic souls Socrates describes in *Republic* 8 and 9 appear not to have: it is their "folly," after all, that aids and abets the tyrant's rise in the first place (575c-d). What if these capacities can be developed? And what if *that* is the education offered by the *Republic*? What if, seeking to counteract the folly that makes people complicit with tyranny, the dialogue aims to educate its readers—ancient and modern—to cultivate our own capacities to scrutinize claims made by power and by knowledge, including claims made by and on behalf of Athens' traditional authorities, those made by philosophical authorities, and those made by citizens on their own behalves? And what if it is by way of *that* education that the *Republic* educates to soul *and* city justice? These are the wagers of this book.

There are good grounds for skepticism. Plato's dialogues, including the *Republic*, mostly depict Socrates engaging in conversation with intellectual, political, and/or economic elites.[38] Does this not indicate that if the *Republic* is concerned with cultivating capacities for self-governance, it seeks to do so in them? Why not argue that the problem depicted in the dialogues is that Athenian leaders have abdicated their authority, and, more pointedly, that they have abdicated

---

37. See also Frank, "How Oligarchy Breeds Tyranny."

38. The slave in the *Meno* is an exception. On the diversity of characters appearing in Plato's texts, see Schlosser, *What Would Socrates Do?*, chap. 2.

it to the *dēmos*?³⁹ What could possibly justify the claim that the dialogues seek to distribute authority *to* the *dēmos*? Are they not also figured as a tyrant in the *Republic*?⁴⁰

That the *Republic* is harshly critical of the Athenian *dēmos* goes without saying. In my view, the dialogue negatively depicts democratic actors and their constitution not out of hostility to democracy as such, however, but rather out of hostility to the overreaching imperial form assumed by Athenian democracy through its development over the course of the long and tumultuous Peloponnesian War, the form of democracy against the backdrop of which Plato set the *Republic*, and in the aftermath of which he wrote.⁴¹ As we will see, Athenian elites were also complicit in Athens' failures during the war. In the *Republic*, that complicity is depicted in part by way of Plato's portrayals of Glaucon and Adeimantus. Some scholars see in the *Republic*'s effort to displace and replace Athenian democratic authorities with the authority of philosophy Plato's chief response to Athens' failures, which culminated in the death of Socrates.⁴² Over the course of this book, I argue instead that the *Republic* represents and enacts challenges to *all* claims to authority, whether elite, tyrannical, or philosophical, and that it seeks to redistribute authority back to those who grant it to Athens' traditional figures and institutions in the first place, namely, the people of Athens. This authority is not the power that cooperated in the overreaching, *pleonexia*, of Athenian imperial democracy, however, nor one based on might or on expert knowledge. Rather, it is bound with an all-too-human wisdom, a *sophia* informed by *phronēsis*.

Malcolm Schofield remarks that "the core meaning of *politeia*," the Greek title for the *Republic*, "is 'citizenship'" or "the condition of being a citizen."⁴³ I read the *Republic* as educating to a new mode of "being a citizen," one that, in keeping with its account of learning to read and following neither "the model of the sage nor the model of democratic mass instruction," reimagines Athenian democratic

---

39. For discussion, see Landauer, "*Idiōtēs* and the Tyrant"; and Landauer, "*Parrhesia* and the *Demos Tyrannos*."

40. I thank John Lombardini for these questions, to which I return in chapter 1.

41. For this way of reading Plato's politics, see, among others, the scholars referenced in note 16 above.

42. On the authority of philosophy as displacing Athens' traditional authorities, see, among others, Allen, *Why Plato Wrote*; Ford, *Origins of Criticism*, 209; Kennedy, *New History of Classical Rhetoric*, 37; Levin, *Ancient Quarrel between Philosophy and Poetry*, chap. 5; Murray, in *Plato on Poetry*, 23–24; Rosen, *Plato's "Republic*," chap. 13; Yunis, *Taming Democracy*, 172. For a different view, see Von Reden and Goldhill, "Plato and the Performance of Dialogue."

43. Schofield, *Plato*, 33.

authority.⁴⁴ It does so not by altering Athens' existing political institutions but by addressing those who participate in these institutions, *hoi polloi* and *hoi aristoi* both, so that, by becoming skilled readers, they can become good citizens.⁴⁵

On my account, Plato's dialogues invite readers to become skilled readers not by accepting the dialogues' philosophical figures as authoritative dispensers of doctrine, although these figures' interlocutors often take them to be such. Rather, as I suggested above, the dialogues stage occasions for those interlocutors to ask questions, to resist, to wonder. These occasions, we will see, take the form of argumentative failures, inconsistencies, and, sometimes, deceptions on the parts of figures of authority, on the one hand, and, on the other, acquiescence and, as noted, missed opportunities to demand transparency and accountability on the parts of interlocutors. These failures, inconsistencies, and missed opportunities create possibilities for the dialogues' readers. As I demonstrate in chapter 1, these possibilities depend on readers *disidentifying* with the characters in Plato's texts, figures of authority and acquiescent interlocutors alike, including Socrates and the other characters often treated by scholars as stand-ins for Plato. Learning to read in this way, by attending to what is obliterated by the dialogues' characters or badly argued—"what's been left out and what isn't a fine product of craft" (401e), as Socrates puts it in *Republic 3*—situates the interpretative mood of this book in a register of negation.⁴⁶

Reading Plato's dialogues negatively is nothing new. Plato's early dialogues are often read as aporetic, undoing Athenian popular understandings of courage, friendship, moderation, piety, virtue, and so on, without putting anything in their place. In a different register of negation, Lloyd Gerson seeks to show "how much of the actual form and content of the dialogues makes sense when we see them as built on a conjunction of . . . five 'antis' and an attempt to unify them in some way." Gerson's "antis"—antimaterialism, antimechanism, antinominalism, antirelativism, antiskepticism—pit the philosophy of Plato's dia-

---

44. This phrase is from Von Reden and Goldhill, "Plato and the Performance of Dialogue," 269, 277, who make an analogous case through readings of the *Laches* and *Lysis*. See also Kastley, *Rhetoric of Plato's "Republic,"* 22.

45. On the distinctively democratic modes of association, *sunousia*, including free speech, accountability, and deliberation, that inform and structure relations among characters in Plato's texts, see Euben, *Corrupting Youth*; Monoson, *Plato's Democratic Entanglements*; Saxonhouse, *Free Speech and Democracy*; Mara, *Socrates' Discursive Democracy*; Schlosser, *What Would Socrates Do?*

46. I am grateful to Melissa Lane for pressing me to elaborate this feature of my interpretative practice. In a different way, Kateb, "Socratic Integrity," too, develops an interpretation based on negation.

logues against a set of positions that are negatively represented in the dialogues to be sure.[47] As we will see, however, the obverses of these "antis" are equally problematized in the dialogues, for both sides of these binarisms of modernity inscribe ethics, politics, and philosophy that the dialogues, as I read them, seek rather to put in question. The register of negation of this book is also not the "not" of disputation or eristic, the not characteristic of what, in *Republic* 7, Socrates calls the "game of contradiction for entertainment's sake, *ton paidias charin paizonta kai antilegonta*" (539c-d), which he associates, in *Republic* 5, with the "purely verbal contradictions, *kat' auto to onoma diōkein tou lechthentos tēn enantiōsin*," that characterize not discussion but competition (454a).

I am interested, instead, in the "not" that appears in the phrase "not tall," when, as in the *Sophist*, for example, we are prompted to take that to signify not "small" but, as Kevin Crotty has put it, "other than tall," which is to say, short, or average, or gargantuan, and so on. This is a "not" that signifies what is "different from" or "other than" tall, something not pregiven as the opposite of "tall," that is, "short," but potentially new.[48] This is a "not" of possibility. Thus, in the chapters that follow, I reread passages in the *Republic, Phaedrus, Symposium,* and *Theaetetus* that have produced dominant interpretative paradigms not to invert their significance but to see what other possibilities they may bring to appearance. I dwell in the space of the "not" not because I seek to resolve the texts' inconsistencies by arguing, say, that Plato's thought developed over the course of his life, or by claiming for it a sublimating unity, or because I seek to correct the argumentative failures the texts display by recurring to an esotericism or to a superordinate metaphysics. My aim is rather to unpack the ethical, political, and/or philosophical possibilities of the "not" of failure, inconsistency, missed opportunity, and disidentification.

This register of negation is crucially bound not only with how we read Plato's dialogues but also with how Plato wrote them, which I describe in chapter 1 as his poetry and its effects.[49] Again, objections could be raised. Isn't a product of *mimēsis* only an image of a copy, situated at a third remove from the form it represents (597e)? Does *Republic* 10 not produce a hierarchy of being and truth that underwrites Plato's contempt for and dismissal of *mimēsis* as altogether false and therefore deceptive? Not in my view. Although mimetic representations are, to be sure, not true, I argue in chapter 2 that the *Republic*

---

47. Gerson, *From Plato to Platonism*, 11–14.
48. Crotty, *Philosopher's Song*, 155–56.
49. Like Gordon, *Turning toward Philosophy*, 77–79, I treat Plato's work as a poetic art. Gordon locates that art in Socratic dialogue. I locate it in Plato's representations of dialogue.

distinguishes the falsity of mimetic things from deception. For, unlike deceptions, which seek to cover over gaps between truth and representation, mimetic things, at least in Plato's texts, prompt attention to those very gaps, and also to our inability to see what does not appear. *Mimēsis* thus turns out to be not at odds with the philosophy of the *Republic*, but rather a condition of its possibility. Against this backdrop, I read the ouster of the mimetic poets from the ideal city as an indictment not of poetry but of the ideal city.

Rereading the *Republic* back to front, chapters 1 and 2 take *Republic* 10's account of *mimēsis* as their point of departure, to make the case for the interpretative approach I have been describing, and to set the stage for how doing so alters our appreciation of the dialogue's ethics, philosophy, and politics as oriented to self-governance. Chapter 3 explores the cognitive and ethical losses as well as the political risks the dialogue associates with the ouster of mimetic poetry from the early educational curricula and the ideal city in *Republic* 2–5. Continuing to focus on the perception, evaluation, and judgment of representations that contribute to self-governance, chapter 4 shows the ways in which the *Republic* develops capacities to see through deception and to resist force in words and hence to call persuasive lies to account. Self-governing citizens also have to reckon with desire. With and against the various contestations of *erōs* articulated in the *Symposium*, chapter 5 argues that the *Republic* orients away from the overreaching desire of fifth-century imperial democratic Athens and tyranny alike, and to an equally overreaching desire for fallible self-knowledge, wisdom, and truth as the basic conditions of ethics, politics, and philosophy. Chapter 6 conducts close readings of the divided line simile, sun-good analogy, and cave allegory of *Republic* 6–7, and draws on the *Theaetetus*, to explore the central role of *aisthēsis*, sense perception, in any adequate appreciation of the *Republic*'s dialectical approach to truth and the good. I close by bringing my findings to bear on justice, the central ethical and political concern of the *Republic*. There are scholars who see in the *Republic* only biting criticisms of Athens' democratic authorities and efforts to supplant those authorities with philosophical authority; only the subjugation of *erōs*, imagination, and sense perception to calculative rationality; and, in Plato's evident artistry as poet and dramatist, only an instrument in the service of philosophical triumphalism and its rule of truth.[50] By foregrounding that artistry and poetry, I seek to bring to light, by contrast, how the ethics, politics, and philosophy of the *Republic* depend on, draw on, and encapacitate desire, persuasion, and the senses, with a view to reimagining democratic authority.

50. Puchner, *Drama of Ideas*, 30–34, 195.

CHAPTER 1

Reading Plato

> The true philosopher and the true poet are one, and a beauty, which is truth, and a truth, which is beauty, is the aim of both.
>
> RALPH WALDO EMERSON, *Nature*

"If one understands by political science political theory, its father certainly is Plato." So writes Hannah Arendt in her essay "What Is Authority?"[1] Treating Plato as the "father" specifically of the rationalism, transcendentalism, and universalism she takes to be characteristic of much of Western political thought, Arendt associates these features, in particular, with the authority of the philosopher-kings in the ideal city of the *Republic*.[2] Acknowledging that the word "authority" and the concept are not Greek in origin, Arendt maintains that Plato, nonetheless, "tried to introduce something akin to authority into the public life of the Greek polis." He does this, she claims, by invoking an extrapolitical source to legitimate rule by philosopher-kings, a source lying beyond the sphere of power and "not man-made," namely, the ideas or what have come to be called Plato's "forms."[3]

The ideas are referenced in the *Republic*'s sun-good analogy, divided line simile, and cave metaphor (507a–509d; 509e–511e; 514a–518b). Establishing a manifold hierarchy, these famous images depict modes of knowing ranging from imagination to belief to understanding to insight, and objects of knowledge ranging, correspondingly, from shadows, images, and reflections to things

---

1. Arendt, "What Is Authority?," 136–37. Similarly, Whitehead, *Process and Reality*, 39: "The safest general characterization of the European philosophical tradition is that it consists of a series of footnotes to Plato."

2. Arendt, "What Is Authority?," 107.

3. Ibid., 104, 109, 111. I engage Arendt on what she calls "Plato's ideas," in Frank, "Circulating Authority."

and artifacts, mathematical entities, and the ideas. The ontological and epistemological trajectory appears to be one of ascension: from the particulars that populate the visible realm of appearances to the transcendent universals populating the domain of true being; from what seems to what is; from what comes into being and passes away to what is unchanging; from affects, emotions, opinions, and desires to thought and insight; from the cave of politics to the light of philosophy.

Taking the ideas to promote philosophical and also political authoritarianism, for, as she explains, "the source of authority in authoritarian government is always a force external and superior to its own power," Arendt identifies Plato with his representation of the philosopher-kings to tell a familiar story.[4] It is one according to which, in the wake of Socrates' death at the hands of democratic Athens, Plato excoriates democracy and seeks to insulate philosophy from politics.[5] On this account, what has come to be called the *Republic*'s "two-world" view presents what appears in the imperfect sensible human world of politics as mere replicas of "real" and perfect "Forms" or philosophical ideas, which exist safely and apart in a separate, intelligible, invisible world.[6] Some interpreters see philosophy's insulation from politics as a good thing. To Arendt, it comes at an unacceptable cost. For when extrapolitical sources of authority govern human affairs, particulars, the world of appearances that they inhabit, and its politics are ordered by what Arendt calls "the tyranny of reason."[7]

Thinkers across the last two centuries endorse versions of this broadly "authoritarian" reading of the *Republic*.[8] For good reason. The dialogue does

4. Arendt, "What Is Authority?," 97.
5. Ibid., 107.
6. For this formulation of the two-world view, see Klosko, *History of Political Theory*, 99.
7. Arendt, "What Is Authority?," 115, 108.
8. In competing philosophical and political traditions and on a variety of different grounds, including Nietzsche, Russell, Wittgenstein, Carnap, and current scholars of the Anglo-American tradition, Heidegger, early Derrida, and Rancière, in Germany and France, and, of course, Karl Popper. What Berger says with respect to Derrida in "*Phaedrus* and the Politics of Inscription," 416, may be applied equally to many of these readers: because Derrida "assimilates Plato to Platonism, because he converts a Platonistic reading of the text to Platonic intentions, . . . far from challenging the Platonistic interpretation, he assumes it, uses it, confirms it. Were he to have challenged it, I think he would have found inscribed in the dialogues a critique of Platonism very similar to his own." On Plato versus "Platonism," see also Heidegger, *What Is Called Thinking?*; and Badiou's 2009–10 seminar at the École normale supérieure in Paris titled "Pour aujourd'hui: Platon!"

introduce the philosopher-kings' access to the ideas to exemplify extrapolitical authority. It does claim that the superior reason of the philosopher-kings, evidenced by their privileged access to ideas, justifies their rule in *Republic* 5's ideal city. And it does present a series of dichotomies—universals vs. particulars, reason vs. desire, truth vs. appearance—that, as Arendt claims, have become authoritative for traditions of Western political thought.[9]

These are features of the *Republic*, to be sure. The focus on them has, however, obscured other aspects of this text that press us in different directions. If the *Republic* exemplifies extrapolitical authority by way of the philosopher-kings' access to the ideas, it also conspicuously subjects to scrutiny and critique that very same authority, its associated universalism, rationalism, transcendentalism, its hostility to what appears, and the ideal city it governs. Over the course of this book, I make the case that the *Republic*'s sun-good analogy, line simile, and cave allegory depict particulars and universals as more mutually implicated than the two-world view suggests. I argue that the dialogue presents *logos*—speech and reason—as intimately bound with practices of *aisthēsis*, the sensation of particulars, and as depending critically and self-consciously on poetry, persuasion, and *erōs*. Highlighting these features of the dialogue's philosophy, more usually associated with Athenian democratic practices, alters how we understand its politics. Rather than legitimating the authority of philosopher-kings and celebrating their rule, the *Republic*, I argue, invites a circulation of authority among the dialogue's interlocutors and also between the dialogue and its readers.

READING, WRITING, FATHERS, AND KINGS

The persuasiveness of my account of the *Republic* depends on how it is read.[10] "Authoritarian" readings of the *Republic* take the relation between Plato and his readers to parallel the one between governor and governed depicted in the ideal city. On this approach, Plato seeks to effect a transfer or displacement of the authority of his readers to himself, that is, to establish for himself, in

---

9. Arendt, "What Is Authority?," 115.

10. For extended and valuable treatments of how to read Plato's texts from which I have greatly benefited, see Allen, *Why Plato Wrote*; Berger, *Perils of Uglytown*; Blondell, *Play of Character*; Cotton, *Platonic Dialogue*; Long, *Socratic and Platonic Political Philosophy*; Peterson, *Socrates and Philosophy in the Dialogues of Plato*; Press, *Plato*; Rowe, *Plato and the Art of Philosophical Writing*; Sayre, *Plato's Literary Garden*; Svenbro, *Phrasikleia*; Szlezak, *Reading Plato*, along with other monographs and articles that appear below.

relation to his readers, the political and philosophical authority attributed to the philosopher-kings.[11] This way of reading brings to mind what Socrates calls "soul writing" in the *Phaedrus*. There, "the good logos" is the product of a "father whose legitimate word is begotten first in his own soul and then in the souls of others, where it defends not only itself but also its father."[12] As a practice of sowing seed (in Socrates' metaphor, *Phaedr.* 276b ff.), soul writing is teaching by implantation or "transmission."[13]

Implying "the learner's passivity,"[14] soul writing pairs well with the practice of reading presented in the *Protagoras*, *Sophist*, and *Statesman*, as discussed in this book's prologue, whereby students learn to read by tracing over pre-written letters, repeating syllables, or following rules of grammar, all given to them by their authoritative teachers. When Plato's dialogues are read as a kind of soul writing, Plato is, in Arendt's word, the "father" of political theory as the father of the Good (*logos*), which, by being inscribed in the souls of his readers, produces and reproduces itself, and thereby the authority of its father, along with his authoritarian politics and philosophy.[15]

As Socrates explains in the *Phaedrus*, however, the medium for soul writing, despite its name, is not writing at all, but oral teaching (276a). Indeed, Socrates' account of soul writing, along with its teaching, sowing, and fathering, as just described, is part of an argument leveled *against* actual writing. Writing, Socrates says, cannot secure the transmission of *logos* because, like paintings, and unlike what Phaedrus calls "living breathing words" (276a), written words are like images that go on saying the same thing forever (275d-e). Socrates says that writing is static, but we might wonder whether that is true.

---

11. Morgan, "The Tyranny of the Audience," 207: "If we accept [Plato's] discourse as the voice of reason, then we acquiesce in [his] 'kingship' over us, the readers"; Annas, *Plato*, 48, 51: it is "relatively clear" which positions Plato thinks are correct and that "Plato is sure he is right on a number of issues."

12. Berger, "*Phaedrus* and the Politics of Inscription," 418, referring to 278a-b.

13. Allen, *Why Plato Wrote*, 27.

14. Berger, "*Phaedrus* and the Politics of Inscription," 420.

15. Halperin, "Plato and Erotic Reciprocity," 61, calls this "male parthenogenesis." Plato represents this phenomenon in the *Lysis*, where the *paideia* of the title character, provided for him by his father, inscribes "as indelibly as possible into his soul the values and beliefs of the older generation," while making him believe that it will make him "powerful and independent." For these phrases and discussion, see Berger, *Perils of Uglytown*, 22–23. For a similar account of *paideia* that brings out shared features with how Athens' elite youths were actually educated in the fifth century, see *Protagoras* 325c–326d. For education in fifth-century Athens, see Robb, *Literacy and* Paideia *in Ancient Greece*.

Letters on a page may remain unchanged, but unless those letters, once they join to make words, signify univocally or determine their own interpretation, and/or unless the sentences and texts these words comprise can somehow, in virtue of being written, defend themselves against interpretation and/or misinterpretation, written words seem *not* to say the same thing forever at all. On the contrary, in written words, as Socrates' and Phaedrus' disparate responses to Lysias' "love" letter in the *Phaedrus* make plain, it is possible for the same person over time and/or for different people at the same time to see and hear different things. The variety of interpretations of Plato's dialogues suggests the same, namely, that people interact with written texts differently.

That Plato has Phaedrus use the term "image" to describe the written word suggests the same as well. Like other "images" populating the lowest segment of the divided line, written words are not static or univocal, but multivocal and in motion. Indeed, it is the very multivocality of written words that informs another argument against writing in the *Phaedrus*. This one appears in an exchange Socrates reports between the Egyptian god Theuth, the inventor of writing, and Thamus, "the king of all Egypt," including the Egyptian gods (274d).[16] When Theuth defends writing as a helpmate of memory and wisdom, Plato has him use, in tension with Socrates' claim that written words are static and univocal, the polysemic word *pharmakon*, poison and/or cure. Thamus, for his part, agrees that writing is a *pharmakon*, but, using it in its other signification, as poison, he disagrees about writing's effect:

> You provide your students with the appearance of wisdom, not with its truth, *sophias ... doxan, ouk alētheian*. Your invention will enable them to hear much, *poluēkooi*, without being taught, *aneu didachēs*, and they will imagine that they have come to know much, *polugnōmones*, while for the most part they will know nothing. And they will be difficult to get along with since they will merely appear to be wise instead of really being so, *doxosophoi gegonotes anti sophōn*. (275a-b)

Framed as an argument about the negative effects of writing on a reader's memory and wisdom, Thamus' disparagement of writing seems to be equally about writing's effects on the power of a king. For if Thamus is right, and by way of writing a king's subjects can learn without being taught, and/or can hear not

---

16. According to Nehamas' notes on the *Phaedrus*, Socrates says "Thamus they call Ammon" (274d). Nehamas (79 nn. 179–80) describes Ammon as "king of the Egyptian gods." For Theuth as the inventor of writing, see also *Phil.* 18c-d.

only the king's voice but "much," and/or can know not only what he says but many things, then, as Harry Berger Jr. has argued, they may well become hard to get along with *for him*, as he will no longer be assured of their obedience.[17] Perhaps Thamus argues against writing, then, because it can weaken if not thwart *his* authority.

Maintaining, on the one hand, that writing is univocal and static, and also agreeing with Thamus' claims about writing's multivocality and mobility (275e), Socrates contradicts himself, a point I return to below. Nonetheless, the arguments against writing presented in the *Phaedrus* converge on the claim that writing does not produce or secure the authority of oral teaching/soul writing.[18] Perhaps Plato, himself not a soul writer but a writer, writes, then, not to effect a transfer of the authority of his readers to himself, and not to establish for himself, in relation to his readers, the authority of a (philosopher-) king, but instead to open the possibility of a different practice of authority.

As noted earlier, soul writing invites a passivity similar to the one involved in the practice of learning to read offered in the *Protagoras*, *Sophist*, and *Statesman*. Actual writing, which is to say, multivocal writing in motion, by contrast, pairs well with the second, more active and experiential, mode of learning to read described in this book's prologue, the one recommended by Socrates in the *Theaetetus* and *Republic*. Learning to read in that way calls not for tracing someone else's letters or being inscribed by their *logos*, but for coming to know by trial and error, forming opinions about letters and syllables based on fallible sensible experiences, looking at everything everywhere. In this mode of reading, authority lies in the capacities of writing's readers to see, hear, and know, as Thamus puts it, many things. It is perhaps for this reason that, in the *Phaedrus*, Socrates says of the written word that "alone, it can neither defend itself nor come to its own support, *autos gar out' amunasthai oute boēthēsai dunatos hautō*" (275e).

Socrates also says that the written word "always needs its father's support, *tou patros aei deitai boēthou*" (275e). If the father of soul writing is a seed sower and authoritative teacher, who is the father of the written word, and what kind of support might he offer? In the *Phaedrus*, Thamus calls Theuth "the father of writing" (275a). Theuth, as we just saw, leaves writing and its authority in the hands of its readers. The support he offers to the written word, then, is to let it be. Socrates says, too, that a written word "rolls about, *kulindeitai*, every-

---

17. Berger, "*Phaedrus* and the Politics of Inscription," 437–41.
18. Ophir, *Plato's Invisible Cities*, 162–63, calls this the "literal core of Plato's critique of writing in the *Phaedrus*."

where, reaching indiscriminately those with understanding no less than those who have no business with it, and it doesn't know to whom it should speak and to whom it should not" (275e). This may be an echo of Thamus' criticism of writing. Or it may simply be an account of the situation of the written word, which Socrates describes using the same word, *kulindeitai*, that he uses to describe justice and opinion in the *Republic*, which, as discussed in this book's prologue, likewise "roll around" (432d, 479d).

Whether positioned for writing or against it, Socrates, Theuth, and Thamus seem to agree about the lack of discrimination of the written word and its anarchy or lawlessness. These together imply a different kind of fatherhood than appears in the *Phaedrus*' account of oral teaching as soul writing and a different kind of authority from the "tyranny of reason" Arendt finds in the *Republic*'s philosopher-kings. The *Symposium* also presents fatherhood and its authority in ways that are at odds with soul writing and philosopher-kings. In that complex dialogue, which I discuss in chapter 5, Plato has Eryximachus call Phaedrus "the father of the *logos*" (177d).[19] More precisely, Plato has Aristodemus remember, and Apollodorus remember and report, that Eryximachus quoted from Euripides when he introduced the topic for the speeches at Agathon's house (177a). The words Eryximachus quotes to indicate that "the speech comes from Phaedrus here" (177a)—that *he* is "father of the *logos*"—are those of Euripides' Melanippe, who says "not mine the tale." And Melanippe says *that* because she tells a tale taught by her mother (fr. 488).[20] As was the case in the *Phaedrus*, the upshot of Plato's embedding in the *Symposium* alters the status of both the *logos* and its father. For if Eryximachus stands for Melanippe, and Phaedrus, the "father of the *logos*," stands for Melanippe's mother, then the father of the *logos* is also a mother. Notice that Plato has Eryximachus introduce Phaedrus as the "father of the *logos*" with a double disavowal: Eryximachus' "not mine the tale" recites Melanippe's "not mine the tale," and this places Phaedrus' *logos* at a third remove from its source and origin.[21] If, then, Eryximachus is Melanippe, and Phaedrus is Melanippe's mother, then Plato, it seems, is Euripides, the mimetic poet par excellence.

19. See also *Phaedrus* 257b: "Blame Lysias, the father of that discourse, *logos*," whose *logos*, too, as noted above, is neither implanted nor transmitted but instead heard, interpreted, and reinterpreted.

20. For these sources, see Bury, *Symposium of Plato*, 18.

21. And brings to mind Socrates' "not Alcinous' the tale," which he announces as he begins the tale narrated by Er (*Rep.* 614b), itself a retelling of the "tales to Alcinous told" in Homer's *Odyssey* 9–12.

If Plato is a mimetic poet, and if, as Socrates tells us in *Republic* 10, mimetic things are at a third remove from the truth (597e), then Plato's writing is at a third remove from the truth. And if Plato fathers *logos* in the way of Phaedrus, which is to say in the way of Melanippe's mother, then the political theory he parents may feature something other than the universalism, rationalism, and transcendentalism associated with the philosopher-kings' authority. And if this is all so, then the politics Plato's dialogues (under)write may turn out to be other than authoritarian. Looking at everything everywhere, as described in this book's prologue, I explore these possibilities by reading Plato's writing as a *pharmakon* in the way of both Theuth and Thamus, which is to say, as a helpmate to memory and wisdom and also as a poison to univocal and static *logos*.

There are good reasons to object. For even if there are grounds for reading the *Phaedrus* and *Symposium* in this way, the same surely cannot be said of the *Republic*, which not only puts forward the figure of the philosopher-kings and their rule in the ideal city but also stages an "old quarrel, *diaphora*, between poetry and philosophy" (607b), sets forth a critique of *mimēsis*, and ousts the mimetic poets from its ideal city. On these grounds, the *Republic* has been regarded as "nothing less than authoritarian" not only in its philosophy and politics but in its attitude to representational art as well.[22] What could justify treating the Plato of the *Republic* as a mimetic poet, and what is to be gained?

My answer to the first part of this question occupies most of the rest of this chapter, in which I read Plato as a mimetic poet and the *Republic* as an example of mimetic poetry by way of *Republic* 10's treatment of *mimēsis* itself. What is to be gained by reading the *Republic* in this way, as will emerge over the course of this book, is an ethics, politics, and philosophy of self-governance. By this I mean the imperative of poetry as *poiēsis*, creation or making, for the self-making and self-authorization that condition self-governance.[23] Depending

22. Halliwell, *Aesthetics of Mimesis*, 73.

23. What I am calling "self-authorization" is aligned in one way with what Gordon, in "Self-Authorizing Modernity," 121–37, describes as the "Enlightenment-era penchant for doctrines of self authorization" (122) and attributes to Hobbes and Rousseau, and especially Kant and Hegel. It is aligned in terms of its ethics and politics, which, as in Enlightenment self-authorization, take their bearings not from the "inscrutable aims of God, or the immutable nature of things," but are instead "self-imposed" (we are creators of our ethics and politics and bound by what we make) (121). However, my account of self-authorization via Plato's *Republic* is not aligned with modern self-authorization in terms of its epistemology. For if, for the German Idealists, we are "sovereign creators" both of ourselves and also of our world, and of the latter insofar as the objects of our world are taken to conform to our knowledge, for the *Republic*'s philosophy, as we will see in chapter 6, it is not the case that objects conform to our knowledge. But neither is it the case that

neither on might nor on extrapolitical truth accessible by reason, and refusing both utility and rationalism, the ethics, politics, and philosophy I associate with Plato's *Republic*, neither instrumental nor idealist, chart a course for citizenship informed by a wisdom that, like the kind Socrates claims for himself in the *Apology* (22e-23b), takes account of its own limitations.

HOW PLATO WROTE

The *Republic* opens with the words "I went down to the Piraeus yesterday with Glaucon . . ." (327a). The voice is Socrates', who is both a fictional character in the dialogue and its narrator.[24] By contrast, Plato, as is widely acknowledged, nowhere speaks in the *Republic*, or in any other dialogue, for that matter. This might turn him into an omniscient narrator who speaks in the authoritative and universal voice of Reason, as he is sometimes read. In the dialogues staged as dialogues, however, there can be no omniscient narrator because there is no narrator at all. And if there can be said to be an omniscient narrator in the narrated dialogues it cannot be Plato for "the Platonic narrator is never Plato."[25] It is most often Socrates, as in the *Republic*, and when it's someone else, as in the *Theaetetus* or the *Symposium*, and even when it is Socrates, the narrator is conspicuously signaled as unreliable, which is to say, not omniscient and not authoritative.[26]

Despite these structural features of the dialogues, scholars often attribute to Plato what Stephen Halliwell characterizes as a *"global and supra-textual principle of ethical responsibility"* via what have come to be called "mouthpiece theories."[27] These theories take named characters in the narrated and

---

our knowledge conforms to objects (not to material objects or to immaterial ones, like forms or ideas). Not yet structured by modernity's binary between subjectivism and objectivism, the premodern practice of self-authorization I develop is an activity of human limitation as well as possibility. It is an activity of human limitation in its relatedness to the world in which we find ourselves, and an activity of human possibility insofar as we have the capacity to affect that world in incremental ways over time, as we affect and effect our humanities.

24. For treatments of poetry and narration in the *Republic*, see Halliwell, "Theory and Practice of Narrative"; Euben, *Tragedy of Political Theory*, 260 ff. On Socrates as narrator, see Saxonhouse, "Socratic Narrative"; Ferrari, "Socrates in the *Republic*."

25. Morgan, "Plato," 359. See also Edelstein, "Platonic Anonymity."

26. For "unreliable narrator," see Booth, *Rhetoric of Fiction*, 158–59. I discuss this feature of these dialogues in chapters 6 and 5, respectively. For the *Symposium* as a nonnarrated dialogue, see Halliwell, "Theory and Practice of Narrative," 15–41.

27. For this formulation in a different context and a critique, see Halliwell, "Theory and Practice of Narrative," 22. For a thorough discussion of mouthpiece theories, see Nails, "Mouthpiece

nonnarrated dialogues alike to speak or stand in for Plato—Socrates, for example, or Diotima or the Eleatic or Athenian visitors—or, in a reversal, claim that "Plato often sees *himself* as *Socrates'* voice (rather than the other way around)."[28] The dialogues give no grounds for assuming that Plato underwrites anything he puts in the mouths of these characters, however, including that of Socrates, who, in any case, says in the *Theaetetus* that "the arguments never come from me; they always come from the person I am talking to, *oudeis tōn logōn exerchetai par' emou all' aei para tou emoi dialegomenou*" (161b).[29] With Plato silent and Socrates' arguments coming from his interlocutors, actual and impersonated and/or, as we saw in the *Phaedrus*, imagined and ventriloquized, there is, as Halliwell claims, "no reliable hermeneutic for tracing a monologic authorial stance (about anything) within Platonic dialogue."[30] Not even by way of the account of narrative Socrates offers in *Republic* 3, for, as neither narration "pure and simple, *haploos*" (393d) nor narration effected through imitation, nor some combination of these (392d), the *Republic*, as G. R. F. Ferrari has noted, "escapes the alternatives" Socrates puts forward.[31] Giving no textual or extratextual guidance about whose say-so to take as true and making no claim to the authority of their author or any claim on the alienation of the authority of their readers, Plato's dialogues, as we will see, regularly and repeatedly invite scrutiny of their own philosophical authority, along with that

---

Schmouthpiece." See also Press, *Who Speaks for Plato?*; and Brumbaugh, *Platonic Studies of Greek Philosophy*, 29–30.

28. The number of scholars who take Socrates to stand in or speak for Plato is too numerous to list. For this last formulation, see Schofield, *Plato*, 19.

29. For Berger, *Perils of Uglytown*, 65, this "is more than a statement of method. It is also an acknowledgment of defeat, and as such it expresses the pathos of Socratic failure: the dilemma of a hero whose spoken words are captured and occupied by the meanings of others, whose mission is frustrated by the very dialogical medium it commits itself to."

30. Halliwell, "Theory and Practice of Narrative," 19. In some tension with her remarks noted earlier above, Annas, *Plato*, 46, writes that "Plato very much wants not to present his own position for the reader to accept on Plato's authority." As Heidegger says in *What Is Called Thinking?*, 71: "Not a single one of Plato's dialogues arrives at a palpable, unequivocal result which sound common sense could, as the saying goes, hold on to."

31. Ferrari, "Socrates in the *Republic*," 20–21. See also Halliwell, "Theory and Practice of Narrative," 41: "Plato's own writing, which is the only place where we can hope to find 'Plato' at all, embodies a cumulative recognition that the scope and operations of narrative, whether in a wider or narrower sense of that category, will always exceed and outrun any attempt to theorise them." For this reason he argues (20, 22–23, 28, 29) that there is a "fundamental gap" between the procedures and assumptions Plato has Socrates present in his account of narrative in *Republic* 3 and Plato's writerly practices.

of the authority figures they put on display. Plato, as Ferrari says, wrote in a way that ensures "that the 'author' should not become a despotic 'authority.'"[32]

If Socrates' narrative theory cannot accommodate Plato's writerly practices, Socrates' practical tips to Glaucon for how to be a skilled reader may be of greater use. Socrates, as we saw in the prologue, recommends looking at the greatest things "and all their kin, and, again, at their opposites, which are moving around everywhere" (402c). He also recommends developing "the sharpest sense for what's been left out and what isn't a fine product of craft" (401e–402b). Reading the *Republic* in this way calls for looking at what Socrates and his interlocutors say and the arguments they make, and the specific dialogical circumstances governing what they say. It calls for considering, too, "why Plato make[s] them say these things," what he makes them leave out, and what he may be "trying to accomplish by putting on this drama for us, the audience."[33] All of this means not treating the speeches of the dialogues' characters as the philosophy of the dialogues' author. It means attending to how the speeches of a dialogue are informed by and revelatory of the characters of the speakers, and to how a dialogue's frame and dramatic cues stage how we are to hear what the characters say. It also means attending to the discursive dynamics among the speakers, and to their styles of argumentation. In short, it calls for reading Plato's dialogues dramatically.[34]

And yet, as Jesper Svenbro maintains, by performing "an internalization of theater in the book," Plato's dialogues may have a dramatic form "without

---

32. Ferrari, *Listening to the Cicadas*, 211. As Halliwell, "Theory and Practice of Narrative," 21, 19, says, we may "refer to 'Plato' only as the author of the text" and must refrain entirely from "treating him as though he were himself an omnipresent voice audible *within* the dialogue." Ophir, *Plato's Invisible Cities*, 162–63, disagrees, arguing that the "task of Platonic writing . . . is not to deny its own authority, but to legitimize itself while being aware of the deficiencies of the medium."

33. Phrases in this sentence are from Press, *Plato*, 186, who calls the levels he disarticulates "logical," "literary," and "integrative." I don't think of them exactly that way but find his taxonomy into registers helpful to think with.

34. For dramatic readings of varying kinds, see, for examples, Badiou, *Plato's "Republic"*; Blondell, *Play of Character*; Gonzalez, *Third Way*; Press, *Plato*; Russon and Sallis, *Retracing the Platonic Text*; Strauss, *City and Man*. See also Monoson, *Plato's Democratic Entanglements*, and Puchner, *Drama of Ideas*, on theatricality and the ways this works with philosophy as *theōria* even as the *Republic* and other dialogues stage their differences from "theatocracy." Dramatic readings sometimes nonetheless treat characters in Plato's dialogues as speaking for Plato. See, e.g., Puchner, *Drama of Ideas*, 14, who argues that "Plato never lets us forget the scene, the situation, the character, the drama," even as he treats what Plato puts in the mouths of his characters as evidence of Plato's own position.

being intended for the stage."[35] As noted in this book's prologue, reading Plato's dialogues and watching them performed are different experiences. This may be because a book takes the time of a reader, whereas a play happens in its own time.[36] It may be because whereas a play runs from start to finish and then it is over, a book can be read in parts and reread, and when it is reread as a whole, it is as if it is being read backward, from finish to start.[37] It may also be because a book, in all its dimensions, can rarely fit the time of a play. Plays based on books tend to leave a lot out. In the case of Plato's dialogues, it is often only upon rereading that aspects of plot, character, and argument become visible to what we might call the "reading I."[38] Indeed, scholars from across divergent schools of interpretation coalesce around the claim that Plato's complexity and artistry indicate that he writes "for readers who can study and re-read his work."[39] Danielle Allen notes that, in the *Republic*, Plato has Socrates use verbs related to art to talk about his production of verbal images, including "*eikazein*, 'to approximate' or 'guess at' with images; *plattein*, which means 'to mold' or 'to sculpt' . . . ; and *graphein*, which means not only 'to paint' but also 'to write' (488a)."[40] Against this backdrop, I advocate for reading Plato's dialogues not only dramatically but also poetically.[41]

Recent work in art history, classics, and ancient history makes the case that the fine arts underwent substantial changes in the years 430–380 BCE, which overlap, on the later end, with Plato's emergence as a writer.[42] Vase painting, mu-

---

35. Svenbro, *Phrasikleia*, 180. See also Burnyeat, "Culture and Society in Plato's *Republic*," 269–70 n. 25; and Gill, *Philosophos*, 12, who maintain that Plato's dialogues are written to be read (and reread).

36. Iser, *Act of Reading*, 148–49, on the time axis of reading.

37. Brogan, "Socrates' Tragic Speech," 32, says that we need to "look backward and forward in order to understand."

38. On the subjectivity of readers, see Iser, *Act of Reading*, 152–59.

39. Ferrari, "Socrates in the *Republic*," 18; Halliwell, "Life-and-Death Journey of the Soul," 445–46, on the myth of Er as "inviting a 'cyclical' reading in conjunction with the preceding dialogue." For examples of staged rereadings in Plato's dialogues, see the *Parmenides* and *Phaedrus*, as cited by Gill, *Philosophos*, 13 n. 37.

40. Allen, *Why Plato Wrote*, 30.

41. Halliwell, *Aesthetics of Mimesis*, 74; Ferrari, "Socrates in the *Republic*," 22: "The poet is Plato"; Brumbaugh, *Platonic Studies*, 20–26, on the aesthetic dimension of Plato's work; Iser, *Act of Reading*, 21. Contra Havelock, *Preface to Plato*, 29: Plato "does not make [the comparison of the poet to the visual artist, the painter] on aesthetic grounds. In fact, it is not too much to say that the notion of the aesthetic as a system of values which might apply to literature and to artistic composition never once enters the argument. Plato writes as though he had never heard of aesthetics, or even art."

42. Osborne, *Debating the Athenian Cultural Revolution*.

sic, and sculpture, in particular, show heightened levels of self-consciousness of presentation, a new focus on perspective, and an increased attention to reception in "the new vibrant arena of what might be called a new aesthetic public sphere."[43] Verity Platt puts it this way: there was "a growing interest in the visual dynamics of mimēsis in the fifth century" that "went hand in hand with a self-conscious experimentation in the power of art to explore its own analytic potential."[44] The *Republic*, written in the mid-300s and set over the course of the Peloponnesian War (the period 431–404), addresses some of these changes explicitly. Socrates criticizes the "new music" (424b-d), for example, and voices more general concerns about the destabilizing effects of innovation, insisting that in the ideal city "the overseers . . . must reject any radical innovation in physical or musical education" (424b).[45] Socrates' criticisms of new music and also of poetry, along with his repeated cautions against innovation, with which he associates poetry as well (600a), have led scholars to conclude that the *Republic* positions itself against the arts and the new.[46]

Consider, however, that Socrates rejects innovation after having proposed an extensive and radical revision of classical Greek education, and also that he criticizes cities that forbid changes to constitutions when they are badly governed (426c). Consider, too, that the *Republic* is itself innovative on any number of fronts. It is sometimes said that the word "philosophy, *philosophia*," is new with Plato, appearing in his writings for the first time, and that the *Republic* is "a radically innovative effort to establish the term's legitimacy."[47] Whether the term "philosophy" is new or not, the content of the philosophy of Plato's dialogues is new, in virtue of, among other things, its differences from both Heraclitean change and Parmenidean unity and sameness.[48] The language of

---

43. See Porter, *Origins of Aesthetic Thought*, 195. See also Lorenz, "Anatomy of Metalepsis"; Schultz, "Style and Agency in an Age of Transition"; and D'Angour, "The Sound of *Mousikē*."

44. Platt, "Likeness and Likelihood in Classical Greek Art," 203. See also Porter, *Origins of Aesthetic Thought*, 179–96, who notes that "the theory of arts in classical antiquity is the province of the artists from the start. . . . By *theory* I mean self-conscious reflection in art" (118).

45. For discussion of the *Republic*'s treatment of music, see Valiquette Moreau, "Musical Judgment."

46. On "Plato's" hatred of the new, see Wallace, "Plato, *Poikilia*, and New Music," 208–9.

47. See Nehamas, *Virtues of Authenticity*, 325; and Press, *Plato*, 26. See, however, Halliwell, *Republic 5*, 201, who maintains that the origin of the words *philosophia* and *philosophos* is "uncertain."

48. For discussion, see Zuckert, *Plato's Philosophers*, chap. 2. I explore this in chapter 6. Bloom, "Interpretive Essay," in *Republic of Plato*, 380, calls the third wave of *Republic* 5 introducing philosophers as kings a "total innovation."

the dialogues is also new, changing "from older adjectival usage" of ethical terms "(e.g. just, *dikaion*, pious, *hosion*, wise, *sōphrōn*) to abstract substantives (e.g. justice, *dikaiosynē*, piety, *hosiōtēs*, wisdom, *sophia*)," which Gerald Press calls "a change from unreflective use of these terms as descriptions that are taken as non-controversial to awareness and critical reflection on the fact that meanings may differ."[49] Plato's writing style is "something quite new in the history of Greek literature," as is his treatment of *mimēsis*.[50]

These innovations are interrelated. Informed by, among other things, its nonconformity to the modes of narrative Socrates put forward in *Republic* 3, the newness of Plato's writing style is bound with his representation of Socrates as a narrator who speaks both in his own person and in the persons of his interlocutors in turn. In thus deploying in his writing representation, on the one hand, and imitation, self-likening, self-assimilation, impersonation, on the other, Plato makes use of the very mimetic features that characterize ancient Greek poetry and are subject to scrutiny in the *Republic*.[51] That these practices of *mimēsis* feature so prominently in Plato's writing makes an initial case for aligning the *Republic* with, rather than opposing it to, art.[52]

There is more to be said, however. For Socrates' imitations/impersonations are *represented* by Plato, as is the dialogue as a whole, of course, and this suggests that like the (other) arts undergoing change in the years 430–380, the

---

49. Press, *Plato*, 28. On the appearance of *dikaiosynē* in Plato, see also Cammack, "Plato and Athenian Justice."

50. On the newness of Plato's writing style, see Ferrari, "Socrates in the *Republic*," 21. On the novelty of *mimēsis*, see Halliwell, *Aesthetics of Mimesis*, 49.

51. See Halliwell, *Aesthetics of Mimesis*, who parses the *Republic*'s account of *mimēsis* into a tripartite schema. He describes the *mimēsis* of Socrates' treatment of narrative in *Republic* 3 as a psychology of "self-assimilation" "whether in first-person verbal recitation or in physical enactment" (80). Two other sorts of *mimēsis* emerge in *Republic* 10: *mimēsis* as a kind of "sympathy" that can draw audiences of poetry into the experiences of the characters depicted, even while recognizing that they are not the same as those characters; and a *mimēsis* that depends on a critical/aesthetic distance enabling understanding and reflection on the different absorptions characteristic of the first two mimetic modes (25, 80–81). My primary focus will be on *mimēsis* as imitation, on the one hand, and as representation, on the other. Halliwell poses and puts to one side for his purposes the question of how Plato's own writing might relate to the different modes of *mimēsis* presented over the course of the *Republic* (84–85). That is the question I take up here.

52. See Naddaff, *Exiling the Poets*, who argues, though on different grounds from those offered here, that the initial oppositions between poetry and philosophy in the *Republic* are, by the end of the dialogue, undone.

Republic may be using techniques of representation and heightened levels of self-consciousness of presentation with a view to experimenting with *its* philosophic potential.⁵³ This, I believe, is exactly what the *Republic* is doing. I make this case next by way of a rereading of part of Socrates' engagement with Glaucon on the topic of *mimēsis* in *Republic* 10.⁵⁴ I then forge a path back to the political and philosophical questions with which this chapter began by showing how the discussion of *mimēsis* bears on how to read the dialogue as a whole.

MIMETIC POETRY

Socrates opens *Republic* 10 confirming "that we were entirely right" that mimetic poetry should be "altogether excluded" (595a-b) from the ideal city of *Republic* 5. If that's the case, why bring it up again? A standard answer is that Socrates seeks to resecure poetry's ouster and cement its displacement and replacement by philosophy, now against the backdrop of the work of the dialogue's middle books. Appearing to endorse that answer, Socrates' conversation with Glaucon over the next ten pages or so concludes with Socrates affirming that "reason or argument, *logos*, compelled us" (607b).⁵⁵ In the "old quarrel between philosophy and poetry" (607b), the compelling force of *logos* overcomes the "spell" of poetry, its "pleasures," "bewitchings," "enchantment," and "magic" (607c-d), its persuasive power, and its emancipation of *erōs*.

Or so it appears. Socrates' words of affirmation repay scrutiny. For he says that "the reasons that we have given, *touton ton logon hon legomen*," for poetry's ouster "we shall *chant* to ourselves, *epa[i]dontes hemin autois*," "like an *incantation, epō[i]dēn*," "as a counter-*charm* to [poetry's] spell, *epō[i]dēn*" (608a, my emphasis).⁵⁶ In so saying, he makes reason work magic, too. Moreover, he treats poetry's magic as the *reason* not only for poetry's ouster but also for its "just return" (607c-d). He then resecures *poetry's* status by offering a series of poetic examples as evidence of the quarrel requiring poetry's ouster.⁵⁷ By thus

---

53. See Farness, *Missing Socrates*, chap. 6, for a reading of the *Phaedrus* against the backdrop of developments in statuary.

54. This is an instance of what Brumbaugh, *Platonic Studies*, 39, calls in reference to the *Charmides* and *Lysis* the "self-referentiality" or "radically reflexive" nature of Plato's philosophy, i.e., that the dialogues perform or enact the topic of which they speak.

55. I explore that conversation at length in chapter 2.

56. For discussion, see Halliwell, "Antidotes and Incantations."

57. I leave aside the question of the status and existence of the quarrel Socrates references, which is debated in the scholarship: for pre-Socratic philosophical critiques of poetry that give

affirming the power of poetry, effacing the differences he has just announced between how philosophy and poetry do their work, and reversing their effects, Socrates also calls into question his own philosophical authority, if that is to be understood in terms of consistency and compelling reason. Glaucon, who had earlier agreed to poetry's ouster, wonders about none of this: not about Socrates' paradoxical invocations of reason's magic and poetry's reason nor about the status and quality of the evidence Socrates offers for the ancient quarrel. This is surprising. It might be expected that he would wonder, given his own extensive knowledge of poetry and his "love" of it, referenced just sentences later by Socrates (607e–608a). If, as Socrates claims in the *Theaetetus*, wonder is the only beginning of philosophy (155d), then Glaucon's failure to wonder signals a philosophical failure on his part, too.

There is still more to wonder about.[58] For if Socrates returns to the topic of mimetic poetry at the start of *Republic* 10 to secure its ouster, and if he does so successfully over the course of his exchanges with Glaucon (a claim I challenge in chapter 2), then why, just after declaring that he and Glaucon have been compelled by reason to affirm that ouster, does Socrates open a loophole, maintaining that "we would be glad to receive [poetry] back from exile" (607c) if the poets themselves or if "lovers of poetry" speaking "in prose on its behalf" can show "that poetry not only gives pleasure but is beneficial, *ōphelimē*, both to constitutions and to human life" (607d)? Why does poetry keep coming back on the scene if poetic authority has been overcome? What is to be made of Socrates' performative contradictions? And what of Glaucon's stolidity in the face of these contradictions?

MIRRORS

Socrates allows the following exception to poetry's censorship: "hymns to the gods and the praises of good men" *are* to be admitted into "our city" (607a). This exception is granted following what he calls "the chief accusation" against mimetic poetry, namely, "its power to corrupt, with rare exceptions, even the

---

evidence of an ancient quarrel, see Heraclitus frr. 40, 42, 56–57, 104, 106 DJ; Xenophanes frr. 1.21–24, 11–12, 14–16 DK, cited in Halliwell, *Aesthetics of Mimesis*, 42 n. 14; for the claim that Plato invented the quarrel, see Nightingale, *Genres in Dialogue*, 60–67. For a response to Nightingale, see Halliwell, review of Nightingale, 455–56.

58. Halliwell, *Aesthetics of Mimesis*, 39, notes that *Republic* 10 is "arguably the most pronounced invitation ever issued to Plato's readers to continue the debate themselves, in dialogue *with* as well as within the work."

better sort, *tous chariesterous*" (605c), who, no less than the many, it turns out, "feel pleasure and abandon [themselves] and accompany the representations of [heroes in grief] with sympathy and eagerness, and praise as an excellent poet the one who most strongly affects us in this way" (605c-d). Socrates says that when their own lives are afflicted by troubles, "the better sort" may, unlike the lamenting characters represented by the poets, instead keep calm and carry on (606d-e), and when they feel pleasure and yield to mimetic representations they may feel shame (605e). But because, as he puts it, "what we enjoy in others will inevitably react upon ourselves" (606b), all mimetic poetry that "waters and fosters" (605b) these feelings must be excluded.

Socrates' comments in these passages appear to reflect the idea of "mimetic identification" as a practice of imitation, the assumption that audiences will copy and so become like what they see. This assumption in turn undergirds what Ruby Blondell calls "mimetic pedagogy," the idea that there is a "relationship between the representation of character (in both dramatic and ethical senses) and education, broadly understood."[59] On the assumption of mimetic identification as imitation, hymns to the gods and praises of good men are exempted from exclusion because such poetry mirrors and also educates the better sort to goodness. The poetry that mirrors the many and enthralls both the many and the better sort is banished so as to avoid an education to vice, with the result that the many, unlike gods or good men and so unable to be educated by the exempted poetry, receive no education at all.[60] Socrates' exception thus appears to confirm not only the negative verdict against (most of) mimetic poetry but also the authoritarian and essentializing politics and ethics often associated with poetry's ouster and with the dialogue as a whole.

This appearance is deceiving, however, for even as Socrates puts forward the idea of *mimēsis* as imitation or mirroring, he also casts it into doubt. As noted above, Socrates describes the better sort as no less enthralled than are the many to the "vexed and complicated type of character, *to aganaktētikon te kai poikilon ēthos*" (605a), represented by the banished poets. This indicates that the better sort are attracted to what is *unlike* them. Socrates also calls into question the pedagogic power of the poetry exempted from the ban, describing representations of "the intelligent and moderate disposition" and

---

59. Blondell, *Play of Character*, 80–83. For discussion of Blondell with which I largely agree, see Cotton, *Platonic Dialogue*, 106–12.

60. For an account of this education, see *Republic* 2–3. For my argument that the education premised on the exclusion of mimetic poetry teaches not goodness but war, see Frank, "Wages of War." I elaborate the consequences of the early education in chapter 3.

of other good characters as "always remaining approximately the same" and, therefore, as "neither easy to imitate nor to be understood when imitated, especially by a festive assembly where all sorts of human beings are gathered in the theater" (604d-e), including, presumably, the better sort. Hymns to the gods and praises of good men thus appear to foster no imitation at all. Bringing neither benefit nor pleasure, the poetry Socrates exempts from the ban is depicted as *failing* to meet the very conditions that, as we hear just pages later, would allow the *banished* poetry's return from exile (607d).

Why does Socrates introduce as an exception to the censorship of mimetic poetry hymns and praises that, by bringing neither pleasure nor benefit, fail to meet the conditions of his loophole? What might Plato be doing when he makes Socrates produce these baffling and contradictory arguments in the context of his account of *mimēsis* as imitation? I suggest next that these arguments mark not only the *distance Republic* 10 takes from *mimēsis* as imitation but also its endorsement of a *mimēsis* of a different kind.[61]

The start of *Republic* 10 lends support to this possibility. Suggesting that Glaucon practice the art of *mimēsis* using a mirror, the exemplary tool of imitation, Socrates says:

> It isn't hard. You could do it quickly and in lots of places, *pollachē[i] kai tachu*, especially if you were willing to carry a mirror, *katoptron*, with you, for that's the quickest, *tachista*, way of all. With it you can quickly, *tachu*, make the sun, the things in the heavens, the earth, yourself, the other animals, manufactured items, plants, and everything else mentioned just now. (596d)

Glaucon responds: "Yes I could make them appear, but I couldn't make the things themselves as they truly are." Socrates lauds Glaucon for seeing the difference between what appears and what truly is (596d-e). Left unsaid is what Glaucon gets wrong, namely, that with a mirror Glaucon *cannot* make appear "everything else mentioned just now." Specifically, a mirror cannot make appear all the things "in Hades beneath the earth" just named by Socrates as products of *mimēsis* (596c).[62] When Glaucon fails to register this (rather obvious) limitation of mirrors, namely, that they reflect only what is visible, he

---

61. I agree with Halliwell, *Aesthetics of Mimesis*, 56, who maintains that *Republic* 10, seeking a definition of "mimesis as a whole" (595c), moves away from *mimēsis* as imitation.

62. Bloom, "Interpretive Essay," in *Republic of Plato*, 428, notes this, too.

claims to be able to see too much. This observation bears on the assumption of mimetic identification when that is understood as imitation. For when hymns to the gods and praises of good men are treated as mirrors of the better sort, what disappears is the possibility, which I explore in chapter 2, that the souls of the better sort, invisible to the eye (like the things in Hades beneath the earth), are not truly good at all. What disappears, too, is the possibility that the better sort may, not unlike Glaucon, see more than is warranted by, say, taking themselves to be reflected in the hymns to the gods and praises of good men. The seeing eye and its possibilities and limitations thus ramify ethically for the seeing I and vice versa.[63]

If, as Glaucon's mistake about mirrors suggests, the relationship between the representation of character and education is not one of imitation, then what might it be? In the mirror passage, Socrates refers five times to how "quickly" mirrors do their work (596d-e).[64] He does so just lines after remarking that "people who don't see well are often quicker, *proteroi*, to see things than people whose eyesight is better" (596a).[65] Socrates' language recalls the "quickest and easiest way, *tachista te kai ra[i]sta*" (541a-b), of coming to understanding that Glaucon sometimes prefers (435d, 504b) to the hard work (511c, 530c, e, 531d) and "longer way, *makrotera kai pleiōn hodos*," of philosophy (435d, 504d). In the mirror passage, Socrates implies, too, that *mimēsis* may do something more than mirror; that, indeed, unlike a mirror, *mimēsis* may be able to bring to appearance what is not visible to the seeing I/eye. Here I agree with Halliwell, who argues, though on different grounds, that "the mirror analogy stands for the threat, not the final assertion of a reductive conception of visual mimesis," and that the arguments of *Republic* 10 "offer a mimetic conception of art at whose core lies a critique of precisely those ideas—truth-to-appearances, verisimilitude, realism, illusionism—that have often been considered to define the mimeticist tradition in aesthetics."[66] But if not a practice of imitation, mirroring, or self-likening, then in what might "mimetic pedagogy" consist? To see, I look next at the poetry *excluded* from the ideal city.

---

63. A point I return to in chapter 6, which focuses on the role of sense perception in the *Republic*'s philosophy.

64. In the Greek: *pollache[i] kai tachu . . . tachista de pou . . . tachu men helion . . . tachu de gen . . . tachu de sauton*.

65. *Proteroi* means "sooner, beforehand"; thus, "quicker" here denotes priority rather than rapidity.

66. For Halliwell's rejection of *mimēsis* as mirroring on other grounds, see *Aesthetics of Mimesis*, 139, 143, and 124–42.

REPRESENTATION

Socrates insists that all mimetic poetry that does not represent the good must be banished. This includes, as he specifies, epic and lyric poetry devoted to representations of "the vexed and complicated, *poikilon*, type of character" that are "easy to imitate" (605a) and will win the poet favor with the many and the better sort alike. On the assumption of mimetic identification as imitation these representations can only reinforce what is not good in each and must be excluded for that reason. If we consider *mimēsis* as representation rather than imitation, however, things appear otherwise.

Consider the word *poikilon*, used here to describe the characters of the banned poetry.[67] It is a word that appears repeatedly in the *Republic* in contrast to what is simple, single, unmixed, unqualified, *haploos* (380d, 382e, 397d, 404b, 404e, 410a).[68] It signifies what is effaced by the education of *Republic* 2–3 through its censorship of poetry (378c) and music (399e), which I discuss in chapter 3. It characterizes the many colors of the democratic constitution, itself full of constitutions of all kinds (557c). It is used multiple times in *Republic* 7 to describe the stars "that paint the skies" (529c-d), to which I return in chapter 6. In these examples, as in *Republic* 10, *poikilia* signifies intricacy, complexity, and also beauty, attributes that, it is often claimed, are excluded or superseded over the course of the dialogue in the name of the simple, the pure, the good, and the one.[69] For this reason, Plato has been called an "enemy" of *poikilia*.[70]

Poikilia is excluded from or superseded in the ideal city, to be sure, but it may be too quick to call Plato an enemy of *poikilia* and too quick to treat the ideal city as a city the *Republic* endorses. Might it be rather that the ideal city's exclusion of *poikilia*, which turns it into what Harry Berger Jr. calls an "*aischropolis*," an Uglytown, and the exclusions of *poikilia* from the curricular reforms

---

67. Wallace, "Plato, *Poikilia*, and New Music," 209, notes that, according to the TLG, Plato uses the term *poikilia* "far more than any other writer."

68. For a similar contrast, see Euripides' *Phoenician Women*, in which Polyneices states, "The word of truth is single, *haploos*, in its nature, and a just cause needs no elaborate interpreting, *poikila hermeneumata*" (469–70).

69. I have more to say about each of these examples in the following chapters on poetry, education, and dialectics, where I disagree that, in the words of Halliwell, *Aesthetics of Mimesis*, 94, the *Republic* regards "all forms of variety and versatility [what is *poikilos*] as subversive of virtue."

70. For "enemy," see Wallace, "Plato, *Poikilia*, and New Music," 202.

of *Republic* 2–3, give grounds for *their* indictment?⁷¹ I explain in chapter 3 why I think this is the case. For now, it is to be noted that, regarding the stars, at least, Socrates does not warn against *poikilia* as such but against taking the complexity, multiplicity, and beauty of the stars to be their whole truth. Socrates issues this warning by drawing a double analogy, first to artistic designs and then to geometry, claiming that "we must use the blazonry, *poikilia[i]*, of the heavens as patterns, *paradeigmasi*, to aid in the study of [the invisible] realities" (529d-e). *Poikilia*, in this case, signifies what is brought to appearance and thus made present by way of what appears.

Complex, various, manifold, plural, *poikilia* also invites a consideration of what is absent (what lies beyond the stars, why this constitution and not that one), what does not appear. In this way, representations of *poikilia* bring "visible and invisible things together in the mind's eye as one coherent fact."⁷² The work of *poikilia* may thus be analogized to Jean-Pierre Vernant's account of the mask on the ancient Greek stage, which showed that

> the "presence" embodied by the actor in the theater was always the sign, or mask, of an absence, in the day-to-day reality of the public. Caught up by the action and moved by what he beheld, the spectator was still aware that these figures were not what they seemed . . . —in short, this was *mimesis*.⁷³

It is precisely the intricacy, complexity, and beauty of *poikilia* as these appear to the seeing eye that orients the seeing I to what does not appear. Socrates says something like this in *Republic* 3 when he uses *poikilia* to describe what summons a soul to reflection about the ideas and their opposites (401a–402c). If *poikilia* and its representations thus invite attention to what does not appear, they make no claim at all to what truly is. Instead they do their work in the register of appearance, sense perception, *aisthēsis*, aesthetics. The *Republic* may offer a critique of *mimēsis* as imitation, copy, verisimilitude, then, but,

---

71. For *aischropolis*, see Berger, *Perils of Uglytown*. Saxonhouse, "Socratic Narrative," also calls the status and place of the ideal city into question, noting that Plato's portrait of Socrates positions him as "the countermodel to the regime he proposes" (741). Unlike what Saxonhouse describes as the Straussian indictment of the ideal city, which finds "tensions in the text that might indicate that the surface meaning might not be the final statement of the author" (745), my interpretation finds reasons to indict the city in what appears on the text's surface.

72. This is Carson, *Economy of the Unlost*, 55, on Simonides' poetry.

73. Vernant, *Myth and Tragedy*, 187–88, quoted in Crotty, *Philosopher's Song*, 115.

in my view, it is a mistake to conclude that it is antimimetic and/or against aesthetics.[74]

On the contrary, as we will see, the philosophy of the *Republic*, and its ethics and politics, critically depend on *mimēsis* as representation. This is because, unlike mirrors, mimetic representations make apparent our *inability* to see what is invisible while inviting us to look harder, more slowly, and again. As such, they prompt and cultivate critical reflection. Indeed, as we will see in chapters 2, 3, and 6, it is the look of a representation, its *eidos*, as that appears to the seeing eye, along with the knowledge that that look is partial and so fails to tell the whole truth, that turns the seeing I toward the idea, also *eidos*. As Berger puts it, "The method is to look for the real only through the opaque screen of an image . . . so constructed as to direct us beyond itself."[75]

Against this backdrop, perhaps Socrates uses the word *poikilon* to describe the characters of mimetic poetry so as to invite his interlocutors to attend to the appearance of these characters and also, and thereby, to what does not appear. If what appears, in the case of mimetic poetry, is, in the language of Socrates' account of learning to read in *Republic* 3, "what isn't fine," then might its *poikilon* characters help to develop "the sharpest sense of what is left out" by prompting and cultivating, as in the case of the stars, critical reflection about how they might be otherwise than they appear? This mode of reflection depends not on imitating what appears, and not on knowing a stable, certain, and universal truth beyond appearance, but instead on being drawn to a representation, on attending slowly to its intricacy and complexity, on seeing it as an appearance, and on wondering about what does not appear, what might be left out. Arendt calls this mode of reflection "representative thinking."[76] We

---

74. See, e.g., Porter, *Origins of Aesthetic Thought*, especially 83–95, who reads Plato's dialogues as seeking purification of all that is *poikilos* and therefore treats Plato as one of the "fathers," with Aristotle, of a "rigorous and austere" aesthetics that leaves no room for "the phenomenal and sensual aspects of art" (86–87). This position is represented in Plato's dialogues, to be sure, but I do not take it to be the position of the dialogues. Taking what is said in the dialogues to reflect Plato's position, Porter concludes that "Platonic aesthetics is a minimal aesthetics. It is grounded in the most intense perception of the least amount of variability and fluctuation (or becoming) and in the greatest degree of changeless, unwavering, unadulterated essences. As a consequence, it is unfriendly to the senses" (87). When we refuse to treat Plato's mimetic representations as his truth, as I am suggesting, the result, as we will see in chapter 6, is a relation to the senses that has much in common with the one for which Porter advocates.

75. Berger, "Plato's *Cratylus*," 216.
76. Arendt, "Truth and Politics," 241.

might also call it imagination.[77] As we will see, the *Republic* treats this mode of reflection as critical to the practice of philosophy.

RESISTANCE AND SELF-AUTHORIZATION

Taking up the principle of mimetic identification as a guide to how to read Plato and treating it as a principle of mirroring or imitation, scholars sometimes recommend that readers of Plato's dialogues imaginatively identify with Socrates' interlocutors, with Socrates, and/or with what is being represented.[78] If a reader imitates Glaucon in *Republic* 10, however, she may, as noted, find herself without wonder. And if she imitates Socrates? The *Symposium* gives readers reason to think twice about imitating Socrates, not least by depicting Apollodorus and Aristodemus, whom I examine in chapter 5, as Socrates "wannabes" and, as a result, as laughable shadows of the alleged "original," who is not himself an "original," of course, but, as already noted, a representation by Plato.[79] In the *Republic*, Plato's representations of Socrates in contradiction with himself, in any case, make imitating him difficult: when someone stands for opposing positions, which one do you choose?

Socrates contradicts himself in any number of ways.[80] Sometimes he does so performatively, as already noted: in the name of defending philosophy against poetry in *Republic* 10, we saw, Socrates instead secures poetry's status;

---

77. Contra Halliwell, *Aesthetics of Mimesis*, 26, 94–96, who describes Plato's "lurking fear of the power of imagination itself" and attributes that fear to the power of the imagination to foster different selves and desires that are "dangerously inimical to reason, precisely because its dynamics are those of self-transformation," "self-creation, self-exploration, and self-renewal." Halliwell recognizes and leaves to one side "the very different uses of the imagination that can be traced at work within Plato's own philosophical thinking and writing—uses that, in their metaphysical and visionary settings, subserve what we might call an alternative, and very different, Platonic 'aesthetic.'"

78. For examples, see Blondell, *Play of Character*; Long, *Socratic and Platonic Political Philosophy*.

79. On the complexity of Plato's representations of Apollodorus and Aristodemus, see Schlosser, *What Would Socrates Do?*, 78–80.

80. For other contradictions in the *Republic*, see, Naddaff, *Exiling the Poets*, 20, 23, 93–94, who discusses the dialogue's differential treatment of mimetic poetry in *Republic* 2–3 and 10, among other things. For Naddaff, the contradictions align Socrates with the poets and sophists, and indicate that Plato is a "self-subverting thinker," "performing dialectics on his own unexamined presumptions," "testing the limits of his philosophical argumentation" (2–3, 70). Noting "inconsistencies" in Plato's *Laws*, Schofield, *Saving the City*, 49–50, describes both an

in the name of affirming *mimēsis* as imitation, he instead criticizes it; he argues against innovation in education after proposing a radical revision of classical Greek *paideia*. Socrates is also inconsistent in the *Phaedrus*, as we saw, insofar as he supports arguments against writing that pull in opposite directions, arguments claiming that writing is static and univocal and also that it is in motion and multivocal. To offer another example from the *Republic*: over the course of a little more than a Stephanus page (433a–434a), Socrates defines justice as "one man:one art," "sharing in common," "minding one's own business," and "the having and doing of one's own and what belongs to one." I explore these definitions, which are not obviously reconcilable with one another, along with others that are given voice in *Republic* 1, in this book's epilogue. For now, it is to be noted that, by way of his contradictions, inconsistencies, and multiplications, Socrates speaks like the exiled mimetic poets who call "the same thing now one, now the other, *ta auta tote men megala . . . tote de smikra*" (605c).[81] Indeed, across the dialogues we hear that it is insofar as poets contradict themselves, and one another, and cannot therefore be cross-examined that they are not to be taken seriously as authorities (*Prot.* 347e; *Meno* 71d; *Lysis* 214–15; *Hippias Minor* 365d). If that is so, then, might Socrates' (self-) contradictions invite a similar questioning of his authority?

The Socrates of the *Republic* does not only speak like a mimetic poet. In virtue of his inconsistencies, he also looks like a character represented in mimetic poetry: vexed, complex, intricate, and, at least according to Alcibiades in the *Symposium*, beautiful (217a), though perhaps not to the seeing eye.[82] Socrates is, in a word, *poikilon*. The same may be said, albeit differently, of the other characters of the *Republic*, who, like the characters of mimetic poetry, are portrayed as not (yet) wise or graceful or good. Perhaps, then, as with the distance *Republic* 10 takes from *mimēsis* as imitation, the relation to *its* characters—both Socrates' interlocutors and also Socrates—the *Republic* as a whole invites is *not* readerly imitation at all but instead, and as with the characters of mimetic poetry, critical reflection on the ways *these* characters are made to appear.[83]

---

earlier interpretative orientation on his part to leave them to one side and how coming to grips with them altered his reading of that dialogue.

81. For discussion of poetic self-contradiction, see Halliwell, "Subjection of Muthos to Logos," 102; Saxonhouse, "Socratic Narrative."

82. Indeed, as Saxonhouse, "Socratic Narrative," 736–37, argues, by the terms of his own arguments, Socrates would be forced to live "well outside the city [in speech] he and his interlocutors found." On Socrates' ugliness, see Nietzsche, *Twilight of the Idols*, 29–34.

83. Along similar lines, Saxonhouse, "Socratic Narrative," 737–38, notes that Socrates' readings of the poems he censors in *Republic* 3 are "flat-footed," portraying "a blindness to

And perhaps Plato represents Glaucon as without wonder in the face of Socrates' contradictions in *Republic* 10 so as to prompt readers to wonder not only about Glaucon's absence of wonder but also about the questions he leaves unasked.

And Socrates? Why present him in contradiction? The dialogue suggests an answer by way of its own attention to contradiction. In *Republic* 7, Socrates maintains that a soul is summoned to reflection when it receives contradictory communications, *hermēneiai* (524b), from the senses. Referring to these contradictory perceptions as provocatives, *parakalounta* (523c), Socrates says that they "awaken reflection" (524d) by giving rise to a puzzle, *aporein* (524a, e; also 515d). Themselves an exemplification of *poikilia*, contradictions invite wonder about the many and opposing things that appear to the seeing eye and so, as we have seen, invite the seeing I to slow down, look harder, and wonder. In Socrates' words,

> If some sort of contradiction of it is always seen at the same time, so that it seems to be no more the one than its opposite, then there would be a need for someone to make a decision about it. In a case like this the soul within him would be driven in its confusion to start searching. It would arouse the capacity for reflection within itself, and ask it what the one itself actually was. (524e–525a)

Like and unlike his representations of Glaucon, then, Plato's representations of Socrates in contradiction invite the reader to slow down, to look harder, and to wonder: to wonder about the topics Socrates is speaking about when Plato has him speak now one way, now another (what is writing? what is *mimēsis*? what is justice?); to wonder about the stability and authority of Socrates' words, which, though presented as oral speech, are, at the same time and in virtue

---

interpretive richness" that is in tension with the complexity and richness of the "interpretive model Plato uses in writing the dialogue." On my view, this is also a case of a "negative example," offered to prompt critical reflection. Contra Long, *Socratic and Platonic Political Philosophy*, 42, 119–20, 154, 166, 172, who sets up the following analogy: Plato's writings:readers::Socrates' sayings:Socrates' interlocutors to argue that just as Socrates helps his interlocutors to become good, so too does Plato's poetic writing turn readers "toward the best." Long rightly calls this "the figure of an idealized Socrates" (7), which he doesn't see as problematic, but I do. As a sophisticated version of a "mouthpiece theory," Long's analogy collapses the distance between Plato the writer and his representation of the character of Socrates and the ways in which, as we will see, Socrates is depicted as failing to bring about goodness/justice in the souls of his interlocutors.

of their inconsistencies, in perpetual motion; to wonder about Socrates' reliability and authority; and to wonder, not least, about truth and appearance themselves.

Read in this way, that is, through the lens of its own treatment of mimetic representation, the *Republic*, like the fine arts of fifth- and fourth-century Athens, invites and prompts not the quick and passive "absorption in naturalistic illusionism" characteristic of *mimēsis* as imitation, but a slow and active, which is to say, a self-conscious and critically aware, engagement with its representations.[84] What, then, is the relationship between the *Republic*'s representation of character and its education? What is its mimetic pedagogy? How might the *Republic*'s representations of complex and vexed characters—its representations of what is not so fine and/or good and/or what is in contradiction—orient the reading I to what is fine and good and in harmony? For some scholars, "the capacity for self-recognition and self-criticism is among the qualities dramatized and recognized" in Plato's dialogues, and it is in this way that a reader "may learn to adopt a critical stance toward herself" and thus be protected from the perils of passive imitation.[85]

I see things otherwise. Indeed, on the reading I have offered so far and fill out over the chapters that follow, it is precisely "the capacity for self-recognition and self-criticism" that is *not* "dramatized and recognized" by the *Republic*'s characters.[86] This means that the *Republic*'s mimetic pedagogy depends not only on slow and careful attention to what appears, but also on a capacity on the part of its readers to resist appearance. By prompting identification not with the being of Socrates and Glaucon (or any other mimetic character) but with their possibility, the *Republic* invites and cultivates mimetic identification as a practice of *disidentification*.[87] What these characters might become, their possibility, is not represented, of course. As the not-yet-actual, it cannot be. For this reason, the mimetic disidentification prompted by the *Republic* depends on and encourages readerly imagination.

---

84. Platt, "Likeness and Likelihood in Classical Greek Art," 198. See Cotton, *Platonic Dialogue*, 116–18: "The emphasis is on self-consciousness, distance, and critical evaluation," practices that she thinks are modeled in the text especially when it draws attention to the activities of interpretation and representation, as in Socrates' commentaries on Thrasymachus' character in *Republic* 1.

85. Blondell, *Play of Character*, 104.

86. This is an example of the "not" possibility, introduced and discussed in this book's prologue. See also Crotty, *Philosopher's Song*, 156–58.

87. See also Cohen, *Thinking of Others*, who treats identification as a practice of metaphor.

Inviting its readers to see, hear, and know many things in the manner of the *Phaedrus*' Theuth, the *Republic* prompts us to ask again and again: "What do *I* see, what do *I* think, and what do *I* make of it?"[88] Mandating, in this way, that its realization and/or actualization is accomplished by its readers,[89] the *Republic* circulates authority to us, with the result that "reading rules" rather than the author or absent writer. We might call this the "democratic spirit" of Plato's writing.[90] I return over the course of later chapters to how a distribution of authority and authorship to separate reading Is can be hospitable to both the democratic spirit and the democratic practice of *collective* self-rule. On the way of reading I propose, the *Republic* is what Ferrari has called a "declaration of Platonic poetics" in at least three senses.[91] It is an artistic *poiēsis*, a work of mimetic poetry by Plato. It is also a *poiēsis* by Plato's readers, an actualization by us. It is, moreover, a *poiēsis* of Plato's readers. For in circulating authority to its readers, the *Republic* prompts us to ask not only "What do I see, think, and make of *it*?" but also "What do I thereby make of *myself*?" and to hear that question as signifying both "What do I take myself to be?" and also "What might I make myself into, who am I to become?"[92] Allen has noted, rightly I think, that, in the *Republic*, reading is "all-important to the formation of the human soul."[93] On my account, the *Republic*'s mimetic pedagogy of disidentification makes reading, for Plato's ancient and contemporary readers alike, a practice of self-creation, transformation, exploration, and renewal that, as such, promotes capacities for self-authorization and self-constitution as well.[94]

88. These are my rewritings of the questions posed by Rancière, *Ignorant Schoolmaster*, 23, discussed in the prologue.

89. Iser, *Act of Reading*, 18–23.

90. I take the phrases "reading rules" (4) and "democratic spirit" (29) from Svenbro, *Phrasikleia*, although he does not use them in reference to Plato.

91. Ferrari, "Socrates in the *Republic*," 21–22. Thanks to Rayna Kalas for prompting me to think about *poiēsis*.

92. Iser, *Act of Reading*, 150: "The reader himself, in constituting the meaning, is also constituted."

93. Allen, *Why Plato Wrote*, 32–33.

94. For this language as a description of what Plato fears, see Halliwell, *Aesthetics of Mimesis*, 95. What I am calling "self-constitution" aligns nominally with what Korsgaard, "Self-Constitution in the Ethics of Plato and Kant," calls the "Constitutional Model" of the soul in Plato's *Republic*, in that for my account, as for hers, "action is self-constitution" (27) and for my account, as for hers, action is attributable to the "whole person" who does it (3). Aligning Plato with Kant, however, Korsgaard takes action to be a matter of "volitional unity," by which she means a practice of reasoned self-government, according to which a person's actions, "all of her actions, in every circumstance of her life, are really and fully her own: never merely the manifestations of forces at work in her or on her, but always the expression of her own choice. She is

In whom exactly? Most of Socrates' interlocutors in the dialogues, including the *Republic*, are, as noted in this book's prologue, the elite of Athens. Some historians argue that literacy in fifth-century Athens, when most of the dialogues are set, was largely confined to small circles of elites.[95] Does this not argue for taking the *Republic*'s education in self-authorization to be directed to them? The arguments of this chapter about writing and reading, together with the expansion of literacy in fourth-century Athens, suggest rather that Plato targeted a broader, more inclusive readership.[96] The proposition that Socrates' conversations with elite interlocutors imply that Plato writes for a readership of the elite assumes that there is a direct inference to be drawn about what Plato is doing from his depictions of what Socrates does. That kind of inference assumes either that Socrates stands for Plato and/or that Plato practices *mimēsis* as imitation. I have discussed earlier in this chapter why there are no grounds for the first assumption, and the *Republic*'s critique of *mimēsis* as imitation gives reason to be wary of the second one. In any case, if we do read Plato as targeting the audience with whom he depicts Socrates conversing, then insofar as, as we will see, Socrates' attempts to educate his interlocutors by and large fail, there would be little to expect of such an education in relation to Plato's readers either.

If, by contrast, we read Plato as writing the *Republic* in the mode of *mimēsis* as representation, we get a different appreciation of what he may be doing when he presents Socrates in conversation with elite interlocutors and another perspective on his target audience. Read in this way, Plato's representations do not produce or reproduce reality but rather invite and cultivate critical reflection about what they bring to appearance. On this way of reading, the dialogues depict failure on the part of Socrates' elite interlocutors (and also, as we will see, on the part of the dialogues' philosophical authorities, including Socrates) for the same reason that they stage contradictions, inconsistencies, and vexed and complex characters, namely, to prompt the mimetic disidentifi-

---

completely self-possessed: not necessarily happy on the rack—but *herself* on the rack, herself even there" (22). On the philosopher's goal being "to be truly invulnerable to evil . . . to transcend the instability of events leading to events and the equivocation of agency compromised by circumstances," see Crotty, *Philosopher's Song*, 20. As we will see in chapter 5, on my account, by contrast, self-government implies an always only incomplete self-possession, according to which one's actions are never fully one's own, and what gives rise to action is a complex combination of experience, reason, and desire, with the last of these doing most of the heavy lifting.

95. Harris, *Ancient Literacy*, 115, claims that literacy became more extensive only in the 370s and 360s, and even then it was still largely limited to elites receiving formal education.

96. See note 3 in the prologue.

cation that gives rise to critical reflection. On this way of reading, the education in self-authorization offered by the *Republic* is directed at any and all readers who do not identify with its representations, whether that disidentification is a matter of character, discursive disposition, class, or anything else. So read, the *Republic* gives force to the claim, put forward in the *Phaedrus*, that written words are available to anyone and everyone, without discrimination (275e).

Anyone who can read, that is.[97] So who exactly were Plato's ancient readers? As noted in the prologue to this book, although he set his dialogues largely in the fifth century, Plato wrote in the fourth century. The question of literacy thus pertains to that later period. If there is scholarly disagreement about levels of literacy in fifth-century Athens, there is broad consensus that in the fourth century literacy was universal for those who participated in the business of politics, which is to say, Athens' democratic citizens.[98] The use of written evidence in forensic speeches by fourth-century orators implies that their addressees, jurors chosen by lot from the *dēmos*, were literate. The compilation and publication of Athens' laws after the Peloponnesian War suggest the same.[99] How advanced were the reading skills of these citizens? Were they good enough, say, to read the *Republic*? On this question, scholars are more divided. Because, as I have been arguing, we cannot simply read Plato's representations as reality, the depiction of Socrates referring at his trial in 399 BCE to the books of Anaxagoras (*Ap.* 26d), and the *Theaetetus*' dramatic frame, which scholars also date to the fourth century,[100] by which Plato stages the dialogue as a reading by a slave, cannot be taken as reliable evidence of how advanced and/or broad literacy levels actually were in this period. As mimetic representations, they can, however, be taken, in Halliwell's words, to "signify and communicate certain hypothesized realities" or "imagined possibilities of experience."[101]

This means that whether or not Athens' fourth-century democratic citizens and/or slaves already possessed the advanced literacy skills required for reading lengthy and complicated political and philosophical texts, they could critically

---

97. Robb, *Literacy and* Paideia *in Ancient Greece*, 13, argues that "craft literacy" preceded "scribe" and "essayist" literacy, with the former in evidence as early as 700–450 BCE, and the latter emerging among Athens' elite in the second half of the fifth century.

98. Missiou, *Literacy and Democracy*; Pébarthe, *Cité, démocratie et écriture*; Harvey, "Literacy in the Athenian Democracy"; Svenbro, *Phrasikleia*; Thomas, "Origins of Western Literacy." See also Burnyeat, "Postscript on Silent Reading"; and Knox, "Silent Reading in Antiquity."

99. See, for discussion, e.g., Harvey, "Literacy in the Athenian Democracy," 596–97.

100. Some to 394, some to 369, and others later, which differences are irrelevant for my purposes.

101. Halliwell, *Aesthetics of Mimesis*, 16.

reflect on the many depictions of such readers in their culture, in plays, for example, on vases, and on gravestones.[102] Even without advanced literary skills, they could read the short passages about learning to read in the *Republic*, say, or in the *Theaetetus*, and they could, by trial and error, build on whatever basic skills they had by reading anything else. In the process of learning to read in this way, that is, by looking at everything everywhere in their culture, and without authorization by the teachers instructing elites, they could come to know more about reading, and more also about their capacities and possibilities as readers, even of the *Republic*.[103] That would not be quick and easy. As we saw, it would take their time. But on the way of reading I have been exploring there is nothing in Plato's text or context that makes it unimaginable that his dialogues target a broad and inclusive audience, and there are good reasons to imagine that they do.

The following question remains: if the *Republic* depicts Athenian imperialism as a symptom of, among other things, the unconstrained authority of the *dēmos*, what could possibly justify the claim that it seeks to provide an education in self-authorization to *them*? Answering that question is the task of the remainder of this book. Using the reading approach offered in this chapter, the following chapters revisit the *Republic*'s treatments of poetry, *paideia*, persuasion, and *erōs*—all key features of Athenian democratic life and character—and show them to be key features, too, of the dialogue's education to self-authorization. Representing fifth-century democratic and imperial versions of these practices, the *Republic*, I argue, offers its fourth-century readers, and later readers as well, opportunities to reimagine them: from being tools of imperial power over others they may become powers of just individual and collective self-rule. Who better to target for such an education than the practitioners of that authority themselves?

The Greek word most often used to signify authority is *exousia*, a correlate of *dunamis*, capacity or power.[104] It appears in *Republic* 2 in Glaucon's rehearsal and amplification of Thrasymachus' praise of injustice, where *exousia* is the

102. Harvey, "Literacy in the Athenian Democracy," 596–97.
103. Rowe, *Plato and the Art of Philosophical Writing*, 13, claims that Plato's "first preoccupation" or primary target of persuasion is his readers or audience. See Morgan, "Tyranny of the Audience," 192–93, 191, who writes that Plato's dialogues thematize "the problem of reception, both explicitly and implicitly," and create "an intimate relationship with the reader." On Plato's concern with his own reception, see also Yunis, "Protreptic Rhetoric of the *Republic*," 13.
104. Thanks to Richard Tuck for the suggestion to look at this term. See Liddell and Scott, *Greek-English Lexicon*, 9th ed., s.v. *exousia*. On the relation between *dunamis* and *exousia*, see Schofield, *Plato*, 266. See also Schofield, "Sharing in the Constitution." The material in this paragraph and the next draws from Frank, "Circulating Authority."

freedom granted by the ring of Gyges to act justly or unjustly without fear of consequence (359c, 360d). It also appears in *Republic* 8 in Socrates' descriptions of the democratic man and regime, where *exousia*, which, in excess, leads to tyranny (563e), is the freedom granted by democracy to refuse to hold office, to refuse to submit to the rule of another, to refuse to follow the law, or to keep the peace (557b, d, 564d). Most often translated as "license,"[105] *exousia*, a "democratical watchword,"[106] may appear, at first glance, to signify only negatively in the *Republic*. A second glance suggests otherwise. Entailing the power to do or refrain from doing "free from all compulsion" (557e), *exousia* locates authority in human capacity, activity, and desire itself. It thus reminds us that, as Peter Euben puts it, authority involves "recognizing oneself as a holder of power."[107]

Writing about the *Crito*, James Boyd White has noted the ways in which that dialogue both "stimulates and frustrates the reader's own desire for an authority external to himself."[108] The *Republic* does the same. This desire, it seems to me, is a feature of what we might call the "democratic condition." This is a condition, which, modern or ancient, confronts citizens with the necessity of developing human capacities for what Arendt calls "building, preserving, and caring" if there is to be a common world of politics, and seems at the same time to produce a longing for an authority that will obviate that necessity.[109] Making legible the necessity *and* desire characteristic of the democratic condition, Plato's *Republic*, as I read it, stages the need to develop human capacities of world-building, preserving, and caring, and stages also the longing for an extrapolitical authority to obviate that need. As we will see, it exposes as well the costs for those very same human capacities when that longed-for authority actually comes into being, along with the more generalized political and philosophical costs of the inevitable failures of the longed-for authority. In staging these failures and costs, the *Republic* also orients to practices of citizenship that are able to avow responsibility and accountability, and sometimes to refuse them, and also, when necessary, to resist even the authority we desire.

---

105. See, for examples, the translations of the *Republic* by Bloom, Shorey, and Reeve. See also Adam, *Republic of Plato*.
106. Adam, *Republic of Plato*, 2:235. In *Civic Conversations of Thucydides and Plato*, 189–92, Mara describes the richness of *exousia* as "one of democracy's contested symbols."
107. Euben, *Corrupting Youth*, 101.
108. White, *Acts of Hope*, 41.
109. Arendt, "What Is Authority?," 95.

CHAPTER 2

Poetry: The Measure of Truth

What matter who's speaking?
SAMUEL BECKETT, *Texts for Nothing*

The people of that time, not being so wise as you young folks, were content in their simplicity, *euētheias*, to hear an oak or a rock, provided only it spoke the truth.

Phaedrus 275b-c

Almost all of the characters in the *Republic* cite and recite poetry. In *Republic* 1, Cephalus quotes from Sophocles on moderation (329b-c) and Pindar (331a) on courage; Polemarchus cites Simonides on justice (331d). In *Republic* 2, Glaucon quotes from Aeschylus (362a-b), and Adeimantus recurs to Pindar, Hesiod, and Musaeus, among others (363b-d, 364c-e, 365b-c). Over the course of the dialogue, Socrates invokes Homer time and again, sometimes with a good deal of poetic license.[1] Socrates also, however, censors and reforms poetry in the proposed curriculum of *Republic* 2–3, banishes the mimetic poets from the ideal city of *Republic* 5, and, as we saw in chapter 1, appears to confirm that ouster in *Republic* 10 (595a-b), where he claims that it is required by the distinction set forth in *Republic* 4 among the parts of the soul (595b).[2] The consensus among scholars is that in the "old quarrel between philosophy and poetry" (607b), poetry, in *Republic* 10, is "overcome."[3] Mimetic poetry is

---

1. On Socrates' license, see Howes, "Homeric Quotations in Plato and Aristotle."
2. Questioning the alleged embeddedness of *Republic* 10 in books 6–7, Halliwell, *Aesthetics of Mimesis*, 58, observes that *Republic* 10 "repeatedly refers back to earlier parts of the dialogue, . . . [but] provides no cross-reference to the metaphysics of the middle books."
3. See, among many others, Ferrari, "Plato and Poetry," 120, 143; Nussbaum, *Fragility of Goodness*, chaps. 5, 7; Rosen, *Plato's "Republic,"* chap. 13; Ford, *Origins of Criticism*, 209; Moravcsik, "Noetic Aspiration and Artistic Inspiration"; *Plato on Poetry*, ed. Murray, 23–24; Levin, *Ancient Quarrel between Philosophy and Poetry*, chap. 5; Allen, *Why Plato Wrote*; Ledbet-

condemned on psychological grounds for appealing to the irrational part of the soul, on epistemological grounds for belonging in the bottommost section of the divided line, on ontological grounds for being at a third remove from the truth, and on ethical grounds for emancipating desire. In the words of Kevin Robb, "The condemnation could not be, Platonically, more complete."[4]

Scholars sometimes treat the *Republic*'s condemnation of poetry as analogous to critiques leveled in the dialogues against Athens' other democratic authorities, particularly, the sophists.[5] This makes sense. Socrates explicitly compares Homer to the sophists in *Republic* 10 (600c), and the sophists of the *Sophist* and *Republic* share features with the mimetic poets: both trade in opinion (*Rep.* 602b; *Soph.* 233c); produce semblances that can deceive (*Rep.* 598b-c; *Soph.* 234b); enjoy reputations for wisdom (*Rep.* 493a, 595c, 598d-e); and engage in play with imagination (*Rep.* 602b, 605c; *Soph.* 234a–235e).[6] These similarities are important. But there are also important differences between how the dialogues portray sophists and poets.[7] As we will see in later chapters, poets do not emancipate the same kind of desire in their audiences as do sophists, nor do they persuade or play with imagination in the same way.[8]

Most relevant for the purposes of this chapter is that poets and sophists do not enjoy reputations for wisdom or deceive in the same ways. In the name of their privileged expertise and to gain political ends, sophists are frequently portrayed in the dialogues as inviting and sometimes manipulating people to alienate their self-rule.[9] Socrates *accuses* the poets of inducing their audiences to hold wrong views about the highest and most important matters, to be sure

---

ter, *Poetics before Plato*, 82, argues that Socrates "attempts to wrest from the poets the authority traditionally attributed to them."

4. For this summary, see Robb, *Literacy and* Paideia *in Ancient Greece*, 220.

5. See, e.g., Nightingale, *Genres in Dialogue*, 54, who claims that, in "Plato's view, . . . the sophists, the politicians and the poets resemble each other insofar as they traffic in wisdom."

6. These similarities are adumbrated by Notomi, *The Unity of Plato's "Sophist,"* 124–33.

7. To say nothing of important differences among the dialogues' portraits of sophists, even of the same sophist, in particular Protagoras, who appears differently in his eponymous dialogue and in the *Theaetetus*, for example.

8. Noting that *peithō* and its cognates do not appear in the discussions of mimetic poetry in *Republic* 10, for example, Belfiore, "Plato's Greatest Accusation against Poetry," 47 n. 11, remarks that the poets do not seek to persuade at all.

9. An important exception, in my view, is Protagoras in the *Theaetetus*, to whom I return in chapter 6. For doubts about the accuracy of the dialogues' depictions of sophists, see Schiappa, *Protagoras and* Logos; and Tell, *Plato's Counterfeit Sophists*.

(383a-c). However, poets are depicted in the dialogues as actually doing no such thing. This is, in the first instance, because dead poets are able to do no inducing at all. Thus, in *Hippias Minor*, for example, Homer is left to one side, "since we are incapable of asking him his thoughts on the verses he had made" (365c-d). Homer's poetry is nonetheless omnipresent in the *Republic*. And Simonides' poetry appears in both the *Republic* (332d, 334b) and *Protagoras* (339a–348a). Still, the multiple and competing interpretations Socrates offers of Homer's poetry and that he and Protagoras offer of Simonides' poetry suggest that these poets offer little guidance about their verses, let alone inducement. Living poets are depicted no differently. When asked to explain their poems, they are portrayed as unable to give an account (*Ap.* 22b-c; also *Ion* 542a). Knowing nothing about whether anything is good or bad (*Rep.* 602b), living poets, like dead ones, and unlike sophists, appear to claim for themselves neither expertise nor authority, not about their own poems or about the highest and most important matters.

Not "self-appointed,"[10] the authority of the poets is, rather, granted to them by their audiences. More accurately, poetic authority is granted by the education of Athens' fifth-century elite, which, as we saw in this book's prologue, mandates the rote memorization of ancient poetry through recitation, imitation, and writing. Conducted by way of the top-down model of learning I analogized to the *Phaedrus*' account of soul writing in chapter 1, that education secures the "transmission of the collective 'wisdom' of the society" by compelling students to read the works of poets and to learn them by heart (*Prot.* 325e–326a).[11] The appeals to poetry by elite Athenian citizens and also metics in the opening books of the *Republic*, noted above, appear to testify to the success of that transmission process. These appeals are not all the same, however. Whereas "virtually everything Cephalus says is spoken in the voice and on the authority of poets,"[12] his son Polemarchus recites only the poet Simonides. And whereas Cephalus quotes poetry for guidance about living well, Glaucon and Adeimantus, marked as sons, too (though not of Cephalus but "of Ariston, godlike offspring of a famous man" (368a)[13]), quote poetry for guidelines

---

10. Cotton, *Education of the Reader*, 163. See also Demos, *Lyric Quotation in Plato*, 60.

11. Gill, "Plato on Falsehood—Not Fiction," 71. See Havelock, *Preface to Plato*, 209. I take up the question of poetry in relation to *paideia* and *Republic* 2–3 in the next chapter.

12. Euben, *Tragedy of Political Theory*, 241.

13. As Socrates puts it, quoting Glaucon's lover.

they would like to reject as vicious.[14] These differences should invite reflection about just how secure the transmission process is, an invitation issued as well by the passing of the torch referenced at the start of the dialogue (328a).[15] If, then, the *Republic* opens by calling attention to differences between fathers and sons, perhaps it seeks to orient inquiry to the relation between "what is old, traditional, and inherited and what is new, innovative, and chosen," which is to say, as we have seen in chapter 1, to the topics of transmission and authority themselves.[16]

Socrates brings to light the ethical and political stakes of this inquiry by way of the following analogy: "Just as poets, *poiētai*, are fond of their poems and fathers, *pateres*, of their children, so money-makers, *chrematisamenoi*, too are serious about money—as their own product, *hōs ergon heautōn*; and they are also serious about it for its use, *kata tēn chreian*, like other people" (330a-c). Presented in the context of a discussion about whether Cephalus' wealth was inherited or earned, Socrates' analogy may be offering moneymakers as the model for poets and fathers. Read that way, poets and fathers "are fond of" their poems and children insofar as these are their "own product." Just as to be serious about money is to be serious about the benefits it brings to moneymakers, so, too, are poems and children to be valued for the benefit they bring to their "makers." Like money, poems and children have value in relation to their maker's "own," which is to say, as their maker's "reflections and extensions."[17] Read this way, Socrates' analogy appears to underwrite the structure of transmission sought by the traditional *paideia* and to generalize it across society, ensuring that by way of their money, poems, and children, moneymakers, poets, and fathers hold sway. The dialogue appears to reproduce this structure of transmission, although not its substance of course, in the revised curriculum presented in *Republic* 2-3. Limiting poetry to "hymns to the gods and the praises of good men" (607a) and seeking to produce rulers who are neither fathers nor moneymakers but philosopher-kings, the revised *paideia*, nonetheless, aims, like the traditional *paideia*, to secure elite authority.

---

14. Euben, *Tragedy of Political Theory*, 271.

15. Ford, *Origins of Criticism*, pt. 3, argues that in fifth-century Athens poetic authority is undergoing a shift. On the relay race and the idea that it is "as agents of *nemesis* that we must read—*nemein*—this document" that is the *Republic*, a torch passed on for us to read and complete, see Russon, "Just Reading," x.

16. Euben, *Tragedy of Political Theory*, 271.

17. For discussion, see Berger, *Perils of Uglytown*, 71-75.

Socrates' analogy may be read as seeking to secure that kind of authority. But it may also be read differently, for as he constructs it, the analogy puts poets *before* fathers and moneymakers. That opens the possibility that he offers poets as models for fathers and moneymakers rather than the other way around. How are poets fond of their poems? Depicted as claiming no authority for themselves, poets appear in this respect to be like Theuth, the Egyptian god from the *Phaedrus*, described as "the father of writing." As we saw in chapter 1, Theuth approached what *he* invented or made by letting it be, allowing to it its separateness and independence, giving it over to the contingencies of interpretation on the parts of readers who saw and learned from writing many things without being taught. This is a different way of showing a father's fondness from one that sees what it makes as the maker's reflection or extension. As we will see shortly, Cephalus, who hands down his wealth and his words/arguments to his son Polemarchus, does not appear to be a father in the manner of Theuth. Nor, as we will see in later chapters, are the founders or rulers of the *kallipolis*. Poets, by contrast, do seem to be like Theuth insofar as they, too, let their words be in their separateness from their makers.

When Socrates' analogy is read as presenting poets as exemplars it thus appears to challenge rather than underwrite the structure of transmission sought, despite their differences, by *both* Athens' traditional education and the *Republic*'s revised curriculum. So read, Socrates' analogy seeks not to secure elite authority but rather to distribute authority, away from its "makers"—poets, fathers, moneymakers, founders, philosopher-kings—and to, what Socrates in *Republic* 10 will call, its "users" (601c-e), which is to say, to poetry's interpreters in the case of the poets, and, in the case of rulers, to the people. I take up the *Republic*'s approach to political authority later. For now, it is to be noted that there is prima facie evidence for this way of understanding the dialogue's approach to poetic authority when Socrates recurs twice to a passage in *Odyssey* 11 to opposite effect: in *Republic* 3 (387c), he expresses concern that "hearing Homer's words [in this passage] would introduce fear into the souls of the guardians"; in *Republic* 7 (516d), he reads the same passage as evoking the courage to "put up with anything." Adducing this example, Bernard Freydberg maintains, rightly in my view, that the dialogue seems to be underscoring that it is "the framework of its interpretation, and not the image created by the poet, [that] is the issue."[18]

In *Republic* 10, Socrates says that "we would be glad to receive [poetry] back from exile" (607c) if the poets themselves (or if "lovers of poetry" speaking "in

---

18. See Freydberg, "Retracing Homer and Aristophanes in the Platonic Text," 101–2.

prose on its behalf") can show "that poetry not only gives pleasure but brings benefit, *ōphelimē*, both to constitutions and to human life" (607d). My goal in this chapter is to fill out the elaborate framework of interpretation offered in the *Republic*'s treatment of mimetic poetry to bring to light the substantial ethical and political benefits of mimetic poetry as these are depicted in and by way of the text of the dialogue. I begin with Socrates' engagement with Polemarchus in *Republic* 1 around the poetry of Simonides.

ALIENATING AUTHORITY, FATHERS AGAIN

Republic 1 is sometimes read as Plato's opening salvo in the dialogue's larger project of usurping poetic authority. There are good grounds for reading it this way. At the home of his hosts, Socrates speaks first with Cephalus, who cites extensively from the poets and then departs to make sacrifices to the gods when Socrates interrogates him about justice.[19] Replacing his father, Polemarchus shores up Cephalus' account of justice by recourse to Simonides, the fifth-century poet, whom he credits with claiming "that it is just to give to each what is owed, *opheilomena*" (331e). Socrates reconfigures Simonides' claim into "a certain art of stealing," which he associates with Homer (334b).[20] Maintaining that these exchanges make manifest the poets' inadequacy regarding the central philosophical question of the dialogue, namely, the question of justice, scholars tend to treat as ironic Socrates' description of Simonides as a "wise and godlike man" whom it "isn't easy to disbelieve" (331e).[21]

I read Socrates' exchanges with Polemarchus about Simonides as inviting a different interpretation of poetic authority. Consider that Socrates engages Polemarchus by offering a series of different formulations of Simonidean justice as "giving to each what is owed" (331e). Checking these one by one with Polemarchus, Socrates asks again and again: can this be "what Simonides means"? "Yes," says Polemarchus each and every time (331e, 332a, 332b, 332c, 332d). Socrates' repeated question calls attention to the fact that Simonides' words

---

19. For valuable treatments of Cephalus, the first two of which are especially attentive to the relations between fathers and sons, see Berger, *Perils of Uglytown*, chap. 4; Euben, *Tragedy of Political Theory*, 241–44; and Steinberger, "Who Is Cephalus?"

20. For discussions of Simonides' controversial reputation as wise poet or greedy poet-for-hire and also of his appearances in Plato's works, see Detienne, *Masters of Truth in Archaic Greece*, 107–16; Thayer, "Plato's Quarrel with Poetry"; Carson, *Economy of the Unlost*.

21. See Ford, *Origins of Criticism*, 213–14; Shorey, in *Republic, Books 1–5*, 331e, note d. Naddaff, *Exiling the Poets*, 14. Contra Ledbetter, *Poetics before Plato*, 117.

don't speak for themselves but require interpretation.²² By focusing Polemarchus on "what Simonides means," Socrates may be referring the interpretation of Simonides' words to the poet's intention. But this quickly proves futile. As Socrates' reformulations, affirmed by Polemarchus, demonstrate, the poet's words accommodate multiple, sometimes conflicting, meanings.

Something similar happens with Simonides in the *Protagoras*, where Socrates and Protagoras offer competing interpretations of Simonides' poem, claiming repeatedly to establish by reference to authorial intent what Simonides meant (339e, 340b, 341c, 341d–342a, 347a).²³ After completing his account of what he thinks "was going through Simonides' mind when he composed th[e] ode" under scrutiny, Socrates underscores poetry's interpretative undecidability, saying: "When a poet is brought up in discussion, almost everyone has a different opinion of what he means, and they wind up arguing about something they can never finally decide" (*Prot.* 347a–348a). Some scholars take Socrates' claims about the indeterminacy of poetic interpretation to demonstrate that "no truth of any importance concerning how one ought to live" can emerge from discussion about poetry. They therefore ally the *Protagoras* with the *Republic* in rejecting poetry in the name of philosophy.²⁴ I agree that the engagements with Simonides in the *Protagoras* and *Republic* open similar questions about the indeterminacy of poetic interpretation. In my view, however, these questions do not set up an opposition between (the indeterminacy of) poetry and (the truth of) philosophy. Instead, I take the indeterminacy of poetic authority in both dialogues to lay the groundwork for philosophy by bringing to appearance the imperative for philosophy of speaking in one's own voice.²⁵

To see this, let us return to *Republic* 1. After Polemarchus maintains that justice is "that which renders benefits, *ōphelias*, and harms to friends and enemies," Socrates asks, "To do good, *eu poiein*, to friends and evil to enemies, then is justice in [Simonides'] meaning?" Here, Polemarchus' response changes. Replying, "I think so" (332d), Polemarchus refers the poet's meaning to his own opinion, thus appearing to shift authority away from the poet and to himself, to speak in his own voice. In acquiescing to Socrates' newest

---

22. See also Naddaff, *Exiling the Poets*, 14.

23. On Socrates' and Protagoras' competing interpretations of Simonides, see Trivigno, "Childish Nonsense?"

24. See, e.g., Weiss, *Socratic Paradox*, 41–43.

25. See Griswold, "Relying on Your Own Voice." For a critique of seeking to establish the sense of the poem by reference to authorial intent, see Ledbetter, *Poetics before Plato*, 109.

definition, however, Polemarchus simply replaces what he has claimed to be Simonides' say-so with the standard formula of Greek conventional morality: helping friends and harming enemies.[26] When Socrates then guides the brief discussion that follows to a definition of justice as "the art of stealing" "for the benefit of friends and the harm of enemies" (334b), the dialogue poses its initial challenges not to poetic authority but to poetic interpretations that disavow their own authority and also to the authority of convention as a standard of justice. It is noteworthy that Simonides is largely absent in this latter series of exchanges between Polemarchus and Socrates. Calling Simonides back into the conversation to check his reconfiguration of justice as the art of stealing, Socrates asks Polemarchus: "Justice, then, seems, according to you and Homer and Simonides, to be a certain art of stealing, for the benefit, to be sure, of friends and the harm of enemies. Isn't that what you meant" (334b)? Appearing to augment Simonides' authority by pairing him with Homer, Socrates at the same time presents Polemarchus and Homer and Simonides as equals, pressing Polemarchus, in his own person ("Isn't this what *you* meant?" [334b, my emphasis]), to take a stand on justice.[27] Replying, "No, by Zeus" (334b), Polemarchus borrows Homer's authority, Zeus, to underwrite his own authority and to reject the meaning Socrates has attributed to the "riddling, *ēinixato*" (332b), poets, Homer and Simonides.[28]

Polemarchus follows up this refusal with "But I no longer know what I did mean" (334b). In so saying, he appears to initiate a different relation to the poets. By admitting confusion, Polemarchus marks the inadequacy of his earlier claims to know what the poet meant. Appearing to recognize that what matters is what *he* knows, he discloses his awareness of the limits of his knowledge. That admission, here, as in other dialogues (*Meno* 84a-b; *Symp.* 201c), is a display of self-knowledge. It is not self-knowledge in its full sense, which, as Socrates' comments at the start of the *Phaedrus* suggest, may be earned, if at all, only over the course of a lifetime (229e–230a). It is, nonetheless, a mode of

---

26. See Blundell, *Helping Friends and Harming Enemies*, esp. chap. 2; Dover, *Greek Popular Morality*, 180–84.

27. For a similar redoubling of poetic authority that at the same time calls attention to the question of in what that authority consists, see *Hippias Minor* 365c-d, where Socrates says this in reference to Homer: "It is impossible to ask him what he meant when he made those verses, but since you come forward to take up his cause, and agree in this which you say is his meaning, do you answer for Homer and yourself in common."

28. On the poets as riddlers, and Simonides as an expert riddler, see Carson, *Economy of the Unlost*, 23.

knowing that, by understanding its own limitations, is, we will see, a necessary condition of philosophy.[29]

By attributing to Homer and Simonides the understanding of justice that Polemarchus has taken as his own from conventional morality, Socrates produces justice as the art of stealing. He also, and not too obliquely, accuses Polemarchus of theft. Neither that definition nor the others that Socrates has come up with over the course of the conversation, and that Polemarchus has appropriated, seem to have belonged to Polemarchus in the first place. Polemarchus' no, his refusal of justice as theft, is also his denial of Socrates' accusation of theft. It opens the way to, though in no way guarantees, a different attitude to authority.[30]

In *Republic* 2, Adeimantus cites another Simonidean fragment (365c), this time without attribution.[31] Displacing anew questions of authorship, the dialogue replays the referential "Plato or Socrates" question, discussed in chapter 1, as the "Plato or Simonides" question. It does so, in my view, to prompt again the consideration that what matters is not who the poet (or philosopher) is, or what he knows, but how auditors take up his words. Indeed, the exchanges between Polemarchus and Socrates about poetic authority say nothing at all about what Simonides knows or about what Plato thinks about the wisdom of the poets. Leaving both as open questions, the dialogue underscores that authority lies not with authors but with their interpreters.

Another exchange in *Republic* 1 gives further force to this reading. Recall that Polemarchus initially entered into discussion with Socrates by interrupting his father. Assuming Cephalus' argument, Polemarchus seems to reinforce a pattern of authority by which the son inherits from the father. Cephalus gladly "hands down the argument" to Polemarchus, who accepts the inheritance, claiming to be the "heir of what belongs to" Cephalus. Cephalus agrees that Polemarchus' inheritance is due, laughs, and leaves (331d). This exchange effects the transition to Socrates' discussion with Polemarchus and prefigures it in telling ways. When Polemarchus takes up Cephalus' argument by interrupting him, is he assuming an inheritance that is his due, or is he steal-

---

29. See Anderson, *Masks of Dionysos*, 128. Polemarchus provides other necessary conditions for the practice of philosophy in the dialogue: as Euben, *Tragedy of Political Theory*, 245, notes, he "brings the interlocutors together and thus makes the dialogue possible," and introduces the contrast between the power of numbers, or force, on the one hand, and the practice of philosophy.

30. See also Ledbetter, *Poetics before Plato*, 117.

31. See Ford, *Origins of Criticism*, 97, on this fragment as Simonidean. See also Carson, *Economy of the Unlost*, 46–62.

ing it? After all, Cephalus is not yet dead. And when Polemarchus shores up Cephalus' account of justice by recourse to Simonides, is he authorizing his father by underwriting Cephalus' say-so with that of the poet, or is he deauthorizing his father by displacing his paternal authority with poetic authority? The dialogue's portrayal of Polemarchus authorizes both possibilities: deference and usurpation. Indeed, Polemarchus appears to represent both possibilities at the same time, in relation to paternal authority, poetic authority, and also convention. His relation to conventional authority comes to light first when, as we saw, after denouncing justice as the art of stealing, he nonetheless cleaves to the conventional formulation of justice, helping friends and harming enemies (334b). Taking the conventional account as his own, Polemarchus only sets it aside to appropriate Socrates' formulation of justice. To Socrates' statement that a just man harms no one, Polemarchus responds: "In my opinion, Socrates, what you say is entirely true" (335d). From father to poets to convention and then to Socrates, Polemarchus moves from theft to deference and back again as he exchanges one authority for another.

Flip sides of the same coin, these movements gesture to a third way of relating to authority, one by way of which inheritances—patrimonial, cultural, political—are taken up not by blind appropriation or by theft but critically, which is to say, by one's own authority. To take up inheritances in this way is to acknowledge their varying sources and to see that though they may belong to us as matters of fact, we must make them our own through understanding. Only by making inheritances our own in this way, which also opens the possibility of refusing them, can we take them up justly. Which is to say, as we will see further when we look at justice in this book's epilogue, that only by having and doing what is our own can we claim that what belongs to us is owed to us or due. That this sort of authority is bound with poetry is suggested by the fact that Polemarchus' insight into his own confusion comes, as we have seen, via his exchanges with Socrates about poetic interpretation.

That connection is confirmed in Socrates' last exchange with Polemarchus in *Republic* 1. Bringing the poets back in to help destabilize convention for a second time, Socrates says: "If anyone tells us, then, that it is just to give to each what is due, and understands by this that a just man should harm his enemies and benefit his friends, he isn't wise to say it, since what he says isn't true" (335e). Generally read as an indictment of Simonides on the ground that it was he who claimed that it is just to give what is owed to each, it is worth underscoring that it was not Simonides but Polemarchus who took that to mean "that a just man should harm his enemies and help his friends," the conventional formulation of justice. As noted, what Simonides said and/

or understood remains an open question. Indeed, in the very next sentences, Socrates implies that he is *not* calling into question the wisdom or truthfulness of the poet when he allies himself with Simonides (and Bias and Pittacus, two of the Seven Sages, both poets, among other things[32]) against those who would put such untruths into the mouths of the poets. Offering Polemarchus another opportunity to take up philosophy with the poets, Socrates invites Polemarchus, whose name signifies "war-ruler," to be his partner in the "battle" against untruth (335e). This time Polemarchus says, "I am ready" (335e). Is he? Or is he simply repeating his earlier error of siding with a set of authorities rather than seeking his own voice? Because Polemarchus is never again Socrates' primary interlocutor in the dialogue, we cannot know for sure.

POETRY SILENCED

If Polemarchus exemplifies the consequences of both deference and usurpation when it comes to poetic authority, Thrasymachus represents the ethical, political, and philosophical costs of its total usurpation. The only major character in the *Republic* to appeal to no poetry at all, Thrasymachus speaks exclusively on his own authority when he bursts in on Socrates' discussion with Polemarchus (336b) to posit justice as the advantage of the stronger (338c). For Thrasymachus, justice "consists of the rules that the strong, those who have political power, impose on the weak, their subjects, who are then obliged to obey the rules, thereby advancing the interests of the strong."[33] Demonstrating his readiness to partner with Socrates, and mirroring a move Socrates had executed on him in their earliest exchange about poetic authority, Polemarchus accuses Thrasymachus of incoherence. Based on claims Thrasymachus has agreed to so far, Polemarchus says, "the advantage of the stronger would be no more just than the disadvantage" (340a-b). Cleitophon steps in to deflect Polemarchus' charge, insisting that what Thrasymachus said was "that the advantage of the stronger is what the stronger believes to be his advantage" (340b). Thrasymachus rejects Cleitophon's reformulation (340c). For Thrasymachus, unlike for Cleitophon, it seems to matter whether the pronouncements of the powerful really work to their advantage.[34] Thus, Thrasymachus appears to stand for justice as a practice of power intelligently exercised.

32. On Bias and Pittacus, see Diogenes Laertius, *Lives of Eminent Philosophers*.
33. Weiss, "Wise Guys and Smart Alecks," 93.
34. Thanks to Gerry Mara for bringing the difference between Thrasymachus and Cleitophon to my attention.

Taking there to be "no justice besides the laws and conventions that the ruled are required by the rulers to observe,"[35] Thrasymachus treats justice as all and only a creature of law (339b).[36] That makes him, in contemporary parlance, a legal positivist. Standing for the position that what is represented as just is just if it is forceful enough to compel acquiescence, Thrasymachus locates the authority of justice in power. When justice is a matter of power (intelligently exercised or not), might (what is) makes right (what ought to be). Justice so understood forecloses "giving to each what is owed" and "the having and doing of one's own and what belongs to one," for these formulations presuppose a gap between how things are and how things ought to be that it is the job of justice to govern.

Maintaining that there was a diplomat from Chalcedon named Thrasymachus who spoke out to "prevent harsh reprisals against his native city" after Chalcedon's unsuccessful revolt against Athens' empire in 407, Stephen White argues that the Thrasymachus of the *Republic* is best read not as a realist on a par with the Athenian generals in the Melian debate for whom "the strong do what they can and the weak suffer what they must" (Thuc. 5.89), but "as an idealist," expressing "the outrage of a man disillusioned and embittered by the brutal realities of fifth-century power politics."[37] Whether the Thrasymachus of the *Republic* is that historical Thrasymachus is undecidable. What matters is that Thrasymachus speaks and Socrates responds to him in ways that make it hard to tell. By obscuring whether Thrasymachus is speaking descriptively or prescriptively, the dialogue represents him as erasing the difference between how things are and how they ought to be.

Thrasymachus also represents the erasure of any difference between truth and representation. The embodiment of words-as-authority, he displaces the poets and their poetry to occupy the position of the poem when it is treated as blindly authoritative, as it was by Polemarchus earlier in *Republic* 1. Staging a world in which self-standing authority backed by force replaces all other modes of authority, Thrasymachus stands with the tyrants in the counterposition Socrates set up at the end of his exchange with Polemarchus between the poets, on the one hand, with whom Socrates allies in the quest for truth about justice, and the tyrants, on the other, whom he holds responsible for the

---

35. Weiss, "Wise Guys and Smart Alecks," 95.
36. This is also Meletus' position in the *Apology* (24b–25a).
37. For the sources of these quotes, in order, see White, "Thrasymachus the Diplomat," 322; Nails, *People of Plato*, 289; *The Landmark Thucydides*, trans. Crawley and ed. Strassler; White, "Thrasymachus the Diplomat," 322.

untruth of conventional morality (336a). As we will see in chapter 3, the ouster of the mimetic poets from *Republic* 5's "city in speech" (369a) is no less an exemplification of words-as-authority than Thrasymachus. And no less tyrannical. The erasure of the distinction between representation and truth thus puts politics in peril. We will see next that it endangers philosophy as well.

FORMS, KNOWLEDGE, LOOKS, SIMULACRA

At the start of *Republic* 10, Socrates gives as his reason for underwriting the dialogue's earlier verdict against mimetic poetry that "it is likely to distort the thought, *dianoias*, of all listeners who do not possess as a *pharmakon* [usually translated as "antidote" but also, as we saw in the last chapter, "poison"[38]] knowledge, *to eidenai*, of what mimetic poetry happens to be like" (595b). Here, as in *Republic* 1, Socrates indicates that when it comes to poetry, it is listeners/interpreters who matter.[39] Maintaining that poetry's ouster is "still more plainly apparent now that we have distinguished the several forms, *eidē*, of the soul" (595a-b), Socrates ties the banishment of mimetic poetry to the dialogue's tripartition of the soul. Starting his inquiry into mimetic poetry with Glaucon using what he calls their "customary procedure," Socrates seeks "a single *eidos*, in the case of the various multiplicities to which we give the same name" (596a). Socrates settles on the couch, echoing Glaucon's invocation of couches when he grew Adeimantus' city of pigs into the luxurious city, populated, for the first time, by "poets and their helpers" (373b).[40]

Socrates begins their investigation of *mimēsis* with reference not to poetry but to painting (596e).[41] Producing what is by now a familiar hierarchy, Socrates explains that there is the form, *eidos*, of the couch, made by a god;

---

38. On Plato's use of *pharmakon* in the *Phaedrus*, see Derrida, *Dissemination*, 63–171. See also Miller, *Postmodern Spiritual Practices*, 144–51.

39. West, "Plato's Audiences," 46, underscores that the judge of a poem is its hearer.

40. On Socrates' choice of the couch as his example, see Burnyeat, "Culture and Society in Plato's *Republic*," 231–36, 245–49; Griswold, "Ideas and the Criticism of Poetry in Plato's *Republic*"; and Janaway, *Images of Excellence*, 84, who associate couches with the luxuries added with the move from the city of pigs to the city with a fever (*Rep.* 372d–373a). See also Berger, *Perils of Uglytown*, 113–21.

41. On how the analogy Socrates draws between painting and poetry works, see Moss, "What Is Imitative Poetry and Why Is It Bad?"; Naddaff, *Exiling the Poets*, 83–91. The analogy is sometimes discussed with reference to a Simonidean fragment: "Painting is silent poetry; poetry paints the speeches": see, e.g., Burnyeat, "Culture and Society in Plato's *Republic*," 265; and, especially, Carson, *Economy of the Unlost*, 46–62.

the artifact of the couch, made by a craftsman based on the god's form; and the *mimēsis* of the appearance of the artifact, made by the painter (597b). That hierarchy may be familiar, but, as scholars have noted, in the context of the dialogue, it is nothing if not strange. Ramona Naddaff remarks that a maker-god appears for the first time here in *Republic* 10, as a *deus ex machina* (see *Cra.* 425d).[42] The form of a particular, sensible artifact—the couch—appears for the first time, too. These innovations suggest that the inquiry Socrates pursues with Glaucon may not be entirely in keeping with their "customary procedure."[43] Glaucon wonders about none of this. He nonetheless seems to get to the heart of the matter when he claims that painted things "look like they *are*; however they surely *are* not in truth, *phainomena, ou mentoi onta ge pou tē[i] alētheia[i]*" (596e). Socrates lauds Glaucon's words (596e), explaining that a mimetic thing *is* not in truth insofar as it is only the "look" of an appearance, situated at a third remove from the form it represents (597e).[44] This hierarchy of being and truth underwrites what is generally treated as Plato's contempt for and dismissal of *mimēsis* as false and therefore deceptive, analogous in its "trickery" to sophistry.[45]

As I have argued in chapter 1, however, there is no ground for inferring what Plato's view may be from what he has Socrates say. On my reading, in any case, treating *mimēsis* as false and therefore deceptive misconceives the work the dialogue associates with *mimēsis*. That Socrates is concerned with trickery in these passages goes without saying. In *Republic* 10, he refers to as nothing short of wizardry, *thaumatopoiia*, arts, including scene painting, *skiagraphia*, and puppeteering, *goēteias*, "and many other such contrivances, *mēchanai*," that exploit errors of vision about size, shape, and color based on, among other things, distance (602c-d). Are these arts exemplars of *mimēsis*? Glaucon thinks so (602d). To him, *mimēsis* is a contrivance and therefore a practice of trickery, hence deceptive.

---

42. Naddaff, *Exiling the Poets*, 73: Socrates is acting like tragic poets "who introduce a *deus ex machine* whenever they are perplexed."

43. For questions about Socrates' claims here, see Halliwell, in *Plato: Republic 10*, 109–18; Griswold, "Ideas and the Criticism of Poetry in Plato's *Republic*," 142; Annas, *Introduction to Plato's "Republic,"* 227–32; Nehamas, "Plato on Imitation and Poetry in *Republic* 10," 54–55; Naddaff, *Exiling the Poets*, 71–75.

44. I take the term "look" from Ferrari, "Plato and Poetry," 127.

45. For discussion, see Carson, *Economy of the Unlost*, 48. For the trickery of sophistry in Plato's dialogues, see Blondell, *Play of Character*, 97 n. 219. For a treatment of the falsity of *mimēsis* as trickery/deception and poetry as the art of illusion, see Naddaff, *Exiling the Poets*, 21–24, 79–83, but see also 34; and Moss, "What Is Imitative Poetry and Why Is It Bad?"

Should we agree with him? Maybe not. For Glaucon is depicted as unreliable when it comes to contrivances. For example, in *Republic* 7, he offers as cases of perceptions that provoke to thought the very arts of wizardry Socrates calls contrivances in *Republic* 10, namely, "distant appearances" and "scene-painting, *skiagraphia*." There, Socrates draws attention to Glaucon's mistake, saying: "You have quite missed my meaning" (523b). In *Republic* 10, as we saw in the last chapter, Socrates offers Glaucon a mirror as the quickest and easiest way to produce tools, plants and animals, including himself, and the earth, and all things in heaven and in Hades and under the earth. Glaucon mistakes the mirror for a contrivance when he fails to notice that a mirror can reflect only what is visible to the eye. An implement of imitation, a mirror cannot bring to appearance what cannot be seen, and so, we saw, it will not (re)produce things in Hades and under the earth (596c-e).

The same cannot be said of contrivances. Indeed, as we will see in chapters 3 and 4, in the *Republic*, *mēchanē*, contrivance, refers consistently to exactly those things that make people see and believe what is not true. For example, the sorceries, *goēteuthentes*, that can strip the guardians unawares of true beliefs are called contrivances in *Republic* 3 (413a-c).[46] As is the ideal city's founding lie (414b-c). Contrivances are designed to deceive. This is how they are false. One might say, then, that the truth of a contrivance is deception. Mimetic things may be false by way of deception as well. Socrates makes this plain in *Republic* 10 when, analogizing the painter to a magician, he refers to the good painter's picture of a carpenter as making "children and fools" believe it to be a real carpenter (598c). Mimetic things deceive when, owing to an inability on the part of the audience to "put to proof and distinguish knowledge, *epistēmē*, ignorance, *anepistēmosunēn*, and *mimēsis*, *mimēsin*" (598d), what is false appears true. It is for this reason that, as in the case of contrivances, knowledge, as Socrates puts it at the start of *Republic* 10, is an antidote, *pharmakon*, to the distorting effects of mimetic things.[47]

Mimetic things and contrivances may be similar in that both may deceive, but they also differ in a key respect. No matter how true to life the painted carpenter appears to be, it makes no claim to truth. In other words, whereas the truth of

---

46. As we will see in chapter 3, the curriculum of *Republic* 2-3 is called a contrivance, *mēchanē*, as well.

47. Knowledge of *mimēsis* can be a *pharmakon* as poison as well as a cure: if while I'm watching the *Eumenides*, say, I spend all of my time analyzing the relation between what it represents and what I don't see, then I will not experience the play. I return to this point in this book's epilogue.

contrivances is to be false by way of deception, the same cannot be said of mimetic things. It is also not the truth of the mimetic things of *Republic* 10 to be true by way of verisimilitude or imitation, as we saw in chapter 1.[48] *Mimēsis* may be introduced as imitation or copying in *Republic* 3 (392d ff.), as when, in Socrates' description, "the poet delivers a speech as if he were someone else" (393a-c). In *Republic* 10's treatment of *mimēsis*, however, words from the *eik*-root, signaling *mimēsis* as a practice of imitation, largely disappear.[49] In the *Ion*, too, Socrates rejects "learning off" the words of Homer's poems as inappropriate to the rhapsode's recitation (530b-c).[50] The mimetic things of *Republic* 10 thus do not represent themselves as imitations. They represent themselves instead as representations.

Putting the lie to *mimēsis* as deception and/or as imitation only, the *Republic* gives its characters license to alter the words of poets and historians, and they do so conspicuously. When, for example, in *Republic* 10, Socrates ventriloquizes the tale narrated by Er, he announces before he begins, "Not Alcinous' the tale" (614b), thereby signaling that his presentation of Er's tale both is and is not a retelling of the "tales to Alcinous told" from Homer's *Odyssey* 9-12. When Glaucon offers his account of the injustice that can be exercised with impunity by the wearer of an invisibility ring in *Republic* 2, he describes it as a "tale," about "an ancestor of Gyges" (359c-e). By calling it a "tale," he signals that he may be taking poetic license with Herodotus' account of Gyges' ring in *Histories* 1.8-11. And, indeed, he does. Herodotus' account is not about "an ancestor of Gyges" but Gyges himself. What Hobbes says about metaphors in *Leviathan* applies to the mimetic representations in the *Republic*, including the dialogue itself.[51] Wearing their falsity on their face, mimetic representations, unlike contrivances, as we will see, prompt attention to, rather than covering over, gaps between truth and representation.

The difference between mimetic things and contrivances is anticipated in the taxonomy of falsehoods Socrates offers in *Republic* 2, which distinguishes between "verbal falsehoods, *to en tois logois pseudos*," on the one hand, and true falsehoods, on the other. True falsehoods bring about "ignorance in the

---

48. Contra the representation of Socrates by Badiou, *Plato's "Republic,"* 320–22, for example, who treats *mimēsis* as a practice of imitative verisimilitude and equates imitation with representation.

49. Halliwell, *Aesthetics of Mimesis*, 63, notes that, unlike in other parts of the *Republic*, Plato, in *Republic* 10, "avoids referring to the products of mimesis" as *eikones* or "by any other term from the *eik*- root." See also Robb, *Literacy and* Paideia *in Ancient Greece*, 220.

50. On *mimēsis* and verisimilitude, see Halliwell, *Aesthetics of Mimesis*, chap. 1.

51. *Leviathan*, chap. 4.

soul, the ignorance of the person who has been deceived, *hē en tē[i] psuchē[i] agnoia hē tou epseusmenou*." For this reason, they are "hated by god and man alike" (382a-d). Insofar as they seek to deceive, contrivances may be characterized as true falsehoods. Dividing the category of "verbal falsehoods" into two, Socrates distinguishes between verbal falsehoods that are "imitations" of the condition the soul is in when it has been deceived, and verbal falsehoods that are "images, *eidola*." Socrates describes "imitations" as copies of true falsehoods (382b-c) that make falsehoods seem like truth (382d). "Images," by contrast, are not copies of true falsehoods for they are not copies at all (382c). As Gilles Deleuze has pointed out, *eidola* seek "to supply not simply a false copy" but instead to place "in question the very notations of copy and model."[52]

Deleuze, like other readers who take Plato to express contempt for mimetic things, reads the *Republic* as dismissing *eidola*, images, or what Deleuze calls "simulacra," which, he says, like "false pretenders," imply "an essential perversion or deviation" from an original model or form in favor of images as "secondary possessors . . . guaranteed by resemblance" to their "original."[53] While Deleuze's characterization of the *Republic*'s distinction between imitations and images seems right to me, unlike him, I take Socrates' taxonomy of falsehoods in *Republic* 2 to express wariness of imitations, and I take the elaboration of mimetic things as images, *eidola*, in *Republic* 10 to anticipate Deleuze's appreciation of images as placing in question the notations of copy and model themselves. Characterizing imitations as verbal falsehoods that are copies of true falsehoods, *Republic* 2, as we just saw, treats imitations as covering over, by claiming likeness, their difference from what they model. Socrates' taxonomy treats images, *eidola*, as verbal falsehoods of a different sort, falsehoods that call attention to their difference from what they represent. These latter kinds of verbal falsehoods, as in the tale of Gyges and myth of Er, make no claim to verisimilitude. Unlike true lies, contrivances, and verbal falsehoods in the mode of imitations, images, *eidola*, may, but need not, and do not seek to, deceive. Making no claim of fidelity to an original, images, *eidola*, wear their falsity on their face.

If, then, the truth of mimetic images is not deception, what might it be? How might the "look" of an appearance at a third remove from the form it represents (597e) be false but not deceptive? Well, what if the truth of the mimetic image, *eidolon*, *is* its falsity to the form and to the artifact? What if its

---

52. Deleuze, "Simulacrum and Ancient Philosophy," 256–57. Thanks to Amanda Jo Goldstein for bringing this essay to my attention.

53. Ibid.

truth is that it *is* neither form nor artifact? Something similar may be said of an artifact, namely, that its falsity to the form and to the mimetic thing is *its* truth (597a).⁵⁴ What would follow from this is that knowledge, *to eidenai*, of *mimēsis* (595b) is knowing that the mimetic image, *eidolon*, *is* all and only a "look," *eidos*, at a third remove from the form, *eidos*, and knowing, too, that the partial or perspectival truth given by a look, *eidos*, is not the same as the truth of a form, *eidos*, or the truth of an artifact (597e). Socrates appears to suggest something like this when he emphasizes that "the picture shows only how the couch appears when viewed from a particular angle" (598a-b). The falsity of the painting is that it is only the look of the artifact of the couch as it appears to the artist from where he stands when he paints it.⁵⁵ And this is also its truth.

Underscoring and representing the importance of perspective and partiality to the truth of *mimēsis*, Socrates switches standpoints in his next exchanges with Glaucon. From looking at what *mimēsis* is like from the standpoint of someone with knowledge of its truth, Socrates moves, as we saw, to consider the standpoint of one who fails to see the truth of the mimetic thing and is deceived (598c-d). And then, switching perspectives once again, he reorients discussion to the sort of knowledge possessed by the mimetic artist, now represented not by the painter but by the poet. *Eidos* and its derivations in some of these passages (596a–597d) signify both "look" and "form," and also the knowledge proper to *mimēsis*, *to eidenai*. The dialogue's exploitation of this shared etymology suggests that the *eidos* represented in *mimēsis* and the *eidos* that is form are not only distinct but also somehow akin. Both *eidenai* and *eidos* are rooted in the stem *(w)id-*, which means "to see."⁵⁶ Perhaps, then, as we saw in chapter 1, the truth of a form or idea, in its invisibility, may be approached only by way of what is visible, that is, its appearance. If this is so, then, in the words of the Simonides fragment quoted by Adeimantus in *Republic* 2, "Appearance constrains even truth, *to dokein kai . . . tan alētheian biatai*" (365c), or, in Anne Carson's translation, "It is in fact upon the world of things needing to be uncovered that the world of merely visible things keeps exerting its pressure."⁵⁷

Carson offers a second, different translation of the same fragment: "Seeming does violence even to truth."⁵⁸ Unlike her first translation, this one seems

---

54. Baracchi, "Another Apology," 7, notes this too.
55. See Burnyeat, "Culture and Society in Plato's *Republic*," 217–324, 263.
56. For discussion and additional references, see Halliwell, in *Plato: Republic 10*, 109–10.
57. Carson, *Economy of the Unlost*, 60. Contra Carson, I read Plato as an ally of Simonides and not only as a rival.
58. Carson, *Economy of the Unlost*, 129.

to elide the distinction between *mimēsis* and deception. As we saw, it is possible for mimetic appearances to do violence to truth. They do so when, like contrivances, they are false by way of deception. Unlike contrivances, however, mimetic things can also be false other than by deception, that is, as partial and perspectival representations of (the) truth (of ideas). When they are understood in this way, that is, as images, mimetic things, making manifest their falsity, do no violence to truth. On the contrary, by making apparent our inability to see what does not appear, mimetic images, unlike mirrors, and also, we may now say, unlike imitations and contrivances, invite us to look harder. Recall, in this context, the passage in *Republic* 7, discussed in chapter 1, in which Socrates extols the stars "that paint the skies" for their beauty and complexity, *poikilia*, while insisting that they fall far short of truth, which is apprehensible by reason and thought but not by sight (529c-d). Warning against taking what the eyes see to be the whole truth, Socrates underscores the limitations of appearances when it comes to truth. He also implies that studying being and the invisible, the *eidos* that is the idea, depends on and is mediated by *poikilia*, the complexity, intricacy, variety, and multiplicity, perceived as appearances by the senses. This suggests that without an *eidos*, the look of an appearance, and without knowing that the look is partial and therefore false to the *eidos* as form, there can be no orientation to the truth of the *eidos* as form. Given this backdrop it is not surprising that the opening passages of *Republic* 10 present the multiple epistemic modalities of *eidos* as entangled and complicit. In an apparent violation of the neat hierarchies and distinctions of *Republic* 6's divided line, to which I return in chapter 6, the *Republic* 10 passages use *eidos* to signify the invisible idea available to insight, *nous*, alone, and also to signify what appears to the senses.

Republic 10 presents *dianoia* as relating to *eidos* (595b) as well. Whereas the line simile positions the "corruptions" that are phantasms, *phantasmata*, and images, *eidola*, in the bottommost domain of imagination, *eikasia*, *Republic* 10 presents *dianoia* as susceptible to these corruptions as well (598b). *Dianoia* is also presented in *Republic* 10 as capable of safeguarding against such corruptions, however, that is, if it possesses knowledge, *to eidenai*, of *mimēsis* (595b). In *Republic* 10, then, *dianoia* and *eidos* both appear on both sides of the division between the intelligible and the visible. Why? And why does *Republic* 10 associate poetry with *dianoia* at all (595b, 603c; also *Ion* 530c-d)? In particular, if *dianoia* is the capacity of the soul associated with mathematical thinking in the line simile, and *Republic* 10 also associates it with poetry, might there be reason to wonder about Socrates' claim that poetry "associates with the part in us that is remote from intelligence, *phronēsis*, and is its companion and friend for no sound and true purpose" (603a-b)? To answer these questions, I turn to poetry's use.

POETRY'S USE

Turning from the perspective of the viewer of a painting to that of the mimetic poet and specifically to an interrogation of the knowledge, *epistēmē*, of Homer (598d-e), Socrates asks: If the poet truly has knowledge of the things he represents, won't he use that knowledge to bring benefit rather than merely putting in words the things he appears to know? Homer's poetry may tell of wars and generalship and governance and education, in other words, but Socrates seems to be saying that the important question for determining the knowledge of Homer is whether he has improved the administration of cities or changed practices of warfare. Are the "many inventions, *epinoiai*, and devices, *eumēchanoi*," reported of others also reported of Homer, he wonders (600a)? Glaucon answers no, and so he and Socrates conclude that Homer's knowledge and, indeed, Homer himself, are utterly useless (599a–600b). With this outcome, the *Republic*'s demonstration of the ethical and political bankruptcy of mimetic poetry is often taken to be complete.

This may be too quick, however. Against the backdrop of the *Republic*'s wariness of contrivances as tools of deception, discussed above, that Socrates describes Homer's poetry as failing as a device or contrivance, *mēchanē*, may be more praise than blame. The same may be said of the charge of uselessness, for that charge applies at least as well to philosophy (*Rep*. 487e–489d, 527d; see also *Gorg*. 484c–486d).[59] That, as counterexamples to Homer's uselessness, Socrates invokes the activities of famed sophists (600c-d) and lawgivers (599d-e), figures who are depicted as masters of contrivance and subject to critical scrutiny across Plato's dialogues (*Rep*. 492a-d; *Gorg*. 515d ff.; *Laches* 186b-d; *Laws* 858e; *Phaedr*. 258a-c, 278c; *Prot*. 315a-b, 343a), might prompt a reconsideration of the negative assessment of the poet as well.[60] Indeed, as in *Republic* 1 and as in the opening of *Republic* 10, the true subject of Socrates'

---

59. Bloom, "Interpretive Essay," in *Republic of Plato*, 430, observes that the charge of uselessness applies to Homer and to Socrates. Kastley, *Rhetoric of Plato's "Republic*,*"* 192, adduces resemblances between poetry and philosophy and concludes that Socrates must therefore do a better job of distinguishing them. In my view, these resemblances underscore the close association the dialogue seeks to establish between poetry and philosophy.

60. For a similar point, see Freydberg, "Retracing Homer and Aristophanes in the Platonic Text," 103.

interrogation at this point may be not the poet or what he knows. What Homer may have known, like what Simonides may have known and/or meant, can only remain an open question. Instead, the multiple references in the *Republic* 10 passages on Homer to what "is told," what "the many say," and what "is reported, *ta legomena*" (598c, 600a, b, c), suggest that under scrutiny may rather be poetry's listeners/interpreters and how they hear, use, and know.

Still, Socrates insists that "all the poets, beginning with Homer, are mimeticists of excellence, *mimētas eidōlōn aretēs*, and of the other things that they create, *poiousin* [or about which they poeticize, "playing with the double meaning of *poiein*"[61]], and do not lay hold of truth" (600e). He maintains, too, that poets produce phantoms, *phantasmata*, not realities (599a) and that "the creator of the image, *eidōlōn*, the mimeticist, *mimētēs*, . . . knows nothing of reality but only the appearance" (601b-c). These statements may indicate contempt for mimetic things as *eidola*, mere images, simulacra, phantoms. Or, as I suggested above, they may simply be telling the truth about the truth and knowledge of *mimēsis*, namely, that mimetic images, *eidola, are* at a third remove from the truth of the ideas, and that, as such, their truth is not to imitate or model reality but, rather, to be false to that reality.

Maintaining that "we must not leave things half said but see them adequately" (601c), Socrates stays with the question of use. Hammering home that what truly matters is what poetry's interpreters know and how they know it, Socrates insists that it is the user who has knowledge (601e). He next analogizes the knowledgeable user of a poem to a flute player who is the knowledgeable user of the instrument and a horseman who is the knowledgeable user of a rein and bit (601c-e). What is to be made of this analogy? Is the knowledgeable user of a poem like the knowledgeable user of a flute or a rein? The rhapsode Ion in his eponymous dialogue thinks so. Treating Homer's poems as artifacts of use, he claims that he should be put in charge of the military based on his knowledge of Homer (*Ion* 541b).[62] Those whom Socrates calls "Homer's admirers" in *Republic* 10 seem to agree, when they celebrate him as "the educator of Hellas," and find that he is "worth studying both for our general education and for the management of human affairs, that we should learn from him and follow this poet in the arrangement and conduct of our own lives" (606e-607a). Socrates, for his part, recurs to Homer's poetry in *Republic* 3 for advice about the food and medicine to use to heal warriors (404b-c). Glaucon

---

61. Shorey, in *Republic, Books 6–10*, 441 note i. See also Belfiore, "Plato's Greatest Accusation against Poetry."

62. For discussion, see Robb, *Literacy and* Paideia *in Ancient Greece*, 168.

indexes poetry to utility as well, acquiescing when, after setting up the analogy, Socrates asks: "Do not the excellence, the beauty, the rightness, of every implement, living thing, and action, refer solely to the use, *chreian*, for which each thing is made or by nature adapted?" (601d).

Glaucon acquiesces. Should we? Let us look again at Socrates' analogy. Referring excellence, beauty, and rightness to use in the case of instruments makes some sense, though, if we recall Socrates' exchange with Thrasymachus in *Republic* 1, we may wonder whether the excellence and possible rightness of instruments might not rather refer to function, *ergon*, which may not be the same as instrumental use (352e–353e). There seem to be no grounds, however, for referring the excellence, beauty, and rightness of living things and actions to utility. In *Republic* 7, for example, Socrates chides Glaucon for instrumentalizing to the ends of war the "useless studies" propaedeutic to dialectics (527d; also 528e–529a). In *Hippias Major*, he argues against referring beauty to use (295c–296a).

What about poetry? Is it a thing of use in the mode of a flute or a rein or a bit? Socrates suggests otherwise when he says that those who judge poetry by its utility don't know anything at all (602b).[63] This is because to use a poem well is a matter of knowing that, like other mimetic images, *eidola*, it is at a third remove from the truth, a point Socrates repeats at precisely this juncture (602c). Knowing that a mimetic poem is at a third remove from the truth, knowledgeable users do not mistake it or its representations for artifacts or ideas. Recognizing the differences between representations, artifacts, and ideas, knowledgeable users understand that what a poem says should not be taken for the truth proper to ideas or to artifacts (602b). When "Homer's admirers," including Ion, Glaucon, and also Socrates, treat Homer's poetry as a tool of use like a rein or a bit, they show themselves to be not knowledgeable users of poetry. Unable to tell the difference between truth and representation, they show that they do not yet possess the necessary antidote to safeguard against mimetic poetry's distorting effects.

POETRY'S REASON

What sort of knowledge safeguards against distorting effects? To Glaucon, guided by Socrates, it is the knowledge belonging to calculative reasoning, *to*

---

63. Contra, e.g., Naddaff, *Exiling the Poets*, 121, and Belfiore, "Plato's Greatest Accusation against Poetry," who both read the *Republic* as taking the measure of poetry to be its utility for philosophy.

logistikon, whose work is "measuring, numbering, and weighing" (602d-e). Located in the part of the soul responsive to "argument, *logos*, and law, *nomos*" (604b), *to logistikon* regulates responses triggered and fostered by poetry, specifically the erotic responses of the inferior part of the soul, and keeps them quiet (606b-d). Calculative reasoning is what Socrates calls "the counter" to the "appearance of the contrary" in deceptive appearances (602d–603b). A. A. Long is not alone in taking "Plato's *Republic* as a whole" to be

> premised on the principle that in the universe, in politics, and in the soul, one thing, and one thing alone, is properly qualified to control and to exercise authority over everything else. That one thing is reason or reasoning, expressed in Greek by means of the noun *logismos*, the adjective *logistikos*, and the verb *logizesthai*.[64]

In *Republic* 10, Socrates appears to force a choice: calculation or desire, law and *logismos* or mimetic poetry. Tipping the scale, he says: "If you admit the honeyed muse in lyrics or epics, pleasure and pain will jointly be kings of your city instead of law and that argument which in each instance is best in the opinion of the community, *anti nomou te kai tou koine[i] aei doxantos einai beltistou logou*" (607a). Yet again, the dialogue's position on poetry seems clear.

Might we not wonder, however, about Socrates' alliance of law with "that argument which is best in the opinion of the community" on the ground that it runs counter to statements he makes earlier in the *Republic* that align law not with the opinion of the community but with the reason of the few (428d, 431c) and that suggest an incapacity on the part of opinion, let alone "the opinion of the community," to rule (484b)? Glaucon does not wonder, and so the choice Socrates puts, in all of its (apparent) starkness, stands. Between law and *logismos*, on one side, and mimetic poetry, on the other, it appears that there can be only one winner.

There can be only one winner because, as Socrates asks Glaucon just before presenting the choice, "Did we not say earlier that it is impossible for the same thing at one and the same time to hold contradictory opinions about the same thing?" Glaucon affirms. Socrates continues: "The part of the soul, then, that opines in contradiction of measurement, *to para ta metra ara doxazon tēs psuchēs*, could not be the same with that which conforms to it." Further, "that which puts its trust in measurement and reckoning must be the best part of the

---

64. Long, *Greek Models of Mind and Self*, 129.

soul, *to metro[i] ge kai logismō[i] pisteuon beltiston an eiē tēs psuchēs*" (602e–603a). With the soul thus divided, and with mimetic poetry opposed to law and *logismos* and awakening the inferior part of the soul and nourishing it, and, "by making it strong, destroy[ing] the calculating part" (605b-c), the choice Socrates presents forces the conclusion that "we should at last be justified in not admitting [the mimetic poet] into a city that is well-governed" (605b-c). Thus is the ouster of mimetic poetry completed.

Or is it? Might Glaucon affirm too quickly? Note that the reckoning and calculation of *to logistikon* are presented as correctives to cases of deceptive contrivances like scene painting and "distant appearances," whereas, as we have seen, mimetic representations or images are not the same as contrivances. Note, too, that Socrates describes the weighing, measuring, and numbering characteristic of *to logistikon* as "charming, *charieistatai*, helpers" (602d) just lines after disparaging the charms, *charieis*, of the mimetic artist (602a). Might this invite a critical distance not only from the charms of *mimēsis* but from those of *to logistikon* as well? As noted in chapter 1, Socrates says that "the reasons that we have given" for poetry's ouster "we shall *chant* to ourselves" "like an *incantation*," "as a counter-*charm* to [poetry's] spell" (607c, my emphasis). Might Socrates thus efface the difference between how reason and poetry do their work?

Even if, like Glaucon, we accept Socrates' claim of the victory of *to logistikon* over mimetic poetry, we might nonetheless wonder what kind of victory that is, especially if we recall that it is Thrasymachus who first introduced the verb *logizesthai* and that he did so as part of his definition of justice as the advantage of the stronger (339a). In this regard, it is worth noticing that in keeping quiet "the emotions of sex and anger, and all the appetites and pains and pleasures of the soul which we say accompany all our actions, *pasē[i] praxei*" (606d), *to logistikon* appears to stymie the motivators of "all our actions," and, thereby, all our actions themselves. Perhaps this is why Socrates, in the *Euthyphro*, calls weighing and numbering, depicted in the *Republic* as "helpers" of calculative rationality, utterly improper measures of "right and wrong, and noble and disgraceful, and good and bad" (7b-d). Calculative rationality seems, in any case, to be an inappropriate metric for application to the human soul, which Socrates describes, not unlike poetry, poetry's audience, and its characters, as itself *poikilon*, "full of multicolored variety and unlikeness, *pollēs poikilias kai anomoiotētos*" (611b).[65] Against this backdrop, it may not surprise that, as we

---

65. For an extended treatment of the failures of calculative rationality when it comes to ethics and politics, with attention to Plato in chap. 4, see Satkunanandan, *Extraordinary Responsibility*.

will see in chapters 3 and 4, when, in the rest of the *Republic*, the laws of a city are associated with *to logistikon*, they are depicted as securing obedience, but not as producing justice, or offering an adequate guide to the good.

If this is so, however, then why does Socrates appear to celebrate *to logistikon* as the counter to the part of the soul "that opines in contradiction"? Here, too, in relation to the dialogue's attitude to contradiction, there is reason to go slowly. For although it is true that Glaucon and Socrates had said "earlier," specifically in *Republic* 4, that "it is impossible for the same thing at one and the same time to hold contradictory opinions about the same thing" (436b, 436e–437a, 439b), Socrates also recommended there, and Glaucon agreed, that they "proceed on the hypothesis that this is so, with the understanding that, if it ever appear otherwise, everything that results from the assumption shall be invalidated" (437a). When Socrates returns to the hypothesis of noncontradiction in *Republic* 10, Glaucon might have brought up that over the course of the dialogue it *has* "appear[ed] otherwise." In *Republic* 7, for example, contradictory perceptions are described as what awaken reflection and summon a soul to philosophy (524d). As we saw in chapter 1, the *Republic* abounds with performative and substantive contradictions, most often in the person of Socrates. We have just seen, too, that Socrates holds contradictory opinions about opinion, specifically, about the capacity of opinion to rule. We will see more contradictions when we turn to the early curricula of *Republic* 2–3 in the next chapter. In Ramona Naddaff's words, Socrates defies "his own golden rule of noncontradiction" almost as often as he follows it.[66]

This is true of the mode of knowing the dialogue calls *dianoia* as well. After appearing to accept Glaucon's affirmation of the hypothesis of noncontradiction in *Republic* 10, Socrates turns to *dianoia*, the mode of knowing to which mimetic poetry appeals.[67] With respect to the *mimēsis* of human action, he asks: "Is a man, then, in all of this of one mind, *homonoētikōs*, with himself, or just as in the domain of sight there was faction and strife as he held within himself contrary opinions at the same time about the same things, so also in our actions there is division and strife of the man with himself?" (603c-d). Without giving Glaucon a chance to answer, Socrates continues: "But I recall that there is no need now of our seeking agreement on this point, for in our former discussion we were sufficiently agreed that our soul at any one moment

---

66. Naddaff, *Exiling the Poets*, 93.

67. For a helpful discussion of how *dianoia* moves from opinion to knowledge, see Morgan, "Belief, Knowledge, and Learning."

teems with countless such self-contradictions" (603c-d).⁶⁸ What Socrates says here suggests that it *is* possible, then, for the same thing at one and the same time to hold contradictory opinions about the same thing. Indeed, the "thing" that appears to work paradigmatically in this way is the soul in its practice of *dianoia*, the epistemic modality that, as Socrates prefigures in the opening passages of *Republic* 10 and repeats here, troubles the neat hierarchies of the line simile by knowing across the division between the visible and the intelligible, a point I return to in chapter 6.⁶⁹

If it *is* possible for the same thing at one and the same time to hold contradictory opinions about the same thing, however, then, as Socrates says in *Republic* 4, all that results from the contrary assumption, that is to say, from the hypothesis of noncontradiction, must be reconsidered. This includes the elevation of *to logistikon* as the best part of the soul, the tripartition of the soul more generally, the city set up by analogy with the partitioned soul, and the education and justice that reinforce that city, in particular the one man:one art principle for which the principle of noncontradiction is a logical analogue. I explore these in the chapters that follow. Also up for reconsideration are the choices Socrates appears to force in *Republic* 10 between reason or desire, and between law or mimetic poetry. I turn to these by way of conclusion.

POETRY'S BENEFIT

Here is the passage, quoted earlier only in part, which is sometimes read as effecting the decisive ouster of the mimetic poets:

> We should at last be justified in not admitting [the mimetic poet] into a city that is well-governed, because he awakens [the inferior] part of the soul and nourishes it, and, by making it strong, destroys the calculating part; just as in a city when someone, by making wicked men mighty, turns the city over to them and corrupts the better sort of citizen. Similarly, we'll say that a poet puts a bad constitution in the soul of each individual by making images, *eidōla eidōlopoiounta*, that are far removed from the truth and by gratifying the soul's irrational part. (605b-c)

Socrates' argument appears to be that mimetic poetry causes harm by bringing about a poor constitution in the soul. To do harm, as we know from earlier in

---

68. Socrates' own argumentative practice of self-contradiction is Exhibit A.
69. Contra Naddaff, *Exiling the Poets*, 80.

the *Republic*, is to be unjust (335e; also *Crito* 48a). Therefore, mimetic poets do injustice. Much hangs on the first premise of this argument, a premise Socrates establishes by way of an analogy to how bad constitutions destroy cities. Let's take a closer look.

How do bad constitutions destroy cities? And who is responsible for them? Who or what, in other words, is the political analogue to the mimetic poet? Consider the beginning of *Republic* 8's account of constitutional change and decline, which, in any case, establishes its relevance to the subject matter of *Republic* 10 by offering Socrates' analysis of constitutional deviation from the ideal city in the voices of the Muses (545d-e). In a gesture to Homer (who regularly signals the introduction of difficult subject matter by invoking the Muses[70]), the dialogue casts Socrates in a position analogous to Homer or, perhaps, to Hesiod, for whom stories of genesis and justice/injustice are stock-in-trade. Is Socrates, then, the political analogue of the mimetic poets of *Republic* 10? Or is it Plato? Is it the Muses? Or is it Homer? Or Hesiod? These poets and/or philosophers offer representations or images of bad constitutions, to be sure, and they are responsible for those representations. But who or what is responsible for the constitutions themselves?

In *Republic* 8, Socrates ventriloquizes the Muses as saying that constitutional decline arises from faction, *stasis*, within a city, which itself arises owing to the failure of the artificial breeding technique of the *kallipolis*. The technique seeks to guarantee that the gold guardians will reproduce themselves. Without this technique, called the "nuptial number," the rulers of the ideal city are unable to judge well the quality of the guardians. With it, however, they also fail to hit their mark (546b). That the technique fails underscores the inadequacy of calculative measures to questions of ethical and political constitution. The result of the failure in the case of the nuptial number is a "chaotic mixing of iron with silver and of bronze with gold," which breeds the civil war and hatred at the root of constitutional degeneration (547a).[71] From this

---

70. Ford, *Homer*, 72, says that Homer invokes the Muses to help him with a daunting task, specifically the task of "get[ting] on with his story, to keep speaking truly in the face of an overwhelming tradition" (82). According to Ford, the same thing occurs in *Euthydemus* 275c, where Socrates says: "It is no small task to take up and go through a wisdom so unmanageably great (*amēchanon*) as theirs. So I, at any rate, must begin my tale like the poets, calling on the Muses and Memory." "The Muses connect the poem to a larger order" (82).

71. It is noteworthy that both the "nuptial number" and the "mixing" (which refers back to the noble lie, a "Phoenician thing," deriving its authority from the poets [414b-415d]) are truths of the Muses, which is to say, representations at a third remove from the truth of ideas.

vantage point, responsibility for bad political constitutions appears to lie with those holding political offices, that is, at the start of *Republic* 8 at least, with the philosopher-kings. Their incapacity to judge well despite or, we might now perhaps say, because of their calculative rationality appears to be responsible for deviation from the perfect city in speech (545d). Are *they* then the political analogues of the mimetic poets of *Republic* 10?

Socrates' story appears to be more complex. In his words (some of them Homer's), constitutions are born not "from oak or rock" (*Il.* 22.126; *Od.* 19.163)[72] but from "the characters of the people who live in the cities governed by them, which tip the scales, so to speak, and drag the rest along with them" (544d-e). As the rest of *Republic* 8 seems to indicate, it is the ways of life of the people living in the cities that bring about the changes in those cities that give rise to their constitutions (547b, 550d–551b, 555b-d, 562c–563d).[73] The engines of bad political constitutions thus appear to be those who empower the rulers by surrendering to them their cities. If this is so, then, by the city/soul analogy invoked in this passage, the engines of bad psychological constitutions are also not the mimetic poets but those who empower the poets by alienating to them their internal cities (592b, 608b), which is to say, the people themselves. What is responsible for their practice of alienation? Socrates attributes the "bad political constitution established" in the tyrannical soul to a lack of education in poetry and music (579c), thus implying that good soul constitutions depend on an education in poetry and music. This cannot be the education in poetry and music provided by Athens' traditional *paideia*, nor, as we will see in the next chapter, is it the early curriculum of *Republic* 2–3 offered as the antidote to that *paideia*, for, as we saw at the start of this chapter, both of *these* modes of education secure elite authority by teaching people to alienate their self-rule to those with privileged expertise.

I have been arguing over the course of this chapter that as its antidote to these educations the *Republic* offers mimetic poetry. But how can this be when

---

72. Socrates invokes this same phrase in *Apology* 34d, using it there to refer to the formation and development not of political institutions but of the human soul, specifically, his own.

73. The *Republic* may at times appeal to the regime "as the most important political fact and the cause of all other facts" (Bloom, "Interpretive Essay," in *Republic of Plato*, 414), and *Rep.* 8 may open with Socrates and his interlocutors maintaining that they will follow their plan and examine constitutions as the engines of regime change first. But, as in the rest of the dialogue, *Rep.* 8 depicts a more complex and bidirectional relation between soul and city. On the dynamic and reciprocal account of self- and regime constitution in *Republic* and *Laws*, see my "Constitution."

Socrates appears to maintain across *Republic* 10, that *mimēsis* has the power to corrupt, and offers as "the chief accusation" against mimetic poetry "its power to corrupt, with rare exceptions, even the better sort" (605c)? Like the other accusations against mimetic poetry examined in this chapter, Socrates' "chief accusation" repays scrutiny. As I show next, the target of this accusation turns out to be not mimetic poetry but the so-called "better sort."

Calling force, *bia*, what prevents the better sort in private from yielding to lamentation when they are afflicted by their own troubles (606a), and calling what restrains them from "playing the clown" outside the theater fear for reputation (606c-d), Socrates describes the better sort in exactly the way he describes the *oligarchical* personality in *Republic* 8. As he puts it there, "Something good of his is holding in check by force, *bia*, the other bad appetites within; not persuading them that they had better not, nor taming them with speech or an argument, *logos*, but by way of compulsion (or necessity), *anangkē*, and fear, because he is terrified of losing his other possessions" (554d). Held in check by force or fear, the oligarch's soul may appear good to others, but it is not truly good. The same appears to be true of the better sort. Maintaining that they treat the pleasures of the mimetic representations to which they abandon themselves as "so much clear gain, *kerdainein*" (606b), Socrates underscores the proximity of the better sort to the oligarch: both are driven by force and fear, and also by the promise of gain. Insofar as the better sort apply the standard of gain to mimetic poetry, moreover, they turn out to be no different from poetry's other "admirers," who, as discussed earlier, take a similarly utilitarian attitude to poetry (606e-607a) and so mistake poetry for a thing of use. Finally, insofar as the better sort are driven to moderate themselves by force and fear, and insofar as the effectiveness of force and fear requires the actual or imagined presence of others, it seems unlikely that they will be able to do any better than the many at moderating themselves in private or than they are able to do themselves in the theater. Socrates refers in *Republic* 10 to the "best element" of the better sort as "relaxing its guard, *phulakēn*" (606a) when it permits grief and/or laughter at mimetic representations in the theater. This element relaxes its guard, he explains, because "it has never been properly educated by speech, *logō[i]*, or habit, *ēthei*" (606a). Thus the better sort, like the oligarch (559d) and the tyrant (579c), *lack* a proper education. And if that is so, then they, too, cannot be truly good.

Why might Socrates present as the better sort those who are not truly good? Perhaps for the same reason that he introduces as an exception to the censorship of mimetic poetry hymns and praises that, as we saw in chapter 1, by bringing neither pleasure nor benefit fail to meet the conditions of his loophole. These, together, seem to underscore that, as Simonides is quoted as saying in the *Protagoras*, "it is hard to become truly good, *hoti andra agathon alētheia[i] genesthai chalepon eiē*" (*Prot.* 339c). Adeimantus quotes Hesiod to the same effect in *Republic* 2 (364d): the road to virtue is long, "rough and steep" (*Works and Days* 290). The road to becoming good is hard and long and steep because a truly good soul will hold *itself* in check, and that, as we will see over the course of the following chapters, takes, in addition to the proper education, time, attention, and above all else, desire. Perhaps, then, the difficulty of becoming truly good is brought to appearance by the poets and in the context of the *Republic*'s discussion of mimetic poetry because mimetic poetry, as we hear repeatedly throughout the dialogue, appeals to and emancipates desire.

Mimetic poetry does not prompt the desire to become good by the principle of mimetic identification as a practice of imitation. As discussed in chapter 1, mimetic poetry's representations of "fretful and complicated" characters (604d-e), however pleasing they may be to the many and the better sort alike, will, by that principle, only reinforce what is not good in each. Instead, mimetic representations provoke the desire to become good, if they do at all, by inviting attention to the appearance of those representations and also and thereby to what does not appear, to possibility. By bringing to appearance a *lack* of moderation or intelligence or grace or goodness, for example, representations of complex and fretful characters may also, and thereby, invite a consideration of how it is possible to become so. That consideration depends not on recourse to a truth beyond representation secured by calculative rationality but on, what I called in chapter 1, the practice of disidentification, a practice that we may now say involves reflection on the relation *between* truth and representation. We might call this mimetic knowledge—that is, knowing that a mimetic representation *is* all and only a "look," and knowing, too, that the partial or perspectival truth given by a look is not the same as the whole truth. Cultivated and informed by mimetic poetry, mimetic knowledge opens the possibility of becoming good by opening possibility. It offers no guarantees.

Socrates says: "We would be glad to receive [poetry] back from exile" (607c), if the poets themselves (or if "lovers of poetry" speaking "in prose on its behalf") can show "that poetry not only gives pleasure but is beneficial, *ōphelimē*, both to constitutions and to human life" (607d). Useless by the lights of any utilitarian calculus, and useless, too, by the lights of what we might call the "epistemic calculus" of *to logistikon*, mimetic poetry brings benefit, if its "lovers" allow it, by appealing to their *erōs*, and specifically, as we will see, to the human soul's desire to know itself, to know others, to know its own good, and thereby to seek to become good, all of which always also remain in question. Moving souls to desire and also to question and thereby, perhaps, to become good would be a benefit "both to constitutions and to human life" (607d). Thus, in its self-presentation as mimetic poetry, and by way of its account of mimetic knowledge, the *Republic*, as I read it, offers an education in mimetic poetry as the very demonstration that Socrates claims at the start of *Republic* 10 to seek.

CHAPTER 3

A Life without Poetry

Everything follows from the direction a person's education takes.

Republic 425c

The first two chapters of this book sought to bring to light the centrality of mimetic poetry to the *Republic*. Why, then, is mimetic poetry censored in the curriculum of *Republic* 2–3 and ousted from *Republic* 5's ideal city? This chapter argues that Socrates works up with Glaucon and Adeimantus the early *paideia*, the laws that structure it, the personalities it produces, and the constitution it fosters to underscore the perils for ethics and politics of a life *without* mimetic poetry.[1]

We saw in chapter 2 that Thrasymachus' exclusion of poetry from his account of the benefits of injustice already staged the perils of such a life. Socrates ostensibly rebutted it.[2] Why, then, does the dialogue stage it again? Perhaps because arguments on behalf of injustice have a powerful hold on Socrates' interlocutors. Announcing at the start of *Republic* 2 that he refuses to accept Thrasymachus' "surrender," Glaucon speaks on behalf of those present when he asks Socrates: "Do you really want to persuade, *hōs alēthōs peisai*, us that it is in every way better to be just than unjust, or is it enough merely to seem to have persuaded us, *dokein pepeikenai*?" (357a-b). Socrates answers that he would prefer "really to persuade you, if I had a choice" (357b). If, as Glaucon says, they are not yet persuaded (a claim echoed by Adeimantus [367a-b]), and if, as Socrates says, he would like truly to persuade, then there is reason

---

1. I discuss the perils for justice in chapter 4 and the epilogue, and for philosophy in chapters 5 and 6.

2. I say "ostensibly" because I agree with scholars who argue that Socrates' rebuttal is not truly persuasive, nor do I think it is meant to be, as we will see in chapter 4.

to expect that Socrates' subsequent engagements with the brothers will revisit Thrasymachean (in)justice as part of his renewed attempt to persuade.

As I demonstrate in what follows, that expectation is not disappointed. *Republic* 2–5 offer an account of justice that, unlike what Socrates put forward in *Republic* 1, *will* definitively vanquish the (in)justice of Thrasymachus. If, as we saw in chapter 2, Thrasymachean justice erased the distinction between truth and representation to underwrite a world in which self-standing authority backed by might replaced all other modes of authority, we will see over the course of this chapter that the counterjustice Socrates offers also erases the distinction between truth and representation to underwrite a world in which self-standing authority backed by knowledge replaces all other modes of authority. If Thrasymachean justice was a matter of might intelligently exercised, the justice of *Republic* 2–5 turns out to be a matter of knowledge coercively exercised.

Despite their important differences, both modes of "justice" are portrayed as producing similar adverse ethical and political effects. Indeed, Thrasymachean justice as a *technē* of political power and the justice of *Republic* 2–5— a *technē* of epistemic power—turn out to be two sides of the same coin. As we will see, justice as a *technē* of epistemic power emerges as a product of the *paideia* of *Republic* 2–3. It is one of the "virtues" Socrates elaborates in *Republic* 4. And it underwrites the ideal city of *Republic* 5, the *kallipolis*. This chapter makes the case that the dialogue's representations of the early education, its associated "virtues," and the constitution of the *kallipolis* prompt readers to be no less wary of the form of justice presented in *Republic* 2–5 than of the justice offered by Thrasymachus in *Republic* 1. Subsequent chapters develop the modes of speaking, desiring, thinking, and justice that I take the *Republic* as a whole to offer to orient away from both *technai* of justice. As discussed in earlier chapters, these are practices of self-authorization informed by mimetic knowledge, which together orient to what I call "poetic justice," and turn to in this book's epilogue. This chapter clears the ground for those developments by way of a reconsideration of the depictions in *Republic* 2–5 of a life without mimetic poetry.

THE BROTHERS' DESIRE

After Socrates expresses interest in truly persuading his interlocutors that "it is better to be just than unjust," Glaucon takes the lead in setting the terms of the discussion that follows. He offers three classes and asks into which class Socrates would place justice: is it desirable in and for itself; in and for itself and for its consequences; or only for its consequences?[3] Describing justice as "that which a man who is to be happy must love both for its own sake and for the results," Socrates claims that justice belongs in the second class, which he calls the most beautiful (357b–358a). Glaucon replies that the many, by contrast, place justice in the third class (358a), and then he and Adeimantus take turns elaborating the force and stakes of that understanding, which they attribute not only to the many but also to Thrasymachus. As we will see in this book's epilogue, Glaucon's taxonomy of justice and the brothers' "augmentations" of Thrasymachean (in)justice are less straightforward than they seem.

Most relevant for now is that, unlike Thrasymachus, the brothers, as we saw in chapter 2, repeatedly reference the poets, emphasizing that their position is the opposite of the instrumental and utilitarian justice they associate, by way of the poets, with both Thrasymachus and the many. Announcing that he would like "to forget about the rewards and results" of justice and injustice, Glaucon places justice in the first class (358b). Saying that he has never yet heard justice discussed as he desires to hear it, he demands from Socrates an "encomium" of justice in and by itself, *auto kath' hauto* (358d). He wants justice stripped bare (361a-c), "scoured clean" like a statue, as Socrates puts it, "purged, *ekkathaireis*" (361d), of the power of invisibility granted by the ring of Gyges (361a).[4] Adeimantus, likewise, asks for justice stripped of its reputation (367b-c). He wants an account of how justice and injustice work on their possessors in and by themselves, by their own inherent force, undetected by gods or by men (366e, 367b-e). Leave it to others, he says, to praise justice only for its consequences (363a), that is, for the rewards and honors that depend on opinion (367d).

Glaucon and Adeimantus want to get rid of seeming, opinion, and appearance (361b, 367b-e), which they blame on the poets. In Adeimantus' words, "to judge by the poets, if I am just without also seeming to be just, I can expect nothing out of it but hardship and clear loss. If I am unjust but have gained a reputation for justice then I am promised a wonderful life" (365b). The brothers are equally anxious about invisibility, and particularly about injustice that escapes detection, *lanthanein* (361a, 367c, 365c-d, 367e), which is to say, the injustice accomplished through stealth and deception that Thrasymachus, in *Republic* 1 (344a), and Socrates, in *Republic* 8–9 (565b, c, 566e, 573e–574b),

---

3. Parry, "Craft of Justice," 30–34, calls the first category of justice an "intrinsic good"; the second, one with "inherent consequences"; and the third, one with "conventional consequences."

4. For "purged," see Adam, *Republic of Plato*, 1:74.

associate with the tyrant. Desiring a justice that will make impossible both perceptible and imperceptible injustice, the brothers want justice unqualified, *haploos* (361b), unmixed, uncomplicated, pure. They want Justice with a capital *J*.[5] Desiring "the opposite" of what Thrasymachus or anyone else might say on the topics of justice and injustice (367a-b), they seek Justice as "a founding virtue of philosophy, conceived as the source of being and the knowledge of what things are in and of themselves."[6]

The brothers' desire for what is unqualified, simple, and pure appears later in *Republic* 2–5 as well. When, in discussion with Adeimantus about styles of poetic narration, Socrates asks which style their curriculum ought to keep—the pure one in which the voice of the poet is heard, the imitative style in which the poet speaks in the voice of another, or the mixed style of epic poetry—Adeimantus chooses to admit only "the unmixed imitator of the good, *ton tou epieikous mimētēn akraton*" (397d). He agrees to the exile of the *diplous* or manifold man in favor of a "more austere and less delightful poet and taleteller" (398a-b). Simple, *haploon*, is how Glaucon describes the perfectly just man (361b). After Glaucon has named the musical modes that conform with the laws of the curriculum regulating speech, and Socrates asks whether their city will support triangles, harps, and flutes, Glaucon acquiesces to the ouster of these "many-stringed and polyharmonic instruments" (399d). As we will see in later sections of this chapter, both brothers support the eugenics programs Socrates sets forth to guarantee the purity and pedigree of the guardian/warriors of the ideal city (460c).

Back in *Republic* 2, when Glaucon (358d) and Adeimantus (367d) ask Socrates to make the case for justice in and by itself exactly as they desire to hear it, Socrates acquiesces (358e, 368c). That might give pause, not least because when justice *haploos* appeared in *Republic* 1, as "truthfulness, and returning anything you may have received from anyone else" (331c), Socrates had rejected it (351a). That Socrates expresses his acquiescence to the brothers using the language of gratification, *charis* (358e; also 430d-e, 472e, 517b), might also give pause, for that is the language Thrasymachus used in *Republic* 1 to describe the answers he gives not truthfully but with a view to pleasing Socrates (351c), and it appears across Plato's dialogues to signify the sophists' "charismatic bondage"

---

5. From here on, to indicate the justice the brothers desire, I write Justice (with a capital *J*).

6. Crotty, *Philosopher's Song*, 116. For Glaucon's desire for the "security of absolute knowledge," see Nichols, "*Republic*'s Two Alternatives," 252.

to their audiences.[7] That Glaucon requests an encomium and Socrates agrees (358d) might give pause as well. For if what Socrates says of the encomia of *erōs* in the *Symposium* is also true of the encomium of Justice in the *Republic*—namely, that encomia offer equal parts truth and empty praise (198c–199c)—then part of that encomium will be true and part empty praise. The situation with Adeimantus is no simpler. Requesting something that will make a man willing to honor Justice even when he has a contrivance or device, *mēchanē*, for dishonoring it (366b-c), Adeimantus asks Socrates for a guarantee against deception, lies, and fraud. Socrates, for his part, agrees to defend Justice as the brothers have defined it but only, he says, because he cannot not defend it. Insisting on his own incapacity—"I don't think I have the ability"—Socrates agrees to do "the best I can do," making "what defense I can" (368b-c).

The brothers' desire for Justice and Socrates' acquiescence to that desire, along with his disclaimer about what will follow, together set the terms for their joint quest for Justice. Those terms, as just described, should prompt the *Republic*'s readers to join that quest with wariness and critical distance, a distance prompted as well by Socrates' repeated "misgivings" (435d, 472a) and disavowals (389a, 403b, 409e, 427d, 458c, 463c, 497d, 527c, 544c). From that distance, the "purged, *kathairein*," city and curriculum (399e) of *Republic* 2–3, the purged virtues and dispositions on display in *Republic* 4 (401b–402a), producing and characterizing the pure, *katharon*, guardians (460c) and underwriting the perfect city and its perfect, *teleōs*, Justice (472c-d), appear, like Glaucon's "purged" statues, as consequences of the brothers' desire.[8] As we will see, these purges, a product not only of the brothers' desire for unqualified Justice but also of their anxiety about what cannot be detected, sideline complexities that also appear along the way as constitutive features of a justice adequate to an ethical and political life.

The brothers may desire a justice that is the "opposite" of Thrasymachean justice, but that desire, I argue, turns out to yield a justice that is the mirror of Thrasymachean justice in both substance and effect. Thus, to "rescue, *boēthein*" (368c), justice in the way the brothers want it to be rescued is to destroy justice and also, and relatedly, to destroy the brothers' ability to

---

7. I take this phrase from Berger, "Facing Sophists."

8. That the action of the *Republic* is responsive to Socrates' interlocutors is noted by others as well; see, e.g., Tarnopolsky, "Plato's Politics"; Weiss, *Philosophers in the "Republic,"* 3, 6–8; Berger, *Perils of Uglytown*, 66; and Peterson, *Socrates and Philosophy in the Dialogues of Plato*, chaps. 4–5.

rescue themselves.⁹ The brothers' desire also sidelines the class of justice that Socrates, for his part, had claimed to find "the most beautiful," namely, justice as good in itself *and* for its consequences, which turns out to have no place in the ideal city where what is beautiful is, instead, opposed to what is good (452d-e). Not a mere aggregation of the first and third classes, this class of justice, I show in this book's epilogue, calls for measures that differ both from the calculative rationality associated with the first class of justice demanded by the brothers and from the instrumental rationality of the third class, which the brothers associate with the many and Thrasymachus alike.

WARRIORS, GUARDIANS, DOGS

When Glaucon requests the encomium of Justice, he asks that Socrates follow his example in exactly the manner he outlines (358d). Beginning with its nature and origin (358e-359b), Glaucon describes a justice inscribed by the terms of a social contract and honored not because it is understood to be a good but "unwillingly," that is, "from want of power, *arrōstia[i]*, to commit injustice" (359b-360d). Socrates, as noted, acquiesces to Glaucon's request. He also follows Glaucon's example exactly as outlined, beginning with the nature and origin of justice in the "healthy city" and then in the city with a fever, going on to describe a justice that, as we will see, is honored, as was Glaucon's contractarian justice, not because it is understood to be a good but "insensibly" (401c), and from a want of capacity to commit injustice. This is the Justice produced by the *paideia* of *Republic* 2-3.¹⁰

Maintaining by way of the soul-city analogy that to see soul justice they would do well to look first at justice writ large (368d-369a), Socrates launches their quest for Justice by founding first, with Adeimantus, a "city for sows" (369b-372d).¹¹ Satisfying its inhabitants' basic needs through a simple division of labor (369d), that city does not satisfy Glaucon, who intervenes to motivate the transition to a second city, the "city with a fever," where desires and appetites grow (372e). To accommodate these appetites requires more goods. Greater production means more jobs and more people, a bigger city to accom-

---

9. This is a paraphrase of Berger's assessment of the *Phaedo* in *Perils of Uglytown*, 48: he says that for Socrates "to save his interlocutors the way they want to be saved is to destroy their ability to save themselves."

10. We will see in the epilogue that the brothers' avowed desire for this Justice is partnered with their disavowed desire for what Adeimantus calls "complete injustice" in *Republic* 1 (366b).

11. On the city-soul analogy, see Ferrari, *City and Soul in Plato's "Republic."* For discussion of the symbolism of sows, see McCoy, "City of Sows and Sexual Differentiation."

modate that growth, increased competition inside the city and also outside it, where conflicts arise owing to territorial expansion. Growth and competition, following on and generating the desire for more, *pleonexia*, give rise to takings from others to satisfy those desires. Such takings are the mark of injustice (349b-c, 362b, 365d), and also the origin of war (373e).

With warfare comes the need for warriors. These are required by the principle of one man:one art (374a-e), which was introduced by Socrates to explain the division of labor in the first city, and to which Adeimantus had agreed (370b-c).[12] Possessing a plurality of traits, which Socrates describes as difficult to combine, the warriors must have keen perception and be swift, strong, brave, high-spirited, gentle (375a-d), and able to guard against enemies from without their city and from within (414b). They must be their own best guardians, moreover, "for fear lest by working injustice, [they] should dwell in common with the greatest evil," in Adeimantus' formulation (367a). Glaucon agrees: "It would be absurd that a guardian would need a guard" (403e). To know whom and what to guard against, when and where to exercise strength, bravery, and/or moderation, what to make of what is keenly perceived, and how best to guard themselves, the guardians must possess gentleness, which Socrates sometimes calls moderation (389d), courage, and the wisdom characteristic of good judgment.

With Glaucon's approval, Socrates associates these characteristics with love of learning, *philomathia*, and also with love of wisdom, *philosophia*, for which, he says, "the criterion of the friendly and the alien is intelligence and ignorance" (376b). After this comes the education to philosophy that prepares the warriors to become guardians worthy to rule, to which I turn below. First, however, I wish to look again at Socrates' opening words in these passages, for, like his engagements with Glaucon and Adeimantus discussed in the last section, they give reason to pause and, as per Socrates' multiple references in these passages, to wonder (375e–376d).

Glaucon approves Socrates' identification of love of learning with love of wisdom.[13] Might he do so too quickly? And what about Socrates' identification of these modes of knowing with the knowledge and ignorance characteristic of a pedigree dog? Socrates says that a dog judges "what it sees to be either

---

12. I return to the one man:one art principle of justice in the epilogue. For now, note that with the introduction of this principle, Adeimantus' city immediately swells (370b–371e), making the cities of the brothers virtually identical except that in Adeimantus' city desires are invisible, whereas in Glaucon's city desires are everywhere apparent.

13. As we will see in chapter 5, he does so again (486c 487a) in the context of Socrates' account of the philosopher by nature, as does Adeimantus (490b).

a friend or an enemy on no other basis than that it knows the one and doesn't know the other" (376b). A philosopher may similarly be a friend to what is known, if, as Hans-Georg Gadamer suggests, being a friend of what is known is being "a friend of... knowledge."[14] But are philosophers enemies of the unknown or unfamiliar? Or might the love of wisdom rather depend on a desire to know what is unknown or unfamiliar?[15] Perhaps because Glaucon does not ask these or like questions, the education that follows informs and underwrites a philosophy based on enmity of the unknown.

There are other things to wonder about, including that Socrates describes the education as starting with stories, *muthoi* (376e–377a), that "are, broadly speaking false, though there is some truth in them, *hōs to holon eipein pseudos, eni de kai alēthē*" (377a). As discussed in chapter 2, Socrates distinguishes two kinds of falsity: true lies and verbal falsehoods (382b), and he divides the latter into falsehoods that "imitate" true lies and those that, as images, wear their falsity on their face. What kind of falsity characterizes the stories the education tells? In *Republic* 3, Socrates refers to the education as a contrivance or device, *mēchanē* (430a), which suggests that the stories the education tells are, like other *mēchanai* referenced in the *Republic*, as discussed in chapter 2, true lies. If this is the case then, in keeping with Socrates' definition of true lies, the education will bring about deception in the souls of its students, and, by bringing about deception, it will bring about not knowledge but ignorance (382b). In the sections that follow I show how the education of *Republic* 2–3 brings about ignorance in its students, and why that is, as Socrates puts it, "the thing everyone wants above all to avoid" (382b). Presented as a true lie to its students, the education of *Republic* 2–3 is presented otherwise to Socrates' interlocutors, for, as noted, they are told that the stories the educational program tells "are, broadly speaking false." Socrates underscores that the educational program should be heard by Glaucon and Adeimantus as a verbal falsehood by calling it "a story" (376d). Stories belong to the "images" category of verbal falsehoods. As we will see over the course of this chapter, however, the brothers take the stories to be imitations or copies, and thus fail to take account of the difference, discussed in chapter 2, between verbal falsehoods as images, *eidola*, and verbal falsehoods as imitations, *eikones*. The result is, as we will see, that the education becomes a true lie to them, too. Like its students, the brothers are deceived by the "contrivance" that is the education (430a). But we needn't be.

14. See Gadamer, "Plato and the Poets," 56.
15. I discuss the necessary lack involved in the desire characteristic of philosophy in chapter 5.

POETS, FOUNDERS, GODS

Republic 2-3 set forth the education of the warriors by way of a *mousikē* that includes poetry, song, and gymnastics for their souls and bodies, teaches good speech, *eulogia*, good accord, *euarmostia*, good grace, *euschēmosunē*, good rhythm, *eurythmia*, and a good disposition, *euētheia* (400d-e), all with a view to what is "simply, purely, reliably good—and nothing but—whose influence and effect would be purely good as well."[16] The education accomplishes this dispositive training by way of patterns, *tupoi* (379a, 383a, 396d, 398b), that are made into laws, *nomoi* (383c), which revise the poetry of Homer and Hesiod to excise references to malfeasance, violence, deception, and transformation on the part of the gods (380c-d, 383a), censor fearful depictions of death, exclude the use of "polyharmonic or multi-stringed" instruments (399c), and, as we have seen, reject practices of *mimēsis*.[17]

I argued in chapter 1 that Plato stages inconsistencies and equivocations to prompt critical reflection about what is being presented. The early education is full of these. Socrates invites Glaucon and Adeimantus to "imagine we are telling a story" when they begin their "design" of the education of the guardian/warriors (376d). Socrates and the brothers thus initially appear as poets. It is as a poet that Socrates, with Adeimantus as his primary interlocutor, says first that the poetry of Homer and Hesiod is to be excised because it is untrue and ugly (377d-e); then that it is (also) to be censored when true, if it is ugly (378a); then that it may be included if it is true (even) when it is ugly, if it is accompanied by an "unobtainable sacrificial animal to make sure the smallest possible number of people hear" it (378a); and, finally, that it is to be permitted when beautiful (378e). What exactly is permitted? And what not? And on what ground? Is truth the criterion of inclusion, or rather, as it appears, beauty?

When a not surprisingly confused Adeimantus follows up with "[So] what stories should we tell?" (378e), Socrates replies, "We are not acting as poets, *poiētai*, at the moment, you and I. We are the founders of a city, *oikistai poleōs*" (378e-379a). Over the course of two Stephanus pages, then, Socrates puts forward a series of equivocal policies to guide the censorship of poetry and then alters his and the brothers' mandate. Are they poets or founders? And what is the difference? Socrates explains: "It is the founders' job to know the patterns on which poets must model their stories, or be refused permission if they use

---

16. For the quoted phrase, see Crotty, *Philosopher's Song*, xiv, citing *Rep.* 379c, 479a-480a, 605a.

17. On the shift from *tupoi* to *nomoi*, see Lane, "Founding as Legislating," 108-9.

different ones. It is not their job to start creating stories themselves." "True" (379a), replies a no longer confused Adeimantus, who thus confirms that founders differ from poets in two ways: founders create not stories but patterns; and they know the ("true") patterns that must regulate the poets' stories. The distinction between poetry and founding appears to resolve the equivocations over the ground of the censorship policies in favor of not beauty but truth.[18]

The patterns of foremost initial concern to the new founders are those having to do with the gods. Saying "We must not allow any stories about the gods warring, fighting, or plotting against one another, for they aren't true" (378c), Socrates goes on, with Adeimantus' help, to enact as laws patterns describing the gods as a cause only of what is good (380b-c), and as themselves "perfect," "beautiful," "good" (380d-381c), "single in form and true" (382e-383a).[19] This appears straightforward enough, but it is not. For, earlier in the dialogue, Adeimantus had raised questions about both the existence of the gods and how much humans can know about them (365d-e). Socrates echoes the latter point as he lays down the censorship laws, maintaining that "we don't know the truth about these ancient events involving the gods" (382d). He returns to this point in *Republic* 4, insisting that "if we have any sense," he and the brothers will leave religious matters in the city "at the founding" to "the traditional authority" because "we do not know about this kind of thing" (427c).

Do Socrates and the brothers know the truth about the gods or not? The answer matters. If they don't, then, in not knowing "the patterns on which poets model their stories," they can't be founders, for they fail to meet the condition of Socrates' definition (379a). And if that is so, then in presenting themselves as founders, which they go on to do for the duration of *Republic* 2–5, they misrepresent themselves. Moreover, if Socrates and the brothers do not know the truth about the gods, then their patterns of what the gods are like, which hold themselves out as imitations or copies of truth, will also be misrepresentations. If Socrates and the brothers do not know the truth about the gods, then, by holding themselves out as true founders and holding their patterns out as true patterns, they cover over the falsity of their misrepresentations.

This is not to say that they therefore act as poets. For although they thereby "create a story," poets, as we saw in chapter 2, unlike Socrates and the brothers,

---

18. Socrates proceeds to hold the poets to a standard of truth when he cites from them in the pages that follow (379d-381e), and produces what Saxonhouse, "Socratic Narrative," 738, rightly calls "flat-footed" readings that portray "a blindness to interpretive richness." That flatness brings to appearance what goes missing when beauty is subordinated to truth.

19. See also Naddaff, *Exiling the Poets*, 73.

create stories that do not hide their status as images, *eidola*. Creating stories that are at a third remove from the truth, poets create false stories or verbal falsehoods, to be sure. Insofar as they make no claim to present the truth, however, poets do not truly lie. The same cannot be said of the founders. For if Socrates and the brothers do not know the truth about the gods, then by holding themselves out as true founders and holding their patterns out as true patterns, and covering over the falsity of their misrepresentations, these misrepresentations become devices, *mēchanai*, contrivances, true lies.

If, by contrast, Socrates and the brothers somehow do know the truth about the gods (despite their hedges noted earlier), then they do not misrepresent by presenting themselves as founders. But their patterns may deceive nonetheless. For Socrates and the brothers present the patterns as capable of molding the guardians in the image of the gods: "We want our guardians to become god-fearing and *god-like*" (383c, my emphasis; also 395b-c). As Socrates tells us in *Republic* 10, however, what is good, let alone perfect, is not easy to imitate (604d-e). This is, in part, because to people of all kinds, good and bad, what is simple and perfect is not as attractive as what is complex, intricate, and vexed, *poikilos*, and so people do not seek to imitate what is simple and perfect. It is also, however, because those who are not (yet) good are not likely to become good by imitating what is good because, being themselves not yet good, they cannot recognize it. If, then, the patterns do tell the truth about the gods, either the student-warriors, being not yet good, let alone perfect, will not be able to mold themselves in the image of the gods, or, in molding themselves in the image of the gods, the student-warriors, not unlike Euthyphro, will (mis)take themselves for the good and perfect gods, with the result that by molding themselves in their image of the image of the gods, they, again like Euthyphro, will mold the gods in *their* image.

What is to be made of all of this? Founders represent their knowledge as truth. Poets, by contrast, represent their knowledge as representation. Socrates' juxtaposition of the founders' representation of their knowledge, which may or may not be a misrepresentation, to poetic representation, which wears its falsity on its face, makes conspicuous the undecidability of the truth and authority of the founders' knowledge. That undecidability is covered over when we read the founding patterns of *Republic* 2–5 as true, and leave unquestioned the founders' authority and their potential deceptions. By contrast, the undecidability of the truth and authority of the founders' knowledge, brought to appearance in *Republic* 2, remains in play when we pay attention to what might be called the poetics of founding, which is to say, when we read the materials that follow the complex introduction to the early education (namely, the early education itself, its virtues, and constitution) as embedded in a "creation story." Attending to the poetics of founding brings to light that the founding patterns may or may not have the epistemic authority they require in order to be what they hold themselves out to be and, hence, that they may or may not be covering over an absence of authority by way of misrepresentation.

SIMPLE MINDS

As noted earlier, *Republic* 3 sets the goal of the warriors' education as teaching good speech, *eulogia*, good accord, *euarmostia*, good grace, *euschēmosunē*, good rhythm, *eurythmia*, and a good disposition, *euētheia* (400d-e).[20] After presenting this goal, Socrates pauses to specify what he means by a good disposition, *euētheia*: "not that weakness of head which we euphemistically style goodness of heart, but the truly good and beautiful, *kalōs*, disposition of character, *ēthos*, and mind, *dianoia*" (400d-e). Why the specification? Perhaps because *euētheia* appeared precisely as "weakness of head" in *Republic* 1, when Thrasymachus had used the term to describe those who accept rule by "the stronger and make him happy by serving him, but themselves by no manner of means" (343c-d). Thrasymachus had also referred to Socrates in this way (343c-d), as well as to the just man who does not desire to overreach other just men (349b), and to the interlocutors in *Republic* 1 who had failed to challenge Socrates (336c). To Thrasymachus, *euētheia* signifies being "simple" or "simple-minded." It is a characteristic of those who, by acting justly, act according to the good of others and, in so doing, to their own disadvantage.[21] Justice so understood Thrasymachus takes to be "a most noble simplicity or goodness of heart" (348c).

Socrates contests Thrasymachus' usage in *Republic* 3. To him, *euētheia* does not signify being oriented to the good of another and so suffering injustice and unhappiness, but being oriented to what is truly good (400e). He recommends pursuing that good "everywhere" where there is "grace or gracelessness": in painting, weaving, embroidery, architecture, in the manufacture of household

---

20. See Porter, *Origins of Aesthetic Thought*, 59, for discussion of these qualities as aesthetic, though he does not treat Plato's *Republic* as an aesthetic text. On good grace, *euschēmosunē*, see also Berger, *Perils of Uglytown*, 23.

21. Liddell and Scott call this the usual "ironical" sense of *euētheia* (*Greek-English Lexicon*, 9th ed., s.v.). Socrates uses the word in this sense later, *Rep.* 529b, when, in rebuking Glaucon for taking astronomy to be a study of the stars based on gazing up at the heavens, he says of himself that perhaps he is *euēthikos* if he thinks that *noēsis* is a product of which direction one looks.

furnishings, and in the natural bodies of animals and plants (401a). "Embroidery" in the arts and crafts Socrates lists translates *poikilia*, the term I discussed in chapters 1 and 2, which signifies complexity, intricacy, and variety.[22] It has appeared so far in the dialogue in descriptions of, among other things, Glaucon's fevered city (373a) and the censored stories of the poets (378c). It appears later in an account of the variety of foods at Sicilian and Syracusan tables (404d-e), and, in *Republic* 7–10, as we have seen, in descriptions of the decorations of the heavens that are the stars (529c-d), the democratic constitution (557c), and the characters of poetry (605a). *Poikilia* is consistently contrasted with what is simple, single, unqualified, *haploos* (380d, 382e, 404b, 404e, 410a).[23] Against Thrasymachus' pejorative use of *euētheia* as simple or simpleminded, then, Socrates presents *euētheia* as oriented to what is complex, plural, variable, and associated with mimetic arts and other crafts requiring discrimination from their opposites of grace, rhythm, and harmony (401a).[24]

Signaling that *euētheia*, understood as the pursuit of the good in complexity, subverts the education that has been set forth so far, Socrates immediately censors the arts and crafts he has just recommended pursuing. He does this, he says, so "that our guardians [will] not be bred among symbols of evil . . . lest grazing freely and cropping from many such day by day they little by little and all unawares, *lanthanōsin*, accumulate and build up a huge mass of evil in their own souls" (401b-c). To prevent the accumulation of evil in the guardian/warriors' souls, they must, "from earliest childhood," be guided "insensibly, *lanthanē[i]*, . . . to likeness, to friendship, to harmony with beautiful reason" (401c-d). Why might Socrates introduce the complex sense of *euētheia* if only to censure it and reaffirm the censored education? What are we to make of the reason Socrates gives for censuring it, namely, that to avoid being implanted unawares, *lanthanōsin*, with a bad disposition, the guardians must be implanted insensibly, *lanthanē[i]*, with a good one (401c-d)? Why bring *in*sensibility into the picture here when, as we saw above, the stated goal of *Republic* 2–3 is to educate the guardian/warriors to keenness of sense perception, among other things (375a-c)? Just in case that goal has been forgotten by this point, Socrates offers a reminder in this very passage, insisting that a proper education would allow someone most quickly to sense or perceive, *aisthanoito* (401e–402a).

Socrates doesn't just recall the imperative of sense perception at this juncture, however; he also affirms, contradictorily, the education censoring the ugly

---

22. Liddell and Scott, *Greek-English Lexicon*, 9th ed., s.v. *poikilia*.
23. For *poikilia* as the opposite of *haploos*, see Adam, *Republic of Plato*, 2:235.
24. For a similarly polysemic use of *euētheia*, see *Hippias Major* 282d, 289e.

so as to prevent it from finding its way to the "inmost soul" (401d) imperceptibly, and then insists, in a further contradiction of what he has just affirmed, that a proper education *would* allow someone most quickly to perceive, *aisthanoito*, *both* what is beautiful *and* what is ugly (401e–402a), the virtues *and* their opposites (402c). Over the course of two Stephanus pages, then, Socrates introduces, contra Thrasymachus' pejorative account, a signification of *euētheia* oriented to complexity, and then submits it to an austerity program, which purges it of that orientation and secures it as a description of minds that know only the good. Why?

Note that Socrates uses the word *lanthanō* to describe how the purged *euētheia* is effected. This word appears early in *Republic* 1 to describe the one who, best at guarding against an evil, is also best at escaping detection when he commits the evil with cunning (333e–334a). It is the word Glaucon and Adeimantus use in *Republic* 2 to express their anxiety about practices of injustice that go undetected (361a, 365c-d, 367c). In light of that anxiety, it might be expected that the brothers would be prompted by Socrates' use of it in *Republic* 3 to wonder about a *paideia* informed by *lanthanō* and also, perhaps, about *its* potential for injustice. Maybe because the purged *euētheia* secures for them the orientation to *haploos* they desire, they do not wonder. But we might. And if we do, we might recall that Thrasymachus also uses *lanthanō*, in *Republic* 1, in relation to tyranny and other acts of "perfect injustice" when they go undetected (348d). Like Socrates in *Republic* 3, Thrasymachus there couples *lanthanō* with *euētheia* to describe minds too simple to see through the "stealth" of a tyrant or to see through what he characterizes as Socrates' duplicitous argumentation, both of which he pairs with force (341a-b, 344a).

So what if Socrates uses *lanthanō* in *Republic* 3 to prompt the question of whether his description of the purged *euētheia* produced by the censored *paideia*, like Thrasymachus' *euētheia*, may involve stealth, deception, injustice, and even tyranny and force? There is reason to think it does. As noted, Socrates calls the implantation of the good disposition "insensible." That already implies stealth. Insofar as the censored education produces minds that are unaware that they have been insensibly implanted, it also implies deception. The purged *euētheia* of the early education resembles Thrasymachus' pejorative *euētheia* in still another way. In the case of Thrasymachean *euētheia*, the politically powerful determine what is good, which is then taken as their own good by those too simpleminded to seek their own advantage. In the case of the purged *euētheia* of the early education, what is good is determined by the founders' patterns, which, as we saw, may or may not themselves deceive. Insofar as the minds of that purged *euētheia* know only what they have been told is good, and know that only as a result of insensible implantation, which is to say, unknowingly, they, too, take as their own a good that has been determined as such by others, namely, the founders.

In taking the founders' good as their own, a good that may or may not be truly good, might the subjects of the early education, like the subjects of Thrasymachus' pejorative *euētheia*, act to *their* own disadvantage? I return to this question in the next section. For now, note only that insofar as they both characterize dispositions that are produced by, and are also unable to see through, stealth and deception, the purged *euētheia* of the early *paideia* and Thrasymachus' pejorative *euētheia* are mirrors of one other. Both characterize the *euēthes* Socrates describes in *Republic* 10, the one who is deceived by "a magician and imitator," having decided that "this man is an expert because he himself is incapable of distinguishing knowledge from ignorance or imitation, *dia to autos mē hoios t' einai epistēmēn kai anepistēmosunēn kai mimēsin exetasai*" (598d).

It is also to be noted that after reaffirming the simplicity of the education's insensible implantation of only the good, Socrates returns to the perception of complexity, of good and bad, beautiful and ugly (401e–402a). "It's just like learning to read, *hōsper ara . . . grammatōn peri tote hikanōs eichomen*," he says (402a). If coming to know is like learning to read, then it calls not for a censored *paideia* but rather, as we saw in this book's prologue, for looking at everything everywhere. And indeed, this is just what Socrates recommends when he describes the pursuit of the good in complexity, as well as in grace, rhythm, harmony, *and their opposites*. Socrates calls the cognitive capacity he associates with an *euētheia* oriented to complexity *dianoia* (400d-e), which, as we saw in chapter 2, appears in *Republic* 10 as a practice of mimetic knowledge able to appreciate *poikilia*. Unlike the simple minds of the purged and pejorative *euētheia* alike, the *dianoia* of complex *euētheia* is capable of perceiving multiplicity, variability, opposition, and contradiction. As we will see in the next chapter, it is able to see and see through duplicity as well.

Glaucon and Adeimantus are not provoked by Socrates' contradictions around *euētheia*. Nor do they wonder why he sometimes distances himself from the laws they enact together by referring to them as belonging not to him but to Adeimantus (334d, 389a) or Glaucon (403b, 409e–410a, 427d, 458c, 463c, 527c, 539a). They don't wonder why, if the education is truly capable of securing the good through insensible implantation, only some of the educated warriors succeed as guardians while the rest are demoted to auxiliaries (414b). Nor why, if the ideal city is ruled by those who succeed, it needs, in order to preserve its constitution, a "permanent overseer, *aei epistatou*" (412a-b), a word that recalls Socrates' earlier description of himself and the brothers as having a duty to supervise/oversee, *epistatēteon*, the storytellers (377c), and that, in fifth-century Athenian politics, recalled the "overseers," *episkopoi*, sent to Athens' colonies with "broad powers to supervise local affairs" and to report back to Athens with a view to serving its imperial interests.[25] The brothers don't ask why the successful guardians, *phulaksin*, will need a guardhouse, *phulaktērion* (424d), even though this goes against their own earlier insistence that good guardians will be their own best guards (403e, 367a). Nor do they ask why, if the guardian/warriors produced by the early education are guaranteed to be good by the laws that govern them, those laws need to be twice secured against injustice, first by the noble lie (414c ff.), which I discuss in the next chapter, and then by the communism of the ideal city (416d–417e). But, again, we might. And if we do, we may be inclined to take a critical distance from the early education even as it is being put forward.

There are other reasons to take that distance. Against the simplicity and unity guaranteed by the laws excising references to and depictions of vice, Socrates suggests in the middle of *Republic* 3 that an adequate education would teach "the different forms of moderation, courage, frankness, highmindedness, and all their kindred *and their opposites, kai hosa toutōn adelpha kai ta toutōn au enantia*" (402c, my emphasis; also 409e, 491b-c). Perhaps most telling is that Socrates poses near the end of *Republic* 3 the very same question that set off the discussion about education in the first place: "How can we be sure that the warriors now will, like dogs, be kind to those they should treat well rather than becoming like wolves or savage masters? Wouldn't a really good education endow them with the greatest caution in this regard?" Glaucon responds: "But surely they have had an education like that." Socrates replies: "Perhaps we shouldn't assert this dogmatically, Glaucon. What we can assert is what we were saying just now, that they must have the right education, *whatever it is, hētis pote estin*, if they are to have what will most make them gentle to each other and to those they are guarding" (416a-b, my emphasis). It seems, then, that, by the end of *Republic* 3, the education the guardian/warriors need if they are to rule well both themselves and others has not yet been presented. Perhaps this is because the gentleness the guardians/warriors need to show toward themselves and each other Socrates associates with the Muse (411c-e) censored by their education.

---

25. On the "overseers" sent to Athens' colonies, see Robb, *Literacy and* Paideia *in Ancient Greece*, 138.

To be sure, there are risks associated with being "bred among symbols of evil" and "grazing freely" among them.[26] As Socrates says, the guardian/warriors may "little by little and all unawares accumulate and build up a huge mass of evil, *kakon*, in their own souls" (401b-c). They may. Or they may not, for, as Socrates points out toward the end of *Republic* 4, it is not the case that "knowledge of good and evil *is* good or evil" (438e, my emphasis). The early education, for its part, seeks and promises to guarantee against evil. There are risks associated with that guarantee as well. In the first instance, as we have seen, it produces an incapacity to see through stealth and deception. There are other risks, too. For if the guardians are implanted only with a disposition oriented to beauty and/or the good and have no knowledge of what is ugly, say, or bad, and if, as just noted, an adequate education would educate to "the different forms . . . and their opposites," then, with no knowledge of "opposites," how might the guardian/warriors judge the beautiful as not ugly, or the good as not bad, to say nothing of the beautiful as beautiful, or the good as good, or the good as not beautiful, or the beautiful as not good? In short, insofar as they know only what they have been taught and are able to stand only for that, how can they judge for themselves at all?

For some readers of the *Republic*, "censorship compensates for a lack of discernment" on the part of children to distinguish between representation and truth, the allegorical and the nonallegorical (378d-e).[27] For others, censorship aids in "the city's efforts to instill in people a sense of their moral agency."[28] If this is so, however, and the early education successfully orients to goodness, then why do the guardians require so many constraints to prevent them from turning "from being allies of the other citizens" into "hostile masters" (417a), to prevent them from changing from dogs into wolves (416b)?[29] In *Republic* 7, Glaucon sounds a note of caution about the early curriculum when he says, "It trained the guardians by means of good habits, without giving them knowledge," and included no study that tended to any such good as Socrates is seeking (522a). On the basis of this, some scholars take the early curriculum to be only a necessary first step toward the dialogue's education to philosophy

---

26. Allen, *Why Plato Wrote*, 31–33, discusses these evils and why Plato might want to foreclose exposure to them.
27. For discussion, see Naddaff, *Exiling the Poets*, 30; Lear, "Allegory and Myth in Plato's *Republic*," esp. 26–28.
28. Crotty, *Philosopher's Song*, 5.
29. See Long, "Who Let the Dogs Out?," 131–45.

proper.[30] But the early education falls short even as preparatory ethical training. Socrates suggests as much in his reply to Glaucon: the education, he says, "really didn't contain anything of the kind we are looking for" (522b). If beginnings make all the difference (377a-b), then the failures of the early education to orient to dispositional and cognitive complexity, and its success in orienting to the good of another, which together create and enforce a lack of discernment and suppress moral agency, should prove to have lasting effects. As I show next, these effects are showcased in *Republic* 4, in the "virtues" Socrates and the brothers associate with the early *paideia*.

OBEDIENCE, DOMINATION, CALCULATION, INJUSTICE

"If the guardians are well educated," Socrates says near the beginning of *Republic* 4, they will grow up into men of good measure, *metrioi andres*, those who are able to judge well what is good for themselves (423e–424a) and also what is good for the city as a whole (428d). Glaucon maintains that this practice of judgment, which Socrates calls *euboulia* and associates with *sophia* and *epistēmē* (428b), "is to be found in the rulers, whom we have just been calling the perfect guardians" (428d). Socrates, for his part "not quite sure how" they found this knowledge, expresses doubts about their procedure, and notes, too, the small size of the class possessing this knowledge. When Glaucon replies that there is "nothing much wrong with the way it was found as far as I'm concerned" (429a), the two move forward in their quest to discover courage, moderation, and justice, treating the "knowledge" characteristic of good judgment as calculative rationality, *to logistikon*, in both city (431c) and soul (441e).

As before, there is reason to join this part of their quest, too, with wariness, for we, like Socrates, have grounds for doubting Glaucon's confidence about the knowledge of his "perfect guardians" and their capacities for good judgment. "If they are well-educated" they will have the appropriate knowledge and judge well, Socrates says. But have they in fact been well educated? Socrates has just raised doubts about this very thing (416a-b). Are their "simple minds" capable of judging what is good? Is good judgment a practice of calculative

---

30. See, e.g., Brann, *Music of the Republic*, 153, 217; Blondell, *Play of Character*, 214–16; Kochin, "War, Class, and Justice in Plato's *Republic*"; Marrou, *History of Education in Antiquity*, 69; and Schofield, *Plato*, 40, who calls the early education only "embryonically philosophical." Contra this divide between ethical and cognitive training, Socrates claims (526b) that one improves one's math skills with practice and training not unlike ethics training.

rationality? If, as I have been suggesting, the dialogue prompts us to answer these questions negatively, then the courage, moderation, and justice produced by the early education and associated with the knowledge of the "perfect guardians" may turn out to be not actually virtues at all. Let's see.

In *Republic* 4, Socrates describes courage as "a kind of preservation, *sōtērian*," that is, of "the opinion formed by education, under the influence of law, about which things are to be feared" (429c).[31] To help Glaucon understand what he has in mind by "preservation," Socrates analogizes the guardian/warriors to wool that is to be dyed. To ensure that the dye remains true, he says, "lengthy preliminary preparation" must be made so that the wool "will absorb as much of the color as possible." "Our soldiers," likewise, must "absorb our laws as completely as possible" (429d–430a). "We want them to possess the right character and upbringing so that their views on danger and other things" are "incapable of being washed out" by pain, pleasure, fear, or desire, "which are stronger than any other detergent" (430a-b). Glaucon is keen to distinguish courage, so understood, from the opinions held by beasts and slaves, for the latter, even if correct, he says, are not the result of education and are therefore not "properly lawful, *panu nomimon*" (430b). With that difference established, Glaucon accepts Socrates' account as courage. Socrates, for his part, demurs, calling the courage he has just defined "political courage" and deferring discussion of true courage to "some other time" (430c).

Glaucon is satisfied with political courage as, in Socrates' words, "the preservation, in all situations, of correct and lawful belief about what is to be feared and what is not" (430b). Perhaps he shouldn't be. For unlike true courage and unlike courage as correct, if uneducated, opinion, for that matter, political courage, as Socrates defines it, is the product of "a power that preserves an imprinted opinion about what is to be dreaded."[32] Lying not in the character of the "soldiers" (430a) but in the law, that power treats the soldiers, as the wool analogy implies, like "passive, inert, material."[33] Who exactly are these "soldiers"? Are they Glaucon's "perfect guardians," whose early education guarantees their passivity and inertia? Or are they the "auxiliaries, *epikourous te kai boēthous*," the warriors who do not become guardians, whom Socrates introduces in *Republic* 3 (414b) and whom Glaucon characterizes, in *Republic* 4, as "obedient dogs to the city's shepherd rulers" (440d)? Perhaps it doesn't

---

31. For *Republic* 4's treatment of political courage, I draw here on Berger, *Perils of Uglytown*, 169–79. See also my "Wages of War."

32. Berger, *Perils of Uglytown*, 171.

33. Ibid., 175.

much matter. For, as the analysis of *euētheia* offered above anticipates, whether auxiliaries and thus "defenders of the *rulers'* belief, *epikourous te kai boēthous tois tōn archontōn dogmasin*" (414b, my emphasis), or perfect guardians/rulers inscribed by the patterns of the founders, political courage, as a practice of preserving laws that have, like dye, been absorbed "as completely as possible," guarantees that the founders' laws, whose questionable legitimacy is, as we have seen, covered over, will be followed. Preserving the power of law thus means safeguarding the power of the founders and doing so "in all situations" (430b), which is to say, whether the laws are good or bad.

Preserving the laws by obeying them, good or bad, and also enforcing them, the courage of the "soldiers"—auxiliaries and guardian/rulers alike—makes them deferential to, and an embodiment of, the laws of the founders, both at the same time. That this has been the goal of the early education is made plain when, referring to it as a contrivance, Socrates says that "the sole aim of our contrivance, *mechanasthai*, was that [the warrior/guardians] should be persuaded to receive our laws like dye" (430a). If it is as a contrivance and therefore as a true lie that the early education produces political courage, then it is no surprise that Socrates defers a discussion of true courage to "some other time" (430c). For, if the Socrates of the *Apology* and *Laches* is to be believed, the hallmark of true courage is not blind obedience to the laws but instead to "stand fast" (*Laches* 190e) to preserve the power of laws only when they are good, and otherwise to resist and disobey (*Ap.* 32a-e).[34] True courage, in other words, is the capacity to say both yes and no to the power of law. It thus depends critically on the very things foreclosed by *Republic* 4's account of political courage, namely, the capacity to discern when to disobey, along with the power to resist.

The moderation cultivated by the early education is similarly problematic, having more in common with taming and gentling, as it is called when first introduced by Socrates in *Republic* 1 (354a), than with the excellence of moderation or self-discipline, which appears as a characteristic of the guardians for the first time only in *Republic* 3 (389d). When, in *Republic* 4, Socrates and Glaucon look for moderation in the ideal city, Socrates calls it something else yet again, namely, "a kind of order, *kosmos*. They say it is a mastery, *enkrateia*, of pleasures and desires and that a person is described as being in some

---

34. For discussion of courage in Plato's dialogues and in democratic Athens, see Balot, *Courage in the Democratic Polis*; Kateb, "Courage as a Virtue"; and Hobbs, *Plato and the Hero*.

way or other master of himself, *kreittō . . . hautou*." Seeming to distance himself from what "they say," Socrates asks, "But isn't the phrase 'master of himself' an absurdity? The master of himself must surely also be the slave to himself, and the slave to himself must be master of himself. It's the same person being talked about all the time" (430e–431a).

Speaking of an individual soul as simultaneously master and slave may be absurd, but it appears that it is not absurd to speak of a city in that way. Thus, as Socrates describes it, a city is moderate when the "desires of the ordinary majority" are "controlled by the desires, *epithumia*, and wisdom, *phronēsis*, of the discerning minority," described by Socrates as simple, *haploos*. Glaucon agrees (431c-d). Moderation, so understood, is the mastery of the desires of the many by those of the few, to whom, if we complete Socrates' analogy from soul to city, the many are thus enslaved. Socrates calls this "a kind of order, *kosmos*." Against the backdrop of his "absurd" introduction, his reference to the "they" who treat self-discipline as the order characteristic of mastery (430e), and Glaucon's claim that it is only in "other cities" and not in "our city" that rulers are "masters, *despotai*, and the common people slaves, *doulous*" (463a-b), we might wonder, however, whether moderation and mastery/order are the same.

That they may not be is suggested by two earlier passages that use the language of order/mastery in regard to pleasures. In *Republic* 3, Socrates asks whether moderation "consists principally in being obedient to their rulers, and being themselves rulers of the pleasures of drink, sex, food" (389d-e). In *Republic* 1, Socrates and Cephalus discuss those same pleasures "and everything connected with those pleasures" (329a). In the early conversation, it is *Cephalus* who defines moderation in terms of orderliness when he claims that being *kosmios*, orderly, or, in one translation, "civilized," is a matter of character (329d).[35] "Impressed" by Cephalus' answer, Socrates asks him to go on, saying, "I suspect most people don't believe you, Cephalus, when you say that. They think it is not your character which makes old age easy for you, but the fact that you have plenty of money" (329e). There are good reasons to disbelieve Cephalus' claim that he takes orderliness to be a matter of character, not least because it follows as a non sequitur from everything he has said so far. After citing with approval Sophocles' claim that it is *age* that offers release from the "fierce and frenzied master" that is *erōs*, Cephalus says, "I thought that a good reply at the time, and I still think it a good one" (329c). Generalizing from sexual appetite to all the appetites he and Socrates have been considering, Cephalus calls age a "final release from a bunch of insane masters,

---

35. For "civilized," see Plato, *Republic*, ed. Ferrari and trans. Griffith.

despotōn" (329d). It appears, then, that what tames the "insane masters" to bring about Cephalus' orderliness, *kosmiotes*, is not his character but rather his age or, perhaps, as "most people" think, his money. If that is so, however, then Cephalus' appetites may be mastered, and he is orderly, to be sure, but is he moderate? The result of mastery, orderliness, *kosmiōtēs*, appears to be moderation in only a "cosmetic" sense, that is, as the appearance and only the appearance of moderation.[36]

We might say that orderliness is to moderation as political courage is to true courage. As we saw, the power to bring about political courage lay not in the "soldiers'" character but in the founders' laws, good or bad. Political courage is thus not a virtue of the soldiers' souls. Orderliness, similarly, regulates a soul not in virtue of its own virtue and/or character but in virtue of something else, in the case of Cephalus, age or money. In the perfect city, Socrates says, the "order" of the many is brought about by the mastery of their desires by "the desires and wisdom of the discerning minority, *tōn te epithumiōn kai tēs phronēseōs tēs en tois elattosi te kai epieikesterois*" (431c-d), which, for their part, are ordered/mastered by "rational calculation, *logismo[i]*," using intelligence, *nou*, and right opinion, *doxēs orthēs* (431c). When the calculative rationality of the few masters the desires of the many, the many may be ordered, but, regulated, like Cephalus, entirely from without, they are not themselves moderate. Moreover, insofar as in being so ordered, they are, in Socrates' word, "enslaved" to the few, it is not obvious how they might ever gain the capacity to moderate themselves.

The "masters," for their part, may be ordered by their own calculative rationality, *to logistikon*, but they nonetheless fare no better. "Masters of themselves," they are, in Socrates' term, "an absurdity": masters and slaves at the same time, although it is "the same person being talked about" (430e-431a). That the political courage and orderliness cultivated and enforced by the early *paideia* are not truly virtues is evident in the descriptions Socrates offers of the guardian/warriors deploying strategies against enemies that orient to excessive brutality and domination (422a-423b, 471a). There is further evidence of the early education's ethical failures in the institutions Socrates sets up at the end of *Republic* 3 and the beginning of *Republic* 4 to protect the people of the

---

36. For "cosmetic," see also Berger, *Perils of Uglytown*, 63. Orderliness is used to signify only apparent moderation in *Meno* 90a as well. In his eponymous dialogue, Protagoras maintains that *eukosmia*, good order, is the goal of the *paideia* described there (325e). The *paideia* that, in both *Protagoras* and *Meno*, is associated with orderliness, *kosmiōtēs*, is the very *paideia* Socrates claims to be seeking to reform by the *mousikē* of *Republic* 2-3 (376e).

perfect city from their potentially "hostile masters" (416d–420a) and also in the plethora of laws enacted in the ideal city having to do with marriage, reproduction, piety, and war (459e, 461b, 468c, 471b). Laws, as such, are not signs of ethical failure. These laws, however, fail to achieve their ends (462e, 613d), and this suggests that, in the absence of true moderation and courage, laws, even (or especially) those modeled on the founding patterns, will not do the trick.

What about the knowledge of the guardian/rulers? Calculative rationality may secure order, but, as we saw in chapter 2, orderliness does not necessarily orient to the good. Here in *Republic* 4, too, Socrates prompts Glaucon more than once to think twice about the intelligence he has associated with the "harmony" his "perfect guardians" achieve. Addressing the "agreement, *hē autē doxa*, to be found among the rulers and ruled . . . about which of them is to rule" (431d-e), Socrates says that it may be "a function of intelligence, if you like, or strength, or again numbers, wealth, or anything like that" (432a). Socrates puts things in a way that associates the intelligence of the rulers with Glaucon ("if you like") and seems to render it commensurate with other principles of rule like "strength, or again numbers, wealth, or anything like that." Earlier in *Republic* 4, Socrates, as we saw, had expressed doubts about the intelligence of Glaucon's perfect guardians (429a), and about their education and judgment. Against this backdrop, perhaps Socrates lines these principles of rule up in this way to prompt Glaucon to wonder how much like "strength, or again numbers, wealth, or anything like that" intelligence as calculative rationality might be. Recall that Socrates had earlier remarked not only on the knowledge of the rulers but also on the small size of the ruling class. Might he return to the latter topic here, too, now against the backdrop of the kind of "agreement" rule by the rulers achieves, to prompt Glaucon not only to question calculative rationality as a principle of rule, but also, as Harry Berger has suggested, to consider whether, when it comes to "strength, or again numbers, or wealth, or anything like that," the power to rule actually lies *not* with the small class of non-property-owning guardians but with those subject to their rule?[37] If Glaucon wonders about neither of these things, Aristotle, by contrast, does. Calling the guardians "a mere occupying garrison" in *Politics* 2 (1264a26-27), he asks "upon what principle" (1264a19-20) the "real citizens" (1264a27-28, i.e., the ordinary majority) of the *kallipolis* would submit to the rule of their rulers.

It is against this backdrop that the discovery of justice takes place, with Socrates describing justice as each part of the city submitting to the rule of

---

37. Berger, *Perils of Uglytown*, 167–68.

calculative rationality (428a–434d). When Glaucon expresses satisfaction with this account, Socrates demurs once again, saying, "Let's not take that as secure just yet" (434d-e). Insisting that they test the account of city justice against soul justice, Socrates characterizes the just soul as regulating well what is truly its own and ruling itself (441d, 586e–587a). Justice is "this business of everyone performing his own task, *to ta hautou prattein*" (433b). Socrates has offered a similar account of the just soul in *Republic* 1, where he called justice the specific excellence without which the soul cannot do its own work (353d–354a). Perhaps it is because, as we have seen, the rationality, order, and political courage Socrates and Glaucon discover in the perfect city are oriented not to "one's own" but to the rationality, order, or rule of another that Socrates calls justice, understood "as a means of producing an excellent city, the ability of everyone to perform his own function . . . apparently a strong *competitor, enamillon*, with the city's wisdom, moderation, and courage" (433d, my emphasis). Soul justice competes with the "virtues" of the ideal city insofar as, unlike them, it calls for not being "forced to rely on an extraneous justice, *epaktō[i] par' allōn . . . tō[i] dikaiō[i]*, for want of a sense of justice of one's own, *aporia[i] oikeiōn*," for that, as Socrates puts it, in *Republic* 3, is "a disgrace and a sure sign of a poor education" (405b).

Still, as Socrates says toward the end of the discussion of the tyrant's injustice in *Republic* 9,

> If you want someone [who is unable to self-regulate] to be under the same kind of rule as the best person, we say he must be the slave of that best person, don't we, since the best person has the divine ruler within himself. . . . Ideally, he'll have his own divine and wise element within himself, but failing that it will be imposed on him from outside so that as far as possible, we may all be equal and all friends since we are all under the guidance of the same commander. (590d)

Ideally, each person will rule himself by bringing about justice in his own soul, but does not Socrates mandate here the imposition of the rule of reason from without over those who are unable to rule themselves? As I explain in the next chapter, I don't think so. For now, it is to be noted that, as in the discussion of moderation as orderliness, Socrates here appears to equate reason imposed from without with slavery.[38] And, in *Republic* 4, he insists, as noted, that to

---

38. For *Rep.* 590c-d as "advocat[ing] that members of the lower classes be 'slaves' to the philosopher rulers so that all citizens are, in one way or another, ruled by reason," see Bobonich, *Plato's Utopia Recast*, 203. For a rejection of this view, see Vlastos, "Slavery in Plato's

be just, a person must, "quite literally, . . . put his own house in order, being himself his own ruler, mentor, and friend" (443d).

Soul justice as a practice of putting one's own house in order is precisely what is foreclosed for the many, however, when the guardian/warriors do all the ruling and the producing classes only submit.[39] It is also foreclosed for the auxiliaries who are mastered as dogs by their shepherd rulers. Finally, it is foreclosed for the perfect guardians themselves who are produced as politically courageous, orderly, and oriented to the simple good mandated by the purged *euētheia* of their early education by the founders' laws (458c). Indeed, as Roslyn Weiss has demonstrated, the guardian/rulers are depicted across the *Republic* as altogether compelled: compelled to ascend to the Good, compelled in their courses of study, compelled to order their souls, compelled to rule the city, and compelled to do so in accordance with the laws of the founder-lawgivers.[40] In the language of *Republic* 10's account of *mimēsis* (596e–598c), we might say that the rule of law in the *kallipolis* is at a third remove from the citizens who are compelled to live under it and at a second remove from the rulers who are compelled to submit to, re-create, and enforce it. Insofar as the capacity of all of these souls, including the guardians, to discern their own good is displaced by recourse to the compulsory authority and institutions of the founders, the souls of the perfect city are incapable of self-justification as that is put forward by Socrates in *Republic* 4. Underscoring the inadequacy of a justice rooted in purged simplicity, orderliness, political courage, and calculative rationality, the myth of Er depicts a man who, having lived in a well-ordered city whose laws have trained him to virtue, a man who thus resembles those who have been educated by the early *paideia*, chooses, for his next life, a life of tyranny (619b-d).

AN *AISCHROPOLIS*

At the beginning of *Republic* 5, in a scene echoing the opening of *Republic* 1, Socrates is stopped in his tracks by a majority resolution initiated by Polemarchus and Adeimantus, who, with the support of Thrasymachus and Glaucon, want to hear more about Socrates' "casual remark," at the end of *Republic* 3, that the guardians and auxiliaries in the city they are cofounding will hold

---

Thought," 151–52, underscoring the distinction between slaves and "providers of upkeep and wages" (560b) referred to in *Rep.* 4.

39. For discussion, see my "Circulating Authority."

40. Weiss, *Philosophers in the "Republic,"* 70, 81–83, 103–12, 118–19, 74–77, with references to the *Republic*.

everything in common (417a-b, 449c, 450c).[41] Socrates responds to the request by expressing worries about the practicability and desirability of his proposals (450c-d) and about misleading his friends on such an important topic. He proceeds, he says, with reluctance (451a-b).

There are good reasons for his reluctance. The "three waves" that institute, structure, and regulate the ideal city are neither consistent with principles Socrates and the brothers have previously agreed to, nor are they consistent with one another. Moreover, as others have noted, they generate regulations that are impracticable and undesirable in the extreme.[42] They nonetheless garner acquiescence, though sometimes with hesitation, from the brothers, who continue to be Socrates' primary interlocutors. Especially notable, perhaps, against the backdrop of the brothers' pointed remarks about the importance of reproduction and the upbringing of children in the constitution of a city (449d-450a, 450c), is their acquiescence to the laws regulating sex. Bringing about what Arlene Saxonhouse has called "the death of eros," those laws regulate who may have sex with and marry whom and when, and when they may have children (459d-461d).[43] Given his insistence that sex in the city will be a matter of erotic necessity (458d), it is especially surprising that Glaucon, himself an avid lover (474d), makes no objection to the laws' displacement of *erōs* by rational calculation or to the policies Socrates proposes proscribing homosexuality (403b-c). Neither brother wonders either about the reappearances of the *erōs* that was supposed to be displaced (458d, 468b-c),[44] or about the multiple appearances of *lēthē* (457e, 459e, 461a), the word that appeared in *Republic* 1 in regard to the stealth and deception of tyranny and in *Republic* 3 in regard to the purged education.

No questions arise either about how the guardians will identify the children of good stock to be taken away and raised communally, about those of impure stock who will be hidden away in a secret place (460c), or about those to be aborted and killed as "unauthorized" or "unholy" (461b-461c) or born out of sequence or born to guardians past the decreed childbearing age or to inferiors or with defects (460c). Perhaps because the brothers wonder about

---

41. This section is titled *Aischropolis*, after the name Berger gives to the *kallipolis* in the title of his work *Perils of Uglytown*.

42. See, for examples, Popper, *Open Society and Its Enemies*; Roochnik, "Political Drama of Plato's *Republic*"; and Vegetti, "How and Why Did the *Republic* Become Unpolitical?"

43. On the "death of eros" in the *kallipolis*, see Saxonhouse, "Eros and the Female," 11. I take up the topic of *erōs* in chapter 5.

44. For discussion, see Halliwell, in *Plato: Republic 5*, 18. For a fictional treatment of Plato's *Republic* that emphasizes how difficult it is to eradicate *erōs*, see Walton, *Just City*.

none of this, Socrates ups the ante. To secure these regulations, he says, the rulers will need to employ many drugs, *pharmaka*, falsehoods, and deceptions (459c-d), including a device, *mēchanē*, to prevent mothers from knowing their children (460c), and a device to contrive some way, *prosmēchanasthai*, to keep the guardian children safe when, as part of their training, they are sent as spectators to the wars fought by the guardian/warriors (467c). Socrates offers the latter contrivance in response to Glaucon's worry that sending the children to war might, if the war is lost, put the children, the guardian/warriors, and the city itself at risk (467b). Glaucon is persuaded, however, that having the children present at war will make fathers better fighters (467b), that the experience of war will be good for the children (467c), that fathers will be good judges of which campaigns are safe enough for the children to attend and which are not (467c-d), and that because the children will be on horseback they'll be able to manage a swift escape, if need be (467e).

Glaucon should not be persuaded. How, he might have wondered, will a guardian/warrior, as Socrates says, "fight better in the presence of its own young" (467b) when, as per wave two, the guardians hold their children in common?[45] And how is the practice of sending children to watch war consistent with the reasons underlying the early education's censorship of representations of warring, fighting, and death? And has Socrates not earlier insisted, in any case, that children should *not* be exposed to anything violent or vicious firsthand because such exposure can bring that viciousness into the child's soul and so corrupt it, making it incapable of sound judgment (409a-e)? Isn't sending children to war to learn about war the very category mistake Socrates warned against in *Republic* 4, when he maintained, as noted earlier, that *knowledge* of good and bad is not to be confused with what *is* good or bad (438d-e)? And how, when, as Socrates maintains, "events are unpredictable" in war (467d), will the guardian/warriors be able to reliably judge in advance the relative harm or safety of a campaign?

Socrates' use of *mēchanē* here, as elsewhere, suggests that in all of this there is a design to deceive. Who is being deceived about what? Is it the children who are being deceived into believing that their safety can be guaranteed under conditions of war? Is it the guardian/warriors who are deceived that the city's restrictive regulations are in their own good? Is it Glaucon and Adeimantus, who appear to believe that the enterprise of *Republic* 2–5 is practicable and good? I think it is all of the above. And that readers are meant to think so. Offered in the name of securing the happiness (421b, 466a), unity (462a), and

---

45. Halliwell, in *Plato: Republic 5*, 184, notes this as well.

agreement (463e) of the whole city, the deceptions and devices of the *kallipolis* are set forth by Socrates to preserve what he calls "the virtuous circle of the constitution, *politeia . . . erchetai hōsper kuklos auxanomenē*" (424a). Socrates goes on: "If you can keep a good system of upbringing and education, they produce naturally good natures. These, in their turn, if they receive a good education, develop into even better natures than their predecessors. Better in general, and better in particular for reproduction. The same is true in the animal kingdom" (424a-b), for "like always produces like, doesn't it, Adeimantus?" (425c).[46]

Socrates says, "If you can keep a good system of upbringing and education" the "natures" these systems produce will be "naturally good." But what if, as I have been arguing, and as Socrates' analogy between the upbringing and education of the ideal city and processes in the "animal kingdom" further suggests, the dialogue presents that upbringing and education as not good? Glaucon, after all, *distinguishes* the education of animals from human education just pages later (430b) on the ground that the former, unlike the latter, is a kind of mindless conditioning.[47] The conditioning of the *kallipolis*'s humans as animals comes up again in *Republic* 5 (466d) after Socrates presents the city's eugenics programs by reference to the techniques Glaucon uses to breed his pedigree cocks and hunting dogs (459a). That, over the course of *Republic* 5, Socrates slides from referring to the guardian/warriors as "guardians of the herd" (451c) to calling them "our herd" (459e) indicates, too, that Adeimantus would have done well to press Socrates on his claims about the goodness of the upbringing and education mandated for the rulers of the *kallipolis*. If the education and upbringing are not good and, as Socrates says, "like always produces like," then the "natures" produced by the education and upbringing will not themselves be good either.

Adeimantus might also have rejected Socrates' suggestion that "like always produces like" (425c), for, in the account of the *kallipolis*, Socrates offers example after example of the reverse. The "noble lie" of *Republic* 3 that founds the ideal city describes those born with gold in their blood as sometimes giving birth to silver- or iron-blooded children, and vice versa (415a-c). In *Republic* 5, as noted earlier, Socrates announces that children born to guardian/warriors will sometimes be "defective" (460c). And the city? If the *kallipolis* is meant to exemplify the "virtuous circle of the constitution" and if "like *always* produces like," then why, in *Republic* 8-9, does Socrates narrate its devolution

---

46. The following two paragraphs draw on my "Constitution."
47. See Mara, *Socrates' Discursive Democracy*, 123; Berger, *Perils of Uglytown*, 158–59.

into tyranny? Or anticipate its *undoing* in *Republic* 5? After all, with only rulers permitted to breed (459d), nondefective ruler children going to war with no way to guarantee their safety (467d), and all other children in the city aborted or killed (461a-c), the *kallipolis* appears doomed from its inception.

Glaucon and Adeimantus appear to see none of this. In failing to see and see through the true lies that found their city, the brothers seem to mirror the guardian/warriors. Exemplars of the purged *euētheia* discussed earlier, the brothers' acquiescence to the founding patterns reveals them to be, and also produces them as, no less politically courageous and orderly, which is to say, obedient and mastered, than the guardian/warriors, and no more educated about what is good.

JUSTICE IN AND BY ITSELF

For the adequate implementation of the whole enterprise of *Republic* 2–5, Socrates, as noted earlier, recommends purging (460c, 560e, 567c, 573b), including, in *Republic* 7, banishing everyone over ten years of age from the new city so that, after removing the usual habits of the remaining children, those can be replaced with the laws and customs of the early education (540e–541a). Scholars raise the practical concern that if adults are exiled there will be no one to rear/educate the children in the new laws.[48] Socrates raises an equally pressing concern about the new laws themselves just pages earlier in a discussion with Glaucon about how an education to dialectics, by offering critique but no alternative, can produce "lawlessness" (539a). To explain to Glaucon what he has in mind, Socrates gives the analogy of a son reared in wealth who becomes aware that his parents are not his true parents. Socrates says that he will most honor his adoptive parents and kin when he does not know of his adoption, but once he finds out the truth, and for so long as he is unable to find his true parents, he will switch his allegiance from his adoptive parents to flatterers, henceforth living by their rule (537e–538b), which is to say, by no rule at all.

When Glaucon says that he doesn't understand the force of the analogy (538c), Socrates explains: the analogues of the adoptive parents are the *dogmata*, unexamined opinions of a society, its conventional morality. Just as the son rejects his adoptive parents when he realizes that they aren't his birth parents, so, too, will a society's conventional morality be rejected with the awareness that there are grounds for calling it into question. And just as when, having rejected his adoptive parents but not found his birth parents, the son turns

---

48. For references and a counterargument, see Adam, *Republic of Plato*, 2:155.

to flatterers, so, too, will the challenge to conventional morality lead to the adoption of a way of life that flatters desires in the absence of a true alternative (538d–539b).

In the *Republic* as a whole, society's conventional morality is exemplified by "helping friends and harming enemies" (332d), one of Polemarchus' accounts of justice in *Republic* 1, as discussed in chapter 2, and also by the understanding of justice the brothers attribute to Thrasymachus and the many, discussed at the beginning of this chapter, justice in terms of its consequences alone, which is to say, the third class of justice according to Glaucon's taxonomy in *Republic* 2. The awareness that there are grounds for calling these moralities into question is exemplified by the brothers' plea that Socrates rescue justice. By the terms of the analogy, Glaucon and Adeimantus, it appears, are seeking their birth parents. It might be expected, then, that when Socrates offers the censored *paideia* and its laws, developed to replace the conventional moralities depicted in the dialogue and to rear the children living in the newly founded city, he gives the brothers their birth parents, namely, the truth about justice.

So it appears. To be the truth about justice, however, the laws Socrates offers would need to be to the children populating the newly founded city as the birth parents are to the adopted son. But in the ideal city there are no birth parents. They have all been banished. Moreover, as discussed, the laws developed to replace conventional morality are based on founding patterns whose truth is in question. Bolstering the textual arguments I have been setting out, the elaborate analogy Socrates offers here appears to confirm that the laws regulating the early education and generating simple or unqualified justice do not offer true justice at all. That in *Republic* 8 Socrates refers to the guardianship of orphans as providing a ripe opportunity of "doing injustice with impunity" (554c) seems to suggest the same. If the laws of the perfect city are not birth parents, however, then, by Socrates' analogy, they must be flatterers, those a son turns to when he is unable to find his birth parents. In the context of the argument of this chapter, that makes sense. As we have seen, Socrates offers the early education, the "virtues" it cultivates, and the constitution it fosters in response to the brothers' desire for Justice. By way of his encomium, he gives them exactly what they want. In giving them Justice, he panders to or flatters their desire, thus confirming that in the ideal city, along with the absence of true courage, moderation, and wisdom, there will also be no truth about justice to be found.

CHAPTER 4

The Power of Persuasion

He who persuades always ends up asking.
ALAIN BADIOU, *Plato's "Republic"*

The opening scene of the *Republic* depicts Socrates and Glaucon stopped in their tracks by a group of young men as they are leaving the Piraeus to return to Athens. The group includes Adeimantus, Glaucon's brother, and Polemarchus, who initiates the following exchange (327c–328b):[1] "It looks to me, Socrates, as if you two are starting off for Athens." Socrates replies, "It looks the way it is, then."

1. Polemarchus: "Do you see how many we are?" Socrates: "I do."
2. Polemarchus: "Well, you must either prove stronger than we are, or you will have to stay here."
3. Socrates: "Isn't there another alternative, namely, that we persuade, *peisōmen*, you to let us go?" Polemarchus: "But could you persuade, *peisai*, us if we won't listen, *mē akouontas*?" Glaucon: "Certainly not." Polemarchus: "Well, we won't listen, *mē akousomenōn*; you'd better make up your mind to that."
4. Adeimantus: "Don't you know that there is to be a torch race on horseback for the goddess tonight?" Socrates: "On horseback? That is novel. Will they hold torches and pass them to one another while racing the horses, or what do you mean?" Polemarchus: "In relays, and there will be

---

1. For ease of presentation, I have arranged this exchange in dialogue form, though that is untrue to how the exchange appears in the *Republic*, which, like the dialogue as a whole, is narrated by Socrates.

an all-night festival that will be well worth seeing. After dinner, we'll go out to look at it. We'll be joined there by many of the young men, and we'll talk. So don't go away; stay."
5. Glaucon: "It seems that we'll have to stay, *eoiken . . . meneteon einai.*"
Socrates: "If it is so resolved, then we must, *ei dokei, . . . houtō chrē poiein.*"

And off they all go to the home of Polemarchus and his father, Cephalus, for the conversation that is the dialogue of the *Republic*. The question before Socrates—should I stay or should I go?—is the question, "what ought I to do?" also the question of justice. Socrates' closing words to Glaucon in this opening exchange foreground the question of justice, even while troubling its positivist orientation in late fifth-century Athens. Socrates' "If it is so resolved" mimics the language used by the assembly to announce the passage of new laws that, by majority rule in democratic Athens, determined justice.[2]

The opening exchange not only sets up the question of justice; it also suggests five possible answers to that question, namely, that justice is determined by (1) the many; (2) the stronger; (3) persuasion; (4) the promise of pleasure or reward; or (5) what appears just whether or not it truly is just. These answers are rehearsed and unpacked in *Republic* 1–2: Polemarchus reprises his initial position in his account of justice as "helping friends and harming enemies" (332d, 334b), a definition he appropriates from popular morality or the many; Thrasymachus expands on the account of justice as the advantage of the stronger (338c); Adeimantus rehearses and augments his opening suggestion by recurring to poetic passages describing justice in primarily consequentialist terms (363a ff.); and, by way of the tale of Gyges, Glaucon elaborates the ways in which what seems or appears can fail to adequately distinguish justice from injustice (359b–361d). Left to one side, it seems, is Socrates' contribution to this exchange when he asks if Polemarchus and his friends might be persuaded to let Socrates and Glaucon go—that is, the suggested link between justice and persuasion.

It might be that persuasion is introduced and then left to one side in order to signal its political and philosophical irrelevance to the question of justice. That way of reading the opening scene fits well with scholarship that treats the *Republic* as hostile to the "work of persuasion" and to the art of rhetoric defined by that work (*Gorg.* 453a). Condemning fifth-century Athenian rhetoric

---

2. See Bloom, "Interpretive Essay," in *Republic of Plato*, 441 n. 6. Socrates' critical response to understanding justice as determined by law is especially evident in his cross-examination of Meletus in Plato's *Apology* (24d–25c).

for its power to manipulate, pander, and deceive in the service of private and/ or political ends, the *Republic* and also the *Gorgias*, it is said, seek to replace rhetoric with a nondeceptive mode of speech based on truth and produced by knowledge of an expert.[3] That expert, a philosophic authority, is represented, most famously perhaps, by the philosopher-king in the *Republic*, but also as the ideal *politikos* in the *Statesman*, the Eleatic visitor in the *Statesman* and *Sophist*, and the Athenian visitor in the *Laws*.[4] Associating the view these dialogues attribute to their figures of philosophic authority with Plato, one scholar concludes that "Plato despairs of persuasion as a political resource."[5]

If some, by contrast, see "hints" of a tacit recognition of a "legitimate art of rhetoric" in some of these dialogues, these scholars, too, maintain that even when it is treated as a "'precious' collaborator" of statecraft and "no longer abandoned in favor of philosophy," rhetoric is accorded by Plato a "strictly subordinate role within the city."[6] If, as others argue, rhetoric in the *Phaedrus*, "properly understood" and/or "reinvented," is, by contrast, "harness[ed] to philosophy" as a "permanent team," it is a team in which philosophy nonetheless has greater pull because rhetoric, not unlike other "genres of discourse," "must be tested by reference to a standard whose essence is absolute truth," a standard that belongs exclusively to philosophy.[7] As one scholar puts it, "For Plato, the task of developing an authentic voice is far more difficult than merely ensuring

---

3. To call it "Athenian" rhetoric may not be so apt, as some of the practitioners and especially the teachers of rhetoric were foreigners who came to Athens to ply their trade (*Prot.* 315a). For discussion, see Nightingale, *Genres in Dialogue*, 21–25.

4. As Rowe notes in his introduction to *Plato: Statesman*, xiii, "The ideal statesman or king of the *Statesman* turns out to be virtually indistinguishable from the philosopher-ruler of the *Republic*." Largely agreeing, Lane, *Method and Politics*, 137–38, 3, nonetheless cautions that the "focus of interest" of the *Statesman* is distinct from that of the *Republic*: "That the [philosophical] knowledge [of the Good] should have political authority is the burden of the *Republic*"; what that knowledge consists in and how it rules are the questions of the *Statesman*. For the Athenian and Eleatic visitors as philosophic authorities and for the argument that they are depicted as conspicuously problematic philosophical authorities by Plato, see Berger, "Plato's Flying Philosopher."

5. Kastley, *Rhetoric of Plato's "Republic,"* 162–63, referencing Klosko, *Development of Plato's Political Theory*, 59–61. On the uselessness of persuasion, see also Rosen, *Plato's "Republic,"* 395–96: "If wisdom is to rule, it can only be through force and lying."

6. These phrases are from Kennedy, *New History of Classical Rhetoric*, 37; Benardete, *Rhetoric of Morality and Philosophy*, 170; and Lane, *Method and Politics*, 2, 145, 185, 201.

7. These phrases are from Yunis, *Taming Democracy*, 172; Kennedy, *New History of Classical Rhetoric*, 38; Benardete, *Rhetoric of Morality and Philosophy*, 127; Nightingale, *Genres in Dialogue*, 170, also 162. See also Warman, "Plato and Persuasion," 49.

that discourse is 'internally persuasive,'" and "authentic discourse can only be achieved by way of philosophical inquiry."[8]

Despite important differences, scholars, broadly speaking, see Plato's dialogues as taking up persuasion in order to distinguish it from, and/or subordinate it to, a rival and more authoritative mode of speaking and knowing, namely, philosophy. The opening scene of the *Republic* appears to lend support to this view: when Polemarchus insists that persuasion depends on listening, something he and his friends will not do, the message seems to be that whether in relation to the immediate question—should Socrates stay or go—or in relation to the larger question of justice, persuasion would be futile and so is best abandoned.

That persuasion does not remain bracketed but reemerges repeatedly and in a variety of forms at critical moments over the course of the dialogue suggests a more salient role for persuasion, however.[9] That Polemarchus announces that he won't listen and then, as discussed in chapter 2, proves to be compliant, deferential, and easily won over, and that Glaucon listens but, as we saw in chapter 3 and will see in this chapter, too, sometimes seems not to hear, invite attention to the ways in which not listening well and/or listening only too well may adversely impact the possibilities of persuasion and justice as much as refusing to listen does.[10] To insist on a salient role for persuasion is not to deny that Plato's dialogues are critical of the rhetorical practices of their time. In my view, as we will see, this is not because the dialogues seek to displace persuasion as such or to subordinate persuasion to philosophy. Instead, I read the *Republic* as developing and also performing a practice of persuasion *as* "internally persuasive" discourse harnessed to philosophy as a "permanent team" of equal partners.[11] As G. R. F. Ferrari puts it in relation to the *Phaedrus*, "If rhetoric must become philosophical, then philosophy must

---

8. Nightingale, *Genres in Dialogue*, 170.

9. *Rep.* 345a-b, 348a, 357a-b, 367a, 388e, 399b, 405b, 411d, 413b, 414c-d, 415c, 430a, 468d-469a, 471e, 476a, 480a, 494d, 498d, 502a-b, 519e, 530a, 545a, 589c-d, 621c.

10. On Polemarchus as pliable, see Blondell, *Play of Character*, 178–79. On the power and ambiguity of listening, consider also *Protagoras* (313e–314a, 314c-e). On listening in Plato, see McCoy, *Plato on the Rhetoric of Philosophers and Sophists*; on listening more generally, see Bickford, *Dissonance of Democracy*.

11. See Tarnopolsky, *Prudes, Perverts, and Tyrants*, 35, who reads the *Gorgias* not as a rejection of "Athenian democracy and rhetorical practices in favor of an undemocratic, expert form of knowledge, but rather to perform an immanent critique of both the Socratic elenchus and the flattering rhetoric [Plato] feared was involved in imperialistic Athenian democratic politics."

acknowledge the extent to which it is rhetoric."[12] Christina Tarnopolsky makes similar claims about what she calls the "mythopoetic form of philosophy that is displayed" in the *Gorgias*.[13] I have begun in earlier chapters to mark the rhetorical qualities and mythopoetic forms on display in the *Republic*, too.[14]

In this chapter, I argue for the centrality of persuasion to the *Republic*'s appreciation of philosophy. I do so by highlighting a particular practice of persuasion, persuasion in the middle voice, a mode of persuasion that is determined not by a philosophic expert but by speakers and listeners acting as agents of their own persuasion.[15] This is an intersubjective practice and a practice of the self at the same time. It is also, we will see, a condition of justice. To clear the way for middle-voice persuasion, the following three sections—on compulsion, deception, and Socratic *elenchos*—explore varying modalities of force the *Republic* depicts as undermining the conditions of persuasion, and links the dialogue forges between these and injustice. I argue that the *Republic* does not, as is sometimes thought, subvert the opposition, standard across antiquity, between persuasion and force but instead upholds that opposition for the sake of justice.[16]

COMPULSION

Persuasion is paired with varying modalities of compulsion, *anangkē*, and force, *bia[i]*, across the *Republic* and other dialogues. The law of the *kallipolis* is depicted in *Republic* 7 as using persuasion and compulsion, *anangkē*, together to bring citizens into harmony (519e). In the *Gorgias*, Socrates suggests that the task of a good citizen/statesman is that of "using persuasion or force, *peithontes kai biazomeno*," to make citizens better (517b). In the *Statesman*, the Eleatic assigns this task to the statesman (304d). In accordance with his innovative "double method," the Athenian, in the *Laws*, argues for appending persuasive preludes to the legislation of Magnesia to render more effective the force of its laws (720a).

---

12. Ferrari, *Listening to the Cicadas*, 38. For this argument with respect to the *Gorgias*, see Tarnopolsky, *Prudes, Perverts, and Tyrants*, chap. 4.
13. Tarnopolsky, *Prudes, Perverts, and Tyrants*, 45, also 126–30.
14. See also Kastley, *Rhetoric of Plato's "Republic."*
15. See *Protagoras* 348c-d; and McCoy, *Plato on the Rhetoric of Philosophers and Sophists*, 71–73.
16. See Buxton, *Persuasion in Greek Tragedy*, for the opposition between force and persuasion in the poetry of antiquity. I argue that the *Laws* upholds this opposition as well in my "Constitution."

For some scholars, "the distinction between persuasion and force is strictly irrelevant to [Plato's] definition of the statesman as acting according to expertise which aims at true benefit."[17] All that matters, according to Harvey Yunis, for example, is whether the combination "accomplishes the goal of leading the citizens to virtue."[18] To Melissa Lane, too, "what makes someone a good (true) . . . statesman, is whether one rules with knowledge and aims to make the citizens as virtuous as they can be." She adds that "the deep Platonic link between knowledge, as attained by reason, and virtue, does not rule out force as a possible means of inculcating virtue." If, for Gregory Vlastos, persuasion, in Plato's dialogues, "means simply changing another's mind. It puts no strings on the way this is done," Lane demurs, maintaining that "whether one uses persuasion or force is not a matter of indifference to politics; it is worth noting, and persuasion should be deployed wherever it has the conditions to be likely to succeed, because it is right for legislators and rulers to seek to be gentle." She concludes, nonetheless, that the distinction between force and persuasion "does not bear on the deepest political questions."[19]

For "Plato's" defense of the use of force and persuasion interchangeably in the service of virtue in the *Republic*, scholars refer to the depiction of the law of the *kallipolis* (519e) and also to Socrates' description, in *Republic* 9, of "good rule" as "slavery" (590c-d). To Lane, for example, good rule "does not involve any constituting role for those ruled, but rather allows their superiors in intellect, who know how to rule, to constitute their psychic structure and values by doing so." Under conditions of good rule, citizens should see themselves not as "authors of the law" but "as its (voluntary) slaves."[20] Force on the part of "superiors in intellect" is permitted, indeed, required under such circumstances, so that those superiors can impose a moral order on a population unable to achieve self-discipline on their own.[21] The ruled, for their part, retain their freedom as "voluntary" slaves. In this way, it is said, the *Republic* makes force and freedom cooperate.

---

17. Lane, "Persuasion et force dans la politique platonicienne"; I quote here and following from the typescript translation supplied to me by the author, "Persuasion and Force in Platonic Politics," 24.

18. Yunis, *Taming Democracy*, 121.

19. Lane, "Persuasion et force dans la politique platonicienne"; Eng. trans., 35, 5, 35; Vlastos, "Slavery in Plato's Thought," 148 n. 5.

20. Lane, "Persuasion et force dans la politique platonicienne"; Eng. trans., 33.

21. Klosko, *Development of Plato's Political Theory*, 59–61.

I see things differently. First, there appears to be nothing "voluntary" about the submission of the ruled, who, as we saw in chapter 3, are rather depicted as mastered, dominated, and ordered in the *kallipolis*. Second, as we also saw in chapter 3, the superior virtue and intellect of the rulers are consistently put in question: the rulers' early education may teach political courage, order, and calculative rationality, but political courage falls short of true courage, order is not the same as moderation—indeed, the rulers are depicted as lacking both true courage and moderation—and calculative rationality is aligned in *Republic* 1 and 4 with questionable principles of rule such as strength, numbers, and wealth. We have seen, thirdly, that souls whose psychic structures and values are constituted for and imposed on them by others cannot become just, for justice depends on souls ordering and constituting themselves. Indeed, in an echo of the account of justice in *Republic* 4 as a practice of self-rule (443c-e), itself an echo of justice as the soul's "own specific excellence, *tēn hautōn oikeian aretēn*" (353d-e) in *Republic* 1, Socrates reminds Glaucon in *Republic* 9, just pages before describing "good rule" as "slavery" (590c-d), that "what is best for each thing is also what is most its own" (586e; also 587a). If the use of force is said to be justified insofar as it brings justice to the ruled, but justice depends on souls ordering and constituting themselves, then by constituting their psychic structures by force from without rulers will necessarily *fail* to bring justice to the souls of the ruled, a conclusion Socrates appears to anticipate when he says, in *Republic* 7, that nothing learned by force, *bia[i]*, stays in the soul (536e). That the *Republic*, as noted, also puts in question the ethical and cognitive capacities of the compelling rulers makes it all the more unlikely that their use of force will be able to meet the conditions of its own justification.

Lane observes that Plato's dialogues nowhere explain *how* virtue may be inculcated by force.[22] In my view, this omission makes sense, for I take that to be a position the dialogues stand not for but against.[23] When Socrates presents the law of the *kallipolis* as combining force and persuasion and/or puts forward the account of "good rule" as slavery, which he does just following his treatment of tyranny, then, perhaps these are to be read not as endorsements of force or slavery in the name of superior reason but instead as invitations to consider the

---

22. Lane, "Persuasion et force dans la politique platonicienne"; Eng. trans., 5.
23. On the counterposition of force and persuasion in the *Laws*, see Bobonich, "Persuasion, Compulsion, and Freedom in Plato's *Laws*."

ways in which rule by epistemic force and rule by the force of might can turn out to be two sides of the same coin. From this perspective, the *Republic* presents examples of rule by force of any kind to open questions about how force may work not to effect but to compromise virtue, and also justice. From this perspective, too, the distinction between persuasion and force in the *Republic* bears on the deepest political questions, including, as noted, questions of virtue and justice, and, as we will see in the pages that follow, questions of freedom and resistance, which is to say, questions of ethical and political agency.

DECEPTION

Anticipating what he says about the use of force by political experts in *Republic* 9 and about the compulsion of the law of the *kallipolis* in *Republic* 7, Socrates maintains in *Republic* 5 that lies are allowed so long as they are made by those with adequate knowledge of the good of the city as a whole and in the service of that good (459c-d). As we saw in chapter 3, Socrates associates lies of all kinds with the rulers of the *kallipolis* and also with the city's founders. In *Republic* 3, Socrates introduces the city's founding lie, which hides from the city's inhabitants the truth about their origins in order to achieve justice as harmony in the city. Like the use of force in *Republic* 7 and 9, the dialogue appears to justify the founding lie on the ground that it brings benefit to cities and/or souls (415d). In this section I make the case that the lie is depicted not as bringing benefit by securing justice or as persuading, for that matter, but, as in *Republic* 7 and 9, insofar as it is a mode of force, as instead undermining both.

Persuasion and its cognates appear across Socrates' account of the lie. He explains that it seeks "to persuade, *peisai*, if possible, the rulers themselves, but failing that the rest of the city" (414c), that their education and training were a dream; that, in truth, they were formed in and by the earth with different kinds of metals in their souls—those born with gold souls rule; those with silver are auxiliaries; those with brass and iron souls are the city's craftsmen and farmers (415a)—and that they, and in particular the guardians (415d), were formed to care for the city and "to regard the other citizens as their brothers and children of the self-same earth" (414d-e). Scholars generally read the founding lie as intended to persuade.[24] I'm less sure. Socrates implies that his initial telling of it will not (or should not) persuade when, as soon as he ends, he asks whether

---

24. They divide, however, between those who, quite differently, treat the lie as a truth told in mythical form (Strauss, Bloom, Burnyeat, Schofield) and those who treat it as a lie all the way down (Carmola). For discussion, see Lear, "Allegory and Myth in Plato's *Republic*," 25-43.

Glaucon has "some device, *mēchanē*, for persuading, *peistheien*" (415c) "first the rulers themselves and the soldiers and then the rest of the city" (414d).[25] If the lie had already been persuasive, there would presumably be no need for *another* device. Glaucon responds that he has no device to persuade the first generation (415d), thus implying both that Socrates' version would not persuade them and also that it had not persuaded him. Glaucon also says that he thinks that the lie *will* persuade the first generation's "sons and successors and the rest of mankind who come after" (415d). He thus signals that he takes the lie to have some persuasive value at least.

Why will it persuade some and not others? Glaucon appears to bind the lie's effectiveness at persuading to its success at deceiving. The "first generation of rulers," he seems to think, won't be deceived because, like him, they will see through its deception. To them, as to Glaucon, to whom Socrates expressly signals the founding lie's falsity, both by calling it a lie, a "noble lie," *gennaion pseudos*, and also by referring to it as a *mēchanē*, device or contrivance (414c), the founding lie will be a "verbal falsehood," in the language of *Republic* 2's taxonomy of lies, as discussed in earlier chapters. To successive generations, by contrast, it will be a "true lie" insofar as it penetrates their souls and thus puts them in a state of ignorance about their origins.

Taking the lie's value as a tool of persuasion to lie in its value as a tool of deception, Glaucon stands behind the founding lie as a true lie if not to the first generation, that is, to the city's rulers, then to the rest. He thus stands behind true lies as mechanisms of persuasion, and also behind persuasion as a practice of deception. Paul Shorey appears to agree with Glaucon when, remarking on these passages, he defines a *mēchanē* as an "ingenious device employed by a superior intelligence to . . . play providence with the vulgar," and explains that "since the mass of men can be brought to believe anything by repetition, myths framed for edification are a useful instrument of education and government." Like other scholars, Shorey attributes this position to Plato.[26] But the dialogue depicts this as *Glaucon*'s position. It is he who, though not persuaded by the lie himself, endorses its usefulness as a tool of deception. As I have shown in earlier chapters, there is no warrant for referring to Plato positions taken up by his dialogues' characters. As I show next, the passages preceding the noble lie, in any case, bring to appearance not the value but rather the *dangers* for city and soul justice of eliding persuasion and deception, which latter they present

---

25. Socrates specifically adds "soldiers" when addressing Glaucon here because, as scholars have widely noted, Glaucon's concerns are largely directed to war.
26. Shorey, in *Republic, Books 1–5*, 300–301 note a; 306–7 note c.

as a mode of force that brings about the loss of one's own, and thus prevents both justice and persuasion.

Just before Socrates introduces the founding lie, he and Glaucon are discussing the question of who should be selected to rule the city from among those reared as guardians. Socrates answers only the "best," whom he defines as those with intelligence, *phronēsis*, who care about the interests of the city (412c-d). Calling these guardians, friends, *philoi*, of the city, Socrates specifies that those most likely to be the city's friends are those who believe that its interests coincide with their own. Indeed, *only* guardians of that true belief, that is, in the coincidence of their self-interest with the interest of the city, are suitable for rule (412d). Turning to the ways in which a true belief may "exit" from the guardians' minds and thus call into question their fitness for rule, Socrates distinguishes between "voluntary" exit—"the departure of a false belief from one who learns better" (also *Gorg.* 458a-b; *Ap.* 22b)—and "involuntary" exit—the departure of a true belief.

At Glaucon's request, Socrates focuses on the latter, explaining that "involuntary exit" of a true belief may occur by force, *bia*, sorcery, and theft (413a). With overtures to Gorgias' *Encomium of Helen*, Socrates elaborates: by force, he means "those whom some pain or suffering compels to change their minds"; by sorcery, he means "those who alter their opinions under the spell of pleasure or terrified by some fear"; and, dividing theft into "forgetting" and "persuasion to change, *metapeisthentas*," a usage that appears only one other time in the *Republic* (399b), he says that, "in the one case, time, in the other *logos*, speech or argument, strips them unawares of their beliefs" (413b-c). By offering deception (both *apatē* and *lanthano*) as an instance of *metapeisthentas* (413c-d), and proposing the founding lie immediately next, Socrates *may* be aligning persuasion with lies, thus underwriting the possibility, discussed above, that the dialogue is indifferent about how persuasion is effected. In my view, however, Socrates sets *metapeisthentas* alongside force and sorcery, as an instance of theft, to bring to light the substantial ethical and political risks of (mis)taking deception, force, or sorcery for persuasion. And I take Glaucon's endorsement of the founding lie as a tool of persuasion to be an *illustration* of that mistake.

What might those risks be? Recall that the true belief that is the condition of good guardianship is the belief that the guardians' self-interest coincides with the polity's interest. Emphasizing the imperative of a sense of one's own for good rule and marking it once again as a constitutive part of justice (413c-414a), Socrates calls "good guardians of themselves" those who succeed at preserving their "indwelling conviction" about the coincidence of their self-interest and that of the polity.[27] It is these guardians, he says, who will be best able to guard "against foes without and friends within, so that the latter shall not wish and the former shall not be able to work harm" (414b). Justice and also the practice of good judgment, along with political rule and self-rule, then, all appear to depend on the capacity to guard one's own against modes of "involuntary" exit, which, in Socrates' words, "strip people of their beliefs unawares." Now note that when, after presenting the founding lie, Socrates refers to "the good effect of the tale in making [the guardians] more inclined to care for the state and one another" (415d), he omits any reference to the self. This makes sense. According to the lie, the city's inhabitants are fully formed in and by the earth and by the metals that determine their rank. That their souls are their own to shape, affect, or effect through education or learning Socrates calls "a dream" (414d). To be a true friend of the city and to rule well, however, depend on a guardian's *self*-interest coinciding with the interests of the polity, and that depends on a sense of one's own. Insofar as the lie produces guardians who care for the state, one another, and the rest of the city's inhabitants but not for themselves, it has the effect of making guardians unfit for friendship or rule, and also incapable of justice, which, as we have seen, likewise depends on self-regulation and a sense of one's own. The ideal city's institutions, which appear on the heels of the founding lie and also evacuate all sense of the guardians' "own" through regulations requiring, among other things, that property, women, and children be held in common (416d-417e), similarly and for the same reason render the guardians unfit for friendship or rule.

In the case of the founding lie, then, as in the early education discussed in chapter 3, contrivances, *mēchanai*, deception, and injustice all appear to cooperate. Presented to the brothers as a verbal falsehood, the early education became a true lie to them when they took it for truth, and that, as we saw, put them, like the warrior/guardians at whom it was directed, in the worst state of ignorance (382a-b). Though not himself persuaded of the founding lie, Glaucon values it as a tool of deception, a true lie. Insofar as he thus seeks to put others in a state of ignorance, and insofar as doing that causes harm, we are invited to wonder, it seems, as much about his capacities for justice and friendship in relation to the city he cofounds as we are about the capacities for justice and friendship of the warrior/guardian rulers.

---

27. See Schofield, "*Fraternité, inégalité, la parole de dieu*," who underscores that the true conviction of the philosopher-guardians lies in political friendship, a practice that combines self-interest with the interests of the polity.

A GRAMMATICAL INTERLUDE

We are also invited to wonder about persuasion. I have been suggesting so far that in relation to the *mēchanē* that is the founding lie (414c, 415c), as in relation to the *mēchanē* that is the early education (430a), true lies are depicted as securing obedience but not persuading. Distinguishing persuasion and obedience is not easy, however. When we do something, it is impossible to tell, by looking at the outcome, whether we've done it because we have (merely) obeyed or because we have been truly persuaded. Distinguishing persuasion from deception is not easy either, as the example of Glaucon makes plain.

The complexity of the relations among deception, persuasion, and obedience is captured in the Greek. Like the English "persuasion," the Greek *peithō* can take the active or passive voice.[28] When active, *peithein*, positioning the subject of the verb as the agent of persuasion, signifies "to persuade," and also to "talk over, mislead." When passive, *peithesthai*, positioning the subject of the verb as the patient of persuasion, signifies "to be persuaded," and also to "obey . . . believe, trust in."[29] The active voice of persuasion does not distinguish persuasion from deception. Neither does the passive voice distinguish persuasion from obedience. Perhaps this is why James Boyd White suggests that *peithein*, taking the active voice, be translated as "to subject to verbal and intellectual force," and that *peithesthai*, when it takes the passive voice, be translated as "to yield to verbal and intellectual force."[30] These translations reflect and well capture depictions in the *Republic* of persuasion when it is paired with force or practiced as deception with a view to securing obedience.

There is another voice of persuasion, however. As Bryan Garsten notes, "in spite of the grammar" in the English "you have persuaded me," the persuadee "is not merely describing something that has happened to him. . . . He is describing something he has done."[31] This aspect of persuasion, missing in English grammar, is accommodated in the Greek by the middle voice. Taking the form *peithesthai*, the middle voice looks exactly like the passive voice, and that means that in grammar, as in life, it is not easy to tell the difference between true persuasion and mere obedience. This makes some sense, for obedience is often *the effect* of persuasion. But obedience can also be the effect of deception and/or force. And so, again, in grammar, as in life, it is by and large only the

---

28. There is also, not in English but in Greek, the middle voice, to which I turn below.
29. On *peithein*, see Liddell and Scott, *Greek-English Lexicon*, 9th ed., s.v. *peithō*.
30. White, *Acts of Hope*, 28–29.
31. Garsten, *Saving Persuasion*, 7.

context that tells the difference.³² In life, it is, more accurately, the *persuadee*'s experience of the context that makes the difference between being persuaded and merely obeying, as it does between being persuaded and being deceived, as discussed in the last section, and also between being persuaded and being forced, as discussed earlier. As I show in the following sections, the *Republic* attends carefully to the experiential differences between obedience due to force or deception, on the one hand, and persuasion, on the other, to develop ethical and political correlates to the grammatical middle voice of persuasion.³³ For now, it is to be noted that Socrates exploits an exception to the grammatical rule that middle and passive voices of *peithō* are indistinguishable by their appearance, when he uses the unambiguous aorist passive participle to say that the sole aim of the early education is to "persuade, *peisthentes*, the guardians that they should receive our laws like dye" so that their faith might be held fast (430a). Socrates seems to be alerting us that the aim of the early education is not to truly persuade but instead to secure obedience. The same may be said of the other conspicuously named devices, *mēchanai*, that appear across the dialogue, including the founding lie. "Stripping people of their beliefs unawares" (413b-c) and abetting the "theft" of one's own, devices do not truly persuade. As I show next, something similar may be said of the *logos*, speech or argument, that is the Socratic *elenchos*.

ELENCHOS

In *Republic* 6, in the name of imaginary listeners, Adeimantus describes as follows what he calls Socrates' "game of question and answer":

> Here is how those who hear what you now say are affected on each occasion. They think that because they are inexperienced in asking and answering questions, they're led astray a little bit by the argument, *logou*, at every question, and that when these little bits are added together at the end of the discussion, great is the fall, as the opposite of what they said at the outset comes to light. Just as by expert checkers players, the unskilled are finally shut in and cannot make a

---

32. Middle and passive voices of *peithō* are distinguishable only by context except in the future and aorist tenses, which, insofar as they have distinct middle and passive conjugations, are distinguishable by appearance.

33. For what I see as an analogous project in Aristotle, see my "On *Logos* and Politics in Aristotle."

move, so they are finally blocked and have their mouths stopped by this other game, played not with counters but with words. (487b-c)

Adeimantus is describing the *elenchos*, for a definition of which scholars sometimes look to the *Sophist*.[34] There the Eleatic visitor, whom Socrates calls "a kind of god of refutation, *elenktikos*" (216b), says that these styles of argument

> cross-examine a man's words, when he thinks that he is saying something and is really saying nothing, and easily convict him of inconsistencies in his opinions; these they then collect by the dialectic process, and placing them side by side, show that they contradict one another about the same things, in relation to the same things, and in the same respect.

He goes on:

> He, seeing this, is angry with himself, and grows gentle, *hēmerountai*, toward others, and thus is entirely delivered from the great prejudices and harsh notions, in a way that is most amusing to the hearer, and produces the most lasting good effect on the person who is the subject of the operation. (230b-d)

One scholar calls the *elenchos* so defined "cathartic and pedagogic."[35] I'm less sure. As Catherine Zuckert has argued, the Eleatic's definition misdescribes the effects of his own elenchic engagements with Theaetetus in the *Sophist*.[36] It also misdescribes the effects of Socrates' language game in the *Republic*.

Consider Socrates' engagement with Thrasymachus in *Republic* 1. A rhetorician himself, so hardly unskilled, Thrasymachus is depicted as modeling his own argumentative style on his account of justice as a *technē* of power when, "hunched up like a wild beast," he flings himself at Socrates and Polemarchus "as if to tear them to pieces" (336b). Using persuasion in its active voice, Thrasymachus offers to persuade, *pepeisai*, Socrates by taking the argument and "ramming it into Socrates' head" (345b), thus literalizing White's definition of active persuasion, noted above, as a practice of "verbal and intellectual force." Although he describes himself as frightened by Thrasymachus (336b) and rendered nearly speechless (336d), Socrates rejects Thrasymachean

---

34. On this topic, I have drawn on Blondell, *Play of Character*, and Tarnopolsky, *Prudes, Perverts, and Tyrants*.
35. Kurke, *Aesopic Conversations*, 359.
36. Zuckert, *Plato's Philosophers*, chap. 9.

justice. He also refuses Thrasymachean "persuasion." As models of force, both fail.

Socrates, for his part, does not threaten physical violence, but his response to Thrasymachus is forceful nonetheless, less perhaps in terms of his arguments, which scholars have described as weak and problematic, than in terms of what may be referred to as his "logic-chopping" and "browbeating" style.[37] In Carol Jacobs' words, "Socrates' power is in his voice. And his battle with Thrasymachus, from the beginning of their exchange, is a struggle for the imposition of voice."[38] Subject to Socrates' forceful voice, Thrasymachus concedes, against his initial claims and unwillingly, that it is the just man, not the unjust man, who is good and wise.[39] Accusing Socrates of refusing to him his power to speak (350e), and exhibiting physical symptoms of psychological duress in acquiescing to a position he opposes, Thrasymachus, Socrates tells us, breaks into a copious sweat and blushes (350c-d).[40]

At the end of *Republic* 1, Socrates describes Thrasymachus as "gentled" or "tamed," *pra[i]os*[41] (354a), but contrary to the Eleatic's claims for the *elenchos*, Thrasymachus is not "angry with himself" but with Socrates. We do not know if the effects of Socrates' arguments on Thrasymachus are "lasting" or "good" because, although Thrasymachus stays for the remainder of the conversation and even participates on the sidelines (450a-b), he does not engage philosophically with Socrates again. By way of Socrates' narration, however, we learn in *Republic* 1 that Thrasymachus has been shamed (350c-d).[42] And that leaves him withdrawn and obedient but perhaps not truly persuaded. Using similar

---

37. See Warman, "Plato and Persuasion," 49; Tarnopolsky, *Prudes, Perverts, and Tyrants*, 68–72; McCoy, *Plato on the Rhetoric of Philosophers and Sophists*, 116–17; Beversluis, *Cross-Examining Socrates*, 237–38; and Weiss, "When Winning Is Everything." For "logic-chopping," see Blondell, *Play of Character*, 187. For "browbeating," see Sachs, *Plato: "Gorgias" and Aristotle: "Rhetoric,"* 7–9, who calls this mode of Socratic engagement "kolastic rhetoric," taking the form of "authoritative rebuke," to contrast it to the pandering or "kolakic rhetoric" characteristic of servile flattery.

38. Jacobs, *Skirting the Ethical*, 190 n. 32.

39. Blondell, *Play of Character*, 182, 183.

40. On the centrality of shaming to Socrates' practices of psychological coercion and an exploration of Socrates' shaming refutation of Gorgias that works in similar ways to his refutation of Thrasymachus, see Tarnopolsky, *Prudes, Perverts, and Tyrants*, chap. 2; and 38–55, for the way Socratic *elenchos*, meaning "to disgrace, put to shame, cross-examine, question, prove, refute, confute, get the better of," is displayed and critiqued in the *Gorgias*.

41. The Eleatic's word in the *Sophist* is *hemeroō*, which, like *pra[i]os*, connotes "being made gentle."

42. For shame as an outcome of the *elenchos*, see also *Sophist* 230d.

language to describe the imaginary speakers who hear his responses to their challenges to his account of the philosopher-kings in *Republic* 6, Socrates says that they, too, are "altogether" "gentled, *pra[i]os*," or tamed. "Persuaded, *pepeisthai*," in what appears to be the passive voice, they are brought to agreement "from shame, if nothing else" (502a). They, too, are made obedient but not, it seems, truly persuaded.[43]

Variously dubbed a "negative" or "destructive" style of argumentation insofar as its primary goal is, as Leslie Kurke has put it, "self-incrimination" or to "force" interlocutors to "bear witness" against themselves,[44] the Socratic *elenchos* may sometimes result in *aporia* (as with, e.g., Polemarchus in *Republic* 1), and that may have a temporary good effect. But it is more often depicted as producing frustration, resentment, and/or anger, all directed at Socrates (consider, alongside Thrasymachus, Protagoras, Callicles, Polus, Euthydemus, Cleitophon, to name a few). That Socrates leaves his interlocutors in *Republic* 1 obedient, gentled, or tamed, but not truly persuaded is suggested by the question with which Glaucon opens *Republic* 2: "Socrates, do you want to seem to have persuaded us, or truly to persuade us, *dokein pepeikenai ē hōs alēthōs peisai?*" (357a-b). He goes on to refer to Socrates as a snake charmer (358b), someone who, like *Republic* 3's "sorcerers," may enchant or mesmerize but has not truly persuaded. Similarly, after being subjected to Socrates' *elenchos*, Callicles puts it this way in the *Gorgias*: "I think you're right, Socrates, but the thing that happens to most people has happened to me: I'm not really persuaded by you, *ou panu soi peithomai*" (513c). Carol Jacobs notes that at the end of *Republic* 1, justice remains "what the stronger insists it is. Or, more correctly: justice is *not*, what Socrates, as the stronger in the eristic argument, insists it is not."[45] Socrates, for his part, seems no more satisfied than his interlocutors, calling himself "none the wiser" and assuming responsibility for their failures in regard to justice (354b-c). Like sorcery, deception, and might, force in argument, it appears, may secure obedience, but it, too, seems to fail to truly persuade. As in the examples discussed in earlier sections of this

---

43. Contra Blondell, *Play of Character*, 178–79, 204–5, for whom being gentled is a sign of philosophic success, but see also 183 for "gentleness" as "sulky silencing."

44. For "negative," see Kahn, *Plato and the Socratic Dialogue*, chap. 4; for "destructive," see Blondell, *Play of Character*, 105, referring to Socrates in *Hippias Minor*; for the phrase from Kurke, see *Aesopic Conversations*, 359. For *elenchos* as a practice of force, see also Reeve, *Philosopher-Kings*, 68.

45. Jacobs, *Skirting the Ethical*, 54.

chapter, failures of persuasion here, too, appear to cooperate with failures of justice.

PERSUADING IN THE MIDDLE VOICE

In the *Gorgias*, Socrates claims that "a good speaker will always give attention to how justice may come to exist in the souls of his fellow citizens" (504d-e). In that same dialogue, he defines power as something that brings good to its possessor (466b). How might the power of speech bring good to its possessor? And how might good speaking bring about soul justice in speakers and listeners alike?

In a kind of primer on persuasion in *Republic* 1, Socrates says to Thrasymachus: "In the first place, if you say something, then stick by what you have said. Or if you change your mind, do so openly. Don't try to do it without our noticing" (345b-c). As we have seen, stealth and deception are modalities of force that compromise the conditions of persuasion by stripping listeners of their beliefs unawares. Does the *Republic* offer a mode of speaking and listening that, unlike the "devices" I have been exploring so far, proceeds by way of the "voluntary" exit of a false belief from the soul of one who learns better, as Socrates puts it in *Republic* 3 (413a; also *Gorg.* 458a-b; and *Ap.* 22b)? The morphology of the Greek middle voice establishes the grammatical possibility that persuadees participate in their own persuasion. As I show next, the text of the *Republic* indicates early on that it is interested in the ethical, political, and philosophical correlates of this grammatical possibility.

Following Thrasymachus' defense of the life of the unjust man in *Republic* 1, Socrates asks Glaucon if he has heard "all the goods that Thrasymachus just now enumerated for the life of the unjust man." Glaucon replies, "I have heard but I am not persuaded, *peithomai*" (348a). Glaucon uses persuasion in the passive or middle voice. Which one? Because this is an instance of *failed* persuasion, it may not so much matter: to be *unpersuaded* manifests the uncoerced agency of resistance either way (also 345a-b). That Glaucon maintains that he has *listened* and is unpersuaded (also 367a-b) sets up a contrast with the opening scene, where Polemarchus threatens to refuse to listen (327c). Socrates follows up Glaucon's remark with "Do you wish us then to try to persuade, *peithōmen*, [Thrasymachus], supposing we can find a way, that what he says is not true?" (348a).

Socrates presents to Glaucon two different ways of trying to change Thrasymachus' mind. One way is for Socrates to "oppose" Thrasymachus by giving "a set speech enumerating in turn the advantages of being just and he replies and we rejoin," whereupon the goods enumerated in each speech are counted up and measured by third-party judges, *dikastai*, who determine the outcome of the speech contest. Another way is for Socrates and Thrasymachus to "come to terms with one another," based on their experiences as "both judges, *dikastai*, and pleaders, *rhetores*, at once" (348a-b). That for both ways of changing Thrasymachus' mind, Socrates names the "judges" *dikastai*, using the word for members of juries in democratic Athens, means that at issue between these two alternatives is not that the second way "suggests another form of rhetoric that would assure [Socrates'] triumph over his accuser and do away with his dependence on popular judgment," but that, unlike the first, which divides the labor of judgment into judge and judged, the second positions the judge and judged as one and the same, arguably a more democratic mode of judgment than was practiced by the *dikastai* at Athens.[46]

The first model, by way of which Thrasymachus' mind would be changed by a verdict issued about his speech by third-party judges, and which judgment he would hear as its subject but in which he would not fully participate, presents him as the passive persuadee of active persuasion. The second, by way of which Thrasymachus' mind would be changed in virtue of his *and* Socrates' judgment, issued by and for them as judges *and* pleaders, presents Thrasymachus as a participant in his own persuasion. The first model, vesting authority one-sidedly, is asymmetrical in its distribution of power. The second, distributing authority across speakers and listeners alike, presumes, acknowledges, and reinforces their equality and mutual accountability.

The second model appears again in Socrates' description in *Republic* 6 of the free and beautiful discussions of philosophy, to which I return below, as well as in his account of musical modes in *Republic* 3 (399a). Speaking with Glaucon in *Republic* 3, Socrates makes plain that he dislikes the first model: "Do you not think it disgraceful . . . to have to make use of a justice imported from others, who thus become your masters and judges, *kritōn*, from lack of such qualities in yourself?" (405a-b). If subjecting oneself to the judgment of others is bad, worse yet, Socrates says, is one who is "persuaded, *peisthē[i]*," to take pride in so subjecting himself (405b). Speaking of "persuasion" in what appears to be the passive voice, Socrates here reinforces the associations between passive persuasion, injustice, and subjection explored earlier. Modeling across speakers and listeners the practice of persuasion in the middle voice, the second mode of engagement presented in *Republic* 1 offers an alternative.

---

46. For the quoted phrase, see Bloom, "Interpretive Essay," in *Republic of Plato*, 446 n. 43. On *dikastai*, see Cammack, "Plato and Athenian Justice."

In *Republic* 1, Glaucon opts for the second model (348b). That the question of how to persuade is put before an interlocutor reinforces the agency of listeners in persuasion. That Glaucon decides in favor of a model in which listeners participate in their own persuasion appears to underwrite this conclusion. That Thrasymachus does not participate in the decision about how Socrates should try to persuade *him*, though he is Socrates' primary interlocutor at this juncture, anticipates the fact that, as we have seen, he appears not to be persuaded by Socrates in *Republic* 1. But even as Glaucon opts for the more equal and symmetrical mode of engaging, his choice of a mode of persuasion *for Thrasymachus* sets *him* up as a third-party judge in relation to Thrasymachus and Socrates' exchange. Glaucon thus positions himself as an "imported" authority (405a-b) despite his stated preference for people coming to terms with one another on their own authority, "as judges and pleaders at once."

It is not unusual to find Glaucon in this position. His endorsement of the noble lie, discussed earlier, is another example of his willingness to participate in practices that secure obedience in the name of persuasion. Something similar happens in *Republic* 5. In the lead-up to Socrates' account of rule by philosopher-kings, the interlocutors become agitated with his presentation of each more radical "wave" that sweeps away their contemporary institutions. When Socrates introduces the third wave—that philosophers will be kings—Glaucon gives voice to the displeasure of the interlocutors with the following warning:

> Socrates, what a phrase and argument you have let burst out. Now that it's said, you can believe that very many men, and not ordinary ones, will on the spot throw off their clothes, and stripped for action, taking hold of whatever weapon falls under the hand of each, run full speed at you to do wonderful deeds. If you don't defend yourself with speech and get away, you'll really pay the penalty in scorn. (474a)

Glaucon charges Socrates with speaking persuasively under the threat of violence. To underscore and foreground that what is at stake here is both the matter of substance (the justice of philosophers being kings) and also Socrates' mode of engagement, Socrates' defense speech is embedded in a subdialogue directed not at his actual interlocutors but at an imaginary listener who is described as an "angry and challenging" lover of sights and sounds. Socrates' task? To "soothe him and gently, *ērema*, win him over" to the idea that philosophers should be kings, "without telling him too plainly that he is not in his right mind" (476d-e, 494d).

Socrates undertakes this task by drawing next what scholars rightly take to be a conspicuously problematic picture of the traits (485b–487a) that are supposed to justify the rule of philosopher-kings to the imaginary lover of sights and sounds.[47] That picture garners ready acquiescence from Glaucon, who, in an echo of his move in *Republic* 1, attempts to enforce his position on the other listeners by again taking up the mantle of a judge, without, however, having pleaded. Calling Socrates' account of the justice of the philosopher-kings "the truth, *tō[i] alēthei*," Glaucon demands obedience to his decree from any who might disagree, using as the word for "obedience" *peithōntai*, persuasion in what appears to be the passive voice. He adds: "To be angry with the truth is not lawful, *themis*" (480a), using *themis* as the word for "law," perhaps to reinforce his self-positioning as authoritative judge: *themis* signifies the positing of law generally issued by the gods, which demands obedience without justification.[48]

Despite the authority vested in Socrates' account of the philosophers-to-be-kings by Glaucon's acquiescence and despite Glaucon's appropriation of that authority to himself, or, perhaps, to render both of these moves to external authority and obedience conspicuous, Adeimantus comes on the scene next to resist. It is at this point that he interjects with his own imaginary listener, who, as discussed earlier, maintains that Socrates' language game has silenced but not persuaded (487b-c), and raises the objection, shared by the many, that those whom Socrates has just described as philosophers worthy of rule are instead "rendered useless to society" by their pursuit of philosophy (487d). Accepting Adeimantus' objections (487e),[49] Socrates puts in question simultaneously the truth of his own account, the justice of Glaucon's verdict in favor of that account, and Glaucon's all-too-ready acquiescence as well. Then, in what appears to be a renewed attempt to justify rule by philosopher-kings, Socrates switches interlocutors and also his mode of engagement. Changing from the argumentative style he used in the embedded subdialogue when Glaucon was his primary interlocutor, Socrates stays within that dialogue to respond to the objection of Adeimantus and *his* imaginary listeners but switches from discussion by way of *elenchos* to "an answer given through image" (487e). Socrates' language here is striking, as he gives agency to the image by his use of the genitive and calls on Adeimantus to listen not to him but to the image and to see it (488a).[50] I return to the persuasive power of images toward the end of this chapter.

---

47. I return to this description in chapter 5.
48. For other appearances of *themis* in the *Republic*, see 398a, 417a, 422d, 480a.
49. For, as we saw in chapter 2, philosophers *are* useless.
50. For discussion, see Miller, *Diotima at the Barricades*, 80–103.

The key point for now is that Glaucon is portrayed in these pages as playing all the parts in the first model of persuasion presented in *Republic* 1, the one he and Socrates had both rejected. He starts off unpersuaded, and then, granting authority to Socrates' account, he submits to the latter's authority in the mode of obedience or passive persuasion, and then, positioning himself as authoritative judge, demands obedience to his verdict. That Socrates endorses Adeimantus' challenge invites us to read these passages as highlighting the failures of the first model of persuasion, and also as a reminder, by way of Glaucon's embodiment of these failures, of the promise and possibility of seeking out the truth of justice by way of the second model. What might the second model of persuasion look like? Not like the *elenchos*, which, as we saw, fails in *Republic* 1 to bring about justice or to persuade. And not like acquiescence, at least in the mode of Glaucon. For although Glaucon, unlike Thrasymachus, willingly acquiesces to Socrates, he sometimes does so when, as we have just seen, he should not. Are there other modes of *logos*, speech or argumentation, depicted in the *Republic* that proceed otherwise than by stripping people of their beliefs unawares, or by force, or by securing willing but passive obedience? Are there modes of *logos* that proceed with awareness and the possibility for listeners to act as agents of their own persuasion? I argue next that persuasion so understood, that is, as persuasion in the middle voice, is exemplified in the practice of analogy.

ANALOGY

In the *Rhetoric*, Aristotle groups analogy, alongside myth, allegory, fable, parable, and simile, under the heading of *ta Sōkratika*. Calling these "invented examples" and "paradigms, *paradeigmatos eidos . . . to auton poiein*," Aristotle treats analogy as the most basic style of persuasive argumentation (1393a22–1394a13).[51] It is, in any case, pervasive in the *Republic*, with Socrates offering analogies between city and soul, the good and the sun, the practice of philosophy and the practice of craft or *technē*, to say nothing of the divided line simile, itself a structure of analogy and the framework of *Republic* 6's account of philosophy.[52]

---

51. With Aristotle I take the structure of analogy to be most basic and so to help to explain how these other modes of *logoi* persuade. On myth, allegory, fable, parable, and simile, see Brisson, *Plato the Myth Maker*; Tarnopolsky, *Prudes, Perverts, and Tyrants*; Morgan, *Myth and Philosophy from the Presocratics to Plato*; Ferrari, *Listening to the Cicadas*, chap. 5; Lear, "Allegory and Myth in Plato's *Republic*"; Kurke, *Aesopic Conversations*. On paradigm or example as a kind of argument from analogy, see Lloyd, *Polarity and Analogy*, 406.

52. I discuss the line analogy in chapter 6.

As with *elenchos*, my treatment of analogy begins with the Eleatic visitor, this time in the *Statesman*.[53] After remarking that "it is quite difficult to make clear anything of importance adequately without the use of paradigms or examples, *paradeigmasi*" (277d), the Eleatic offers the following, what G. E. R. Lloyd calls a "paradigm of a paradigm," to help explain what he means to the young Socrates, his interlocutor.[54] Choosing the case of learning to read as an analogy for knowledge acquisition and, as discussed in this book's prologue, concerned specifically with "the easiest and best way to lead [children] to letters which they do not yet know," the Eleatic recommends taking children "first back, *anagein*, to those cases in which they were getting these same things right" (278a), that is, to short syllables in which they are already able to distinguish individual letters well enough (277e). The next step is to set

> these [letters] beside what they're not yet recognizing. By comparing them, we demonstrate that there is the same kind of thing with similar features in both combinations, until the things that they are getting right have been shown set beside all the ones that they don't know . . . and so become models, *paradeigmata*. (278a-b)[55]

On Lloyd's analysis, from this example we learn three things about analogy: that analogy is a "practice in method"; that it has a "didactic function"; and that it is a method of "discovery." He elaborates: analogies "not only provide useful practice in the method to be used on more difficult subjects"; they also are "a means of teaching a person by leading him from something he knows to something which he does not yet know but which is similar to what he knows." If, as it turns out in the case of reading, the "instructor . . . clearly knows [in advance] the letters in each of the combinations in which they occur," then, in Lloyd's words, "to some extent, no doubt, Plato has emphasized the element of search and discovery . . . simply for dramatic or literary purposes."[56]

I agree that analogies have a didactic function and that they are also a practice in method. I also agree that, in the Eleatic's account of learning to read, the element of discovery is missing. If, as the Eleatic insists, the key to knowledge acquisition is starting with right opinions (278d-e), then the *only* way to learn

---

53. On analogy as a principal form of argumentation in Greek thought, see Lloyd, *Polarity and Analogy*, part 2.
54. Lloyd, *Polarity and Analogy*, 398.
55. For discussion, see Lane, *Method and Politics*, 66–67.
56. Lloyd, *Polarity and Analogy*, 399–400.

to read or to come to know anything at all, for that matter, is to be given or led to right opinions by someone who already has them. Similarly in the *Sophist*, as we saw in this book's prologue, the Eleatic maintains that learning to read requires being taught a *technē*, in that case the art of grammar (253a-e). As we have also seen, however, learning to read is depicted differently in the *Republic* and also in the *Theaetetus*, which is often treated as the first in a trilogy comprised of the *Theaetetus, Sophist*, and *Statesman*. If, for the Eleatic, learning to read is a function of being taught or led to right opinions by an authoritative teacher, a third-party judge, so to speak, Socrates, in the *Republic* and *Theaetetus*, presents learning to read as a function of the learner giving an account of the letters and syllables he sees from out of his own sense perceptual experiences (*Theaet*. 203a, 206a, 207d; *Rep.* 402a-b). If, in the Eleatic's example, the element of search and discovery is "simply for dramatic or literary purposes," in Socrates' analogy it seems to be for real.[57]

For unlike in the Eleatic's analogy, where, as Lloyd put it, analogies are "a means of teaching a person by leading him" because the teacher, an authority, already knows, in Socrates' examples, analogies appear to open the way for learners, including, as we will see, Socrates, to move from what is familiar to what is new by way of their own authority and respective experiences put into words. Taking learners, rather than teachers, as the locus of learning alters both the didactic function of analogy and the practice in method it offers.[58] As the *Republic* suggests more than once, analogies depend on their uptake (368d ff., 434e ff.). They require what Lloyd calls "verification."[59] This is because there are no a priori rules or criteria for judging analogousness. Dependent on how they are received no less than on their makers, analogies, like middle-voice persuasion, arise in and depend on the context of discursive exchange.[60]

Theaetetus does not say how he learned to read. A "pliant" and "tractable" listener, he turns out to be just the sort of interlocutor the Eleatic seeks in the *Sophist* (217d).[61] Back in the *Republic*, Glaucon, too, does not engage actively to "verify" Socrates' analogies. As discussed in chapter 3, although it is open to him in *Republic* 4, he does not apply the test of soul justice to the city. Similarly, in the case of the analogy between the sun and the good, which I explore

---

57. Allen, *Why Plato Wrote*, 52, disagrees, calling Socrates' "language of discovery . . . a cheat."
58. At *Physics* 207b7-24, Aristotle also locates learning in the learner.
59. Lloyd, *Polarity and Analogy*, 400.
60. On analogies, see Frank, *Democracy of Distinction*, 96–97.
61. See Stern, *Knowledge and Politics in Plato's "Theaetetus,"* 206, 218–19.

in more detail in chapter 6: even after Socrates invites his especial vigilance (507a), Glaucon offers only intermittent questions of clarification and then accepts Socrates' statement (507b–509a) that "as the good is in the intelligible region with respect to intelligence and what is intellected, so the sun is in the visible region with respect to sight and what is seen" (508c). Their discussion of the sun-good analogy ends with Glaucon returning to the good as pleasure, an identification that Socrates, just passages before, attributed to the many (505b) and that he seeks, by way of the analogy, to attenuate. By accepting the sun-good analogy without having sought to verify its terms, Glaucon continues to think what he thought before, namely, that nothing is more beautiful than pleasure. Socrates' response to Glaucon, *euphēmei* (509a), generally translated as "hush," suggests that Glaucon has not been listening well and that he would do better, perhaps, to keep silent.[62]

By not taking up the didactic function of Socrates' analogies and the practice in method they offer, Glaucon fails to participate in middle-voice persuasion. But we might. If, unlike Glaucon, we apply the test of soul justice to the *kallipolis*, as we did in chapter 3 and again earlier in this chapter, then we might challenge the authority of the philosopher-kings on the ground that it fails to bring justice to the souls of the ordinary majority by preventing their self-regulation. And if, unlike Glaucon, we attend more carefully to how Socrates sets up the analogy between the sun and the good? Socrates calls what he offers "just the interest, *tokos*," which is to say, the effect but not the thing itself, describing the sun as "an offspring, *ekgonon*, of the good" (507a), "begot in a proportion with itself, *egennēsen analogon heautō[i]*" (508b). Socrates warns Glaucon that he might in some way "unwillingly deceive in rendering the account of the interest fraudulent" (507a), and also that Glaucon will "see ugly things, blind, and crooked, when it's possible to hear bright and beautiful ones from others" (506c-d). In short, what Glaucon sees as "uncontrived beauty, *amēchanon kallos*" (509a), Socrates presents as a contrivance or device, *mēchanē*: not beautiful but, instead, aligned here, as in *Republic* 3, with ugliness and deception.

After issuing these warnings to Glaucon in *Republic* 6, Socrates reopens the possibility of the beautiful conversation he just called into question. Seeking to come to terms with Glaucon on their own authority, as judges and pleaders at once, taking the good into account, he makes plain that his concern lies in how they will speak and listen together. Socrates seeks agreement (507a) about

---

62. "Avoid all unlucky words, during sacred rites: hence, as the surest mode of avoiding them, keep a religious silence" (Liddell and Scott, *Greek-English Lexicon*, 9th ed., s.v. *euphēmeō*).

what he and Glaucon have so far defined together in their speech (507b) as well as about the powers of the senses, and he calls particular attention to their sensible experiences, how things are seen and heard (507b-c). He points out that in the case of hearing, unlike in the case of seeing, there is no "third thing" (507c-d) giving the power to see, a point I return to in chapter 6. For now, it is to be noted that at stake in coming to terms by way of the practice of analogical argumentation in all of these examples is a mode of speaking and listening that, like the second model of persuasion presented in *Republic* 1, depends on parties to the exchange relying not on the power of third parties but engaging by way of their own authority, which is to say, on middle-voice persuasion. Earlier in *Republic* 6, Socrates refers to this mode of speaking and listening as the "free and beautiful discussions" of philosophy.

FREE AND BEAUTIFUL DISCUSSIONS

Offering the following corrective to the way contemporary cities practice philosophy, Socrates says:

> Nowadays, those who take it up at all are lads fresh from childhood; in the interval before running a household and making money, they approach its hardest part and then drop it. . . . I mean by the hardest part that which has to do with speeches or words or discussion, *tous logous*. In later life . . . they believe it's a great thing if they are willing to listen to the philosophical discussions of others, thinking it ought to be done as a hobby or by-work, *parergon*. (498a-b)

When Adeimantus replies that however enthusiastically, *prothumōs*, Socrates speaks, his listeners are even more enthusiastic in their opposition and will remain unpersuaded, *oude peisomenous* (498c), Socrates answers: "It is no wonder that the many are not persuaded, *me peithesthai*," for of the thing spoken of here—"free, *eleutherōn*, and beautiful, *kalōn*, discussions whose sole aim is to seek out the truth" (499a)—"they have never beheld a token, but only the willful, *exepitedes*, chiming, *homoiomena*, of word and phrase" (498d-e).

Claiming that neither have the many seen "a man 'equilibrated' and 'assimilated' to virtue's self perfectly, so far as may be, in word and deed, and holding rule in a city of like quality," Socrates associates, by way of their rarity, free and beautiful discussions that seek out the truth with excellence in soul and city. Underscoring the significance of such discussions, he maintains: "We will spare no effort until we either persuade, *peisomen*," any who may not agree about their importance, or "achieve something that will profit them when they come to that life in which they will be born again and meet with such discussions as these" (498d). Free and beautiful discussions, involving speaking and listening well with a view to persuasion, taken up not as divided labor or over time but together, and associated with ethical and political excellence, are thus presented as a propaedeutic to philosophy, if not as philosophy itself (also 399b-c). In *Republic* 9, Socrates isolates *logoi*—speech, discussions, arguments—as the instrument, *organon*, of judgment of the philosopher (582d). If, as it appears, free and beautiful discussions of philosophy are the site of persuasion, then any exploration of the *Republic*'s understanding of persuasion will call for examining those discussions.

Where might they be found? Shorey reads the passages in *Republic* 6 as referring to "the difference between the artificial style and insincerity of the sophists and the serious truth of [Plato's] own ideals."[63] If that is right, then we should find the free and beautiful conversations of philosophy in the *logoi* displaying that "serious truth." For the scholars referenced at the beginning of this chapter, for whom, as for Shorey, the *Republic* presents the "authentic discourse" of political experts as based on knowledge and truth, Plato's "serious truth" appears by way of the philosopher-kings. I have argued against identifying Plato with his characters. There are, in any case, other obstacles to treating the philosopher-kings as the site of the free and beautiful discussions of philosophy. For one, as noted in chapter 3, the activities of the philosopher-kings are consistently described in the *Republic* as "compelled" (500d, 515c-d, e, 520a, 521b, 526a-b, e, 540a-b), and, if that is the case, then there is reason to wonder about how free their conversations may be.[64] Second, as we also saw in chapter 3, what Socrates calls Glaucon's beautiful city, *kallipolis* (527c), is conspicuously depicted as an "uglytown," an *aischropolis*, and, if that is the case, then there is reason to wonder also about the beauty of the conversations of those who rule that city.[65] Most telling, perhaps, is that the philosopher-kings in the city in speech never actually speak. When, for example, the philosopher-kings order the desires of the "ordinary majority" (431c-d), they are not depicted as doing so by discursive methods.[66] When, in yet another scene of compulsion (520a), they are ordered back to the cave by Socrates, who speaks

---

63. Shorey, in *Republic, Books 6–10*, 62 note c.

64. On the compulsion of the philosopher-kings, see Weiss, *Philosophers in the "Republic,"* 74–77, 81–83, 107–12.

65. For *aischropolis*, see Berger, *Perils of Uglytown*.

66. Contra those who refer to the "imperative discourse" of the philosopher-kings. See, e.g., Yunis, *Taming Democracy*, 164–65.

in the name of the laws of the ideal city's founders (520b-d), the philosopher-kings are addressed but offer no audible response. If the "serious truth" of the *Republic* is to be found in the free and beautiful discussions of philosophy, then that truth, it seems, here, as in *Republic* 2–5, is *not* to be associated with the philosopher-kings.

Might, then, the free and beautiful discussions of philosophy appear in the *logoi* of Socrates? This chapter has argued against that possibility as well. Socrates and his interlocutors may speak and listen, but their discussions turn out to be no more free and beautiful than the modes of engagement Socrates seeks, in *Republic* 6, to correct. This is sometimes because Socrates and his interlocutors exercise discursive force, as we saw in the exchanges between Socrates and Thrasymachus. It is sometimes because Socrates and his interlocutors do not seek after ethical and political excellence and/or truth, as we saw in Socrates' engagements with Glaucon.

If this is so, however, and the free and beautiful discussions of philosophy do not appear in the *Republic*, then why might Socrates bring up their promise and possibility? And why might the dialogue stage only failures of persuasion? I have argued in earlier chapters that Plato's dialogues present failures in order to prompt readers to disidentify with the dialogues' characters and also and thereby to prompt wonder about the questions and topics about which the dialogues' characters do not wonder. When, for example, as we have seen, Plato puts Socrates in contradiction in the *Republic* around poetry or simple-mindedness, or has Socrates present virtues, laws, and institutions that thwart soul and city justice, and Glaucon and Adeimantus offer no resistance, these representations may prompt *readers* to engage. With Christopher Rowe, then, I take the dialogues' primary targets of persuasion to be their readers.[67]

James Kastley, for his part, has called the *Republic* a "mimetic representation of an act of persuasion" that seeks "to constitute an audience who can rethink its cultural heritage and value justice in a radically new way."[68] I agree that the *Republic* seeks to constitute its readers by prompting our rethinking. In my view, however, the *Republic* does its prompting not as a "mimetic representation of an act of persuasion" but instead as a mimetic representation of *nonpersuasion*. Offered no "doctrines" by Plato, and, if my reading so far has been persuasive, seeing and hearing no "serious truth" represented by the *Republic*'s characters, readers are like the imaginary speakers and listeners

---

67. Rowe, *Art of Philosophical Writing*, 21.
68. Kastley, *Rhetoric of Plato's "Republic,"* xiii and passim. Kastley also calls the *Republic* a "mimetic poem," whose "subject is persuasion" (80).

presented in *Republic* 5, 6, and 7 (476d-e, 487b-c).[69] Overhearing the dialogue's discussions, and finding the characters' words and modes of speaking largely *unpersuasive*, the imaginary speakers and listeners of the *Republic* challenge the arguments on offer. In my view, readers are prompted to do the same.

The *Republic* thus reinforces by exemplification Socrates' claim that the many "have never beheld a token" (498d) of "free and beautiful discussions whose sole aim is to seek out the truth" (499a). It thereby leaves philosophy to another place and time (498d). If, as noted, the free and beautiful discussions of philosophy are sites of persuasion, then their nonappearance in the dialogue leaves persuasion, too, to another time and place. I take that to be the time and place of engagement between readers and text. Unpersuaded, disidentified with the characters, and invited to intervene not by imitating the represented conversations but by questioning what appears, readers are prompted to open a parallel dialogue with the text, and also with other readers, about the topics raised but not persuasively addressed in the dialogue's represented discussions. Thus, as I have shown in chapters 2 and 3, when the *Republic*'s characters do not challenge Socrates' contradictory arguments about the truth of mimetic poetry, the good of simple minds, or the early education and the dispositions and constitution it underwrites, such discussions are shifted to the dialogue's readers.

If readers are, and are meant to be, unpersuaded by the conversations we read, however, how could we possibly be Plato's targets of *persuasion*? As with the other mimetic representations discussed in earlier chapters, readers may be prompted by the *Republic*'s unpersuasive conversations to wonder about how *persuasion* does its work. Seeing Socrates' association of persuasion with free and beautiful discussions and the dialogue's staged failures of persuasion, we may consider how the dialogue's speakers' words undermine freedom and beauty, and how listeners, for their part, sometimes fail to resist exercises of unfreedom and ugliness in words, and/or how they listen, as Socrates puts it in *Republic* 6, as merely a "by-work" or hobby. Seeing Socrates associate free and beautiful discussions that seek out the truth with soul and city excellence, we may wonder, too, about how persuasion might matter for ethics and politics. Seeing the manipulations, deceptions, and compulsion of the dialogues' characters, and seeing the complicity in these practices on the parts of the philosophic figures of authority and interlocutors both, we may also take account of the deprivation of self-authorization these practices of nonpersuasion

---

69. Also *Phaedr.* 243e–244a, 252b; *Theaet.* 163d, 188d, 195e. Burnyeat, in *Theaetetus of Plato*, 61, also notes the presence of imaginary listeners in the *Theaetetus*.

condition. Exercising our readerly self-authorization by disidentifying with the dialogues' characters, we may learn to see through and also perhaps to resist exercises of deception and argumentative force. We might also and thereby create the conditions for our own "beautiful and free discussions."

Why does Socrates stay in the Piraeus? It's implausible to answer that he stays *because* he fears Polemarchus' threats (playful or not), for, as we saw in his engagement with Thrasymachus, he is not compelled or persuaded by fear. And yet Socrates, for his part, makes no attempt to persuade Polemarchus to let him go. Susan Bickford has noted that it's after Adeimantus intervenes, promising a torch race, that Socrates says no more about leaving.[70] Why? Socrates might stay in order to watch the torch race. But insofar as Adeimantus' offer of the torch race anticipates his fuller consequentialist account of justice in *Republic* 2, which Socrates rejects, it is unlikely that Socrates stays *because of* the promise of that reward. Socrates might be persuaded to stay because Glaucon and all the rest wish him to do so. Given, however, that Socrates' reply to Glaucon—"If it is so resolved, then we must"—mimics the language of the democratic assembly, and that Socrates opposes the equation of majoritarianism with justice, it is implausible that he stays simply because that's what *they* desire.[71]

What, then, persuades Socrates? Promised a torch race, Socrates asks: "On horseback? That is novel. Will they hold torches and pass them to one another while racing the horses, or what do you mean?" (328a). Apparently intrigued by the spectacle Adeimantus describes, Socrates seems to be trying to imagine it. Polemarchus' follow-up—"In relays and there will be an all-night festival that will be well worth seeing, *axion theasasthai*. After dinner, we'll go out to look at it, *theasometha*. We'll be joined there by many of the young men, and we'll talk"—fills in the picture of what might lie ahead for Socrates if he stays: novelty, sensory experiences, *erōs*, and conversation. That the torch race hasn't happened yet does not prevent Socrates from experiencing the spectacle in and through the power of words. Socrates and the rest never attend the torch race, but this confirms rather than undermines that power: occupied with the words that make up the text of the *Republic*, they participate in a world that is entirely built up and experienced through words, a kind of subjunctive world that arises from representation. So understood, what Adeimantus offers, anticipating his recourse to the poets in *Republic* 2 and his invocation of the

---

70. Bickford, *Dissonance of Democracy*, 3–4. Also Kastley, *Rhetoric of Plato's "Republic,"* 25.

71. Socrates' action here is thus to be distinguished from his responsiveness in speech to the brothers' desire discussed in chapter 3.

imaginary listener in *Republic* 6, is a glimpse of the play of imagination in persuasion, portrayed as bound with *aisthēsis* and *erōs*. Indeed, sensations, affects, and desire, as these are summoned by words and images (487e–488a), appear to be the conditions of persuasion. As we will see in this book's epilogue, they are also the conditions of justice when it belongs to what Socrates, in *Republic* 2, calls the most beautiful class (358a).

In the *Gorgias* (461d–462a), when Polus replaces Gorgias in discussion with Socrates, Socrates demands that Polus keep his speeches short and to the point. When Polus asks: "Won't I be free to say as much as I like?" Socrates replies that Polus has every reason to expect to speak freely, especially in Athens, "where there is more freedom, *exousia*, of speech than anywhere else in Greece." Socrates continues: "But look at it the other way. If you spoke at length and were unwilling to answer what you're asked, wouldn't I be in a terrible way if I'm not to have the freedom to stop listening to you and leave?" In contrast to Gorgias' definition of rhetoric, that is, to persuasion as a practice of asymmetrically distributed freedom, visible across the *Republic*, as we have seen as well, the *Gorgias* here, like *Republic* 6, describes a mode of engagement in which speakers and listeners are free to acquiesce or resist, to stay or to go.[72] Unlike force, sorcery, and deception, and unlike certain styles of argumentation, such freedom invites and depends upon active practices of listening, of speaking up, and also on the capacity to remain unpersuaded, which is to say, to resist. Persuasion thus seems to depend on something in the listening soul moving itself. That something, as I explore next, is desire.[73]

---

72. These possibilities play out in the dialogues: for just two examples, consider Socrates' threat to leave the discussion with Protagoras (*Prot.* 335a-e) and Callicles' refusal to continue discussing in the *Gorgias* (505e). Consider also Anytus and Euthyphro, who likewise walk away. For Socrates' underscoring of the degree to which the speaker is "always subject to the power of the listener," see *Prot.* 334d-e. For discussion, see Saxonhouse, *Free Speech and Democracy*, 194–95.

73. Mara, *Socrates' Discursive Democracy*, 11, similarly notes that "rhetoric would appear to be dispensable only under the humanly unattainable condition of the silence of desire."

CHAPTER 5

Erōs:
The Work of Desire

Erōs is the desire to give birth in beauty.
Symposium 206b

What "drives the tyrannical man on to *hubris*, murder, and eventually out-and-out tyranny," Socrates says in *Republic* 9, is the "internal tyrant" who rules his soul (572d–573d), whom Socrates names *erōs* (575a), desire, passion, love.[1] The actual tyrant, who is overrun while awake by desires that in most people are confined to their dream life (572b), Socrates calls *erōs* "incarnate" (573b). *Erōs*'s perils—in souls and/or cities—are on abundant display across the *Republic*: from the luxurious city full of "relishes" produced in response to Glaucon's *erōs* in *Republic* 2 (372c), a mirror of Athens in the 420s, in which, alongside *erōs*, injustice appears in the city for the first time (372e), to the regime changes described in *Republic* 8–9, where the more "the sting of desire" is dominant, the lower the constitutions rank (573a), to the tyrant, who, "always either master or slave, . . . never tastes freedom or true friendship" (576a).[2] The signal feature of *erōs* in all of these contexts is *pleonexia*, an overreaching driven by the desire for more, which first appears in *Republic* 1 as the defining characteristic of an unjust soul (349c, 350c).

Checks on desire are equally abundant. As we saw in chapter 3, the early education of *Republic* 2–3 is designed to produce rulers who are able to master not only their own desires but also those of the "ordinary majority" to bring

---

1. See, for discussion, Wohl, *Love among the Ruins*, 186.
2. See Hughes, *Hemlock Cup*, 92, who describes Athens in the 420s as becoming a mecca for "the best Chian chianti," "fine fabrics from the backs of the sheep of Miletus," "lapis from Afghanistan and saffron from the volcanic island of Thera," and peacocks. For "the sting of desire," see Bloom, "Interpretive Essay," in *Republic of Plato*, 422.

order to the perfect city, as described in *Republic* 4–5.³ The education to philosophy outlined in *Republic* 7, to which I turn in chapter 6, appears similarly to subjugate *erōs* to *logos*. We saw in chapter 2 that mimetic poets are ousted from the perfect city because their poetry "emancipates" (561a) and "thematizes" *erōs* (568a-b; 604b–605b).⁴ Based on this evidence, the *Republic* is often seen as presenting *erōs* as a problem for justice, and, indeed, for ethics, politics, and philosophy, and as offering as its solution the *kallipolis*, which, like the philosopher-kings' souls and their reason, is purged of the perils brought on the scene by *erōs*.⁵

The dialogue also displays a different attitude to *erōs*, however. In *Republic* 6, for example, Socrates describes the philosophical soul, moved by what he calls the *erōs* of truth (485b-c), in the following terms:

> Never losing his edge, never abandoning his passion, *erōtos*, he kept on going until he grasped, *hapsasthai*, the nature of what each thing itself is with that part of his soul—the part akin to it—which is equipped to grasp this kind of thing. And it was only when he used this part of his soul to get close to and be intimate, *plēsiasas kai migeis*, with what really is, so engendering understanding and truth, *gennēsas noun kai alētheian*, that he found knowledge, true life, nourishment, and relief from the pains of the soul's childbirth, *ōdinos*. (490b)⁶

The *erōs* of truth, Socrates says, leads the choir (490a-c). This implies that *erōs*, which, in philosophical souls is ruled over by virtue, wisdom, and/or reason, also somehow orients those same souls to philosophy in the first place.⁷

Acknowledging the centrality of *erōs* to the *Republic*'s account of philosophy, some scholars seek to dissociate the dialogue's philosophic *erōs* from the *erōs* that, according to historians and classicists, characterized both tyranny and later fifth-century Athenian imperial democracy alike. Following what Ian Morris

---

3. Tecusan, "*Logos Sympotikos*," 239.

4. For "emancipate" and "thematize," see Bloom, "Interpretive Essay," in *Republic of Plato*, 347, 421, 422.

5. Rosen, *Plato's "Symposium*," 6: "Eros appears in human form in the *Republic* only to be criticized."

6. The *Republic*'s reproductive imagery resonates powerfully with similar language in the *Symposium* and has generated valuable commentary: see, e.g., Hobbs, "Female Imagery in Plato," 252–57; Saxonhouse, *Fear of Diversity*, chaps. 6–7.

7. For the idea that *erōs* is "ruled over" by virtue, wisdom, and/or reason, see Irwin, *Plato's Moral Theory*, 237–41; Zuckert, *Plato's Philosophers*, 201.

describes as "the end of restraint c. 425 B.C.," Athenian democracy exemplified a desire to possess people(s) and cities with a view to power, glory, and honor.[8] In Aristophanes' *Frogs*, performed in 405, Dionysus describes in similar terms the *erōs* of the *dēmos* for Alcibiades, the prominent Athenian statesman and general: they "long for him and hate him and want to possess him" (1425).[9] The desire of possession also appears to characterize Alcibiades himself, whose alleged profanation of the mysteries in 416 Mark Munn describes as an "arrogance of appropriation."[10] With the figure of *erōs* emblazoned on his shield and exhibiting sexual and material appetites more commonly associated with tyrants, Alcibiades, who changed his political allegiance multiple times over the course of the Peloponnesian War, loved and hated and wanted to possess other cities, the Athenian *dēmos*, and also, if we are to believe the Alcibiades of Plato's *Symposium*, Socrates.[11] Alcibiades' *erōs* is, writ small, the *erōs* of both tyranny and Athenian imperial democracy. There is good reason to be wary of this *erōs*.

In order to "purify" or "purge" *erōs* of its possessive element, the *Republic*, according to Paul Ludwig, for example, introduces an "impersonal" *erōs*.[12] Ludwig claims that "owing to the nature of the objects [philosophers] desire," namely, the ideas, which are "common property for anyone who wants them and has the capacity," "impersonal" or "philosophical" *erōs* is detachable from ownership.[13] Along similar lines, other scholars treat the *Republic*'s philosophical *erōs* as the "rational desire for what is good," located in and/

---

8. Morris is cited in Munn, *School of History*, 52, who, at 118–19 and 374 n. 31, describes "the tyranny of Athens . . . [as] exercised over subject-states, although the image of *Demos* in the *Knights* also implies tyranny over domestic subjects." For evidence of Athenian democracy qua tyranny, see Thuc. 1.122.3, 1.124.3, 2.63.2, 3.37.2, 6.85.1; Ar. *Knights* 1111–14, cited in Munn, 76. On the *dēmos* as tyrant, see Morgan, *Popular Tyranny*. In *Love among the Ruins*, 182–83, 195–96, Wohl elucidates what she calls the master/slave dialectic at play in both the *erōs* of tyranny and that of fifth-century imperial democratic Athens.

9. Cited and discussed in Wohl, *Love among the Ruins*, 144 ff.; and Nussbaum, *Fragility of Goodness*, 169 ff. On the paradoxical cooperation of love and hate in *erōs*, see Carson, *Eros*.

10. Munn, *School of History*, 107.

11. Socrates in *Alcibiades 1*, 103c, 105a, characterizes Alcibiades' *erōs* as a perpetual desire to have more, *pleonexia*. On Alcibiades' *pleonexia*, see also Wohl, *Love among the Ruins*, 143–44; Munn, *School of History*, 111; and Balot, *Greed and Injustice in Classical Athens*, 166–72. See also Farenga, "Paradigmatic Tyrant."

12. Ludwig, "Eros in the *Republic*," 209–24.

13. Ibid.

or identified as "the rational part of the soul," specifically *to logistikon*, the calculating part,[14] and/or as "a psychological, and even physiological, drive to learn," a natural element of some souls that channels desires away from the appetitive and toward philosophy or toward the good.[15]

These approaches set out to give broad scope to the play of *erōs* in the *Republic*. They, nonetheless, despite their important differences, substantially and similarly limit *erōs*'s effects. Naturalized *erōs* is partnered with and subordinated to virtue and thereby made safe for philosophy, ethics, and politics. Rationalized *erōs*, under whatever description, is already safe because assimilated to or allied with reason's rule. By naturalizing and/or rationalizing *erōs*, these approaches revalue *erōs* so it can become its own solution. In so doing, however, they approximate the very interpretations they position themselves against, interpretations that, despite passages like those in *Republic* 6, take the *Republic*, in the name of philosophy, to eradicate appetitive influences altogether and also and for that reason to sublimate *erōs*, or to transform the *erōs* of philosophy into *philia* (hence *philo-sophia*), a mode of "Platonic" love they see as "higher" than *erōs* owing to its evacuation of passionate desire.[16]

There are good reasons to take the *Republic* to be anxious about passionate desire. As noted, the dialogue makes plain that *erōs* may just as soon, and often sooner, channel toward vice and exercises of power without limits as it will toward truth and the good. And yet the *Republic* also seems to represent a passionate, grasping, and productive *erōs* as the condition of philosophy. This chapter explores *that erōs*. I argue that even as the *Republic* proliferates strategies for obviating the perils of *erōs* characteristic of tyranny and fifth-century Athenian imperial democracy alike, it also underscores the dangers of succeeding at such strategies. In my view, the *Republic* brings to appearance the risks associated with pleonectic *erōs* and also makes manifest the costs of seeking to guarantee against such risks. The *kallipolis*, its philosopher-kings, and their knowledge—whether exemplifications of naturalized and/or rationalized

---

14. See Kahn, "Plato's Theory of Desire," 80; also 90, 92; see also Kahn, *Plato and the Socratic Dialogue*, 261; Cooper, "Plato's Theory of Human Motivation," 8; Hobbs, "Plato and the England Riots."

15. The quoted phrase and "toward philosophy" are from Lane, "Virtue as the Love of Knowledge," 45; "toward the good" is from Zuckert, *Plato's Philosophers*, 199.

16. On Plato's sublimation of *erōs* in the *Republic*, see Nussbaum, *Fragility of Goodness*, 155, and chap. 5 more generally. On *erōs* as a mode of *philia*, see Hyland, "Eros, Epithumia, and Philia in Plato," 37–38.

erōs, or as purged of *erōs*—represent the dangers of that guarantee. As we will see, to purge, rationalize, or naturalize *erōs* is to deprive the *Republic*'s philosophy and its associated ethics and politics of their signal motivator.[17]

PHILOSOPHER-KINGS, PHILOSOPHERS BY NATURE, PHILOSOPHICAL EROTICS

Republic 6 opens with Socrates confirming with Glaucon that "after a long and weary and winding way" their discussion "has at last made clear who are the philosophers or lovers of wisdom and who are not" (484a). Their "winding way" was necessary in order to justify the "third wave" Socrates presented in *Republic* 5, namely, that there will be "no end to suffering" unless "either philosophers become kings in our cities, or the people who are now called kings and rulers become real, true philosophers—unless there is an amalgamation of political power and philosophy" (473c-e). Summing up his justification, Socrates says, now in conversation with Adeimantus:

> Truth compelled, *hupo talēthous ēnangkasmenoi*, us to say that no city, constitution, or individual man will ever become perfect until either some chance necessity compels, *anangkē tis ek tuchēs peribalē[i]s*, the few uncorrupted philosophers who are now called useless, *achrēstois*, to care for the city, whether they want to or not, and compels the city to obey them, or until some divine inspiration, a genuine passion for true philosophy, *alēthinēs philosophias alēthinos erōs*, takes possession either of the sons of those in positions of authority or sole rule, or the actual holders of those positions. (499b-c)

Prompted by Socrates, Adeimantus expresses skepticism that the many will endorse either account of rule. Socrates admonishes him, saying:

> If instead of indulging your love of victory, *philonikōn*, at their expense you soothe, *paramuthoumenos*, them and try to remove their slanderous prejudice against the love of learning, by pointing out what you mean by a philosopher and by defining the philosophic nature and way of life . . . they'll realize that you don't mean the same people they do. (499e)

---

17. See also McCoy, *Plato on the Rhetoric of Philosophers and Sophists*, 19, who argues that "the *Republic*, *Phaedrus*, and *Symposium* all place love rather than knowledge of the forms at the heart of philosophy."

The larger context of this passage suggests that the many mistake sophists for philosophers (492a–493e, 495c–496a).

Less transparent is what Socrates, Glaucon, and Adeimantus mean by "a philosopher" and/or what the dialogue may mean. These are questions worth asking because, although Socrates confirmed at the start of *Republic* 6 that the question of who is a philosopher had been settled (484a), he has by this point reopened it at least three times (484a, 486e, 488e). As if to underscore the ongoing provisionality of what Socrates and the brothers come up with in *Republic* 6, Socrates asks the same question again in *Republic* 7 (521c). This is not an abstract question. Against the backdrop of the third wave, at stake, as Socrates indicates at the start of *Republic* 6, is who should be "leaders in a city" (484b).

What is meant by "a philosopher"? By this point, three descriptions have emerged in *Republic* 6: first, those "capable of apprehending what is eternal and unchanging" (484b) and, having fixed "their eyes on the absolute truth, and always with reference to that ideal and in the exactest possible contemplation of it, establish in this world the laws of the beautiful, the just, and the good" (484c-d); second, those who are neither "lovers of money" nor "braggarts" nor "cowards" nor "unsociable" nor "savage" nor "unjust," but are instead "orderly" and "gentle" and graced "by nature" with magnificence, memory, measure, and aptness to learn (486b, 487a, 490c); and third, those whose souls are led by an *erōs* for truth (490a, c). The first description fits the philosopher-kings introduced in *Republic* 5; the second characterizes those Socrates dubs "philosophers by nature"; the third I'll call erotic philosophers or philosophical erotics.[18]

At issue in *Republic* 6, it seems, is whether the qualities associated with these three kinds of philosopher can combine in the same person (485a). Thus, it might be expected that Socrates' summary justification of who qualifies to lead the city in the passage quoted above (499a-c) would point to something like the "erotic philosopher-kings by nature." Socrates' summary appears instead to leave to one side philosophers by nature, and to offer as alternative candidates for rule "the few uncorrupted philosophers who are now called useless," on the one hand, and, on the other, those who are inspired by a genuine passion for true philosophy.

---

18. Weiss, *Philosophers in the "Republic,"* calls the first, philosophers by design; and the second, philosophers by nature. I agree with and use her treatment of the first in the following pages. For my differences with her treatment of the philosophers by nature, see Frank, "By Nature and by Design," which I also draw on below. In Weiss' view, Socrates himself presents a third paradigm of philosophy. For discussion, see Schlosser, review of *Philosophers in the "Republic."*

Who are "the few uncorrupted philosophers who are now called useless," and why might Socrates counterpose them to those who are inspired by a genuine passion for true philosophy? The language of compulsion Socrates uses to describe the first candidates for rule identifies them as the philosopher-kings, who, as discussed in earlier chapters, are characterized repeatedly across the *Republic* as compelled. The philosopher-kings, as we saw in chapter 4, "compel the city to obey them" by way of the law of the *kallipolis* combining persuasion with force (519e). *Republic* 7's cave allegory presents the philosophers-to-be-kings as "released from their chains" and "compelled" by a series of exercises of force to "stand up, turn his head, start walking, and look towards the light" (515c-e). With no apparent authors, these compulsions appear to be the "chance necessities" Socrates refers to in his summary. Compelled by the founders of the perfect city to return to the cave to rule in order to repay the debt they owe to the city (519d–520d), the philosopher-kings rule "whether they want to or not."[19]

Why present the philosopher-kings as *alternative* candidates for rule to those possessed by a genuine passion for true philosophy, the philosophers characterized under the third description above as souls led by an *erōs* for truth? Because, in the *Republic*'s depiction, the philosopher-kings turn out to be devoid of such passion. Compelled entirely from without, these "philosophers by design," as Roslyn Weiss calls them, have, as she puts it, "nothing internal to propel them" toward philosophy.[20] Compelled by their education to love philosophy, compelled by the just-mentioned "chance necessities" to take the final ascent to the good, and "compelled to order their own souls" by the institutions of the *kallipolis*,[21] philosopher-kings are also regulated by the "geometric necessity" of the *kallipolis*'s eugenics laws (458d), which seeks to thwart their sexual passion, already ostensibly "mastered" by their compelling *to logistikon*, as we saw in chapter 3.[22] If the *erōs* of truth characteristic of

19. On the conspicuously problematic nature of the argument compelling the philosophers to return to the city to rule and its resemblance to the definition of justice Socrates rejects in *Republic* 1, see Weiss, *Philosophers in the "Republic,"* 98–107, 114; and Kastley, *Rhetoric of Plato's "Republic,"* chap. 8.
20. Weiss, *Philosophers in the "Republic,"* 109.
21. Ibid., 70, 74–77, 53, 69–72, 81.
22. In *Fear of Diversity*, 154, Saxonhouse notes that after having eliminated possessiveness from the *kallipolis*, Socrates nonetheless "relies on the citizens' eroticism . . . for the sexuality necessary to repopulate the city" when he treats women as "prizes for the man who has performed well in battle." See Halliwell, in *Plato: Republic 5*, for the reappearances of *erōs* in *Republic* 5.

philosophy is the passionate *erōs* Socrates describes in *Republic* 6 (490b), then that *erōs* appears to be unavailable to the philosopher-kings.

After Socrates presents rule by compulsion, Adeimantus agrees that such rule will, as Socrates puts it, "altogether tame and convince" the imaginary interlocutors who were brought on scene to challenge the philosophers-to-be-kings when they were first introduced (501a). The imaginary interlocutors are tamed and convinced "so that for very shame, if for no other reason, they may assent" (501e–502a). This language of taming and shaming, which resonates with the forceful tactics Socrates used himself and also experienced in his discussion with Thrasymachus in *Republic* 1, invites strict scrutiny. It reflects, at the rhetorical level, the compulsion being described at the political level as a mode of rule. When, as discussed in chapter 4, acquiescence is thus secured, however, interlocutors and readers should think twice about the argument on offer. Socrates has already invited Glaucon and Adeimantus to think twice, and indeed three times, by asking repeatedly "who is the philosopher." They do not. And yet, despite the "assent" of the imaginary interlocutors to rule by philosopher-kings, and the assent of the brothers as well, Socrates, for the second time in *Republic* 6, reopens the question.

Moving on as if to consider the alternative candidates for rule he had named, that is, those inspired by a genuine passion for true philosophy, Socrates brings back into the picture the philosophers by nature, asking: "Will anyone contend that there is no chance that the offspring of kings and rulers should be born with the philosophic nature?" (502a). Are, then, philosophers by nature and erotic philosophers one and the same? Weiss thinks so, for she takes the *erōs* that moves the philosophic soul to be granted by nature.[23] I'm not sure. *Adeimantus* may accept Socrates' claims that it is not impossible that "over the course of time" one or all offspring born with a philosophic nature could be saved from corruption, that the "occurrence of one such is enough, if he has a state which obeys him, *polin echōn peithomenēn*," and that "it's not impossible that citizens would be content" with the laws and institutions ordained by such a one (502b-c). But perhaps he should not. For Socrates exposes this mode of rule as at best a kingship, if the one "saved" is "tamed" by *logos* or partnered with virtue, but also, perhaps, a tyranny, because, as Socrates has noted pages before, the "natural" virtues can, in the absence of *erōs* and "when environment and nurture are bad" (495a), corrupt the philosophic nature.

Socrates goes on to say that "it is from men of this type," namely, philosophic natures, "that those spring who do the greatest harm to communities

---

23. Weiss, *Philosophers in the "Republic,"* 12, 84.

and individuals" (495a). Because in the absence of an *erōs* for truth the gifts of nature will tend "to corrupt the soul" and "divert it from philosophy" (491b), philosophers by nature will be true philosophers, hence fit for rule, only when *erōs* already guides their nature. Nature seems to be the helpmate of *erōs*, not the other way around. The brothers are silent in the face of the possibility that philosophers by nature may rule as tyrants. That might be because Socrates' profile of the philosophers by nature offers a mirror to *them*. Neither "lovers of money" nor "braggarts," "cowards," "unsociable," "savage," or "unjust," but instead "orderly" and "gentle," and graced "by nature" with magnificence, memory, measure, and aptness to learn (486b, 487a, 490c), philosophers by nature possess the characteristics of aristocratic Athenian gentlemen, the "*kaloi kagathoi*."[24]

Whether Glaucon and Adeimantus' silence signals their acquiescence to and/or desire for rule by philosophers by nature, or they have been tamed by Socrates' compelling justification of rule by philosopher-kings, or for some other reason, Socrates does not return to the philosopher candidates moved by the true *erōs* for true philosophy in *Republic* 6. Against the backdrop of the threat of tyranny associated with philosophers by nature and the perils of compulsion associated with philosopher-kings, however, the erotic candidates for philosophical rule repay scrutiny. Socrates appears to speak on behalf of these candidates in the passage directly following his summary justification (499a-c). Describing the compelled and compelling philosophers as populating a "boundless past" or "some outlandish country, presumably, far removed from our view," Socrates highlights the temporal and spatial *distance* of philosopher-kings from the discussion at hand. He continues:

> There is one thing we shall be prepared to take up the cudgels over: it is when the Muse of Philosophy is mistress in the city, *hotan hautē hē Mousa poleōs enkratēs genētai*, that the constitution, *politeia*, we have described either has existed, or does exist, or will exist. It's not impossible, *adunatos*, for her to be mistress, so we are not talking about impossibilities, *adunata*. That it is difficult, we would none of us deny. (499c-d)

Socrates says he is prepared to go to bat now for a regime guided by the muse of philosophy. If, as I argued in chapters 1 and 2, the muse of the *Republic*'s philosophy is mimetic poetry, then Socrates' turn here to the constitution guided

---

24. For the aristocratic nature of these virtues and of Socrates' interlocutors, see Blondell, *Play of Character*, 203.

by that muse makes sense. For, unlike philosopher-kings, the mimetic artist, Socrates says in *Republic* 10, is not compelled by anyone or anything (601e–602a). *Mimēsis* is rather "a form of play, *paidian*" (602b),[25] one that, both the *Republic* (561a, 603b) and the *Symposium* (209b) tell us, involves *erōs*.

Establishing the muse of philosophy as mistress in the city calls for play. It also calls for work: as we saw in chapters 1 and 2, there is nothing "quick and easy" about the practices of political and self-constitution prompted by mimetic poetry. "That it is difficult," Socrates says in *Republic* 6, "we would none of us deny" (499d). Who can do this "difficult" work and thereby, as Socrates suggests here, qualify for philosophical rule? Not the philosophers-to-be-kings, whose absence of *erōs* is disqualifying. Perhaps, then, it is those who Socrates twice presents as their alternative, namely, "the people who are now called kings and rulers," the "actual holders of positions of authority and their sons," if, that is, they are possessed by a genuine passion for true philosophy (473d, 499c). Who are *these* candidates for rule? The "actual holders of positions of authority and their sons" in fifth-century Athens when the *Republic* is set are the people of Athens. Might Socrates be suggesting that the people qualify for philosophical rule?

That cannot be. How can the people, driven by their imperial democratic, which is to say, as we have seen, tyrannical *erōs*, be candidates for philosophical rule? Recall Socrates' response to Adeimantus' skepticism about the many. When Adeimantus doubts the capacity of the many to accept the candidates for philosophical rule Socrates offers, Socrates admonishes him, saying that rather than indulging his love of victory at the expense of the many, Adeimantus should try to remove the slanderous prejudice of the many against the love of learning (499e). In this passage, Socrates speaks to Adeimantus about the prejudice of the people. He also speaks to Adeimantus and Glaucon about their own prejudice, and to the *Republic*'s readers as well. Socrates' point seems to be that if the people of Athens could only learn to love learning, and if the brothers could only learn to love learning more than they currently love power, glory, and reputation, and if the dialogue's readers could learn to do all of the above, then they/we could all become true philosophers.

Learning to love learning more than honor, power, glory, and reputation is no more quick and easy than acquiring mimetic knowledge. Letting go of prejudices is not quick and easy either, especially when, as it turns out, the people were right to be suspicious of rule by philosopher-kings, and, as we saw, there is reason, too, for them to fear rule by philosophic natures. Learning

---

25. See Freydberg, *Play of the Platonic Dialogues*.

to love learning can be all the more difficult when, as under the conditions of fifth-century Athenian democratic imperialism, love of profit, typically associated with the democratic many, and love of honor, typically associated with the aristocratic few, coalesced and reinforced one another in the desire to possess other cities, peoples, and things described at the start of this chapter. Orienting *erōs* away from love of honor and/or profit and to love of learning may be "difficult," but, as Socrates repeats three times, it is not impossible, *adunaton* (499b, 499d). In light of the alternatives, it may well be "the minimum change," ideally, "the single change," or "failing that, two, and failing that, as few as possible in number and as small as possible in impact" (473b), that Socrates recommends in *Republic* 5. How might the people, the brothers, and the dialogue's readers transition from what Stanley Rosen has called "the Eris [strife, discord] of war" to "the Eros of philosophy"?[26] Plato's *Symposium* suggests that for that transition there may be no better helpmate than *erōs* itself.

DESIRING POSSESSION

Staging the *erōs* of imperial democratic Athens in an aristocratic setting, the *Symposium* brings to light the risks posed to the *erōs* of philosophy by the love of honor, victory, and/or profit. Speaking first, Phaedrus praises *erōs* and specifically paiderastic *erōs*—the love between an active, older, generally aristocratic male lover and a younger passive male beloved whom the lover socialized into practices of Athenian citizenship—for guarding against shameful cowardice and for producing courage on the battlefield and hence military power and glory for Athens (*Symp.* 178e–179b).[27] Speaking next, Pausanias praises paiderastic *erōs* of the "higher" or "Uranial" sort (180d) for producing courage, friendship, and virtue (182b-c, 184c-e, 185b), instrumental to the social and political life of Athens (185c). Eryximachus, for his part, celebrates *erōs* for bringing good fortune and harmony to human society and to the cosmos (188d). Attributing to *erōs* the power of curing human incompleteness, which he calls "the wound of human nature" (191d, 189d), Aristophanes celebrates paiderastic *erōs* in particular for producing powerful politicians (191d–192c). In bringing these benefits, the encomiasts maintain, *erōs* produces honor (178d,

---

26. Rosen, *Plato's "Symposium,"* 6.

27. On the institution of *paiderastia*, see Brisson, "Agathon, Pausanias, and Diotima"; see also Monoson, *Plato's Democratic Entanglements*, chaps. 3, 7; Dover, *Greek Homosexuality*; Halperin, *One Hundred Years of Homosexuality*; and Winkler, *Constraints of Desire*.

179a, 180a-b, 185b). It is, as Phaedrus puts it, "the cause of our highest good" (178c), namely, as the others agree, happiness (188d, 189d, 193b, d).

Speaking last but for Socrates, Agathon claims that "all of those who have spoken before me did not so much celebrate the god [Eros] as congratulate human beings on the good things that come to them from the god. But who it is who gave these gifts, what he is like—no one has spoken about that" (194e-195a). Agathon criticizes the other encomiasts for focusing on *erōs* as a means for securing ends like military success, honor, profit, harmony, and for neglecting to ask what/who Eros is. Agathon is on to something. With Phaedrus, the "father of the *logos*" (177d), setting the terms for the symposiasts' encomia, and, as Mary Nichols notes, with "*chrestos* appear[ing] to be Phaedrus' favorite word of praise," the gold standard for *erōs* across the encomia is what is "worthy" or "good" in the register of instrumentality.[28] Agathon, focusing, by contrast, on who Eros is, celebrates the god for being young (195c), delicate (196a), moderate (196c), just and good (196b-c), brave (196d), wise (196e), and beautiful. When Socrates takes his turn to speak, he commends both the beauty of Agathon's speech and also its focus on the sort of being *erōs* is before addressing *erōs*'s gifts (198b-c). It's not that Socrates accepts Agathon's characterization of *erōs*, however. On the contrary, he finds it too beautiful. As from the other encomiasts, Socrates says that from Agathon he has heard only the "highest and fairest qualities, whether the case was so or not" (198e).

Receiving permission from Phaedrus to put "some little questions to Agathon" (199b), Socrates presses two aspects of Agathon's speech. Bringing into play the work of necessity, *anangkē*, which Agathon had only opposed to *erōs* (195c, 197b), and taking issue with Agathon's characterization of *erōs* in substance, Socrates asks whether "not as a likelihood, but as a necessity, *anangkē*, consider if the desiring subject must have desire for something it lacks, and again, no desire if it has no lack, *epithumein hou endees estin, ē mē epithumein, ean mē endees ē[i]*" (200b). Socrates, for his part, is "perfectly sure it is a necessity, *anangkē*," for "all who feel desire feel it for what is not at hand and not present, what he does not have, and what he is not, and that of which he is in need; for such are the objects of desire and love" (200e). Establishing in discussion with Agathon that, if *erōs* desires beauty, justice, virtue, and wisdom, the god cannot already be beautiful, just, virtuous, wise, and so on, Socrates brings to light that *erōs* necessarily depends on lack. Agathon agrees (200b), admits to having been confused (201b), and, together, Socrates

---

28. Nichols, *Socrates on Friendship and Community*, 37.

and Agathon settle on the "truth" that if Eros "lacks beautiful things and good things are beautiful things, he must lack good things too" (201c-d).[29]

Socrates' engagement with Agathon makes manifest that *erōs* involves necessity, *anangkē*, the same word that described the compulsion of the philosopher-kings in the *Republic*. If, however, the philosopher-kings, as we saw, are compelled from without, the necessity characteristic of *erōs*, as we will see below, is of a different kind. Socrates' engagement with Agathon also makes manifest that possession, the achievement of satisfaction in relation to the desired object, brings with it the end of that desire, which is to say (tautologically) that achieving the end of desire is achieving the end of desire. As Leo Strauss puts it, "The copresence of desire and satisfaction is impossible."[30] If this is true, then the *erōs* lauded by Agathon's speech and the *erōs* eulogized by the earlier encomiasts not only differ but are similar as well. Whether a cause of the possession of honor, victory, and harmony, as the early encomiasts claim, or already in possession of the virtues and goods, as Agathon had claimed, *erōs*, under both descriptions, brings about its own negation. The tone and style of the speeches of the early encomiasts reflect this outcome. Rosen has noted that they are characterized "by a sober and rational effort to win pleasure through a detachment—or freedom—from Eros."[31] By praising *erōs* as a means to particular ends and practicing *erōs* in this way as well, these encomiasts, like Lysias in the *Phaedrus*, are what we might call technicians of *erōs* or eroticians.

For many readers, Diotima's speech stands as a corrective to the accounts of *erōs* presented in the other encomia.[32] Unlike them, her speech gives an account of the being of *erōs* (201d-206a), and, unlike them, it orients *erōs* to goods of the soul rather than to goods like military success or political power (206b-212a). These differences are exemplified in the part of her speech sometimes dubbed the "ladder of love." In my view, by contrast, Socrates presents Diotima's ladder of love to make manifest the ways in which its account of philosophical *erōs*, like the *erōs* of the other symposiasts, also brings about its own negation. I make this case in the following section, turning after that to what I take to be the dialogue's alternate account of philosophical *erōs*, which I find in Socrates' presentation of Diotima's genealogy of Eros as the child of Poros, resource, and Penia, need (203b-d).

---

29. For valuable discussion, see Miller, *Diotima at the Barricades*, 251–66.
30. Strauss, *On Plato's "Symposium,"* 182.
31. Rosen, *Plato's "Symposium,"* 2nd ed., 34.
32. Neumann, "Diotima's Concept of Love," is an exception.

LADDERS, IMMORTALITY, INSTRUMENTALITY

On Diotima's account of the ladder of love, man ascends from desiring particular beautiful things to beautiful learning, finally coming to know, at the topmost rung of the ladder, "the very essence of beauty" (211c). Moving from bodily generation to that of the soul, *erōs* reaches for the "ever existent," "certain and singular," "independent" (211b) knowledge of the beautiful, which neither comes into being nor perishes, neither waxes nor wanes (211a-d), and is altogether beautiful and in no part ugly (206c, 209b, 211a). The vision of beauty reached by climbing the ladder of love enables the one who has it, by way of his "resourcefulness" and without ever "begetting upon the ugly" (209b), to become "immortal" (212a). On its way up the ladder, *erōs* produces among its "offspring" poetry and laws (209d), which, fair and deathless (209c), "procure for [their makers] a glory immortally renewed in the memory of men" (209d, 208e). Diotima says that all are "in love with what is immortal, *tou ... athanatou erōsin*" (208e), and "a mortal thing partakes of immortality, both in its body and in all other respects," by what she names "the device, *mēchanē*," of *erōs*. "By no other means can it be done" (208b).

If there are, as noted, important differences between Diotima's account of *erōs* and the *erōs* of the earlier encomiasts, there are also noteworthy parallels. Her speech, like theirs, especially that of Pausanias, quantifies and compares amounts of *erōs* based on units of value (210a-d). The style of her speech resonates in rhythm and language with some of the other speeches, which, in turn, borrow in their style and content from Prodicus and Hippias, famed sophists, who, in the *Protagoras*, are depicted as mentors of Agathon and Pausanias, Phaedrus and Eryximachus, respectively (315b-d).[33] Perhaps this is why Socrates refers to Diotima as "a perfect sophist" (208c), an authoritative teacher who offers a program of education (209a-c) that Daniel Boyarin has called "as penetrative and hierarchical as Pausanian pederasty."[34]

Moreover, in taking *erōs* to secure immortality, Diotima, like the other encomiasts, treats *erōs* as a means.[35] Indeed, the ladder of love portion of Diotima's

---

33. For discussion and sources, see Bury, *Symposium of Plato*, 125.

34. Boyarin, *Socrates and the Fat Rabbis*, 310. Identifying Plato with Diotima, Boyarin offers this as a critique of Plato. I agree with this assessment of the ladder of love but, refusing to treat Diotima as speaking for Plato, I take Plato to present the ladder of love account of philosophical *erōs* not to advocate for it but rather, as we will see, to prompt a critical distance from it.

35. Neumann, "Diotima's Concept of Love," 44, 45, 47, also argues that Diotima is an instrumentalist: as he puts it, for Diotima, "knowledge, even of absolute beauty, is a tool for gaining undying fame" (44).

speech is explicitly signaled as her response to Socrates' question of *erōs*'s use, *chreian* (204c). Like the earlier encomiasts, Diotima indexes *erōs* as a means to the love of honor and glory, a similarity to which Plato prompts attention by having her offer Alcestis and Achilles as examples of this *erōs* (208d), as had Phaedrus (179b–180b). Perhaps it is in order to highlight these similarities between her ladder of love and the speeches of the earlier encomiasts that Diotima refers to "the men around" Socrates as the point of departure for her account of the love of honor (208c). Whether we take Diotima to be referring to "the men around" Socrates at the time of the discussion he claims to be reporting from years earlier, or to the encomiasts present at Agathon's symposium, these men, all aristocratic democrats, love *erōs* as a means to the end of honor, which they treat, once secured, as a settled possession.

On the ladder of love, *erōs* is a means not only to the end of honor but to the end of immortality, which, once secured, becomes itself a settled possession as well. As Diotima puts it, he who ascends the ladder of love becomes, "above all men," immortal (212a). If, as discussed earlier, "the copresence of desire and satisfaction is impossible," then to achieve the end of *erōs*, whether that be honor or immortality, is to bring about the end of *erōs*. In Diotima's speech, as in the speeches of the early encomiasts, *erōs*'s instrumentality effects its negation. Marking the continuities between Diotima's speech and those of the other symposiasts, Socrates heaps praise on Diotima and her speech (206b, 207c, 208c) in ways that mirror what scholars uniformly call his "ironic praise" of the other encomiasts.

John Cooper remarks that "Diotima seems an invention, contrived by Socrates (and Plato) to distance Socrates in his report of [her speech] from what she says."[36] Scholars sometimes read this distance as a function of Socrates' youth and inexperience compared with Diotima's age and wisdom and philosophical prowess, and as putting the lie to claims Socrates makes in the *Sympoisum* on behalf of his own expertise in love matters (177e, 198d). On such readings, Diotima is sometimes treated as speaking for Plato.[37] For reasons already adduced, I reject any identification of Diotima with Plato. I nonetheless

36. See his short introduction to the *Symposium* in *Plato: Complete Works*, 457.
37. That Diotima's speech represents the philosophy of the dialogue is a dominant position in the scholarship, though scholars differ on whether Diotima represents Plato's philosophy or that of the mature Socrates: see, e.g., Bury, *Symposium of Plato*, xxxix, who says that "it is only for the purpose of literary art that Diotima here supplants the Platonic Socrates: she is presented, by a fiction, as his instructor, whereas in fact she merely gives utterance to his own thoughts." On Diotima-as-Plato, see Rosen, *Plato's "Symposium,"* 197–277. An important exception is Belfiore, *Socrates' Daimonic Art*, pt. 2, to which my discussion of the *Symposium* is indebted.

agree with Cooper that Plato presents Diotima as a contrivance, a point I return to below. As we have seen, her ladder of love account of *erōs* is also called a contrivance, *mēchanē* (208b). I suggest next that, as with the contrivances that appear across the *Republic*, Plato has Diotima call her account of *erōs* a contrivance to mark his distance from her ladder of love and to prompt readers, too, to take a critical distance from its *erōs*.[38]

Consider that before she offers the ladder of love, Diotima, in conversation with Socrates about the desire for good and/or beautiful things (204d-e), turns the question of that desire into a question of possession: "What will he have who gets good things?" Together, Socrates and Diotima answer, "happiness," which they call a desire "common to all mankind" (205a) to possess the good forever (206a). Having turned the desire for good things into a desire for the good, Diotima then translates the desire for the good into love of honor, as noted above, and, by way of the ladder of love, as we saw, into the desire for immortality (207a). Even before Diotima's questionable translation of love of the good into honor, Socrates begins to wonder. He wonders about Diotima's claim that "all men love the same things always," when she explains this as singling "out a certain form of love, and applying thereto the name of the whole," which "we call love, *erōs*" (205b). Then, and each time he expresses wonder or uncertainty thereafter (206b, 208c), Diotima responds by advising Socrates to cease to wonder (205b, 207c, 208b), to be certain (208c). If, as Socrates says in the *Theaetetus*, wonder is the only beginning of philosophy (155d), then Socrates' wonder should prompt readers to wonder, along with him, about the claims that provoke his wonder.[39] Is the question of the desire for good and/or beautiful things a question of possession? What is the relation between the desire for good and/or beautiful things and the desire for the good and/or the beautiful? Is happiness a desire to possess the good forever? Is that a desire "common to all mankind"?

That Diotima actively thwarts Socrates' wonder about these matters should give readers reason to wonder about her practice of philosophy as well, and also about the *erōs* it will generate. Do "all men love the same things always"? Is *erōs* a certain form that applies to the name of the whole? Is the desire to possess the good forever a desire for honor and/or immortality? Is philosophical *erōs* an *erōs* for nonsensual essences or forms? Or, as the depiction of her

---

38. Contrivances appear in Aristophanes' speech in the *Symposium* (190c, 191b) as well.

39. For the philosophy of Plato's dialogues as an "interrogative stance" or a stance of wonder, see Hyland, *Virtue of Philosophy*, 16.

practice of philosophy here suggests, might Diotima orient to an *erōs* and also and thereby to a philosophy that spells the death of both?[40] What if, in other words, the description of Diotima as seeking to "teach" Socrates to "become a master of love matters, *deinos . . . ta erōtika*" (207c), is a prompt not to accept her status and authority in matters of *erōs* and its philosophy but instead to be wary of the very "mastery" she seeks to teach?

Inviting precisely these questions, Diotima says: "If you believe that love is by nature bent on what we have repeatedly admitted, then you may cease to wonder" (207c). *If* you believe that *erōs* desires essences characteristic of immortal forms, *then* you may cease to wonder. Being certain, you will cease to desire to know, that is, you will cease to be philosophical. What is the problem with the "ever existent," "certain and singular," "independent" (211b) knowledge of the beautiful, which neither comes into being nor perishes, neither waxes nor wanes (211a-d), and is altogether beautiful and in no part ugly (206c, 209b, 211a), that characterizes the *erōs* presented at the top of the ladder of love? The problem is that, insofar as the immortality Diotima claims to be the cause and effect of *erōs* is godlike, self-sufficient, unchanging, and fully knowing, it already possesses everything it desires. Like the Eros of Agathon's speech, and the very opposite of the *erōs* Diotima describes in the genealogy she offers in the early part of her speech, to which I turn below, the *erōs* of the ladder of love denies the "necessity" of lack for the being of desire about which Agathon and Socrates earlier agreed (201a-201c). And that brings about not only the end of *erōs* but the end of philosophy.

Socrates concludes his account of Diotima's speech saying, "I myself am persuaded, *pepeismai d'ego*; and being so persuaded, *pepeismenos*, I try also to persuade, *peithein*, others" (212b).[41] If, as I have been arguing, the *Symposium* seeks to prompt distance from the ladder of love, this is an odd thing for Socrates to say. Notice that Socrates uses the ambiguous middle/passive voice to describe his own persuasion. As discussed in chapter 4, that could mean that Socrates participated in his own persuasion and was thus truly persuaded, or it could signify that he was only passively persuaded, that is, not truly persuaded by, but instead made to "obey . . . believe, trust in," Diotima's account of *erōs*. That Diotima repeatedly thwarts Socrates' wonder about the premises of her ladder of love argument, thus foreclosing his active engagement in

---

40. Halliwell, in *Plato: Republic 5*, 206, 208–12. See also Saxonhouse, *Fear of Diversity*, 159, who takes Diotima's vision to lead back to the *kallipolis*.

41. For discussion, see Belfiore, *Socrates' Daimonic Art*, 155–60.

his own persuasion, suggests that he may have been passively persuaded. By contrast, Socrates uses the active voice to describe his persuasion of others. That might signify that Socrates seeks to persuade others about the truth of Diotima's ladder of love, to make them believe its truth. Given, however, that he appears himself to be only passively persuaded, that seems unlikely.

As we saw in chapter 4, the active voice could also signify that Socrates seeks to persuade others by deceiving them about the truth of the ladder of love. But this seems unlikely as well. For just before Socrates presents his encomium of *erōs* by way of Diotima, he claims that now that he has heard the prior encomiasts, he will not take his turn to praise *erōs* as he had initially promised. He had thought they were going to tell the truth about *erōs* but instead he has heard empty praise (198c–199c). Thus his speech, he maintains, will not say what is most beautiful, as he had first intended (198b), but will speak what he calls the "mere truth, *ta ge alēthē*," in a way that "will not rival" (199b) the earlier speeches. Indicating that, so as not to become a laughingstock (199b), he will present, by way of Diotima's speech (199b), the truth of the earlier encomia of *erōs*, Socrates announces that he is saying "good-bye to his bond" to tell the truth (199a-b). He thus flags for his audiences that his presentation of Diotima's speech will be, in the language of *Republic* 2, a "verbal falsehood" (382b).

Reminding his audience of the status of the ladder of love as a verbal falsehood when he finishes giving Diotima's speech, Socrates, having earlier marked the inadequacies of encomia when it comes to truth (198c–199c), requests that Phaedrus "be so good as to consider this account as an *encomium of love*," or else that he "call it by any name that pleases [his] fancy" (212c, my emphasis). Twice, then, before and after giving it, Socrates advertises the untruth of his speech on behalf of Diotima, that is to say, the falsity of *erōs* instrumentalized and/or mastered, whether that be in the service of honor, immortality, or knowledge of the eternal and unchanging ideas. If, then, Socrates' revelation of the untruth of Diotima's ladder of love indicates that he seeks neither to deceive nor to persuade that it is true, what does he seek to persuade about? Perhaps he seeks to persuade that approaching *erōs* in these instrumentalizing and/or mastering ways offers no adequate account of *erōs* at all. Perhaps he also and nonetheless seeks to persuade "that human beings can find no better *sunergon*, workmate, for acquiring knowledge than *erōs*" (212b), if, that is, *erōs* is something other than a device, an instrument in the service of other ends, or that end itself. To explore what else *erōs* might be, I turn next to the "rather long story" (203b) Diotima tells in the *Symposium* about the genealogy of *erōs*.

GENESIS, REPRODUCTION
IN DIFFERENCE, BELONGING

In "the right and regular ascent" of the ladder of love, Diotima says, a man will suddenly "have revealed to him, as he draws to the close of his dealings in love, a wondrous vision, beautiful in its nature" (210e). Although described as a product of resourcefulness (209b) and of the climb up a ladder, that vision, in its "singularity of form independent by itself" and "affected by nothing" (211b), springs as if from nowhere. In a similar vein, the speeches of Phaedrus and Pausanias explicitly deny parentage to *erōs* (178b, 180d). In discussion with Agathon, Socrates seems to see things differently when, trading on the genitive "of," he exclaims: "How absurd it would be to ask whether love is *erōs* of a mother or a father!" (199d). To some readers, Socrates poses here, in the context of his initial approach to *erōs*, "the fundamental problem of incest."[42] That may be. By claiming that it is absurd to ask whether *erōs* is "of a mother or a father," Socrates may also, however, be indicating, contra the other symposiasts, that of course *erōs* is of, that is to say, comes from and belongs to, a mother and a father. By asking after the genesis of *erōs*, Socrates reopens Agathon's inquiry into the question of who/what *erōs* is and also opens an inquiry into what kind of possession the belonging of *erōs* might be. These questions are pursued in Diotima's genealogy of *erōs*, the part of her speech focusing on who/what *erōs* is before she turns, as discussed above, to *erōs*'s use.

In Diotima's genealogy, Eros appears as the child of Poros and Penia. Originating in wealth or resource or means, as his father, and in poverty or need or necessity, as his mother, Eros is, like his father, "resourceful in his pursuit of intelligence, *phronēsis*, a lover of wisdom, *philosophon*, throughout his life, ensuing the truth" (203d). He is like his mother, too, shoeless and homeless, hard, parched, and poor (203c-d). It is as "the intermediate sort" between wisdom and ignorance (203e) that Eros, in Diotima's description, is "a friend of wisdom, *philosophon*" (204b). In wonder and in need, Eros is not beautiful or ugly, not rich or poor, not only a means nor an end in itself. Not a god but a *daimōn*, Eros passes between being and becoming (202a-202e). Despite all of these "nots," and unlike the *erōs* of the encomiasts and of Diotima's ladder of love, the Eros of resource and need does not generate its own negation.

Instead, and positively, Eros, the offspring, is both a being in its own right, a named particular, and also always in relation, a third, one might say, though not in the way of the "external" third thing or in the way of the third-party

---

42. Rosen, *Plato's "Symposium,"* 211–15.

judge, both discussed in chapter 4. Eros is, instead, a middle. This Eros is unlike Aristophanes' *erōs*, the "desire to be complete" (192e–193a) that drives the quest to return to a primordial unity in an erasure of difference and relationality signaled by the absence of speech between the unified parts (192c-d). It is unlike Eryximachus' *erōs*, which harmonizes discord by eradicating it (187b-c), or Agathon's Eros, which is counterposed to necessity (195c, 196b), or the *erōs* of the ladder of love, which depends on resourcefulness (209b) but not need (211d), and is oriented to what is godlike and immortal. Eros, in Diotima's genealogy, is a product of need and excess. Navigating between the opposites it relates, Eros brings those opposites into a unity that does not overcome their difference but instead exposes and preserves their relationality and interdependence. Eros does this insofar as, as an offspring, a third that is a middle, it joins within itself the oppositional relationality of its parents.

On this genealogy, Eros is like the mortal children situated on the lowest rungs of the ladder of love, who "never obtain honor" for their parents (209e) and thus fail to secure their parents' immortality. This Eros belongs to his parents not as a possession that secures their self-reproduction but as a safeguard of the necessity, if Eros is to be what he is to be, of their difference.[43] Eros' parents, Penia and Poros, belong to him in a similar way (203b-c). Generating Eros as a middle of be(-)longing oriented to reproduction in difference, Diotima's genealogy stands in stark contrast to the other encomia. A tribute to himself as poet/Eros and his self-externalization by way of his poems, Agathon's speech, readers are told by the *Symposium*'s narrator, was as much about Agathon himself as it was about the god Eros (198a).[44] Treating as most useful to the city the *erōs* of *paiderastia*, the other early encomiasts celebrate an aristocratic institution that, perpetuating dominant social configurations with a view to consolidating power on the ground of wealth and birth, depended on lovers producing their beloveds in their own image. Dubbing the ladder of love "the right method of boy-loving" (211b), Diotima marks the proximity of its *erōs* to that of the early encomiasts, insofar as it, too, orients to reproduction in what she calls "the semblance of the original" (208b).[45] The *erōs* of Diotima's genealogy is, by contrast, oriented to reproduction in difference.

Two figures in the *Symposium* most resemble this genealogical portrayal of Eros: Alcibiades and Socrates, the latter, though usually shoeless like Penia,

---

43. Contra Rosen, *Plato's "Symposium,"* 242, who says that "parents love their own children in whom they see their completion."

44. See also Nichols, *Socrates on Friendship and Community*, 57.

45. In "Diotima's Concept of Love," Neumann calls this "psychical reproduction" (42).

wears, on the occasion of Agathon's symposium, "his best pair of slippers" (174a), like Poros. Socrates and Alcibiades are both depicted as resourceful and questing (Soc.: 223a; Alc.: 217d) and also as needy (Soc.: 207b; Alc.: 216a, 219e). Both are depicted as middles (Soc.: 213b; Alc.: 213a-b). Both are depicted as lovers and also beloveds (222b), attracted to the beautiful Agathon, whose name also signifies the good (Soc.: 174a-b; Alc. 212d).

Arriving late to Agathon's symposium, Alcibiades, impressing the other symposiasts with the freedom of his speech, *parrhēsia* (222c), and describing himself as a truth teller, *parrhēsiastēs*, at least six times (214e, 216a, 217b, 217e, 219c, 220e), announces that no one should be persuaded by Socrates' speech on behalf of Diotima (214c-d). Though he has not heard it, Alcibiades insists and then goes on to show by way of images (215a) how "the case is quite the contrary" of what Socrates has said about *erōs* through Diotima (214d). If the ladder of love emphasizes the right and regular order or ascent of *erōs* (210a, e) leading to "a certain single knowledge" (201d-e) oriented, as noted, to "love of the whole" (205b), Alcibiades' encomium substitutes Socrates for *erōs* (214d), highlighting that *erōs* is oriented to particularity and materiality. Giving free rein to the wonder he experiences in relation to Socrates (213e, 215b, 216c, 217a, 219c, 220a, 220c, 221c, 222e), Alcibiades offers a poignant treatment of Socrates' virtues and faults (222a-b), his beauty and ugliness (215b, 216e-217a).[46] In style and content (215a), Alcibiades' speech displays the destabilizing and haphazard effects of *erōs*, the way it works as itself a possessor (216c).

As we have seen, there is good reason for Alcibiades to reject Diotima's ladder of love. Does his speech harbor the dialogue's alternative account of philosophic *erōs*? Yes and no. For, even as his speech and he himself, too, exemplify that *erōs*, he and his speech are also governed by the means-end logic of the *erōs* of possession characteristic of the other encomiasts and of Diotima's ladder of love. Striving to determine some use to which to put Socrates (216c) and desiring to swap his physical beauty and/or his property or that of his friends for Socrates' wisdom (217a, 218c, d), Alcibiades' *erōs* is oriented to the acquisition and possession of Socrates whom he wants as his "commanding partner, *sullēptora*," in his quest to become the best he can be (218d). Agathon had demanded the same (175c). When Socrates refuses Alcibiades' terms or

---

46. On Alcibiades' attention to Socrates' particularity and physicality, see Nussbaum, *Fragility of Goodness*, chap. 6: she takes Diotima to stand for Plato and so reads Alcibiades as offering a counter to philosophic *erōs*. Refusing to identify Diotima and Plato, I see Alcibiades as a key step in the direction of the philosophic *erōs* the dialogue as a whole brings to appearance.

offers his own, Alcibiades runs away (216b, c). In response to Socrates' refusal, Alcibiades, like Agathon (175e), accuses Socrates of *hubris* (215b, 219c, 222b, 221e). Socrates is guilty, to be sure. But unlike *hubris* in its usual legal sense, which refers to an arrogance of appropriation—a public dishonoring or humiliation of another by treating their person or property as one's own—Socrates' *hubris* as it is depicted in the *Symposium* lies in his refusal to accept another's person or property as his own, and in his refusal to be treated as an object of possession. Socrates' *hubris* is, in other words, an arrogance of disappropriation. Seeking to articulate a different mode of possession, one that, like that of the Eros of Poros and Penia, is able to safeguard difference, requires that Alcibiades and Agathon turn not to Socrates as their resource or commanding partner but to a need and resource, or helpmate, *sunergos*, of their own, namely, *erōs* itself.

Debra Nails remarks that "when *erōs* is directed to wisdom and truth, Socrates' active participation, or even his presence in the dialogues, can diminish . . . and disappear."[47] Rosen notes that the *Symposium* signals at the start that "Socrates' absence is as important as his presence."[48] Socrates' absence *may* signal the moment of impersonal truth, his identification with the *erōs* of Diotima's ladder of love, which orients to ideas by displacing materiality and passion as does the rationalizing tendency in the scholarship discussed at the beginning of this chapter. Or that absence, a signal feature of Socrates' arrogance of disappropriation, may instead underscore that while *erōs* originates between Socrates and his needy interlocutors, *erōs* must do its work not only interpersonally but also intrapersonally, which is to say, within individuals, in their self-relation, as both needy and resourceful. Like Penia in Diotima's genealogy, who, as Paul Allen Miller points out, "is the one who contrives a *poros*, not Poros himself . . . [and] does so precisely to the extent that she becomes aware of her own *aporia*," Socrates, too, is both resourceful and needy, with *poros* and also in *a-poria*.[49] Perhaps this is why Socrates plays both parts in his ventriloquized "dialogue" with Diotima, to which I return below.

Erōs, so understood, is also brought to appearance in the midwife metaphor Socrates uses to describe himself in the *Theaetetus* where he says, "My interlocutors never learnt anything from me but they on their own and from themselves found and gave birth to many beautiful things" (150d). The job of Socrates the midwife is to witness a mode of production that, like physical

---

47. Nails, "Tragedy Off-Stage," 197.
48. Rosen, *Plato's "Symposium,"* 27.
49. Miller, *Diotima at the Barricades*, 254.

pregnancy, depends on the hard work of the one giving birth to create something new and different: an offspring, a middle, a third. What is this new and different third? In life, it is a child, of her parents and also, as we have seen, a subject of possession in her own right. In Plato's dialogues, the offspring is an interlocutor, engaged with others and also giving birth to himself as a desiring, that is to say, a needy and resourceful, self. Unlike the inscriptive practices of self-reproduction powered by the *erōs* of the encomiasts' speeches, by Diotima's ladder of love, and exemplified as well in Thucydides' Pericles' view of Athenian imperial democracy as "the school for all Hellas" (2.41.1), reproduction powered by *erōs* as *sunergos*, modeled on physical pregnancy and witnessed by Socrates the midwife, generates within the birther and also with what comes out a relationality hospitable to need and difference.

FRAMING DESIRE

To see more explicitly how the *Symposium* scrutinizes and critiques *erōs* as a possessive and instrumental practice of ethical and political self-reproduction in the semblance of the original and what it points to instead, consider the dialogue's frame. What we read as the *Symposium* is presented as Apollodorus' retelling to an unnamed companion of the speeches and events of the night at Agathon's based on an account Apollodorus originally heard from Aristodemus, who attended Agathon's symposium as Socrates' guest.[50] Aristodemus is portrayed as a disciple of Socrates, doing anything Socrates may bid him to do (174b), and emulating Socrates' original style and dress (173b).[51] Also striving to be faithful to an original by making it his daily business to "know whatever Socrates says or does" (172c), Apollodorus reports that he authenticated Aristodemus' story with Socrates (173b), and then he proceeds to tell "the whole story from the very beginning, as Aristodemus told it to me" (173e–174a), reporting twice that he knows the story "pretty well by heart" (172a, 173c).

Noting that Apollodorus and Aristodemus are portrayed as capable only of imitation, David Halperin maintains that they "function entirely as sites of Socratic inscription."[52] Insofar as inscription "maintains identity . . . by eliminating change," whereas *erōs* works "by continually producing something new

---

50. For a helpful chart of the characters in the dialogue's frame, see the opening pages of Halperin, "Plato and the Erotics of Narrativity."
51. Aristodemus goes shoeless to Agathon's, for example.
52. Halperin, "Plato and the Erotics of Narrativity," 114.

to replace what is being lost," the frame of the *Symposium*, Halperin argues, sets the dialogue up as "an act of intellectual insemination by the teacher" represented "from the teacher's perspective as an exercise in male parthenogenesis, an attempt to reproduce himself and his doctrines in the student."[53] On this reading, Plato figures philosophy as "homotextuality," upholds the same penetrative and hierarchical norms as do Diotima's ladder of love and the Pausanian paiderasts, and the erotic philosophy of the *Symposium* shares their understandings of *erōs* as the possessive desire for immortality figured as the reproduction of oneself as/in another.[54]

It is true that Apollodorus and Aristodemus are portrayed as seeking to reproduce themselves as Socrates. They are also, however, depicted as Socratic *failures*. Lacking Socrates' physical and intellectual stamina (176c, 220a), Aristodemus falls asleep before the evening at Agathon's is over (223d), and his memory is signaled as faulty even while he is awake (177e, 180c). Apollodorus reports that he checked Aristodemus' story with Socrates who authenticated it in part (173b). With Apollodorus reporting this, we may wonder about the parts Apollodorus didn't check, especially after he reports, too, that "the entire speech in each case was beyond Aristodemus' recollection and so too the whole of what he told me is beyond mine" (178a). Although he is asked to relay only the actual speeches presented at Agathon's symposium (172b), Apollodorus can only reproduce the whole account "by heart" (172a, 173c), and, regularly finding fault with everyone (except Socrates) (173d), he is presented, in contrast to Socrates, as a misologue and also as a misanthrope.[55] Apollodorus and Aristodemus may be portrayed as "sites of Socratic inscription," but, as such, they are portrayed as singularly un-Socratic. Anticipating what emerges over the course of the rest of the dialogue, they are marked as failures, in my view, precisely insofar as, as disciples, they, like Alcibiades, desire that Socrates be their "commanding partner," that is to say, insofar as they desire to *be* the reproduction of another.[56]

That the *Symposium* goes to such lengths to underscore the failures and unreliability of the reports of Apollodorus and Aristodemus, and that all we

---

53. Ibid., 116–17.
54. Ibid., 117.
55. He is also called "maniac" (173e), and that may connote "divinely inspired."
56. Contra Bury, *Symposium of Plato*, xvi, for whom "the way in which Aristodemus, the primary source, and Apollodorus, the secondary source, are described is evidently intended to produce the impression that in them we have reliable witnesses."

as readers get is Apollodorus' report, are taken by Freddie Rokem as evidence of the dialogue's "radical critique of mimetic representation by pointing at its limitations": Apollodorus' report, the *Symposium*, is twice removed from what it represents, Agathon's symposium, with Aristodemus' report standing in between, at one remove from the actual event.[57] To read the *Symposium* this way is to presuppose a real symposium at Agathon's, a true event, of which Aristodemus and Apollodorus offer "mere" (i.e., unreliable) imitations. For that presupposition, however, the dialogue gives no grounds. *We* may wish to turn Plato's *Symposium* into "a semblance of the original" (208b) by seeking, for example, to settle its date of composition by reference to historical events mentioned in the dialogue. But, although the dialogue refers to Agathon's victory (173a) and populates his symposium with historical events and characters, the complex temporal embedding performed by the dialogue's frame makes it impossible to settle, by reference to historical events and/or people, the dramatic date of the *Symposium* as a whole.[58] In the language of earlier chapters, the dialogue presents itself not as the copy of an original but as a mimetic representation, an "image."

Plato draws attention to the dialogue's repeated play with the very idea of an original, when, as discussed in chapter 1, he has Aristodemus remember, and Apollodorus remember and report, that Eryximachus quoted from Euripides when he introduced the topic of *erōs* (177a). The words Eryximachus quotes are those of Euripides' Melanippe, who says "not mine the tale." Eryximachus quotes Melanippe because, as he says, "the speech comes from Phaedrus here" (177a). So Eryximachus introduces the topic of *erōs*, which belongs to Phaedrus, and the words Eryximachus quotes belong to Melanippe, or rather, as the rest of her line indicates, to her mother, since she speaks a tale taught by her mother (fr. 488).[59] To whom does Phaedrus' speech, put forward by Eryximachus quoting Melanippe's tale from her mother, belong? However we cash out these embedded references, their effect is that mimetic representation is all we get. There is, it appears, only the here and now. For an original, we are given an absent mother.

This point is replayed in the dialogue's figuration of Diotima as, in John Cooper's word noted earlier, a "contrivance." Halperin writes that Diotima turns out "to be not so much a woman as a 'woman,' a necessary female

---

57. Rokem, *Philosophers and Thespians*, 25, 23.

58. "The evidence" in the dialogue leads to different dates: Nussbaum chooses 404, Bury opts for 400; Nails for plus or minus 400.

59. For these sources, see Bury, *Symposium of Plato*, 18.

absence—occupied by a male signifier—against which Plato defines his new erotic philosophy."[60] Is Diotima "a necessary female absence"? Yes. In marked contrast to the Old Comedic poets who put the female on stage, body and all, "in the form of actors dressed as Muses, Comedy, Poetry, and Music,"[61] Plato gives Diotima no physical representation in the *Symposium*. Is Diotima's absence "occupied by a male signifier"? Yes. Diotima is ventriloquized by Socrates, and identified by scholars, falsely, in my view, as "the Platonic Socrates," a "thinly disguised Plato," and a "purified Agathon."[62] Is Diotima's absence that "against which Plato defines his new erotic philosophy"? I don't think so. I think rather that her "necessary absence" is that *in terms of which* the dialogue offers its readers a new erotic philosophy.

An analogue not only of Melanippe's mother but of Penia as well, Diotima figures the necessary lack without which there can be no *erōs*. As such, she is the condition of Socrates' *aporia*. It is in conversation with her that he comes to see that he is unable to answer what someone will have who gets beautiful things (204e), that he realizes that he does not understand whether the question of the desire for good and/or beautiful things is a question of possession, or what sort of desire the desire for happiness is. Before she is depicted as thwarting Socrates' wonder, Diotima helps to bring to appearance for Socrates that and what *he* does not know. These questions are opened for Socrates by Diotima or, more accurately, by Socrates-as-Diotima to signal, perhaps, that, as suggested earlier, *erōs* does its work not only interpersonally but intrapersonally as well.

More accurately still, the questions are opened by the dialogue for its readers, who are left by the symposium at Agathon's, and by the *Symposium*, to wonder about *erōs*, to wonder about philosophy, and to wonder, too, about our own needs, resources, and desires when it comes to desire. From start to finish, then, whether because of the unreliability of its reporters and/or because the dialogue breaks off with Socrates in midsentence owing to the fact that Agathon and Aristophanes, according to what Apollodorus recounts from Aristodemus' report, needed to sleep (223b-d), and/or because of the representations of the symposiasts, in short, because of the dialogue's mimetic poetry, the *Symposium* leaves its readers with and without the means or resources,

---

60. Halperin, "Why Is Diotima a Woman?," 149.

61. Hall, "Female Figures and Metapoetry," 415.

62. For the last two phrases, see Rosen, *Plato's "Symposium,"* 203, who rejects the first but accepts the second. See Reeve, "Telling the Truth about Love," 101, for the second; and Bury, *Symposium of Plato*, xxxix, for the first.

a-poros, that is, in *aporia*, and at the same time desiring to determine what it might tell us about *erōs*. That *experience* of desire is itself the positive content about *erōs* we may have been seeking in the form of a doctrine or proposition. Giving only *erōs* as something to be desired, the dialogue offers *erōs* as *sunergos*, performing its account of *erōs* phenomenologically, which is to say, by thematizing and emancipating the *erōs* of its readers.

ERŌS AND PHILOSOPHY

If the being of *erōs* is need and resource together, what, then, is *erōs*'s work, *ergon* (*Symp.* 201d-e)? What is *erōs* for? Not for securing the objects the erotician desires, for that, as we have seen, spells the death of *erōs*. Not self-reproduction in/as another. Instead, the *Symposium* suggests that to be an erotic is to desire oneself desiring, to be pleonectic for *erōs*. This means that the being of *erōs* and its work as *sunergos* are the same: namely, to be forever in desire in relation to things that can never be fully and entirely possessed. In the *Republic* and in the *Symposium*, these appear to be the good and the beautiful and their truth. The work of *erōs*, this suggests, is, as we have seen, the possibility of philosophy. Are we then back to the ladder of love? No, because, as we saw, to sit atop the ladder of love is to possess what one desires, to know the essence of beauty, and to become, as such, immortal. By contrast, to be forever in desire is bound with mortality, with wanting to possess good and beautiful things, with wanting to become a good and beautiful thing, not in the mode of Aristodemus or Apollodorus, who want to become Socrates, but instead as someone who, as Socrates says of himself in the *Symposium*, understands erotic things (177d-e, 198c-d).

Catherine Zuckert points out that when Socrates says that he understands erotic things, it is "basically the equivalent of his saying, as he will in the *Apology of Socrates*, that his wisdom consists in his knowing that he does not know, and why Socrates often states, as in the *Phaedrus*, that he seeks self-knowledge first and foremost."[63] What is the relation between philosophic *erōs*, human wisdom, and the quest for self-knowledge? Links among these are forged not coincidentally in *Alcibiades 1*, where Socrates first reasserts the difference, present, as we have seen, in the *Symposium*, between what we possess and who we are: "Is he cultivating himself when he cultivates what he has?" Socrates asks (*Alc. 1*, 128a). No, he explains. Only "if we know ourselves, then we might

---

63. Zuckert, *Plato's Philosophers*, 203. We see this in the *Symposium* as well when, on his way to Agathon's house, Socrates stops to "turn his attention upon himself" (174d).

be able to know how to cultivate ourselves, but if we don't know ourselves, we'll never know how" (129c-d). Self-cultivation, becoming the best one can be (128e), can only come about by way of self-knowledge, knowing this particular thing that I am. Possessions are not beside the point, for self-cultivation involves knowing oneself and one's belongings (133e). But insofar as knowing one's possessions involves understanding what can and what cannot be possessed, and insofar as *erōs* is central to this understanding, *erōs*, along with its perpetual orientation to the always-not-yet possessed good and/or beautiful, makes possible the self-knowledge that Socrates, in the *Apology*, calls human wisdom (20b-c). Characteristic of human wisdom is, then, a certain kind of self-seeking. This self-seeking does not take shape as a practice of material self-expansion or *pleonexia* in the manner of the tyrant, Athens' imperial *dēmos*, Alcibiades, or the encomiasts of *erōs* at Agathon's symposium, including Diotima's erotic who, in desiring immortality, seeks to become a god.

Rather, the characteristic self-seeking of the true erotic emerges as the quest for self-knowledge as such.[64] As we have seen, the waxing and waning, coming into being and perishing, that characterize human bodily generation as well as *erōs* are obviated in the self-reproduction of the same that are the immortal ideas, *paiderastia*, the originary unity of Aristophanes, and/or Agathon's poesy. By contrast, the generation of self-seeking philosophic *erōs* is the perpetual production in and of oneself as a middle or third by way of an *erōs* of the always-not-yet good or beautiful. This is a mode of production that, as a work in progress, is, like *erōs* itself, waxing and waning and coming into being and perishing. In thus representing the being and work of *erōs*, the *Symposium* and *Alcibiades 1*, read in conjuction with the *Apology* and *Phaedrus*, open the way to an *erōs* directed not toward the conquest and possession of other souls and cities, but instead toward self-knowledge and its mortal limitations, and hence, toward philosophy.

These dialogues suggest that there is no route to *erōs* as *sunergos* short of repeatedly learning the lessons of what can and cannot be possessed. Not only is there no route toward this understanding of *erōs* except experience, but the experiences that teach us about the impossibility of possessing such things as beauty, the good, and/or truth will also always involve *erōs* toward particular beautiful and good things, and ugly and bad ones, too. Perhaps this is why Socrates balks when, as we saw, Diotima singles "out a certain form of love," applies to it "the name of the whole," and describes that love as that which all men love always (205b). It is, in any case, why Glaucon should demur rather

---

64. See also Zuckert, *Plato's Philosophers*, 235.

than agree when Socrates says in *Republic* 5 that to call someone a lover of something is to describe them as desiring not one particular but the whole class (475b), as "loving the whole thing" (474c). For, as Socrates' examples go on to show, Glaucon's desire, whether for a boy with a snub nose or one with a beak or one who is dark or white or honey-pale (474d–475a) is, like thirst (437c, 439b), always oriented not to the whole but to a particular.

Contrary to Diotima's representation in the ladder of love, and contrary, too, to the so-called theory of forms, the good and the beautiful, this means, are not objects of a discrete kind of *erōs* but rather what each of us pursues by pursuing the other ordinary things that we desire, like food or lovers, slaves or territory. For these reasons, *erōs*, ultimately, cannot be made safe for politics or philosophy. The understanding it involves is only earned, if it is earned, by courting its risks. It follows that philosophic *erōs* also bears in itself the risks of everything from which it is also differentiated.[65] This is, among other things, the proximity of Socrates to Alcibiades in the *Symposium*, and, as we will see next, the proximity, too, of the philosophical erotic to the tyrant in the *Republic*.

NECESSITY, TYRANNY, AND DEMOCRACY

In the *Symposium*, as we have seen, *erōs* is figured as a matter of necessity, *anangkē*. It is this very necessity, the lack that conditions the possibility of desire, the always-ongoing presence of *a-poria*, that also defines the erotic philosophers of *Republic* 6 and qualifies them for rule (499c-e). That necessity, a product of their own need, is not the same as the necessity characteristic of the philosopher-kings, whose necessity or compulsion, *anangkē*, by the institutions of the *kallipolis*, its *paideia*, and other "chance necessities," is entirely external. But there immediately arises another question: how are we to distinguish the erotic philosopher's internal necessity, *anangkē*, from that of the tyrant, whose *erōs* is also described in terms of *anangkē* in *Republic* 9 (577d–579e)? Is there any difference between *these* two?

Socrates appears to anticipate this question at the end of *Republic* 1, where, after successfully taming and shaming Thrasymachus, as discussed in chapter 4, he describes himself in curiously pleonectic terms. So far, Socrates says, he has learned nothing about justice because, like a glutton, *lichnos*, he has snatched at and tasted from every dish without properly enjoying each, having proceeded without first asking "what justice is" (354b-c). Socrates' self-description as

---

65. Thanks to Patchen Markell for this formulation.

a *lichnos* affiliates him with the tyrant who is likewise described as snatching at everything without discrimination in regard to justice (344a-b, 573e–574e). Socrates also suggests a different approach to justice in *Republic* 1, however, one that involves not indiscriminate grasping but instead asking questions, like "what justice is" (354b-c). An alternative to exercises of both the literal and the metaphorical *pleonexia* associated with tyranny, it seems, is to be "curious or inquisitive," which is exactly how *lichnos* is defined by Liddell and Scott in what the dictionary calls its "metaphorical sense."[66] This metaphorical way of being a *lichnos*, which is at a third remove from the literal *lichnos*, is explicitly denied to the tyrant in *Republic* 9, for, insofar as he lives in isolation and privacy to avoid harm from enemies (579b), and has no taste of freedom or true friendship (576a), a tyrant has no one to ask questions to and/or with.

C. D. C. Reeve has called the link between *erōs* and asking questions the "nontrivial play on words facilitated by the fact that the noun *erōs* ('love') and the verb *erōtan* ('to ask questions') sound as if they are etymologically connected."[67] If what orients to questing after justice, beauty, and good, in a word, to philosophy, appears, in the *Republic*, as in the *Symposium*, to be one's own pleonectic *erōs* itself, that is distinguishable from the tyrant's pleonectic *erōs* in that seeking the learning that is bound with self-knowledge, self-seeking, and self-possession by asking questions with and of oneself and others is not the same as seeking the profit, glory, and/or honor bound with the possession of others. And yet, as we have seen, philosophic *erōs* bears in itself the risks of everything from which it is also differentiated.

Still, the self-possession powered by philosophic *erōs* is not self-mastery as that is modeled by the philosopher-kings of the *kallipolis*, who, like the philosopher atop the ladder of love, fix their gaze on those things "which are always the same," "spending [their] time with what is divine and ordered" and "imitating and trying, as far as possible, to resemble those things," so as to become "as ordered and divine as it is possible for a human being to be" (500c-d). That is to desire to be a "semblance of an original," a copy of the "forms." Nor is the self-possession powered by philosophic *erōs* self-sufficiency in the mode of the tyrant, whose pleonetic *erōs* makes him a slave to his desires while striving to become *auto-nomos*, a law unto himself, which is to say, subject to no necessity at all.[68]

---

66. For the different senses of *lichnos*, see Liddell and Scott, *Greek-English Lexicon*, 9th ed., s.v.

67. Reeve, *Plato on Love*, xx. See also Reeve, "Plato on Friendship and Eros." The connection between *erōs* and *erōtan*, Reeve says, is "explicitly mentioned in the *Cratylus* (398c5-e5)."

68. For discussion, see Wohl, *Love among the Ruins*, 186.

Unlike the tyrant who is unable to tell the difference between sleeping and waking (*Rep.* 574d–575a, 576b), and so takes his dream of self-possession to be true, and unlike the philosopher-kings and the erotician of Diotima's ladder of love who, possessing complete wisdom, are beyond wonder and so do not dream, the erotic philosopher, as we have seen, remains always in desire. Always in desire because, while desiring to be self-possessed, he is not, this always-not-yet-self-possessed erotic is a lover of his "own." This is his quest, and it is always in question. In desire and in question, resourceful and in need, the one possessed by *erōs* in this way is Eros, the child of Poros and Penia, and also the philosophical soul of *Republic* 6, who, neither a philosopher-king nor a philosopher by nature, and also for now not a tyrant, lives the dream of self-mastery as a dream.

In *Republic* 8, Socrates describes democracy as the regime whose unnecessary and useless desires produce and also result from an "insatiable longing" for freedom (562b). The freedom granted by democracy is the power to do or refrain from doing "free from all compulsion" (557e). In democracies, each person is free to "organize his life . . . just as it pleases him" (563d): there is freedom to refuse to hold office, to refuse to submit to the rule of another, to refuse to follow the law, or keep the peace (557b, 557d, 564d). Democratic freedom, in its excess, may lead to pleonectic democratic imperialism and its mirror, tyranny (562b-c, 563e), both driven by the *erōs* of possession. Democracy may also, however, be the only constitution that, precisely in virtue of its absence of external compulsion, is hospitable to the need or internal necessity upon which philosophic *erōs* depends. As the conditions of late fifth-century Athens make plain, democracies offer no guarantee. That absence of guarantee may also be the source of democracy's erotic and therefore philosophical promise, which promise, however fragile, provisional, and defeasible, is better than no promise at all.

CHAPTER 6

Dialectics: Making Sense of *Logos*

> Phenomena are a sight of the unseen.
> ANAXAGORAS, fr. B21a DK

In *Republic* 7, Socrates defines the philosopher as "the man who is able to exact a *logos* of each thing" (534b), and describes his art, dialectics, as proceeding "by means of arguments, *tō[i] dialegesthai . . . dia tou logou*, without the use of any of the senses—to attain each thing that is" (532a).[1] The dialogue's sun-good analogy, line simile, and cave allegory appear to hierarchize insight or intellect, *nous*, over sense perception, *aisthēsis*, to produce the *Republic*'s understanding of philosophy.[2] Socrates seems to anticipate the psychology, metaphysics, epistemology, and ontology associated with that philosophy when he asks in *Republic* 3, isn't it "true that if images of writings should appear somewhere, in water or in mirrors, we wouldn't recognize them before we knew the things in themselves?" (402b).

Other evidence of the dialogue's subordination of *aisthēsis* to *logos* is not hard to find. Instead of supper, the apparent impetus for Socrates' return with Glaucon to the house of Cephalus and Polemarchus at the start of *Republic* 1 (328a), there are *logoi*, which is to say, speeches, conversations, and argumentation. *Republic* 5 appears to juxtapose the lover of sights and sounds with the philosophic lover of truth (474d). *Republic* 8–9 figure the decline of regimes and

---

1. Because the Greek *aisthēsis* and *logos* have multiple meanings in English—with *aisthēsis* referring to both sensation and perception and *logos* including speech, statement, definition, argument, account, discourse, structure, reason, rationality—I'll stay, for the most part, with the Greek terms. See Liddell and Scott, *Greek-English Lexicon*, 9th ed., s.vv.; for discussion see Desjardins, *Rational Enterprise*, 46, 123, 200 n. 4.

2. Reeve, *Philosopher-Kings*, 70, calls this noetic knowledge over doxastic knowledge.

the specific corruptions of democracy in terms of their appeal to the senses.[3] And the *kallipolis*—the city in *logos* (369c)[4]—neutralizes and regulates individuated sensations and sensibilities, making common the guardians' pains, pleasures (462b-e), and sexual relations (457d, 459e-461e), and ousting the mimetic poets (398a) because the images they offer the senses emancipate *erōs* (603b). Reflecting its commitment to the distinction between what appears and what is, the *Republic*'s subordination of *aisthēsis* to *logos*, it is said, underpins the "celebrated Platonic doctrine that true reality is a nonsensible realm of changeless being, the Forms, and it is in these alone that knowledge can find its objects."[5] Thus, in the view of Myles Burnyeat, for example, the *Republic* is "full of hostility towards perception and everything it represents." The dialogue's "charge against perception is that it offers itself as a dangerously seductive rival judgment-maker to reason."[6]

The *Republic* treats *aisthēsis* as a "judgment-maker," to be sure. In my view, however, the dialogue makes manifest that *aisthēsis* is not only a rival but also a condition of *logos*, and, indeed, of dialectics itself. Thus, my goal in this chapter is, in the words of its title, to make sense of *logos*, by which I mean to make legible the ways in which the *logos* of the *Republic*, often associated, as we saw in chapter 1, only with rationality, universality, transcendence, unity, being, order, and stability, is also sensible, particularistic, immanent, partial, changing, and potentially disruptive.[7] In short, I seek to bring to light the constitutive work of *aisthēsis* in the *logos* of dialectical philosophy.

Legible? Bring to light? It is all too easy, one might say, to find in the *Republic* attention to *logos* in terms of legibility and light. As we have seen repeatedly, learning to read is put forward as an analogy for coming to know (402b). Socrates frequently uses metaphors of light (508e) and sight (518c-519a) to make philosophical points. It is by way of his eyes, for example, that the figure of Leontius in *Republic* 4 plays out the battle between desire and reason (439e-440a). The soul is summoned to philosophy to make sense of contrarieties appearing before the eyes in *Republic* 7 (523a-525b). In the *Phaedrus*, the eyes are called the windows to the soul (250d-e, 251a-b). Noting associations between *logos* and *aisthēsis* when it comes to the sense of sight, scholars argue that sight

---

3. For discussion, see Panagia, *Political Life of Sensation*, 125-27.

4. *tō logō ex archēs poiōmen polin* (369c): Shorey and Grube treat *logos* here as theory, Bloom as speech.

5. Burnyeat, in *Theaetetus of Plato*, 8, 36-37. See also Kottman, *Politics of the Scene*, 35.

6. Burnyeat, in *Theaetetus of Plato*, 60-61, referring to the *Phaedo* as well.

7. See also Tarnopolsky, "Plato's Politics of Distributing and Disrupting the Sensible."

is an outlier among the senses for the distance it preserves between the person and what is being sensed. Paul Kottman maintains, for example, that in the philosophy of the *Republic*, "wonder (*thaumazein*, which also derives etymologically from *thea*, 'sight') is transformed into the contemplation of noetic objects (*theoria*)."[8] What is important about seeing as the attitude toward what is seen is that it preserves the remoteness, the cognition, the unbodily. From that vantage point, one might allow that the sense of sight is important in the *Republic*, and maintain that the dialogue nonetheless (or in so doing) elevates the theorist (from *thea* as well) over the sensate being.

I see things differently. When, after offering the allegory of the cave in *Republic* 7, Socrates refers to drawing the eye away from darkness to light, he says that this can only happen "by turning the whole body" (518c). This implies, as we will see further over the course of this chapter, that seeing belongs together with the other senses and with the body, and that these belong with philosophy. Indeed, across the *Republic*, the senses appear to be entangled with philosophy in ways that belie an opposition between *aisthēsis* and *logos*. This is especially so in the case of hearing, sounds, music, listening, and voice.[9] As we saw in chapter 4, the *Republic* opens with Polemarchus implying that there would be no dialogue at all if there were no listening (327c). In *Republic* 6, as also discussed in chapter 4, Socrates maintains that philosophy depends on the speaking and listening characteristic of free and beautiful discussions (498a–499b). In *Republic* 2, he characterizes his defense of justice as occurring in sound (368b-c).[10] References to and analogies from music frequently appear where the dialogue treats of philosophy.[11] And, as noted in the prologue, lovers of sights *and* sounds are not only counterposed to the philosopher in *Republic* 5 but also marked, by way of analogy, as similar (475e).

If *aisthēsis* appears to be bound with philosophy in these ways, the relation works in the reverse as well, that is, from the *logos* of philosophy to *aisthēsis*. As discussed in chapter 3, when Socrates describes the characteristics suitable to the guardians in *Republic* 2, he twice in the same passage marks the importance of "keenness of perception, *aisthēsis*" (375a). In *Republic* 3, he underscores

---

8. Kottman, *Politics of the Scene*, 34. See also Cavarero, *For More Than One Voice*.

9. Contra Cavarero, *For More Than One Voice*, 33–41, for whom Plato is primarily responsible for philosophy's overall "devocalization of *logos*." The word *akouein*, to listen, and its cognates appear over 130 times in the *Republic*. Thanks to Janet Safford for running these numbers.

10. Thanks to Christina Tarnopolsky for bringing this to my attention.

11. For an extensive and valuable treatment of the relation between music and philosophy in Plato, see Valiquette Moreau, "Musical Mimesis and Political Ethos in Plato's *Republic*."

that a proper education to philosophy would allow someone most quickly to perceive, *aisthanoito* (401e–402a). In *Republic* 8, the rulers of the ideal city are said to require *logos* with *aisthēsis* if they are to succeed at generating the best offspring (546b), and, in *Republic* 9, Socrates describes the healthy soul as seeking the perception, *aisthanesthai*, of anything "it knows not what, whether it is past, present, or future" (572a).[12] After seeming to isolate *logoi* as the philosopher's instrument, *organon*, of judgment in *Republic* 9 (582d), Socrates partners *logos* with experience, *empeiria*, and practical wisdom, *phronēsis* (582a), both of which, we will see, critically involve *aisthēsis*.

Against this backdrop, the *Republic* 3 passage that appeared at the beginning of this chapter deserves another look. For although in it Socrates appears to prioritize knowledge of "the things in themselves" over the perception of images (402b), he makes this remark in the context of an analogy between coming to know and becoming musical and surrounds it with two references to *aisthēsis* (401e, 402b-c). The second appears when, in summarizing his position on coming to know, Socrates asks,

> So, in the name of the gods, is it as I say: we'll never be musical—either ourselves or those whom we say we must educate to be guardians—before we recognize the forms, *eide* . . . and all their kin, and, again, *their opposites*, which are moving around everywhere, and *perceive, aisthanōmetha*, that they are in whatever they are in, *both themselves and their images, en hois enestin . . . kai auta kai eikonas autōn*, despising them neither in little nor big things, but believing that they all belong to the same art and discipline, *tēs autēs . . . technēs einai kai meletēs*? (402b-c, my emphasis)

Recognizing the forms and perceiving appear to be somehow related. We will see something similar in the *Republic* 7 passages (532a, 534b) I adduced at the beginning of this chapter as well. How might these ways of knowing "belong to the same art and discipline"? How might they work together, as Socrates says, to produce philosophical knowledge, to orient to dialectics, and, as he indicates across the *Republic*, to orient also to good political rule?[13] In the following section, I take up these questions in the context of *Republic* 7's education to philosophy, which I see as an education to statecraft as well. Unlike those for whom the *Republic*'s joint orientation to politics and philosophy must needs

---

12. This formulation is from Reeve's translation, *Republic*, in *Plato: Complete Works*, 1180.
13. On the imperative of a combination of *aisthēsis* and *logos* for the cognitive reliability of the rulers, see also Reeve, *Philosopher-Kings*, 114.

orient to ideal theory, I read the *Republic*'s political philosophical project as altogether practical.[14]

PROVOCATIVES

The curriculum Socrates sets forth in *Republic* 7 presenting the *Republic*'s education to philosophical politics or political philosophy includes the studies of number and calculation, geometry, stereometry, astronomy, and harmony, all of which are said to be preparatory for dialectics (536d). The centrality of *aisthēsis* to these studies is made apparent near the start of Socrates' account of number and calculation. It is when the soul receives contradictory communications, *hermeneiai* (524b), from the senses, he says, that it "summons to its aid the calculating reason, *logismon*," as when, for example, the soul perceives three fingers, each of which appears to be both big and small depending on where it is relative to the other fingers (523e). Referring to these contradictory perceptions as provocatives, *parakalounta* (523c), Socrates claims that they "awaken reflection" (524d) by giving rise to a puzzle, *aporein* (524a, e; also 515d). Sensing opposites, the soul is provoked to wonder how the same thing can be big and small at the same time.[15]

What is perceived as a unity and in contradiction, namely, big-and-small at the same time, the rationality associated with number and calculation, *to logistikon*, resolves into two separate and simple unities to ask: What is the big? Or what is the small?[16] Glaucon, Socrates' interlocutor here, finds the separate and simple unities generated by the reason of number and calculation most compelling (524c). This should not surprise. As we have seen in earlier chapters, Glaucon longs for what is *haploos*, simple, unified, unqualified.[17] As we have also seen in earlier chapters, however, the *Republic* repeatedly raises

---

14. For a treatment of some ways in which the politics and the philosophy of Plato's dialogues may be opposed, see Schofield, *Plato*, chap. 4.

15. As I have been bringing to appearance over the course of this book, the text of the *Republic* itself throws up opposites to the senses—in, among other things, Socrates' contradictions and inconsistencies, as discussed in chapters 1–3—to provoke puzzlement if not in Socrates' interlocutors then in its readers. Especially pertinent to the argument of this chapter is Socrates' contradictory affirmation and dispraise of "insensibility" in *Republic* 3, as discussed in chapter 3.

16. Adam, *Republic of Plato*, 2:111–12.

17. Weiss, *Socratic Paradox*, 177 n. 15, cites Ferrari, *City and Soul in Plato's "Republic,"* 16, who notes "Glaucon's desire to keep the goodness of justice pure, confined to the soul and untainted by the worldly goods to which it might lead." On Glaucon, see also Nichols, "*Republic*'s Two Alternatives."

the possibility that the rationality associated with *to logistikon* will be inadequate as a philosophy addressed to ethical and political matters. Perhaps this is why Socrates emphasizes not the compelling unity of calculation but rather the moment of *aporia*, the puzzle posed by the contradictory sense perceptions themselves, which "awaken reflection" and provoke judgment (524e). Perhaps this is also why Socrates invites Glaucon to think about the unity of number by analogy with the provocatives of sense perception (524d). Thus encouraged, Glaucon maintains that in the case of number, too, "we see the same thing at once as one and as an indefinite plurality." As if to press Glaucon further in this direction, Socrates asks: "If this is true of the one . . . the same holds of all number, does it not? . . . and calculation and arithmetic are wholly concerned with number?" (525a-b). Socrates seems to be asking Glaucon to imagine mathematical thinking not in terms of a compelling unity alone but "as one and as an indefinite plurality" at the same time. Linking this way of imagining explicitly to *aisthēsis*, Socrates positions himself against mathematicians who refuse to discuss "numbers attached to visible and tangible bodies." Referring to those who leave "the region of generation" entirely behind (525b) as clever, *deinos* (525d-e), Socrates seems to imply that, in reference to the education to philosophical politics at stake in *Republic* 7, they may not be truly wise.[18]

The rest of the education elaborated in *Republic* 7 indicates, too, that turning away from the region of generation and its change and multiplicity is neither compulsory nor desirable for the politics and philosophy the dialogue seeks. Indeed, the power of particular perceptions in opposition to awaken reflection, to provoke to thought, to summon to philosophy, appears repeatedly in the accounts of the remaining branches of study. For example, Socrates opens the discussion of the study of geometry, the second of the studies preliminary to dialectics, by alluding to the "direct contradiction" between the science, *epistēmē*, of geometry and the language employed by geometers: "They speak as if they were doing something and as if all their words were directed to action. . . . Whereas in fact the real object of the entire study is pure knowledge" (527a). Glaucon does not ask about this contradiction. But there is reason to wonder: why do geometers, if they are seeking "pure knowledge," *epistēmē*, speak in terms of activities like "squaring and applying and adding and the like" (527a)? Asking this question might awaken reflection about the start of the *Theaetetus*, where, for Theaetetus, young Socrates, and Theodorus,

---

18. For a similar contrast between being clever and being wise, see *Phaedrus* 229c–230a. For a different reading of the mathematicians, see Reeve, *Philosopher-Kings*, 75.

the knowledge of surds, or mathematical powers, begins in and depends on their representation to the senses of squares and oblong rectangles through images and illustrations (*Theat.* 147d–148b).[19] In the case of these geometers, their words, directed to and by the action of their representations, disclose the source and origin of their mathematical knowledge *in* these representations. As Socrates says, in the realm of *dianoia* or thought, mathematicians use models, objects, or figures *as* images (510b). *Dianoia*, the mode of knowing to which mimetic poetry also appeals, as we saw in chapter 2, is the epistemic modality that, moving between what does and does not appear to the senses, has the capacity to hold contradictory opinions about the same thing.

After geometry, Socrates and Glaucon turn to astronomy. Rebuking Glaucon for suggesting that gazing at the heavens with one's eyes "compels, *anangkazei*, the soul to look upward" (529a), Socrates insists that no other study "turns the soul's gaze upward than that which deals with being and the invisible" (529b). Extolling the beauty and complexity, *poikilia*, of the stars "that paint the skies," Socrates, using poetic language, calls the stars "adornments" or "embroideries, *poikilmata*," while insisting that they fall short of truth, which can be apprehended only by reason and thought and not by sight (529c-d). This is often taken as proof positive that philosophy must turn away from sense perception and becoming to reason and being. It is worth noticing, however, that Socrates only warns against taking what the eyes see to be the whole truth. It is worth noticing, too, that he issues that warning by drawing a double analogy, first to artistic designs and then to geometry, claiming that "we must use the blazonry, *poikilia[i]*, of the heavens as patterns, *paradeigmata*, to aid in the study of [the invisible] realities" (529d-e). In astronomy, as in geometry and number, studying being and the invisible, and perceiving, appear to be interrelated. With *poikilia* and its derivations coming up repeatedly in these passages (529b, c, d), it seems here, as in relation to mimetic representations, discussed in chapters 1 and 2, that the soul is provoked to orient to being and invisibility *by* the intricacy, loveliness, and multiplicity perceived by the senses.

Just after remarking that the study of being and the invisible is not a matter of gazing at the heavens either haphazardly or by compulsion but of turning the soul's gaze upward, Socrates notes that "if any one tries to learn about things of sense, *aisthētōn*, whether by gaping up or blinking down, I would say

---

19. The *Theaetetus* and *Republic* mirror each other not only in their treatments of geometry but also in the other studies that Theaetetus undergoes, which map onto the studies of *Republic* 7, including astronomy, harmony, and calculation (145d). For discussion, see Zuckert, *Plato's Philosophers*, chap. 9.

that he never really learns—for nothing of the kind admits of true knowledge—nor would I say that his soul looks up, but down" (529b-c). In insisting that one fails to learn in matters of becoming and the visible *and* in matters of being and invisibility alike when one gapes or blinks, which is to say, when one looks without seeing or when one is, in Glaucon's word, by contrast, "compelled, *anangkazei*" (529a), Socrates appears to be suggesting that truly noticing things of sense perception, like truly attending to being and the invisible, is a purposive attitude of soul. Perhaps this is why, in the *Republic* 3 passage quoted earlier, Socrates insists that recognizing the forms and perceiving them "belong to the same art and discipline" (402b). What might a purposive soul practice of *aisthēsis* look like? And how might such a practice relate to the *logos* of philosophy? I return to these questions below through a reading of the *Theaetetus*.

For now, continuing to explore the studies leading to dialectics in *Republic* 7, we can see the imperative of sense perception also to the account of harmonics, which Socrates and Glaucon discuss after astronomy. Rejecting Glaucon's criticism of those who use their ears to stimulate their minds, Socrates insists that such is part of any investigation of the beautiful and the good (531a–531c). "Our other injunctions will be of the same kind if we are to render what is due, *ophelos*, as lawgivers," he says (530c). Alluding to legislative possibilities that seem quite different from the laws of *Republic* 2-3, and 5, which, through their censorship of the mimetic poets and orientation to simple Justice delimit rather than expand what is available to the senses, Socrates gives content to the new style of law when he announces the "law, *nomos*, which dialectics recites." It reads: "When anyone by dialectics attempts through discourse of reason and apart from all perceptions of sense, *tō[i] dialegesthai . . . aneu pasōn tōn aisthēseōn dia tou logou*, to find his way to the very essence of each thing and does not desist till he apprehends by thought itself the nature of the good in itself, he arrives at the limit of the intelligible, *tō[i] tou noētou telei*" (532a). If this law appears to demand precisely the rejection of the senses I have been seeking to attenuate, that appearance is deceiving. Asking whether this law is "finally the true tune or theme which the study of dialectics plays" (532a), Socrates uses a musical metaphor to describe an embodied dialectics reciting or performing an appeal to organs of sense, to ears, in the first instance, and then to eyes, when he calls the law of dialectics, in Paul Shorey's rendering, "an imitation" of how we see (532a-b). So conspicuously at odds with his insistence on intelligibility apart from perceptions of sense, Socrates' account of the law of dialectics invites a second look. Socrates' performative contradiction here, like the contradictions of geometry and astronomy, might have "summoned" (524d) his interlocutor's soul, awakening its reflection (524b) on the question of the *relation* between what is intelligible and universal, on the one hand, and what is particular and perceptible, on the other. But Glaucon does not ask.

Perhaps it is for this reason that Socrates articulates their quest for the good, which directly follows, in similarly contradictory terms: "And, if I could, I would show you, no longer an image and a symbol of my meaning, but the very truth, as it appears to me, *oud' eikona an eti hou legomen . . . all' auto to alēthes*—though whether rightly or not I may not properly affirm" (533a). Sometimes read as a decisive turn away from the sensible, Socrates' words instead open doubt about whether the intelligible—"the very truth"—may be shown by way of something other than what appears. Telling of "the very truth" "as it appears to" him, Socrates' words refer truth to what he sees (see also 523a, 525b).[20] The education to dialectics of *Republic* 7 thus appears to involve not the compelling unity of *Republic* 2, 3, 5, but instead the play of difference between the sensible and the intelligible, which, in its complexity, *poikilia*, induces *aporia* and prompts judgment.[21]

The play between sensible and intelligible in *Republic* 7 is anticipated by the line simile in *Republic* 6, which, likewise, establishes continuities, by way of its structure and content, among the modes of being and knowing it represents as divided. What have been variously called the "models," "diagrams," or "figures" of mathematical or scientific thinking, *dianoia*, positioned in the intelligible world above the line are also likenesses, *eikones*, of the living things and objects of belief, *pistis*, positioned in the visible world below the line (510b, e, 511a). These objects of belief, *doxa*, are, in turn, the doxastic "originals" of the images of imagination or conjecture, *eikasia*, occupying the bottommost and smallest segment of the line. This is what we just saw in the case of *Republic* 7's account of geometry, and also in Theaetetus and young Socrates' practice of it near the beginning of the *Theaetetus*. Some scholars treat these continuities as symptoms of "intellectual unclarity" on Plato's part.[22] Another possibility is that Plato has Socrates represent the divided line, itself an image, in a way that brings to appearance that its allegedly distinct epistemologies, ontologies, and metaphysics are actually interdependent. That the line simile is structured as

---

20. See also Miller, *Diotima at the Barricades*, 80–103.

21. For more on the puzzlement and judgment prompted by *poikilia*, see "Representation" in chapter 1 and "Simple Minds" in chapter 3.

22. See Annas, "Understanding and the Good," 149–50. For clarification, see Reeve, *Philosopher-Kings*, 79–81.

an analogy supports this latter understanding, for the separate terms of analogies stand in mutually constituting relations.

The sun-good analogy, appearing just before the line simile, raises similar questions about the knowledge, being, and truth of an independent nonsensible realm. The analogy runs as follows: just as the sun gives the power, *dunamis*, of sight to the eye, so too does the idea of the good give the power, *dunamis*, of knowing to the knower and the truth to things known (508e). We saw in chapter 4 that Glaucon acquiesces to the analogy without questioning it. By contrast, scholars have raised any number of concerns, specifically about the account of the good implied by the analogy.[23] Claiming that "Plato" assumes but "offers no direct argument" for there being an "unqualified Good" that is "objectively, just good, not good relative to anything," Julia Annas, for example, wonders why "Plato" helps "himself to the claim that the Good, the object of all human strivings, is the Form of the Good," positioned as "the supreme object of knowledge" but with "nothing to do with one's *own* good." Maintaining that "Plato" treats the "Form of the Good" as "beyond being" (509b) and as "simply and unqualifiedly good," rather than as "what is good for the seeker, or good for others, or good in relation to anything or anyone," Annas concludes that "Plato has forsaken the practical philosopher for the contemplative one."[24] Annas is right to wonder about all of these features of the sun-good analogy. But, in my view, she is wrong in assuming that the analogy represents "'Plato's Good'" as the "Form of the Good," or that this, therefore, is the good the *Republic* endorses.[25] If we refuse to draw inferences about what the dialogue may or may not endorse from the words Plato puts into Socrates' mouth, and take a second look at those words, the text appears to prompt the very concerns Annas raises.

As noted in chapter 4, Socrates claims that he offers "just the interest, *tokos*." Describing the sun as "an offspring, *ekgonon*, of the good" (507a) "begot in a proportion with itself" (508b), he indicates that he presents an effect but not the thing itself. Saying, as he introduces the analogy, that he may in some way "unwillingly deceive in rendering the account of the interest fraudulent" (507a), Socrates warns Glaucon that he will "see ugly things, blind, and crooked, when it's possible to hear bright and beautiful ones from others" (506c-d). Glaucon,

---

23. To Ophir, *Plato's Invisible Cities*, 131, for example, the form of the good is an "ultimate Other... archetype of all despots."

24. All in-text quotations are from Annas, "Understanding and the Good," 145–47, 158, 159–60. She makes similar charges against the line simile and cave allegory.

25. Annas, "Understanding and the Good," 146.

as we saw, calls the analogy an "uncontrived beauty, *amēchanon kallos*" (509a). But by aligning it explicitly with deception, Socrates seems to be prompting Glaucon to hear it instead as a contrivance, *mēchanē*. That Socrates ends his account of the analogy by insisting that he has left a lot out (509c) further highlights its questionable status. In all of these ways, Socrates seems to be inviting a critical distance from the analogy, even as he puts it forward.

From that distance, we may notice that Socrates situates the sun-good analogy in the register of *aisthēsis* by calling specific attention to how things are seen and heard (507b-c). We may also notice that Socrates depicts the power to see, in the analogy, as depending on the "third element" of light (507c-d), "an overflow from the sun's treasury," and maintains that light gives power to sight (508b). Light thus appears like the "Good itself," which, as Annas notes, is "brought in from outside the discussion":[26] just as in the visible region, when we turn our eyes "on things illuminated by the sun, they see clearly," so, too, in the intelligible region, when the soul fixes its attention on things "illuminated by truth and what is, it understands, knows, and appears to possess understanding" (508d). The sun is a source of light to be sure, but why, we may wonder, does the analogy treat the sun's light as the *cause* of the power of sight (507e-508b)? Does not the power to see lie also in the eye? And if Socrates truly seeks what is "objectively, just good, not good relative to anything," and if, as Annas claims, that is what the analogy gives, then why does the good of the analogy produce only *apparent* understanding? Might Socrates present the sun-good analogy in the ways he does, including by warning about its deception, to bring to light that, like the line simile, and the *Republic* 7 education, it seeks not to endorse an "unqualified Good," but rather subjects that kind of good to scrutiny? I return to these questions toward the end of this chapter.

For now, consider Socrates' repeated use of the word *idea* in these passages. He uses it first to draw the distinction between "one class of things," which "can be seen but not thought," and another class, which "can be thought but not seen," which latter Socrates calls the ideas (507b-c). He uses it again to invoke the idea as a measure, with reference to light's power to "yoke together" the sense of sight with the power of being seen (507e-508a). He uses it, finally, to refer to the power of the idea of the good to give knowledge and truth to the one who seeks to know (508e). If we take *idea* in its primary signification, that is, as "the appearance of a thing" or "how it looks," then, with reference to the good here, in anticipation of his comments about "the very truth" (533a), which I discussed earlier, Socrates appears to be questioning any hard and fast

26. Ibid., 145.

distinction between what is thought and what is seen. Here, as in the law of dialectics, the idea of the good—like its study—appears to be mediated by experience, specifically by what looks good to those who seek good. Read in this way, the upshot of the sun-good analogy is not to locate the power, *dunamis*, of sight and/or knowledge in some external "third thing" (be that sunlight and/or an objective unqualified "Form of the Good"), but instead to locate it in, or, as we will see next, largely in, seers/knowers themselves. I explore this appreciation of *dunamis* next in the context of the *Theaetetus*, Plato's dialogue explicitly addressing the relation of *aisthēsis* to knowledge.

WHAT DO I SEE? OR, THE POWERS OF SENSE PERCEPTION

Providing what one author has called an "uncharacteristically elaborate theory of sensation,"[27] Socrates' engagement with his interlocutor Theaetetus around the latter's account of knowledge as "nothing but *aisthēsis*" (151e) occupies more than half of the *Theaetetus*. After this first definition, Theaetetus offers two other definitions of knowledge over the course of the dialogue: knowledge as true opinion, *alēthēs doxa* (187b, 200e); and knowledge as true opinion with *logos, meta logou* (201c, 206c). I explore these definitions in the sections that follow. I take the relation among them and the knowledge they delineate to be exemplified in midwifery, the practice by which Socrates introduces himself to Theaetetus near the start of the dialogue (148e–151a) and to which he returns at critical junctures (157c-d, 160e, 210b-c). As Socrates explains, knowing in the mode of a midwife includes being able to tell, on the basis of *aisthēsis*, whether a woman is pregnant; assaying the health and product of the pregnancy, which is to say, judging, based on opinion, which offspring will be viable; and giving an account of that viability (149c-d). Involving all three ways of knowing in combination, midwifery depends on the *empeiria* of *aisthēsis* for its judgment about viability and for its ultimate *logos*.[28]

Socrates indicates the philosophical stakes of Theaetetus' first definition when he situates it in relation to the positions of Protagoras and Heraclitus,

---

27. Desjardins, *Rational Enterprise*, 83.

28. Recognizing that to do justice to the complexity and difficulty of the dialogue requires more space than I devote to it here, the following draws on and also, as indicated, departs from the rich and excellent scholarship on the *Theaetetus*, including: Burnyeat, in *Theaetetus of Plato*; Zilioli, "Wooden Horse"; Penner, "Wax Tablet, Logic, and Protagoreanism"; Desjardins, *Rational Enterprise*; Gill, *Philosophos*, chaps. 3–4; Polansky, *Philosophy and Knowledge*; Stern, *Knowledge and Politics in Plato's "Theaetetus."*

on the one hand, and Parmenides, on the other. Lining Theaetetus up with Protagoras (152a) and Heraclitus, both of whom he further allies with the poets, Socrates reports that Homer "said that all things are the offspring of flow and motion" (152e; also 180c-d). Melissus and Parmenides, by contrast, "teach the opposite of this," for they maintain "that everything is one and stationary within itself, having no place in which to move" (180d-e).[29] Socrates appears to want Theaetetus to choose between these positions when, just over halfway into the dialogue, he asks: "What shall we do with all these people, my friend? For, advancing little by little, we have unwittingly fallen between the two parties, and, unless we protect ourselves and escape somehow, we shall pay the penalty, like those in the palaestra, who in playing on the line are caught by both sides and dragged in opposite directions" (180e–181a).

The choice between Heraclitus and Parmenides comes after multiple refutations of knowledge as *aisthēsis*. It might be expected, then, that Theaetetus would choose Parmenides' "Motionless, the name of which is the all" (180e) over Heraclitus' "Nothing ever is but is always becoming" (152d). And, indeed, Theaetetus says he would like to hear more about Parmenides' position. Socrates refuses (183d). This may be because Parmenides is implicitly omnipresent in the dialogue, a possibility I consider below when I address the dialogue's frame. Or it may be because Parmenides is a nonstarter, for, as Socrates puts it later in the dialogue, "if we stay still, we shall discover nothing" (200e–201a). Whatever is the case with Parmenides, Socrates appears to reject Heraclitus outright when he claims that "we are not going to grant that knowledge is *aisthēsis*, not at any rate on the line of inquiry which supposes that all things are in motion" (183c).[30] Socrates continues: "We are not going to grant it unless Theaetetus here has some other way of stating it" (183b-c). Is there "some other way" to say that knowledge is *aisthēsis* without committing to the radical flux endorsed by the Heracliteans? Theaetetus does not offer another way, but I suggest below that Socrates does, by way of the "secret doctrine" (152c) he associates with some of Protagoras' students, whom he calls "the subtle thinkers, *komposteroi*" (156a).[31]

As we will see, this means that I read the *Theaetetus* as wittingly falling between Heraclitus and Parmenides, and doing so by way of Protagoras. That

---

29. But see 152e, where Socrates names only Parmenides as on the side of the motionless and one.

30. For an illuminating engagement with Heraclitus, see Brann, *Logos of Heraclitus*.

31. Zilioli, "Wooden Horse," 172–79, identifies the "subtler thinkers" as Cyrenaics. Farrar, *Origins of Democratic Thinking*, 57, claims that this account is "a Platonic argument."

when he speaks for Protagoras Socrates accuses himself of unfairness in his initial representations of the sophist's account of knowledge as *aisthēsis* prompts Socrates' audiences (including Theaetetus and Theodorus in the dialogue and the dialogue's readers as well) not only to reconsider the viability of how Protagoras says we perceive, judge, and know the world, but also to consider how we speak with and act toward one another. Socrates foreshadows the stakes of his engagement with Protagoras when he says that he is bringing the sophist back to life to, as he puts it, assist Protagoras "in the name of justice" (164e). We may recall that assisting in the name of justice was something Socrates said he was afraid he would be unable, *adunaton*, to do in the *Republic* (368b). This suggests that the stakes of this dialogue about knowledge may not be only philosophical, but ethical and political as well.

The "secret doctrine" (152c) Socrates associates with Protagoras' students goes like this:

> According to this theory, black or white or any other colour will turn out to have come into being through the impact, *prosbolēs*, of the eye upon the appropriate motion; and what we naturally call a particular colour is neither that which impinges nor that which is impinged upon, but something which comes into being between the two, *metaxu ti hekastō[i] idion gegonos*, and which is private to the individual percipient. (153e–154b)

Scholars take this account of *aisthēsis* to be refuted by Socrates over the course of the dialogue as part of his overall rejection of Heraclitean flux and relativism. I disagree. For although there is, to be sure, a lot of motion in this account, indeed, Socrates says that it "begins from the principle on which all that we have just been saying also depends, namely, that everything is really motion" (156a; also 156d), the motion that characterizes this understanding of *aisthēsis* is not the same as the motion of the Heracliteans.[32]

For Protagoras' students, according to Socrates, *aisthēsis* consists in being moved and acted upon as a species of qualitative change (156d) involving "impact" (153e). They claim that "what we naturally call a particular colour is neither that which impinges nor that which is impinged upon, but something which comes into being between the two" (153e–154b). As Socrates explains in a long passage worth quoting in full,

---

32. I agree with Gill's analysis, *Philosophos*, chap. 3, of the dialogue's critique of Heraclitean motion. As we will see, I disagree that it defends Parmenideanism instead.

Thus the eye and some other thing—one of the things commensurate, *summetrōn*, with the eye—which has come into its neighbourhood, generate both whiteness and the perception which is by nature united with it (things which would never have come to be if it had been anything else that eye or object approached). In this event, motions arise in the intervening space, sight from the side of the eye and whiteness from the side of that which cooperates in the production of colour. The eye is filled with sight; at that moment it sees, and there comes into being, not indeed sight, but a seeing eye; while its partner in the process of producing colour is filled with whiteness, and there comes into being not whiteness, but white, a white stick or stone or whatever it is that happens to be coloured this sort of colour.

This account of course may be generally applied; it applies to all that we perceive, hard or hot or anything else. . . . All things, of all kinds whatsoever, are coming to be through association with one another, as the result of motion. For even in the case of the active and passive motions, it is impossible, as they say, for thought, taking them singly, to pin them down to being anything. There is no passive until it meets the active and no active except in conjunction with the passive, *oute gar poioun esti ti prin an tō[i] paschonti sunelthē[i], oute paschon prin an tō[i] poiounti*; and what, in conjunction with one thing, is active, reveals itself as passive when it falls in with something else, *to de tini sunelthon kai poioun allō[i] au prospeson paschon anephanē*. (156d–157a)

How is it that "sight from the side of the eye and whiteness from the side of that which cooperates in the production of colour" come together in the activity of *aisthēsis*? And what comes into being as between the two "which would never have come to be" otherwise? *Aisthēsis*, Socrates says, happens between two commensurate things. But how can an eye and a stick be commensurate with one another? Socrates explains: "At that moment it sees, there comes into being, not indeed sight, but a seeing eye; while its partner in the process of producing colour is filled with whiteness, and there comes into being not whiteness, but white, a white stick or stone or whatever it is that happens to be coloured this sort of colour."

There are similarities here to Aristotle's account of sense perception. For him, too, if a perceiver is to be moved to sense, what acts upon the relevant sense must be "like" the sense (*De an.* 416b35). As he explains in *De anima*, "The sensitive faculty [i.e., the eye] is potentially such as the sensible object [the stick] is in actuality" (*De an.* 418a3-5). This means that what is perceived is not the stick as such but the actuality of its whiteness. And what sees is the physical eye, but only when its potentiality, *dunamis*, is actualized as a seeing eye. What are commensurate or like one another are not the things, eye and stick, but their actualities, which come into being only in the activity of *aisthēsis* itself (*De an.* 425b26-426a26).[33] In the *Theaetetus*, Socrates puts the same idea on behalf of Protagoras' students in this way: "There is no passive until it meets the active and no active except in conjunction with the passive" (157a). It is the simultaneous and dual actualization of sense organ and sensed object that "comes into being between the two," which is to say, between the eye and the stick in the activity of *aisthēsis*. Socrates says that "if it had been anything else that eye or object approached," the eye and the stick "would never have come to be." Thus, "from the union, *homilias*, and friction of these two are born offspring infinite in multitude but always twin births, the object of sense and the sense which is always born and brought forth together with the object of sense" (156a-b).

Motion is central to this understanding of *aisthēsis*. To repeat from the long quotation above, "all things, of all kinds whatsoever, are coming to be through association with one another, as the result of motion." As for the Heracliteans, this account does not involve an ongoing, separate, and existent perceived (the stick) or on an ongoing, separate, and existent percipient (the eye). Instead, the sensing organ and the sensed object somehow come into being with the activity of sense perception and disappear once that activity is complete. At the same time, however, it is not the case that everything is all and only motion, for *aisthēsis* depends on the ongoing presence of a capacity, *dunamis*, power or potentiality, in the percipient,[34] and also on an ongoing *dunamis*, capacity, in what is being perceived, even when these capacities are not being actualized in use. It is the ongoing capacity or power, *dunamis*, to see and be seen that makes possible the stable as well as changeable identity over time of the (potentially) sensing organ and sensed objects.[35] Thus, everything is not all and only motion insofar as *aisthēsis* depends on capable and potentially actualizable sense organs and objects.

Actualized in and by way of inter-action (between sense organs and sensed objects), *dunamis is* not. That is to say, it *is* not before it is actualized. As such, *dunamis* is the not-(yet)-being of actualization. Since, when the inter-action is

---

33. Contra Zilioli, "Wooden Horse," 177, who claims that Aristotle is committed to a "strong sense of 'essence.'"

34. *Theaet.* 184e, 185c, e, 186b-c.

35. For the relation between potentiality and actuality in Aristotle, see Frank, *Democracy of Distinction*, 45-49.

over, *dunamis* ceases to be actualized, it is, in this sense, the not-(anymore)-being of actualization as well. In both senses, *dunamis* is not-being. This is the anti-Parmenidean flux side. At the same time, the actualization of *dunamis*, as temporary and temporal, depends on there being an ongoing capacity (something one, so to speak, holds for use). This means that *dunamis* is in being as potential. This is the anti-Heraclitean stability side. That there is on this account of *aisthēsis* a being in being, something that "abides in its own nature" (182e), preserves the possibility of identity over time, though that identity will, to be sure, be changeable.

Dunamis, signifying capacity, ability, potential, possibility, is implicitly and explicitly thematized across the *Theaetetus*.[36] As Paul Stern notes, its importance is signaled by Socrates' regular references to what is and isn't "*in our power*" (191a, 201e), what we may or may not be able to do and/or show (168c, 209a), and what is and is not possible (159a, 184e, 185a, 185e).[37] It makes its first implicit appearance in the dialogue's frame, which compares the mature Theaetetus, who is near death, with the boy "so full of promise thirty years ago."[38] *Dunamis* also comes up in Theaetetus' account of the geometric theory he and young Socrates have developed, which he and Socrates discuss near the beginning of the dialogue. In the words of Myles Burnyeat and M. J. Levett, that theory gives a "new" use to "power," namely, to "denominate a species of line, viz., the incommensurable lines for which the boys wanted a general account" (147d-e, 148b, d).[39] In contrast to the "square," the boys' theory of powers, *dunameis*, like the *dunameis* of sense perception, preserves the lines' difference even as they unite to become "oblong."[40]

Theaetetus remarks that Socrates seems to want regarding knowledge what the boys have come up with for geometry, which, he claims, in the case of knowledge, to be unable to offer. Socrates agrees that this is the kind of knowledge he is after, here, as in *Republic* 7. Socrates appears to disagree, however, that Theaetetus lacks the capacity, *dunamis*, to offer it (148b). What might an account of knowledge look like that, as a unity that can accommodate difference, involves a kind of commensuration that does not obviate incommensura-

---

36. Liddell and Scott, *Greek-English Lexicon*, 9th ed., s.v. dunamis.
37. Stern, *Knowledge and Politics in Plato's "Theaetetus,"* 236, 237–38, 284.
38. Ibid., 17.
39. Levett, with Burnyeat, in *Theaetetus of Plato*, 266 n. 3.
40. Polansky, *Philosophy and Knowledge*, 101, who also notes the analogy between Theaetetus' account of surds or geometrical powers, *dunameis*, and the *dunameis* of *aisthēsis*, says that in both cases the powers are "united."

bility? The possibility of such an account, these passages seem to suggest, lies in *dunamis*. Thus, *dunamis* appears to preserve not only the possibility of identity over time, as noted above, but the possibility of change over time as well, as Socrates' response to Theaetetus' own capacity implies. From this vantage point, it is not surprising that each time Socrates claims to reach an "impossible result if we say that knowledge and perception are the same," it is because the account of knowledge as sense perception he and Theaetetus have been examining has failed to take *dunamis* into account (164b; also 157d, 158e–159a, 165c). Indeed, the central conundrum of the dialogue—how it is possible to come to know—is itself a question of *dunamis*. As Stern puts it, "The idea of potential raises the possibility that our knowledge is not wholly present or wholly absent, that it may exist in varying degrees of actualization depending on the degree to which we have actualized our latent power."[41] So understood, knowledge itself is like what the *Theaetetus* refers to as a "wind-egg" (151e), somehow mediating between being and not-being.[42] Knowledge is also like the contradictory perceptions Socrates refers to as provocatives in the *Republic* (523c), which, owing to their appearing to be and not-be what they are at the same time, "awaken reflection" (524d) and give rise to *aporia* (524a, e; also 515d), as we saw above. Such contradictions appear in the *Theaetetus*, too, where Socrates describes them, as in the *Republic*, as provocative of the wonder that is the beginning of all philosophy (154c–155d).

WHAT DO I THINK? OR, HAVING AN OPINION

If, owing to *dunamis*, everything is not all and only motion in the account of *aisthēsis* Socrates associates with Protagoras' students, it is not all and only motion for another reason as well. *Aisthēsis*, Socrates says, produces "*in being*" (my emphasis) an in-between. The in-between—the dual actualization of sensing organ and sensed object in the activity of *aisthēsis*—is the here and now of the sensory experience that subsists with some, albeit temporary, stability over time. Socrates describes that experience as "private to the individual percipient" (154a). "Private" here does not mean that the sensory experience inheres in the percipient, for, as we have seen, the sensory experience is generated by the coactualization of the sense organ and sensed object to create an in-between. "Private" signifies rather that each occurrence of perception is individuated and unique to the particular occasion (159c–160a). Since "that

---

41. Stern, *Knowledge and Politics in Plato's "Theaetetus,"* 226.
42. Stern, *Knowledge and Politics in Plato's "Theaetetus,"* 133, makes a similar observation.

which acts on me is to me and me only, it is also the case that I perceive it and I only" (160c). As singular and individuated, the experience of *aisthēsis*, in motion and also ongoing, is private and, for this reason, infallible and unfalsifiable (152c): "To me my perception is true; for in each case it is part of my being and I am . . . the judge of the existence of the things [i.e., the perceptions] that are to me and of the nonexistence of those that are not to me [and in this sense] I am an infallible judge, *kritēs . . . apseudēs*" (160c7-d1).[43] In the case of *aisthēsis*, the judgment-maker, which, as we saw, Burnyeat calls "the rival judgment-maker to reason," is, in the language I introduced in chapter 1, the seeing I/eye, and also, we may now say, the hearing ear, the touching hand, the tasting tongue, and so on.

Are these judgment-makers rivals to *logos*? I suggest otherwise by looking next at how the in-between that is actualized between percipient and perceived in the private, individuated, infallible, and unfalsifiable experience of *aisthēsis* becomes part of the in-between of a shared world and as such subject to scrutiny and contestation, which is to say, accountable and falsifiable. Just after presenting the account of *aisthēsis* on behalf of the students of Protagoras, Socrates says to Theaetetus: "You must have courage and patience; answer like a man whatever appears to you to be true about the things I ask you" (157d). Opening the possibility that the private in-between of *aisthēsis* is also constituted as an in-between between human beings, Socrates invites Theaetetus to give his opinion about what appears to him. In doing so, he anticipates Theaetetus' second definition of knowledge as true opinion, *doxa* (187b, 200e).[44] He also marks that, in the account before them, sensing and judging, *aisthēsis* and *doxa*, go together, as is already implied in the words *dokei moi*, in which, as Cynthia Farrar has noted, "the term translated as 'appears' can refer both to what someone perceives and to what he thinks."[45]

Aisthēsis and *doxa* go together in that *doxa*, like *aisthēsis*, is private. As Socrates puts it, "I define forming opinion as talking, *legein*, and opinion as talk, *logos*, which has been held, not with someone else, nor yet aloud, but in silence with oneself" (190a). Opinion may be silent, but it is still talk. Thus, just as Theaetetus' first and second definitions of knowledge go together, so, too, does Theaetetus' second definition anticipate his third, namely, knowledge

---

43. Quote taken from Desjardins, *Rational Enterprise*, 84.

44. Burnyeat, in *Theaetetus of Plato*, 65 and passim; and Gill, *Philosophos*, 101 and passim, translate *doxa* as "judgment."

45. Farrar, *Origins of Democratic Thinking*, 56.

as true opinion with a *logos*. Opinion may be silent, but insofar as opinion is "thought . . . manifest in the manner of speech," it is also unavoidably public.[46] Our opinions may be our own, and yet, insofar as they are in language, they cannot be wholly private or wholly on one's own terms, for those very terms— the language we speak when we talk, even to ourselves—always and inevitably come from and refer to a common world. In James Porter's words, "The language through which experience is expressed, and the very frames of reference through which experience is allowed to appear at all, can never be private but can only be publicly shared, because it is culturally given."[47]

Does the appearance of *logos* through *doxa* at the scene of aisthetic experience stabilize, order, fix, and secure the characteristic motion of *aisthēsis*? It can. The *logos* of the *politikos* in the *Statesman*, for example, makes sense of the experience of the *dēmos* by commanding it, as does the calculative rationality of the philosopher-kings in relation to the ordinary majority of the *kallipolis*, as we saw in chapter 3. In the *Theaetetus*, by contrast, Socrates explains the *logos* that goes with *doxa* and *aisthēsis* in terms of a conversation: "When it thinks," he says, "the soul is merely conversing, *dialegesthai*, with itself, asking itself questions and answering, affirming and denying" (189e–190a). In the middle voice, *dialegesthai*, in Eva Brann's account, "betokens turn-and-turn-about, that is, reflexivity, coming together, even in opposition, in a dialogue; hence 'dialectic,' which will come to name the powerful engine of developing rational thought as it posits, opposes, and composes itself," as we saw in *Republic* 7.[48] The material of the *logoi* of *dialegesthai* is vocal sound (*Theat.* 206d; also *Crat.* 389d–390a).[49] Like all other sounds, these *logoi* are available for *their* actualization only through *aisthēsis*. This makes the *aisthēsis* of *logos* no less private, individuated, particularistic, phenomenological, and infallible than any other sensory experiences. *Logoi*, like *doxa*, are also, and for the same reasons, however, unavoidably public. It is this paradox of *logos*, its amphiboly[50]—as the object of sense experience and as the medium by way of which such

---

46. Arendt, "Philosophy and Politics," 89.
47. Porter, *Origins of Aesthetic Thought*, 196.
48. Brann, *Logos of Heraclitus*, 12.
49. For discussion of the "arising of linguistic meaning from mere sounds through their combination into syllables," see Desjardins, *Rational Enterprise*, 67.
50. For discussion and examples, although not with reference to Plato, see Condren, *Status and Appraisal of Classic Texts*, 242–52; Ober, "Tyrant Killing as Therapeutic Stasis," 243–45; and Morgan, "Tyranny of the Audience," 181–213.

experiences are shared—that appear to give the Greek *logos* its multiple significations in English as speech, word, statement, discourse, and also as definition, argument, account, structure, reason, rationality.[51]

WHAT DO I MAKE OF IT? OR, MEASURING, INCOMMENSURABILITY, RELATIONALITY

Socrates speaks of the object that appears to me in a particular way as "that against which I measure myself, or that which I touch." He speaks of the organ that is sensing as "that which did the measuring off, or the touching" (154b).[52] What sort of measuring is this? The account of *aisthēsis* offered on behalf of Protagoras' students suggests, in the first instance, that the sensing organ is the measurer, insofar as it is the *dunamis*, power, of, for example, the eye to see, actualized in seeing, that measures the stick. The sensing organ is also the measured, however, insofar as it is the *dunamis*, power, of the stick to be seen, actualized in being seen, that measures the seeing eye. On this account of *aisthēsis*, contra the sun in the sun-good analogy discussed earlier, there *are* powers, *dunameis*, in the seeing eye.[53] On this account, too, the measure is not "outside and beyond"[54] what it is supposed to measure but inheres in the percipient and in the perceived, in between the two, where they touch. At first glance, this account of measure, located in between "person" and "thing," and neither Heraclitean nor Parmenidean, seems opposed to Protagoras as well.[55] This is because Protagoras' "Man is the measure, *metron*, of all things, of the things that are, that [or how] they are, of the things that are not, that [or how] they are not" (152a) is generally interpreted as Heraclitean fluxism and is, therefore, said, like it, to locate the measure of all things entirely in the per-

---

51. Arendt, "Socrates," 23: "The identity of speech and thought, which together are *logos*, is perhaps one of the outstanding characteristics of Greek culture."

52. Derrida has noted that to listen, *entendre* in French, is to tender, to offer, to give; and Manning, *Politics of Touch*, 12–13, has added "to reach out toward" in order to underscore the connection of hearing to touch.

53. *Rep.* 507c, e, 508a, 509b. Light encapacitates seeing and being seen but, unlike in the sun-good analogy, is not their cause.

54. This is how Arendt, "What Is Authority?," 109, characterizes the ideas in the *Republic*.

55. Penner, "Wax Tablet, Logic, and Protagoreanism," 200, claims that "as is generally granted ... Plato rejects the Protagoreanism of this part of the *Theaetetus*." Desjardins, *Rational Enterprise*, 88–89, is an exception.

son. Socrates' refutation of Heracliteanism is thus often read as a refutation of Protagoras' radical relativism and subjectivism as well.

As we just saw, however, Socrates does not quite refute so much as amend Heracliteanism, by way of the account he attributes to Protagoras' students. Protagoras and Heraclitus, this suggests, should not be too quickly assimilated. If Protagoras may stand for something other than Heracliteanism, however, what might that be? Martin Heidegger glosses Protagoras' man-measure principle like this:

> Man does not, from out of some detached I-ness, set forth the measure to which everything that is . . . must accommodate itself. Man who possesses the Greeks' fundamental relationship to that which is and to its unconcealment is *metron* (measure [*Maß*]) in that he accepts restriction [*Mäßigung*] to the horizon of unconcealment that is limited after the manner of the I.[56]

To acknowledge what the man-measure principle, on Heidegger's gloss, does not leave up to the "I," we might characterize its relativism and subjectivity as relationality and intersubjectivity. When, as in the account of *aisthēsis* Socrates associates with Protagoras' students, what is being sensed is no less and no more a subject or object than is the seeing I/eye, there is a dual subjectivity that, as such, distributes the power of actualization of both subjects across the relation between perceiver and perceived.[57] It follows that *aisthēsis*, though infallible and unfalsifiable, does not depend on the perceiver alone.

To be sure, how and what I sense critically depends on my sensing capacities, *dunameis*. And these depend on my capaciousness, my openness to being, in Socrates' words, touched or moved. In being touched or moved, I do not only measure what I perceive, however. What I perceive measures me at the same time. How I comport myself in relation to what I sense thus affects what and how I come to know *and* who I come to be. It is for these reasons and in these ways that the practice of *aisthēsis* is, as Socrates implies in *Republic* 7, an attitude of soul, a point to which I return later. For now I want to emphasize that the production in being by *aisthēsis* of the unity of actualization of the *dunameis* of sense organs and what is sensed makes measure relative to *both* human and perceptible thing and, by making it relative to both *at the same time*,

---

56. Heidegger, "Age of the World Picture," 145–46.

57. Zilioli, "Wooden Horse," 177, 182, reads this account of perception as one of the positions against which the *Theaetetus* is written.

stabilizes the relativism by way of that difference-in-unity, at least for now.[58] Between people, this is the work of *doxa* and *logos*.

Heidegger, like many commentators, takes Plato and Socrates to attribute only relativism and subjectivity to Protagoras. In my view, Socrates rather anticipates Heidegger's gloss on Protagoras when he says: "Then you know that [Protagoras] puts it something like this, that as each thing appears to me, so it is for me, and as each thing appears to you, so it is for you—you and I each being a man?" (152a; also 170a). There is no "detached I-ness" here but instead what Edward Schiappa has called attentiveness to "frames of reference," such that "To the form 'A is B' must be added the notion 'for C.'"[59] Socrates puts it this way:

> It remains only . . . that it and I should be or become . . . for each other; necessity binds together our existence, *hēmōn hē anangkē tēn ousian sundei*; but binds neither of us to anything else, nor each of us to himself; so we can only be bound to one another. Accordingly, whether we speak of something "being" or of its "becoming," we must speak of it as being or becoming for someone, or of something or towards something; but we must not speak . . . of a thing as either being or becoming anything just in and by itself. (160b-c)

I show next that the attentiveness to frames of reference that Socrates attributes to Protagoras may also be seen in Socrates' own attentiveness to frames of reference when he detaches from his "I-ness" to impersonate Protagoras.

After ostensibly bringing "the Protagorean tale, *muthos*, to naught," and, with it, Theaetetus' definition of knowledge as perception, Socrates insists that they revisit it anew, this time in the company of the tale's "father," Protagoras himself.[60] If Protagoras were alive, Socrates says, "he would have had a good deal to say in his defence. But he is dead" (164d-e), like the poets with whom Socrates had earlier allied him (152e). And so, as he sometimes does with the poets, Socrates, at "Protagoras'" request ("Protagoras," because it is Socrates

---

58. On the "broadly stable as well as locally variable" nature of human interaction with the world, see Farrar, *Origins of Democratic Thinking*, 49.

59. Schiappa, *Protagoras and* Logos, 126, who also, 129–30, displays, rightly in my view, skepticism about the appropriateness of the language of subjectivity and objectivity in the Greek context, owing to anachronism. For this reason, perceiver and percipient are better understood as simultaneously subject and object.

60. I return to this passage in "Impostures, Images, Truth" below.

speaking in the person of Protagoras), turns to Protagoras' writings (166d-e), to which he had also referred earlier (161c), and will later again (171b). Farrar provides a thorough treatment of the arguments Socrates presents on behalf of Protagoras over the course of the dialogue, referring to the Protagoras of the *Theaetetus* as "Platagoras" to mark the differences between the dialogue's representations and the real-life sophist.[61] Michel Narcy argues, by contrast, that Socrates quotes directly from Protagoras' work, titled *Truth*, and that, in so doing, seeks to limit his engagements with Protagoras "to answers that could be given by Protagoras himself."[62] Despite their differences, Farrar and Narcy both treat Plato's representations of Protagoras in the *Theaetetus* as the "semblance of an original," to use the language of the *Symposium* discussed in chapter 5.

But what if we read the dialogue's depictions of Protagoras and of "Protagoras" not as copies but as representations? And what if "Protagoras" refers Socrates to Protagoras' writings not to establish their "truth" but to make manifest that in relation to writing, as in relation to all perceptible things, for man to be the measure is, as Socrates puts it a few pages later, now speaking on his own behalf, "to take ourselves as we are, and go on saying the things which seem to us to be" (171d)? What if by way of "man is the measure," Plato's Protagoras and Socrates' "Protagoras" seek not to avoid but to explain promiscuities of interpretation, which is to say, to practice interpretation, give opinions, and form judgments based on what is perceived? Finally, what if, given the nature of how we perceive, that is, by way of our different and potentially incommensurable frames of reference, to relate to writing, as we saw in the context of the *Phaedrus* in chapter 1, as to relate to all things, is, *eo ipso*, to be involved, "like the many," in "all sorts of difficulty" (*Theaet.* 168b-c)? In short, what if "Protagoras" refers Socrates to Protagoras' writings precisely to bring to light the futility of seeking a guarantee against different and potentially incommensurable frames of reference by recourse to *Truth*?

This is, indeed, what the dialogue appears to show us when, after he has finished impersonating Protagoras, Socrates explores with Theodorus, also called a "measure, *metron*" (169a), the difficulties around what they take Protagoras' writings and "Protagoras," too, to have said (169d-172b). Over the course of their exchange, Socrates twice calls Theodorus "Protagoras" (170a, c). In doing so, he seems to underscore the promiscuity of "Protagoras" himself, and also to be implying that he and Theodorus both have the capacity, *dunamis*, to speak on behalf of Protagoras, to be his measures, despite

---

61. Farrar, *Origins of Democratic Thinking*, 53–77.
62. Narcy, "Why Was the *Theaetetus* Written by Euclides?," 163.

Theodorus' earlier refusal and Socrates' later disavowal of his own status as measure (179b). Like other sense perceptibles, "Protagoras," Protagoras, and *Truth* are also the measures of Socrates and Theodorus. When Theodorus refuses to exercise his capacity to speak on behalf of Protagoras, for example, he shows himself to be unwilling to come to the assistance of his friend (164e). Socrates, for his part, has been speaking on behalf of Protagoras since the beginning of the dialogue but, from "Protagoras'" point of view, he has been doing so unfairly and ungenerously (166a-c, 168b, d). In these passages, the hallmarks of the account of sense perception Socrates has associated with Protagoras' students—*dunamis* and attentiveness to frames of reference—are thus associated, by way of "Protagoras," with Protagoras' man-measure principle, too. As we will see next, they appear in the *Theaetetus'* frame as well.

FRAMING KNOWLEDGE

Plato presents the dialogue between Socrates and Theaetetus as a transcription by Euclides of a conversation that took place many years before. In an echo of his treatment of Protagoras' writings, discussed above, Michel Narcy writes that the *Theaetetus* is the "only Platonic dialogue in which, instead of being criticised (as in the *Phaedrus*), writing is presented with emphasis as a guarantee of truthfulness in reporting the words or thoughts of an absent speaker."[63] I see things differently. For one thing, while there is criticism of writing in the *Phaedrus*, that criticism, I argued in chapter 1, effectively discloses writing's promiscuity, power, and promise for its many readers. Narcy's assessment of the status of Euclides' writing in the *Theaetetus* is open to question as well. In my view, rather than "a guarantee of truthfulness," Euclides' writing is presented as thoroughly unreliable. I do not see this as a criticism of writing, however, but rather as a criticism of the "guarantee of truthfulness" Euclides' writing appears to seek to claim for itself. By making manifest its *un*reliability, the dialogue thus exposes the falsity of writing that claims to guarantee truth. Like the *Phaedrus* and like Protagoras' *Truth*, as just discussed, the *Theaetetus'* frame locates the truth and authority of writing, even (or especially) writing about knowledge, in its readers.

Anticipating the argument Socrates presents toward the end of the *Theatetus*, proving "the nonidentity of knowledge and true judgment" using the example of jurors whose judgments rest not on eyewitness testimony but on

---

63. Ibid., 150.

"hearsay" (201c), Euclides' transcription, we are told, is not of the actual conversation it reports.[64] Euclides was not present at that conversation. Instead, his report is based on Socrates' memory of the conversation that Euclides has written down on the basis of his memory of Socrates' report. Like Apollodorus and Aristodemus in the *Symposium*, discussed in chapter 5, Euclides is presented as an unreliable narrator.[65] Unlike Socrates, who was able to recount his early conversation with Theaetetus from memory, Euclides says he is unable to recall what Socrates reported to him about that conversation except by looking at notes he made "as soon as I reached home," where "at my leisure, as I recalled things, I wrote them down, and whenever I went to Athens I used to ask Socrates about what I could not remember, and then I came here and made corrections; so that I have pretty much the whole talk written down" (143a). Euclides' description of his writing practice is a little odd. If, as Narcy suggests, his "writing is presented with emphasis as a guarantee of truthfulness in reporting the words or thoughts of an absent speaker," then why does Euclides tell us that he waited until he got home to Megara to make his notes? Why does he not make them while speaking with Socrates, especially given that, as he also tells us, there were things that he could not remember when he got home? Euclides says that he checked his notes with Socrates but also only corrected *these* when he got home. Given the unreliability of his memory, what guarantee is there that his corrections, made from memory, are accurate? It may be that Euclides consulted with Socrates about his corrections as well. But, despite the detailed account he offers of his writing practice, he does not say that, saying instead that he has "pretty much the whole talk written down." As with Apollodorus, as noted in chapter 5, this may leave us wondering which parts Euclides may have forgotten or left out.

Euclides cannot tell us what he may have forgotten, of course. He does tell us some of what he left out by explaining the method he followed for his transcription: "I have not made Socrates relate the conversation as he related it to me, but I represent him as speaking directly to the persons with whom he had this conversation. . . . I wanted, in the written version, to avoid the bother of having the bits of narrative in between the speeches—I mean, when Socrates, whenever he mentions his own part in the discussion, says 'And I maintained' . . . or 'He would not admit this'" (143b-c). Euclides avoids the bother of superfluous utterances, which, according to Narcy, are a mark of eristic,

---

64. The quoted phrase is from Burnyeat, in *Theaetetus of Plato*, 124.
65. Zuckert, *Plato's Philosophers*, 600, comments on Euclides' unreliability as well.

whose school, the Megarian School, was founded by the historical Euclides.[66] Avoiding superfluities is also the mark of Eleatic monism or the Parmenidean unity of being and of knowledge, also advocated by the historical Euclides.[67] By omitting all signs of Socrates' narration, Plato's Euclides effectively erases the genealogy of the *logoi* of Socrates and his interlocutors, thus rendering them sourceless and timeless, which is to say, universal and unchanging. The Euclides of the *Theaetetus* is thus presented as making stable and secure what is actually in motion, and doing so in a way that erases motion's traces. The great success of "Euclides' transcription" and of Parmenideanism more generally is attested to by Narcy's claim that Euclides' writing acts as a guarantee of truthfulness.

John Cooper claims, in his introduction to the *Theaetetus*, that "since ancient sources tell us of Socratic dialogues actually published by Euclides, it is as if, except for the prologue, Plato is giving us under his own name one of Euclides' dialogues!"[68] I agree that Plato appears to be giving us one of Euclides' dialogues. The result, if we ignore the prologue's framing references, is a hypostasization of the *logos* of the dialogue and its identification with that of Parmenides. By having Euclides flag his omissions, however, especially after the mimetic stage has been so carefully set, the dialogue points to his erasures and thereby discloses the partiality and situatedness of the representations that follow. In the language of *Republic* 2, the prologue of the *Theaetetus* presents the dialogue to its readers as a "verbal falsehood." By conspicuously underscoring in its frame the unstable, contingent, and fallible genealogy of the dialogue's *logoi*, the *Theaetetus* prompts readers to wonder not only about the power of writing and memory to put *logos* in motion but also, and again, about what Gerald Mara describes as the phenomenological nature of *logos* itself.[69] To leave to one side these lessons of the dialogue's frame of reference is to do to the *logoi* of the dialogue what Euclides does to Socrates' *logoi*, which is to say, to act in an eristic fashion by representing as unchanging, eternal, stable, and fixed what the dialogue's frame presents rather as intersubjective and relational, subject to scrutiny and contestation, accountable and falsifiable.

---

66. On superfluities and eristic in the *Euthydemus*, and on Euclides as the founder of the Eristic school, see Narcy, "Why Was the *Theaetetus* Written by Euclides?," 164 and 151, with references at n. 5.

67. On the historical Euclides as a Parmenidean, see Zuckert, *Plato's Philosophers*, 597; and Nails, *People of Plato*, 145.

68. Cooper, in *Plato: Complete Works*, 158.

69. Mara, *Socrates' Discursive Democracy*, 158.

The staging of the reading of the transcription, "its literary intricacy and self-consciousness," underscores the mimetic and mediated quality of the *logoi* that follow, even as Euclides' omissions do the reverse.[70] That the transcription is read by Euclides' slave, who is at a third remove from the *logos* he is presented as presenting, underscores the self-consciousness of the dialogue's mimetic representation. This is underscored as well in Socrates' impersonation of Protagoras, to which I return next.

IMPOSTURES, IMAGES, TRUTH

As we have seen, after ostensibly bringing "the Protagorean tale, *muthos*, to naught," and, with it, Theaetetus' definition of knowledge as perception, Socrates insists they revisit it anew, this time in the company of Protagoras, the tale's "father." If Protagoras were alive, Socrates says,

> he would have had a good deal to say in his defence. But he is dead, and we are abusing the orphan. Why, even the guardians whom Protagoras has left—one of whom is Theodorus here—are unwilling to come to the child's assistance. So it seems that we shall have to do it ourselves, assisting him in the name of justice. (164d-e)

I have alluded to aspects of this passage earlier in this chapter, but there is more to notice. One thing is that, in the space of a few lines, Socrates characterizes Protagoras as both a father and a child. The origin of his tale, Protagoras is a "father" in a metaphorical sense. At issue at this point in the dialogue are the status and worth of his metaphorical offspring, specifically, his "tale, *muthos*," of knowledge as *aisthēsis* by way of man as the measure. In the terms of the account of midwifery, introduced by Socrates earlier in the dialogue, the question is whether by this tale, Protagoras' mind, *dianoia*, has brought forth an "image, *eidolon*, an imposture, *pseudos*, or a fertile truth, *alēthes*" (150c). Claiming that it is "out of the question" for him "to allow an imposture, *pseudos*, or to destroy the true, *alēthes*" (151d), Socrates says that if, after examination, he thinks something is "a mere image, *eidolon*, and not real," he will "quietly take it" and abandon it (151c). Opposing "real offspring" to "mere wind-eggs" (151e), Socrates appears to treat images as impostures and both as failed wind-eggs.

We have seen in earlier chapters, however, that the *Republic*, at least, distinguishes images and impostures. The taxonomy of falsehoods Socrates offers in

---

70. For the quoted phrase, see Halliwell, "Theory and Practice of Narrative," 16.

Republic 2 (382a-d) treats images, *eidola*, as verbal falsehoods, which, by announcing their falsity, do not seek to deceive, and distinguishes these from true lies, which deceive by covering over their falsity. That the *Theaetetus* uses the same word for "imposture" that the *Republic* uses for "true lie," namely, *pseudos*, may caution against too quickly assimilating images and impostures. There are further grounds for caution. As we will see, the bright line that Socrates seems to draw at this point, near the beginning of the *Theaetetus*, between real offspring and infertile wind-eggs is blurred over the course of the dialogue, as Socrates rehabilitates wind-eggs whose infertility has ostensibly been established. Harboring a fertility of their own, some wind-eggs, it seems, are worth rearing. Is Protagoras' "tale" an image, imposture, or true? Is his offspring a wind-egg worth rearing, an infertile wind-egg, or a real offspring? That Socrates has treated Protagoras' identification of knowledge and perception as a wind-egg but rehabilitates it any number of times gives reason to take it to be neither infertile nor an imposture. Is it, then, an image, or is it true, a wind-egg worth rearing or a real offspring? What are the relations among these? And what are the stakes of their differences?

A metaphorical father of a metaphorical offspring, Protagoras is also presented as himself an offspring, specifically, an "orphan," whom Socrates marks in the passage above as vulnerable to abuse (see also *Republic* 495c), especially when, as in the present case, his guardians, including Theodorus, are unwilling to come to his aid. What kind of offspring is Protagoras? And what kind of metaphorical offspring is "Protagoras," Socrates' representation by impersonation of Protagoras? In the terms of Socrates' account of midwifery, is "Protagoras" an image, an imposture, or the truth? At first glance, we might say, an imposture, for, as we saw in chapters 2 and 3, impersonation, a form of imitation, seeks, as a rule, to cover over the fact that the impersonator is not the one he impersonates. This is not the case here, however, for Socrates announces that he will speak as Protagoras. "Protagoras" is thus a "verbal falsehood," whose truth is to be false but not deceptive (*Rep.* 382a-d).

Is Socrates' "Protagoras," then, an image or a truth, fertile wind-egg or real offspring? By the measures of the *Theaetetus* and *Republic*, "Protagoras" appears to be both. "Run around the hearth" by his metaphorical father in the *Theaetetus*, namely, Socrates, Protagoras survives the rite Socrates describes as determining the worthiness of offspring to be reared (160e–161a). As a verbal falsehood, whose paradigmatic exemplifications are images, as we have seen in earlier chapters, Protagoras and/as "Protagoras" is also an image. By the art of midwifery, too, Protagoras/"Protagoras" seems to be both: though orphaned, and abandoned by his guardians, he has not been quietly taken and abandoned by Socrates, which is what Socrates says he will do if he thinks after examination that something is "a mere image, *eidolon*, and not real" (151c). Instead, he is rehabilitated time and time again. "Protagoras" thus appears to be an image and a truth both, which suggests that, in the *Theaetetus*, as in the *Republic*, images have a truth of their own.

Where does this account of Protagoras/"Protagoras" leave us in relation to his offspring, the "tale" that knowledge is *aisthēsis*? The *Theaetetus* ends with Socrates maintaining, in the name of midwifery, that all three definitions of knowledge forwarded by Theaetetus have been refuted: "Our art of midwifery declares to us that all the offspring that have been born are mere wind-eggs and not worth rearing." Theaetetus agrees (210a-b). But perhaps he should not. For although the art of midwifery has declared repeatedly that Theaetetus' offspring are wind-eggs, it has taken a different attitude to their rearing. Regarding all three definitions, whenever Socrates has claimed that he and Theaetetus will have to start afresh, from a clean slate, from the beginning, as if to erase what has come before (151c-d, 187b, 200d), Socrates has instead breathed new life into what had appeared to be a "mere wind-egg" (151e, 157d, 161a), even when Theaetetus agrees that he has been refuted and is prepared to move on (162d–163a, 164c-e, 179c-e). The fertility of "mere wind-eggs" aligns them, contra Socrates' closing statement, with offspring who *are* worth rearing.

Rearing by whom? Socrates' practice in the *Theaetetus* suggests that the viability of offspring depends on their midwives. It also depends on their birthers, which is to say, in the case of the dialogue's three definitions, Theaetetus. How does he fare? On the one hand, he appears to fare well, for his offspring survive until the very end of the dialogue. They do so, however, with not too much assistance from Theaetetus, who, instead, as noted, repeatedly accepts Socrates' refutations. Socrates, by contrast, rehabilitates Theaetetus' first definition of knowledge by treating it as Protagoras' offspring, which he takes up and defends and also challenges. The fertility of wind-eggs and their rearing thus appear to depend not only on midwives and birthers but also on myriad others, including Plato's Protagoras and Socrates' "Protagoras." Perhaps, then, Socrates' closing declaration that Theaetetus' definitions have been refuted signals only that Theaetetus' definitions *as midwifed by Socrates* have been refuted. If that is so, then they may still be taken up by anyone who is willing, in the mode of a midwife and/or birther, actual or metaphorical, to speak on their behalves. Read in this way, the dialogue's ending exemplifies the understanding of knowledge it had been presenting all along by way of Theaetetus' definitions: dependent on plural and varying perceptions, opinions, and accounts, knowledge, so understood, *is* a matter of *aisthēsis*, *doxa*, and *logos*, which is to say, that knowledge is perspectival, partial, provisional, revisable, and integrally bound to speech.

Burnyeat concludes that, for the *Theaetetus*, "the problem of knowledge is ultimately a problem of determining the powers and limits of human reason."[71] Agreeing, I have sought to show how the aisthetic and doxic dimensions of *logos*, made conspicuous in the *Theaetetus* and in the *Republic* as well, challenge "two-world" views of the dialogues' philosophy by making manifest the ways in which the allegedly detached world of ideas is bound to a world of appearances. My goal has also been to show how bringing sense perceptions to appearance by way of *logos* is a power or capacity, *dunamis*, of soul and how judgment—the *logos* we find in reflection on *aisthēsis* (186d)—is, as it were, the child of sense experience.

WILLING TO PAY ATTENTION, AN ATTITUDE OF SOUL, *PHRONĒSIS*

Near the end of the dialogue, when they are considering Theaetetus' final definition of knowledge as true opinion with a *logos* (201c, 206c), Socrates asks Theaetetus about letters and syllables (202e–208b). At issue is whether syllables and/or letters may be given a *logos* and thereby be known. Inviting a turn to the experiential, and specifically to the practice of self-examination, Socrates says: "Let us, then, take them up and examine them [letters and syllables], or rather, let us examine ourselves and see whether it was in accordance with this theory, or not, that we learned letters" (203a). While waiting to hear from Theaetetus about his experiences, Socrates appears to change tack with the following words: "First, then, syllables have a *logos*, but the letters are *alogos*?" (203a). What follows is a discussion of the knowability of complexes or wholes that concludes with Socrates rejecting "the statement of any one who says that the syllable is knowable, *gnoston*, and expressible, *rheton*, but the letter is not" (205e). When Theaetetus agrees with Socrates' claim about what is and is not sayable, one that cuts against his initially expressed intuitions, Socrates responds: "Wouldn't you rather accept the opposite belief, judging by your own experience when you were learning to read?" Going on to describe that experience by references to sight and hearing (206a), and pressing Theaetetus not to forget his experiences (207d), Socrates underscores that in

---

71. Burnyeat, in *Theaetetus of Plato*, 234–41, 241.

learning to read, an analogue, as we know, for coming to know, Theaetetus, like the students of dialectics in *Republic* 7 (525b), should not leave the "region of generation" behind.[72] No adequate *logos* of knowledge can leave out experience, and specifically sensible experience.

If this is so, however, then what are we to make of the *Theaetetus*' famous digression (177c)? Socrates contrasts those whose eyes are "fixed upon the whole" (175a) and "the investigation of abstract right and wrong" (175c), who are concerned with "what a human being is and what is proper for such a nature" (174a-b), and abstain from all political activities (173d-e), on the one hand, with "worldly men," on the other, those "clever, *deinos*" (177a), men, who "knock about in the lawcourts and such places" (172c).[73] In language resonant with *Republic* 7, discussed earlier, what most distinguishes the first type of man from the second is the capacity, *dunamis*, to calculate, *logizesthai* (175a, b). Scholars sometimes take the digression to be advocating for the first type, "who have been brought up in philosophy and other such pursuits" (172c), and who recall, in some aspects, the philosopher-kings of the *Republic*, and also, as Mary Louise Gill has suggested, Parmenides: they all exercise their *to logistikon* to compel unity, believing, as Gill puts it, describing Parmenides, that "all things are one and unchanged (180e)";[74] they all seek to become as "god-like" as possible (*Theat.* 176b; *Rep.* 383c). The digression, Gill remarks, "portrays a philosopher of a very different stripe from the Protagoreans and Heracliteans who dominate" much of the rest of the *Theaetetus*.[75]

Theodorus, Socrates' interlocutor, favors this kind of philosopher, saying that if all men could be persuaded of his truth, "there would be more peace and fewer evils among mankind." Socrates, for his part, appears to distance himself from this type by referring to him as the one "whom *you* [i.e., Theodorus] call a philosopher" (175e, my emphasis). To Socrates, "it is impossible that evils should be done away with, Theodorus, for there must always be something opposed to the good." He adds that philosophers, moreover, "cannot have their place among the gods but must inevitably hover about mortal nature and this earth" (176a). The philosopher of the digression, like the philosopher-kings discussed in chapter 3, may *seek* good without evil, and that kind of unity

---

72. Contra Burnyeat, in *Theaetetus of Plato*, 187, 209, 213, who calls these passages "a simple lesson in spelling."

73. For "worldly men," see Gill, *Philosophos*, 87.

74. Gill, *Philosophos*, 86–89. Gill underscores, and I agree, that these philosophical types also all differ from one another.

75. Gill, *Philosophos*, 89.

without opposition may be available to gods, but unless we "escape from the earth" (176b), it appears that finding that good is not possible for mortals.

Is it not nonetheless humanly desirable to strive to become "most nearly perfect" by becoming like a god "so far as this is possible" (176b-c)? If that means becoming like Theodorus' philosopher, then, on my reading, the digression answers no. Gill disagrees. Reading the digression as a plea "for the objectivity of moral values," Gill argues that the distinction between the digression's philosopher and the "worldly man"—"two patterns, *paradeigmata*," Socrates says, that distinguish "the divine, which is most blessed, and the godless, which is most wretched" (176e–177a)—maps onto a contrast between what she calls "mental perception," defined as "the direct awareness of stable, intelligible objects," and sense perception. She maintains that the digression marks this contrast, which we may recognize as another instance of the two-world ontology, in order to create space by way of the first and against the second, for a Parmenidean account of knowledge against the Heraclitean/Protagorean accounts that have come before.[76] Gill makes her case by attending to contrasts the digression makes between "perceptual awareness" and what she calls "failure to notice," *lanthanein*. "So keen was he to know things in heaven," Socrates says, describing the philosopher Thales, "that he failed to notice the things right at his feet, *lanthanoi auton*," and so fell into a pit (174a-b). The digression's philosopher also fails to notice, *lelethen*, his neighbor, "not only ignoring his activities but scarcely knowing whether his neighbor is a human being or some other creature" (174b). In Gill's view, the philosopher's failure to notice "transient sensible objects" underwrites his attunement to "mental perception," which allows him "to escape from earth to heaven" and to exemplify the paradigm of the divine and blessed. The worldly man, by contrast, does not see what the philosopher sees, namely, "all the earth" (174e) and "all time" (175a). Failing to perceive "stable objects," including "the nature of man, justice, and happiness," he acts unjustly. In his folly, he fails to notice, *lanthanousi*, that by his unjust actions he exemplifies the paradigm of godlessness and wretchedness (176e–177a).[77]

The appearances of *lanthanein* words in the digression repay scrutiny. As we saw in chapter 3, *lanthanein* and its derivations punctuate the *Republic*'s account of the early education of the philosophers-to-be-kings. There, too, as in the account of the philosopher of the digression, they signify a failure to notice sense perceptibles and an orientation instead to stable objects like

---

76. Ibid., 87–89.
77. Ibid.

Justice *haploos*, and the good. *Lanthanein* words also punctuate the *Republic*'s accounts of tyranny, where they mark failures to notice when one is being deceived into acting for the good of another rather than in one's own good. In the context of *Republic* 2–5, I argued that Socrates uses *lanthanein* words across the *Republic* to prompt questions about, rather than to underwrite, the early education's orientation to Justice, and to prompt questions, too, about the ways of being good that follow from failures to notice sense perceptibles.

In my view, the *lanthanein* words in the digression in the *Theaetetus* do similar work, prompting questions about both the worldly men and the philosopher. That the digression prompts us to question the "wretched" and "unjust" worldly men and their failures to notice their own injustice and wretchedness (176d) seems clear enough. What about the philosopher? His mind "borne in all directions," he gazes upward at the stars "above the sky," and also "below the earth" (173e), at everything except what is around him on earth, including, as noted, his neighbor. Thus, when he hears an encomium of a tyrant or a king, "he fancies he is listening to the praises of some herdsman" (174d). Interested in "the investigation of justice and injustice themselves," he rises "above the level of 'What wrong have I done you or you me?'" (175c). Unable to distinguish either between tyrant and king, or between those with and without power, and unaware whether he has done or been victim to injustice, the philosopher of the digression may be a good "calculator," but as we have noticed about *to logistikon* in relation to the philosopher-kings of the *Republic*, that will make him singularly ill-equipped to attend to matters of ethics and politics, including his own good. Thus depicted as failing to notice his own actual and potential wretchedness and injustice, which is not surprising given that, as we saw at the beginning of this section, self-knowledge in the *Theaetetus* is depicted as a matter of sense perception (203a), the philosopher of the digression bears the same problematic marks as the worldly men. What Socrates says "we must tell" the worldly men, then, appears no less relevant to the digression's philosopher, namely, "that just because they do not think they are such as they are, they are so all the more truly" (176d).

If, then, it may not be humanly desirable to strive to become "most nearly perfect" in the mode of the philosopher of the digression, for the costs, as for the worldly men, are self-knowledge and justice, might it be desirable to strive in some other way? Socrates says that to become like a god "so far as this is possible" is to become just and pious, with practical wisdom, *phronēsis* (176b). To become just is, at least, to do no harm, to oneself or others. I explore justice further in the epilogue. To become pious is, at least, to acknowledge a difference between being human and being a god, which may open a doubt about those who desire "to escape from earth to the dwelling of the gods as quickly as we can" (176a-b). In any case, Socrates tells us that to strive to become humanly just and pious is to strive with *phronēsis*. In the *Republic*, *phronēsis* is associated with a practice of philosophy that does not reject but rather depends on *logos* and *empeiria*, experience (582a, d). In the *Theaetetus*, too, Socrates appears to recover the man-measure principle for philosophy by marrying it to *phronēsis* (183b-c). What sort of knowledge is *phronēsis*, the attitude of soul that orients human beings to justice and allows us to measure things not in our detached I-ness but by being toward them? Not *logistike*, calculation, for, as we have seen, *to logistikon* is an inadequate measure of things like justice. Instead, it is a mode of knowing that, in the form of philosophy, as we saw in chapter 5, understands and accepts that to be what it is to be depends on failing to secure once and for all what it seeks.[78] The *sophia* of philosophy, this means, is, as *phronēsis*, the always not-yet of knowledge. Near death in the *Phaedo*, Socrates remembers his decision to study the *logoi* of human beings and not the things themselves (99d–100a). On my way of reading, this is a decision Plato seems to have shared, which is to say that he, like his Socrates, appears to offer, by way of the *Theaetetus* and *Republic* at least, studies of *logos* that open to contestation and scrutiny in the practice of dialectics, *dialegesthai*, the all-too-human things that constitute what Davide Panagia has aptly called "the political life of sensation."[79]

A CITY IN *LOGOS*

If *logos*, *doxa*, and *aisthēsis* interrelate in the ways I have suggested, then what are we to make of the view that the *Republic*'s sun-good analogy, line simile, and cave allegory strictly hierarchize noetic knowledge over doxastic knowledge and sense perception, *aisthēsis*? We have seen that the line simile, structured as an analogy, represents not a fixed hierarchy at all but rather, like all analogies, puts its terms in mutually constituting relations. I have argued that the sun-good analogy, too, problematizes rather than inscribes an idea of the good divorced from *aisthēsis*. What if we read the cave allegory along similar lines?

Taking shadows for things, sounds of puppets for human voices, and the light and warmth of a fire for the sun (514a–515c), the cave dwellers are pre-

---

78. On *phronēsis*, see also Stern, *Knowledge and Politics in Plato's "Theaetetus,"* 122, 200, 254, 291; Polansky, *Philosophy and Knowledge*, 30, 109, 142.

79. See Panagia, *Political Life of Sensation*.

sented as mistaking sense perceptual particulars. Might it be that their philosophic failure is tied to *these* mistakes? Fettered to sense only what is straight ahead of them, might they be unable to actualize the "indwelling capacity, *dunamis*," to sense with their souls *because* their fetters prevent them from turning their whole bodies (518c)? Might those very fetters foreclose the experiences they would need to have to sense this lack? Compelled to emerge from the cave, the philosopher, for his or her part, is described as seeing what is by way of the images, reflections, and refractions of the sun's rays (532c), which is to say, as Socrates did (533a), by way of their look, how they appear. When, by contrast, the philosopher looks directly at the sun, the analogue of the good, to see beyond what appears, that, Socrates says in the *Phaedo*, would be blinding (99d–100a). What if, then, the cave allegory, like the line simile, sun-good analogy, and the law of dialectics, prompts us to see *aisthēsis* as a condition of the possibility of *logos* and not only as its rival?

What we might call an aistheticized *logos* is a *logos* that, like mimetic poetry, professes its inconstancy, even as it stabilizes, fixes, and secures through names an order, and makes common our individuated sensory experiences. The *Republic* and *Theaetetus* bring to appearance that it is by way of expressing our opinions, *doxa*, in speech, *logos*, about that aistheticized *logos* that we constitute ourselves as a contingent and differentiated unity, actualized in a here and now, whose terms and conditions of association, namely, conversation, *dialegesthai*, are no less contestable, contingent, and fallible than the doxastic *logos* that constitutes it. This is not the city or the *logos* of the city in *logos* (369c, 473d-e) of the *Republic*, in which there is orthodoxy, which is to say, right opinion, but, as we saw in chapter 4, little, if any, speaking. That city, so called because it emerges in conversation over the course of the first half of the dialogue, is instead established by *to logistikon* of its founder-lawgivers who by their laws fix its *logos*. Melissa Lane explains: there is first the founding of the city by founder-lawgivers "articulated in terms of the framing of laws," then the upbringing and education of the city's rulers, then the laws of the city, produced by the rulers in keeping with the "significant" laws first established by the founder-lawgivers, and finally, the city's laws, which, as determined by the rulers, "inculcate the values which support them through education in a virtuous circle."[80]

Lane points out that the founder-lawgivers of the city are "in a sense extra-constitutional." So, too, is its governing body, for the establishment of the

---

80. Lane, "Founding as Legislating," 111–12, 110. These paragraphs draw from my "Constitution."

philosopher-kings as rulers of the *kallipolis* is not itself legislated.[81] From their position outside the constitution, the founder-lawgivers determine, and the philosopher-kings legislate and enforce, the laws that govern the institutions and way of life of the city. Thus, to Paul Kottman,

> Plato's philosophy evolves around the problem of ordering action, subsuming action to an order, and keeping people together within some kind of orderly framework. And in Plato's writing, this amounts to turning the harmonious but unpredictable spectacle of political life, or of human actors on the world stage, into the stable, eternal spectacle of Ideas . . . to which [political life] is hierarchically subjugated.[82]

From this vantage point, there is no question that the calculative rationality of the philosopher-kings, courtesy of the calculative rationality of the founder-lawgivers, stabilizes, orders, fixes, and secures, often, as we have seen in earlier chapters, by compulsion, the "unpredictable spectacle" that is the aisthetic life of the ordinary majority. Indeed, in *Republic* 6, Socrates calls the founder-lawgiver a "constitution-painter" (501c). A *technē* in Aristotle's sense, this art of constitution designs its product according to a blueprint, an idea, *eidos*, originating in the soul or mind of the artist, and lying outside the product as its cause, principle, or rule, *archē* (*Metaph.* 1032b23; *Eth. Nic.* 1140a10), namely, in the calculative rationality of the founder-lawgivers.[83]

The clear and apparent advantage to approaching constitutionalism by reference to an extraconstitutional art of rule is, as Lane notes, that when constitutions are thus established, their virtuous circularity appears to be guaranteed. As Socrates puts it in *Republic* 4, "Once it gets off to a good start, our constitution will be a virtuous circle" (424a-b). In order to "get off to a good start" constitution-painters must, as Socrates says in *Republic* 6, wipe the slate clean, "refusing, right from the start, to have anything to do with any individual or city, or draft any laws, until they were either given a clean slate or had cleaned it for themselves" (501a). The "slate" of the *kallipolis* must not only be cleaned at the start by banishing everyone over the age of ten (541a), as discussed in chapter 3. It must be kept clean as well, hence, as we have seen, the extensive eugenics programs and abstraction from one's own mandated by the laws of *kallipolis* (459d–461e).

---

81. Lane, "Founding as Legislating," 113.
82. Kottman, *Politics of the Scene*, 35.
83. For the "absurd atemporality" of the city in speech, see Ophir, *Plato's Invisible Cities*, 114.

Is the *kallipolis* the *Republic*'s final word? Is the philosophy of founder-lawgivers and/or of the philosopher-kings "Plato's philosophy"? It could be that the *Republic* presents the ordering by the calculative rationality of the founder-lawgivers and philosopher-kings as a guarantee of constitutional virtue. Or, as I have sought to show over the course of this book, it could be that Plato offers the city in speech produced by that ordering to bring to appearance the risks, dangers, and costs of seeking that guarantee. What if, in other words, the clear and apparent advantage of approaching politics by reference to the unaistheticized and nondoxastic *logos* of the founders and philosopher-kings turns out to be only apparent? Under the *kallipolis*'s conditions of compelling *logos*, as we have seen, we hear nothing about speech or opinions, let alone free and beautiful conversations. Feeling "the greatest community of pain and pleasure" (464a), the inhabitants of the *kallipolis* are "all as nearly as possible subject to the same pains and pleasures." This commensuration of *aisthēsis* guarantees that everyone will have "a single opinion about what belongs to them [and] the same goal to aim at" (464d). It thus guarantees against the difference, incommensurability, and plurality that are the conditions of ethics and politics. If, then, as we have seen in earlier chapters, Plato depicts the founder-lawgiver-artists of the *kallipolis* as rivals of the tragic poets, perhaps he does so to position himself in his artistry as their ally in the project of bringing to appearance by way of his mimetic poetry the costs of displacing by an unaistheticized orthodox *logos* the irreducibly unstable, contingent, and falsifiable *logoi* of ethics and politics whose truth is established, if it is at all, in and through discussion, which is to say, dialectically.

EPILOGUE

Poetic Justice

But how could I think of being just through and through? How can I give each his own? Let this be sufficient for me: I give each *my* own!

NIETZSCHE, *Thus Spoke Zarathustra*

At the start of *Republic* 2, Glaucon divides goods into a threefold classification and asks to which class justice belongs (357b-c). Is justice good in and for itself? Is it good in and for itself and for its consequences? Or is it good only for its consequences? Glaucon's classification seems straightforward enough. He (358a) and Adeimantus (363a–364a) associate the many with the justice of the third class of goods, which Glaucon describes as "unpleasant but beneficial." To the many, the brothers say, justice is like physical exercise, undergoing medical treatment, and earning a living, goods we choose, as Glaucon puts it, not "for their own sakes, but only for the payment or other benefits which result from them" (357c-d). Socrates, for his part, places justice in the second class, which he calls "the most beautiful" (358a), and in which Glaucon places "things like thinking, seeing, being healthy," goods "we value both for their own sake and because we desire their results" (357c). Demanding from Socrates Justice unmixed, pure, and simple, as we have seen, Glaucon and Adeimantus appear to place justice in the first class, that is, as, in Glaucon's words, "a good of the kind we would choose to have because we value it for its own sake, and not from any desire for its results" (357b).

The terms and parameters of the *Republic*'s inquiry into justice appear to be set by this classification, and yet the brothers' speeches in *Republic* 2 also seem to call it into question. Arguing not for justice but instead for "complete *injustice*" (360e–361d, my emphasis), the brothers, one scholar maintains, introduce a way of thinking about justice that falls completely outside of the classification's parameters. Taking the rest of the *Republic* to respond to the brothers' *Republic* 2 representations of injustice, M. B. Foster contends that

Plato made a mistake when he included the threefold classification at the beginning of *Republic* 2, and concludes that "[a] true interpretation of Plato's meaning in the *Republic* requires us to dismiss what he says in that passage," for "it seems quite clear that Plato [is] simply confused."[1] There is, indeed, much that is confusing about *Glaucon*'s classification. In my view, as we will see, the confusions bring to appearance the vexed nature of Glaucon's and also Adeimantus' relationship to justice, in the language of chapter 1, its complexity, *poikilia*. Let us look first, however, at the brothers' speeches directly following the classification, for there is reason to find them confusing, too.

It's not only that they make a case for injustice, which appears to lie outside of the parameters of Glaucon's classification, but that they make a case for *"complete* injustice," which Adeimantus defines as injustice "coupled with counterfeit respectability, *met' euschēmosunēs kibdēlou*" (366b), and Glaucon exemplifies in his tale of Gyges' ancestor's invisibility ring (359c-e). It is also not only that they make a case for complete injustice, but that they do so in the name of Thrasymachus (367a) when that is not his position. Thrasymachus advocates for justice as another's good, which, in the case of rulers, as we have seen, is tantamount to injustice, to be sure. But Thrasymachus stands behind injustice as a practice of power, and that makes *appearing* just, a defining characteristic of "complete injustice," beside the point and unnecessary. There is more, for Adeimantus attributes the desire for complete injustice not only to Thrasymachus but also to "anyone else for that matter" (367a), calling it the opinion of experts and most people (366b). By the brothers' own account, however, as noted, the many endorse not injustice but justice for its beneficial consequences, though they find it unpleasant.

In short, the brothers' speeches introduce a new category of (in)justice and do so by falsely attributing it to (many) others. Why the false and also excessive misattribution? Might the brothers seek to distance themselves in these ways from the injustice they introduce in order to cover over that this is actually what *they* desire? Might *they* want the beneficial consequences of justice by appearing just without actually being so (360e-361d)? Seeing things this way helps to make sense of why the brothers are so anxious about the stealth and deception they associate with tyrants, discussed in chapter 3. It also helps to explain why, when he responds to the brothers' speeches, Socrates wonders whether he can trust that they have *not* been truly persuaded by what they have said about complete injustice. "On the basis of the arguments themselves," he says, "I would distrust you. And the more I trust you, the more I'm at a loss as

---

1. Foster, "Mistake of Plato's in the *Republic*," 390.

to what I should do" (368a-b). What *does* Socrates do? As we have seen, to meet the brothers' avowed desire for "a good of the kind we would choose to have because we value it for its own sake, and not from any desire for its results" (357b), Socrates gives the brothers, by way of the philosopher-kings, their education, their city, and their ideas, complete and unqualified Justice. Is this, then, the counter to the brothers' disavowed desire for "complete injustice"? Or its fulfillment?

Let us return to Glaucon's classification. The brothers, as noted, treat the Justice they demand from Socrates as an exemplification of class one justice, that is, as a good valued for its own sake and not from any desire for its results. When Glaucon introduces the classification, he offers as examples of class one goods "enjoyment" and "pleasures which are harmless and produce no consequences for the future beyond enjoyment for the person who possesses them" (357b). How can Justice, the route to which Glaucon repeatedly says is a matter of sustained difficulty and hard work (530c, 531c, d, 532d), and whose task is to harmonize souls, belong to the same class of goods as fleeting pleasure and inconsequential enjoyment? As noted, the brothers also treat the Justice they demand as different from the consequentialist justice of class three, but this, too, is odd. For, as we saw in chapters 3 and 4, Glaucon approves, for the sake of the ideal city's justice, the deceitful measures deployed in the *kallipolis*, including the noble lie. It is also he who converts Thrasymachus' definition of justice in terms of advantage to one in terms of profit (347e). If, then, as it appears, Glaucon is a consequentialist when it comes to justice, why does he not place justice in class three?

What if the brothers place justice among the fleeting pleasures of class one because they desire Justice *as* fleeting pleasure or enjoyment? Seeing things this way helps to explain why they do *not* put justice in class three, which they associate with the many, for whom, they claim, as noted, that justice is *"unpleasant but beneficial."* Insofar as the brothers want justice to be not unpleasant but pleasant, and to "produce no consequences for the future beyond enjoyment for the person who possesses" it, the justice they desire *is* different from the justice they attribute to the many. Still, insofar as they want the benefit of justice to lie in its inconsequential enjoyment, they, too, attach a consequence to justice, even as they claim otherwise. From this vantage point, it appears that the brothers' Justice belongs in class one *and* class three. Insofar as they want justice to be fleetingly pleasant and inconsequentially enjoyable, the brothers appear to indicate that they may not be willing to do the hard work justice may entail, a point I return to below. If that is so, however, then, in desiring these consequences of justice without doing the work, the brothers appear to want to appear just without actually being so, which is exactly Adeimantus' definition of "complete injustice," namely, injustice "coupled with counterfeit respectability" (366b). Against this backdrop, the brothers' avowed desire for pure and simple or complete Justice and their disavowed desire for complete injustice appear to be one and the same. And what Socrates offers as Justice appears to be responsive to what we may now see as the brothers' equally problematic avowed *and* disavowed desires for Justice/injustice.

Is this, then, where the dialogue leaves us on the question of justice? The scholarship is divided. Some scholars take the *Republic* as a whole to endorse class one justice, into which they place unqualified Justice. In my view, by contrast, as I have sought to demonstrate over the course of this book, the dialogue performs a critique of this Justice even as it is put forward. Other scholars take the dialogue to advocate for class two justice, which they see as a combination of class one and class three, whereby the philosopher-kings' privileged access to Justice brings about as its consequence justice in their souls and in the souls of the other inhabitants of the *kallipolis*.[2] In my view, by contrast, as I have sought to show as well, the *Republic* depicts the philosopher-kings as *failing* to bring about justice in any souls, including their own. The dialogue is, in any case, critical of class three's consequentialist justice, especially, that is, when it takes the form of instrumentalization and/or utilitarianism. We have noticed this in the cases of other human activities, excellences, and goods in earlier chapters. For example, when, as discussed in chapter 3, moderation is a means to the end of order, as it is in the *kallipolis* in *Republic* 4, both the ordinary majority and the philosophical few are deprived of the capacity to become moderate. Similarly, as we saw in chapter 5, the symposiasts' treatment of *erōs* as a means to the end of honor and happiness in the *Symposium* results in the death of *erōs*. In these cases, instrumentalizing human activities and goods to further ends negates the being of the activity or good in question.

That this is true of justice as well comes to light over the course of Socrates' engagement with Thrasymachus in *Republic* 1, which begins with Thrasymachus' demand that Socrates stop asking questions about justice and start giving answers instead. Thrasymachus accompanies his demand with a list of "forbidden, *hōn proeipes*" (337b, c), answers: "Don't be telling me that [justice] is that which ought to be, *to deon*, or the beneficial, *to ōphelimon*, or the

---

2. Mabbott, "Is Plato's *Republic* Utilitarian?," displays this additive approach. Although strictly speaking it is anachronistic to speak of "utilitarianism" in the context of the *Republic*, the approach taken to ethical and political topics by characters in this dialogue and others warrants use of this term. For discussion, see also Creed, "Is It Wrong to Call Plato a Utilitarian?"

profitable, *to lusiteloun*, or the gainful, *to kerdaleon*, or the advantageous, *to sumpheron*" (336d). Claiming uncertainty about the positive content of justice, which, only a page before, he had called the excellence of human being (335c), Socrates invites Thrasymachus to define it (336e–337d, 338a). Happy to do so, Thrasymachus offers that justice is "nothing else than the advantage of the stronger" (338c–339a). Socrates notes that Thrasymachus' definition uses one of the terms he has just prohibited (339a-b), agrees that "the just is something that is of advantage," but demurs on Thrasymachus' reference to "the stronger" (339b), orienting advantage instead to a consideration of those who are ruled (342e).

Paul Shorey calls Socrates' acceptance of the just as "something that is of advantage" "Plato's so-called utilitarianism."[3] But that is a better description of Thrasymachus' position. For it is he who links justice not only to advantage (344a, c) but to profit (348b, 344c), and also to nearly all the other terms he has forbidden, including benefit and gain (343e). Using these terms interchangeably, moreover, Thrasymachus highlights the utilitarian's commitment to commensuration. The only forbidden term that does not reappear in Thrasymachus' speeches is justice as "that which ought to be," but this should not surprise. As we saw in chapter 2, Thrasymachus' understanding of justice erases the distinction between what is and what ought to be, thereby erasing the gap that it is the job of justice to govern. As with moderation and *erōs*, then, treating justice as an instrument or tool negates the being of the activity or good in question.

Unpersuaded by Thrasymachean justice, Socrates maintains at the end of *Republic* 1 that "injustice can never be more profitable than justice" (354a). Disagreeing with how Thrasymachus values justice, Socrates calls the pursuit of justice more precious than the pursuit of gold (336e). That, near the end of their exchange, Socrates regrets that he has so far failed to pursue "what justice is" (354b) suggests that, by the close of *Republic* 1, Socrates has turned away not only from injustice as a source of profit or gain but also from gain, profit, and other such considerations as measures of justice. Socrates had already indicated that he would not pursue justice along such lines when, in earlier discussion with Polemarchus, he described justice as "useless" (333d). Orienting inquiry away from instrumentalist and utilitarian considerations, Socrates instead, as we have seen in earlier chapters, foregrounds the question, "What is x?": What is *mimēsis*? What is persuasion? What is *erōs*? What is *logos*?

And, at the end of *Republic* 1, What is justice? (354c). Socrates answers in *Republic* 2 when he places justice in class two, that is, among goods "we value

---

3. See Shorey, in *Republic, Books 1–5*, 50 note a.

both for their own sake and because we desire their results" (357c). But how can *that* be when, as we have just seen, the dialogue as a whole appears to reject class three justice and, as I have been arguing, it rejects class one justice as well? I show in the remainder of this epilogue that the *Republic* does not endorse a combination of classes one and three justice, at least not as that is desired by the brothers. But neither does it set aside Socrates' desire for class two justice. Instead, the dialogue represents as class two justice an alternative to both the ideal and/or fleeting justice of class one and also to the instrumentalized or utilitarian justice of class three, taken separately and/or together. Binding the good of justice as an activity to its results, and the actuality of justice to its appearance, class two justice, I argue, counters the brothers' avowed and disavowed desires for complete Justice/injustice by avoiding both idealism and instrumentalization. It does so by way of what Socrates calls "the most beautiful" class of justice (358a), and what I call "poetic justice," which, in the formulation attributed to the poet Simonides in *Republic* 1, seeks "to give to each what is owed, *to ta opheilomena hekastō[i] apodidonai*" (331e). To unpack class two justice so understood, I begin one last time with Socrates' engagement with Polemarchus in *Republic* 1.

SEEMING, BEING, DOING

As his first account of justice, Polemarchus offers Simonides' definition: it is just to give to each what is owed (331e). In ancient Greek, this word for "what is owed," *opheilomena*, shares a common root with the word for "benefit," *ōphelia*, with the only difference being in the vowel quantity of the first letter: omicron for what is owed; omega for what is of benefit. The relation between these two Greek words is analogous to the relation between the English "owed" and "ought."[4] Over the course of the exchange with Polemarchus, Socrates brings forward the relation between these two seemingly quite different understandings to open the possibility that justice is an activity that seeks to bring benefit by giving what is owed. This is the "advantage" of justice.

Socrates responds to Polemarchus' Simonidean definition with a case in which rendering what is owed may bring harm: "If one took over weapons from a friend who was in his right mind and then the lender should go mad and demand them back ... he who did so return them would not be acting justly" (331c). Socrates then alters Simonides' definition by transforming "what is owed" into "what is fitting, *prosēkon*" (332c). At Socrates' prompting, Polemarchus

---

4. I owe this point to Michael Kicey.

explains what is fitting as that which renders benefits, *ōphelias*, and harms to friends and enemies (332d), offering as his revised account of justice, as we saw in chapter 2, late fifth-century Athens' conventional morality: helping friends and harming enemies. To which Socrates responds: "By friend do you mean those who seem to a man to be worthy or those who really are so, even if they don't seem, and similarly of enemies?" and asks: "Don't people make mistakes in this regard?" (334c). Socrates' questions across these exchanges appear to seek to direct Polemarchus' attention to the potential gaps between the way things seem and the way they may be, to bring to light the ways in which all of the definitions Polemarchus offers depend on partial and fallible judgments about particulars.

Altering this definition, too, Socrates next translates helping friends and harming enemies into justice as doing/acting well, *eu poiein*, to friends and badly, *kakōs*, to enemies (332d), another context-relative and also agent-based practice. To Socrates' question about what are the action, *praxei*, and work, *ergon*, of the just person, *dikaios*, which amount to doing/acting well, *eu poiein* (332d-e), Polemarchus answers: "Making war and being an ally" (332e), and, in peacetime, depositing money and keeping it safe (333c), which Socrates elaborates by remarking that it is when money, being kept safe, is idle or useless that justice is useful in relation to it (333c-d). Generalizing from there, Socrates asks whether "in the use of each thing, justice is useless, *achrēston*, but in its uselessness useful, *chrēsimos*?" Polemarchus replies, "It looks that way" (333d), and, from here, it is a short way to Socrates' reformulation of justice as theft, a definition that, as we saw in chapter 2, Polemarchus disavows (334b), endorsing instead Socrates' claim that "in no case is it just to harm anyone," not even when they are one's enemies, a position Socrates maintains is a more apt reflection of Simonides' formulation of justice as rendering to each what is owed (335e), a point to which I will return.

For now, notice that by orienting away from usefulness to goodness,[5] and from justice as a means to justice as an activity and work of well-doing (332d-e), Socrates offers justice as the work of becoming good by acting well. This is a context-relative and particularistic practice of rendering what is owed, which is to say, what is fitting. The "useless" *and* consequential benefit of justice as this kind of activity of well-doing is that it brings about good. Measured not by

5. On Socrates' shift from usefulness to goodness, see Weiss, *Socratic Paradox*, 171 n. 7, referring to *Rep.* 334b-d. Socrates adds a consideration of goodness to those who are useful at 333b as well.

"the idea of the good" of which we can, in any case, have "no adequate knowledge" (505a), or by its utility, this good, Socrates says, is a kind of possession (505b). Contra the encomiasts of *erōs* in the *Symposium,* it is not a possession that we hold apart from our activity. Instead, as the capacity we have to make our own souls good by well-doing and, in so doing, to bring about what is good for ourselves and others, justice is the good consequence of just acts (444e). Taking its measure from the "useless" benefit of the good, an intersubjective and relational human, or, in the terms of chapter 6, what we might call a Protagorean, measure, justice is a matter of acting justly, and acting justly depends on being just.

Socrates' exchanges with Polemarchus thus bring to light that acting justly is a matter of being just, that allowing to each what is owed *is* giving to each what is proper to each, which is to say, *its* own, and that doing that depends on attending to particulars so as to render what is fitting to *them*. Socrates' engagement with Polemarchus also brings to light that doing that requires what chapter 6 called the attitude of soul that the *Republic* and *Theaetetus* associate with *phronēsis*. This is because attending to particulars so as to render what is fitting to them depends on judgments about people, contexts, and things, and also on the justice-seeker's awareness that these judgments about what appears to her senses rest (only) on her own opinions about fit, that what appears to her to be the case with respect to the particulars may not actually be so, and that what may be fitting today might not be tomorrow. The activity of justice that emerges in these exchanges thus relies on partial judgments about imagined and contingent possibility based on perceptual experiences and their representations, in short, on what I have called mimetic knowledge.

JUDGING, APPEARANCES, IMAGINATION

Such judgments are explored in *Republic* 9.[6] Returning to the question Glaucon and Adeimantus initially posed in *Republic* 2 about whether the unjust tyrant is happiest or most miserable, Socrates asks:

> [Is not] the person who is fit to judge, *krinein*, someone who in thought can go down into a person's character, *ethos*, and examine it thoroughly, someone who doesn't judge from the outside, the way a child does, who is dazzled by

---

6. The material in this section draws on and adds to my "Wages of War."

the façade that tyrants adopt for the outside world to see, but is able to see right through that sort of thing?" (577a)

The tyrant may appear to be happiest owing to his boundless power, but a fit or worthy, *axios*, judge, Socrates explains, does not judge by appearances in the way of a child. The difference between a child who is dazzled by facades and a good judge is not that the child sees only appearances while the good judge sees appearances and truth. Rather, a good judge sees what appears, while also recognizing that there may be more both to what appears and to what is than meets the eye. For this reason, Socrates pairs the fitness qualification with a competency criterion based on experience. Someone is competent to judge the happiness or misery of a tyrant when he has lived in the same house with a tyrant and witnessed his behavior at home and his treatment of members of his household when he is stripped of his facade, and has also seen how he behaves when in danger from the people (577a-b). Differences in context and perspective matter. As does time.

After setting forth these criteria of judgment, Socrates asks Glaucon: "Do you want to make believe, *propoiēsōmetha*, that we are among those who would be able to judge and have already met up with such men [i.e., tyrants] so that we'll have someone to answer what we ask?" "Certainly," Glaucon replies (577a-b). Mobilizing the soul-city analogy, Socrates invites Glaucon to draw inferences about the happiness or misery of a tyrant based on the happiness or misery of a city ruled by a tyrant. Assessing such cities as enslaved, subject to force, impoverished, and full of terrors, alarms, and lamentations, and so most miserable, Glaucon draws the same conclusion about the tyrant. Socrates demurs, insisting that the misery of someone with a tyrannical temper who lives his life in private is far less than that of an actual tyrant. Glaucon agrees with that, too. Socrates invites Glaucon to slow down: "It is not enough to suppose such things. We must examine them thoroughly" (577c-578c). The thorough examination Socrates proposes begins with a thought experiment. Inviting Glaucon to suppose (after warning him against doing so just lines before), Socrates pictures the tyrant caught up "by a god" and "set down in solitude," alone with his family and fifty slaves, where, without his monopoly over power, he will be vulnerable to those he oppresses (578e).

It is against the backdrop of this thought experiment that Socrates calls on Glaucon to act "like the judge, *kritēs*, who makes the final decision, [and] tell me who among the five—the king, the timocrat, the oligarch, the democrat, and the tyrant—is first in happiness, who second, and so on in order"

(580a). Socrates appears to prompt Glaucon to judge as he would a theatrical spectacle (580b).⁷ That is, in any case, how Glaucon seems to hear Socrates' prompt when he quickly answers: "That's easy. I rank them in virtue and vice, in happiness and its opposite, in the order of their appearance, as I might judge choruses" (580a-b). Is judging choruses as "easy" as Glaucon claims? In Sara Monoson's account of fifth- to fourth-century Athenian practices of theatergoing and "audience performance," judging theatrical spectacles involved both seeing what appeared on stage and seeing what appeared as appearance, which she describes as part of the "active, possibly even creative (that is not merely passive and observational), contributions of the audience to the theatrical experience."⁸ Socrates invites Glacuon to be active, to be sure, to see what appears as appearance, which is to say, in the language I used in chapter 1, to resist taking appearances for truth. By way of his thought experiment, Socrates prompts Glaucon to imagine as well what does not appear, which is to say, to be creative. The kind of judgment Socrates seeks from Glaucon is like the spectatorship of theatergoers in these ways.

It also appears to be different. For, as discussed in chapter 1, and as noted above, it takes attention to multiple perspectives and contexts, and, most especially, it takes time, to engage in the kind of "thorough examination" and practice of imagination Socrates invites by the thought experiment he proposes. Bound to the time of the play and attending to *its* multiple perspectives and contexts, theatergoers who examine thoroughly and imagine otherwise in the ways Socrates proposes might well lose track of the play. The creativity and time involved in *Republic* 9's account of judgment, in my view, invites rather a spectatorship of the kind associated with what Jesper Svenbro calls "theater in the book," or reading.⁹ As we saw in chapter 1, reading targets the same audiences as fifth- to fourth-century Athenian theater, but differs from theatergoing by taking the time of the reader, who can read and reread, forward and backward, with a view to looking at everything everywhere, at the things that

---

7. Bloom, "Interpretive Essay," in *Republic of Plato*, 470 n. 5; Grube, in *Republic*, 227 n. 5; and Adam, *Republic of Plato*, note on 580a-b, 2:340. For a discussion of some controversies around Socrates' request that Glaucon act like "a judge to make the final decision," see Adam, *Republic of Plato*, 2:373–76.

8. Monoson, *Plato's Democratic Entanglements*, 206–26; quotations are from 222 n. 29 and 210.

9. For "theater in the book," see Svenbro, *Phrasikleia*, 180.

appear, at their images and representations, and who can also imagine what does not appear, all without losing her place.

How does Glaucon fare as judge in *Republic* 9? By asking Glaucon to pretend after he has set forth criteria for judging based on experience, Socrates implies that Glaucon may not have the experience necessary to judge the tyrant. He also suggests that under such conditions, judging well will call for a double dose of insight: pretending that they are well positioned to imagine the tyrant's soul while recognizing that they are not. Despite his confidence in his ability to pretend to such knowledge, or perhaps because of that confidence, Glaucon shows himself to be unequal to the challenge. Judging without subjecting king, timocrat, oligarch, and democrat to thorough examination, Glaucon fails as readerly judge. Judging strictly in order of appearance, he fails as a theatrical judge as well. Glaucon's failures are forecast by his misplaced confidence in his ability to see, by his overly hasty conclusion about the tyrant's misery based on the analogy of city and soul, and by his uncritical response to Socrates' thought experiment. Taking appearance for truth, Glaucon fails to see what appears as appearance, and supposing only what Socrates places before him, he does not imagine what does not appear. Using language of stealth and deception, *lanthano*, in *Republic* 9, Socrates asks whether he should add to Glaucon's decree about the unhappiness of the tyrant that "this is so whether the character [of each ruler] is known or not known, *lanthanosin*, to all men and gods." Glaucon says yes (580c). As discussed in chapters 3, 4, and 6, stealth and deception decouple appearance from actuality to make it possible to appear just without actually being so. Glaucon's "yes" to that decoupling in this instance gives force to my earlier suggestion that, despite his disavowal in *Republic* 2, Glaucon does in fact desire "complete injustice," which, as we saw, effects the same decoupling.

Even without Glaucon's misplaced confidence and desires, the practice of judgment Socrates invites in *Republic* 9 is difficult and demanding. As we saw in the last section, such judgments about imagined and contingent possibility based on perceptual experiences and their representations call for the attitude of soul characteristic of *phronēsis* and depend on mimetic knowledge. Combining seeing and critical reflection, they appear to be comprehended by the Greek *theōros*, who judges not as a lover of sights and sounds alone or as a lover of wisdom alone, but rather as a lover of sights and sounds and wisdom together, to both of whom, as we saw in this book's prologue, Socrates, in *Republic* 5, gives the name "spectators" (475d-e). Anticipating that the practice of judgment bound with "the most beautiful" class of justice will call for seeing *and* thinking, these activities appear together as examples of goods that we desire for their own sakes and for their consequences in class two of Glaucon's threefold classification (357c).

Even when we see appearances for what they are, resist taking them for truth, and imagine what may lie beyond what appears, there can still be no guarantee that we will do justice, however. Perhaps this is why Socrates supplements his first account of judgment in *Republic* 9 with an account calling not only for proximate experience, perception, and imagination, but for speech as well, *empeiria[i] te kai phronēsei kai logō* (582a, d). Judging well depends on speech because, as we saw in chapters 4 and 6, it is through conversation, *dialegesthai*, that we disclose what we are seeing, judging, and imagining. Giving our accounts to ourselves and others may thus allow us to see and imagine what we may have failed to see and imagine in the first instance. In conversation, we also disclose who we are, to others and also to ourselves, if only partially and for now, to which we may sometimes respond by desiring to become otherwise.[10]

NO HARM, ONE MAN: ONE ART

Given the necessary opacity of what does not appear, we may fail to allow to each their own even when we exercise judgment by using engaged and proximate experience, perception, and imagination, and even when we share what we see and think in speech. Thus, Nietzsche asks, in the aphorism that serves as the epigraph for this epilogue, "How can I give each his own? Let this be sufficient for me: I give each *my* own!"[11] Is giving to each my own enough? Or would that simply make justice another exercise of domination, as the imposition of my own as/on your own? We have seen across this book that giving to each my own can be an exercise of domination, as when, for example, it prevents others from bringing about justice in their own souls and/or is tantamount to the advantage of the stronger. Perhaps it is in recognition of this that Socrates, in *Republic* 1, supplements justice as allowing to each his own with justice as "do no harm," a negative "ought," what is not "owed," what I can not do, which, he says, approximates the justice of the poet (335e).[12]

It is justice so understood to which Socrates returns in *Republic* 6, in the figure of the philosopher who, "standing aside under the shelter of a wall in a

---

10. For disclosure of the who in plurality, see Arendt, *Human Condition*, 180.
11. Nietzsche, *Thus Spoke Zarathustra*, 69. But see Satkunanandan, *Extraordinary Responsibility*, 43–44, who distinguishes the *Republic*'s account from Nietzsche's.
12. Links may be drawn here to Agamben on inoperativity in "What Is a Destituent Power?"

storm . . . , is satisfied if he can somehow lead his present life free from injustice, *adikias*, and impious acts and depart from it with beautiful hope, *meta kalēs elpidos*, blameless and content" (496d–e). Some scholars see this as a positive mandate for philosophers to remain detached and aloof, with the goal of keeping philosophy safe from politics.[13] For others, it signals a passive, retreatist, or pessimistic position for philosophy relative to politics.[14] Because Socrates refers in this passage to a philosopher who, "happening upon a constitution proper or fitting, *prosēkousē[i]*, to the constitution of his soul, is able to preserve his own and what is common, *meta tōn idiōn ta koina sōsei*" (497a), still others take Socrates to be describing the philosopher-kings of the *kallipolis* as uniquely able to refrain from individual acts of injustice and to bring about city justice owing to their superior wisdom and knowledge of the ideas.[15] We have seen that justice is not, however, a matter of the *kallipolis*'s philosopher-kings' philosophical expertise, their calculative rationality. Is it, then, merely personalist, relativist, and substantially apolitical? Socrates suggests otherwise. When Adeimantus signals his appreciation of the man who "remains quiet and minds his own affairs" and is content if he can keep from injustice, Socrates chides him, saying that such a person accomplishes no great thing by comparison to one who is able to save both his soul and his city (496d–497a).

The words Adeimantus and Socrates use to describe how one preserves one's own soul—minding one's own affairs—appear repeatedly in the dialogue, most often in *Republic* 4 where they are used to define justice as "doing one's own business, *ta hautou prattein*, and not being a busybody, *polupragmonein*" (433a, b), and as "the having and doing of one's own and what belongs to oneself, *hē tou oikeiou te kai heautou hexis te kai praxis*" (433e–434a). Based on the description of the inhabitants of Adeimantus' city in *Republic* 2 (370a-b), who "mind their own affairs, *ta hautou prattein*," by performing the tasks to which they are fitted, and similar descriptions elsewhere (441d–442a), "minding one's own affairs" is often read as underwriting "one man:one art" as the dialogue's principle of justice for a city. In *Republic* 4, however, Socrates calls this understanding a "phantom, *eidōlon*," or image of justice (443c), thereby signaling that one man:one art is, in the language of *Republic* 2, a "verbal falsehood" (382b). Its status as verbal falsehood is, in any case, made manifest when it is first introduced, also in *Republic* 2 (370c), in the context of Socrates' conversation with Adeimantus about the first hypothetical city, the one that is the product of

---

13. For discussion of this position, see Arendt, "What Is Authority?," 107.
14. See, e.g., Roochnik, "Political Pessimism of Plato's *Republic*," 103.
15. Ferrari, *City and Soul in Plato's "Republic,"* 108.

need (369c). Dismissing it as a "city of pigs" (372d) for its modesty and simplicity, Glaucon misses what Socrates makes plain by his roster of what is required to meet the city's needs. In addition to farmers, builders, and weavers, Socrates says, the city needs shoemakers, carpenters, blacksmiths, skilled workers, cattlemen, shepherds, other herdsmen, importers, exporters, traders, merchants, seafarers, and laborers (370c–371e), and more (371a). The first city may be established to achieve self-sufficiency or self-rule, *autarcheia*. But because, as Socrates says, owing to our needs, "we are not, any of us, self-sufficient, *ouk autarkēs*," on our own (369b), a city based on one man:one art needs itself to grow infinitely, which is to say, it can never be self-sufficient at all. One man:one art, it seems, cannot be the principle of justice for a city.

It may, however, exemplify justice in a soul. Indeed, the truth, Socrates says, "as it seems," is that

> justice apparently *was* something of this kind, [yet] it was not concerned with the external performance of a man's own function, *ou peri tēn exō praxin tōn autou*, but with the internal performance of it, *alla peri tēn entos*, genuinely concerning himself and those things which are his, *hōs alēthōs peri heauton kai ta heautou*. (443c-d, my emphasis)

If we take Socrates' use of the word "was" here to refer back to *Republic* 1, he appears in *Republic* 4 to be confirming what he had put forward earlier, in conversation with Thrasymachus, namely, that the soul can perform its function only if it has its "own specific excellence, *aretēn . . . tina psuchēs*," namely, justice (353d-e). Echoing *Republic* 1, 4, and 6, Socrates reiterates the imperative of soul justice in *Republic* 9 as well: such a person would "keep his eyes fixed on the constitution in his soul" (591e). To Glaucon's claim that those so concerned "will not willingly take part in politics," Socrates responds: "In his own city he certainly will, yet perhaps not in the city of his birth, unless some divine chance, *tuchē*, comes to pass." Glaucon takes Socrates to be referring to the *kallipolis*, but Socrates does not say that: it seems to be the politics of the person's own city that matters (592a-b).

No great thing (497d), saving the constitution of one's soul. But no small thing either, as the whole of the *Republic*, devoted to this question, makes plain by showing how demanding and self-(re)forming to the end of actualizing the good it is. No obvious thing either, as is implied by the reference to the soul of Odysseus in the myth of Er, which chooses the life of "an ordinary citizen who minded his own business, *idiōtou apragmonos*," after finding that life "lying in some corner disregarded by the others" (620c).

POLITICAL PHILOSOPHY

Is the beneficiary of poetic justice, then, the agent of justice alone, who does no harm, minds his own affairs, considering not the advantage of another but only his own? I don't think so. Practicing poetic justice in these ways is an activity of and toward the self, to be sure. Thrasymachus is thus wrong to call justice the good of another (343c). And Nietzsche is right that to act justly is a matter of my own. At the same time, *giving* my own only happens in and by way of our relations with others, which always also affect who we are. To do justice when I am safekeeping the weapon of my friend, for example, requires that I judge how what I do may alter my soul (my own), how it may affect my friend (her own), how it may affect our friendship, to say nothing of the safety and well-being of others who may be affected by my judgment. And it requires that I do all of that without knowing whether I will get it right. No small or obvious thing, such complex, particular, contingent, and partial judgments depend, like the practice of midwifery, and like the practice of learning to read, on knowledge built up from patterns perceived in firsthand experience to which must be applied the power of attention, the basis of which is an exercise of reflection, analysis, and synthesis. In the case of midwifery, as discussed in chapter 6, perceiving and thinking are completed in and by way of giving an account. So, too, as we have seen, in the case of justice. The same may be said of learning to read. In all of these cases, the outcome may be a failed "windegg" (*Theaet.* 151e), which may sometimes, nonetheless, be worth rearing. In any case, there can be no guarantee.

Learning that doing justice is by way of the always fallible authority of one's own experiences, perceptions, opinions, imagination, and conversation *is* what I take to be the *Republic*'s education to ethical, political, and philosophical self-governance. Concerned first and foremost with soul justice, the *Republic* is also and as such concerned with city justice and politics.[16] It is about city justice by being about soul justice because there can be no city justice, at least where citizens rule themselves, if citizens cannot bring about justice in their own souls. And it is about politics because soul justice is, as we have seen over the course of this book, a matter of self-government, self-constitution, and self-authorization in and by way of relations with others.[17]

---

16. It nonetheless offers no account of social or distributive justice in the mode of an Aristotle or a Rawls. For discussion, see Kamtekar, "Social Justice and Happiness in the *Republic*."

17. See also Mara, *Socrates' Discursive Democracy*, 74–82.

In the myth of Er, Socrates recommends that one neglect all other studies to

> seek after and study this thing—if in any way he may be able to learn of and discover the man who will give him the ability and the knowledge to distinguish the life that is good from that which is bad, and always and everywhere to choose the best that the conditions allow. (618c)

Who is the man that will give him the ability to know? The one who, "with his eyes fixed on the nature of his soul," "will be able to make a reasoned choice, *sullogisamenon haireisthai*, between the better and the worse life" (618c-e). That is to say, none other than the seeker himself, if and only if, that is, he undertakes the work, *ergon*, of seeing and thinking together, which, as we have seen, combine to make possible poetic justice. Offered as an aside during his narration of the myth, this advice Socrates directs to Glaucon to underscore what has come to light repeatedly over the course of the dialogue, namely, that Glaucon is reluctant to seek such (fallible) knowledge himself, and thus to do the work that becoming just requires. In light of Glaucon's reluctance, Socrates does, in the myth of Er, what he has been doing all along. He positions himself as "the man who will give [Glaucon] the ability and the knowledge to distinguish the life that is good from that which is bad." Does Socrates thereby do Glaucon justice? Perhaps. It may be, however, that Socrates' gift to Glaucon, like his encomium of Justice that is sometimes taken to be the gift of the dialogue as a whole, will, like any *pharmakon*, make the very seeing and thinking Glaucon needs to make his own good choices and to become himself just less rather than more attainable.

Disputes over questions of justice and injustice cause wars within souls, within cities, and between cities. They may also, as the *Republic* attests, summon a soul to philosophy. When the summoning fails, it may be because a soul is driven by pleonectic desires to declare that its judgments rule based on power alone. That is the mode of the tyrant described in *Republic* 9 and anticipated in the figure of Thrasymachus. Or it may be because a soul passively acquiesces to the rule of another. That is the mode of the warrior as figured by Polemarchus. Tyrants or warriors may always triumph. Or both may: witness Glaucon. Or warriors may be(come) philosophers: witness Socrates. Or tyrants and philosophers may become friends: witness Thrasymachus and Socrates (450a-b). In a time in which the polis and its resources were being evaluated for their war-usefulness (526d, 527d), the *Republic* articulates spaces of ethics, philosophy, and politics that are not reducible to war. These are spaces of shifting alliances among a plurality who attain a harmony, if they do, not because of a pregiven set of forms, categories, or rules, or owing to the exercise of force, but through the comity of conversation among incommensurable parties.

In *Republic* 9, Socrates says that the one "to whom we ought all to listen is he who has this capacity of judgment" (577a). Who is that? Not the philosopher-kings, whose compulsory education in calculative rationality orients them to unity without difference, and whose ideas are divorced from experience, and also not consequentialists if they are guided by instrumental rationality. Rather, we should listen to, though not necessarily allow ourselves to be persuaded by, those who, awakened to reflection by the *aporia* of their experiences, are summoned to seek an understanding of how and why their opposite judgments about the same thing could be held at the same time. Souls thus summoned to philosophy may generate new categories and rules from out of their conversations and may thereby produce in thought and also in action a harmony that involves neither an eradication of one or the other of their incommensurable opinions nor the sublation of them through abstraction. Instead, the mimetic work that the *Republic* performs and also sets for judgment and, hence, for justice, both within souls and cities and between these, is holding conflicting opinions together in a harmony that depends on, even as it mediates, their differences—that is to say, the work of political philosophy.

WORKS CITED

PRIMARY WORKS

Aristotle. *Metaphysics, Books I-IX*. Translated by Hugh Tredennick. Loeb Classical Library. Cambridge, MA: Harvard University Press, 1933.

———. *Nicomachean Ethics*. Translated by Joe Sachs. Newburyport, MA: Focus, 2002.

———. *On the Soul* and *On Memory and Recollection*. Translated by Joe Sachs. Santa Fe, NM: Green Lion Press, 2001.

———. *The Physics, Books I-IV*. Translated by P. H. Wicksteed and F. M. Cornford. Loeb Classical Library. Cambridge, MA: Harvard University Press, 1957.

———. *Politics* and *The Constitution of Athens*. Edited by Stephen Everson and translated by Benjamin Jowett. Cambridge: Cambridge University Press, 1996.

Diogenes Laertius. *Lives of Eminent Philosophers*, vol. 1. Translated by R. D. Hicks. Loeb Classical Library. Cambridge, MA: Harvard University Press, 1972.

Euripides. *Helen. Phoenician Women. Orestes.* Translated by David Kovacs. Loeb Classical Library. Cambridge, MA: Harvard University Press, 2002.

Gorgias. "Encomium of Helen." In *The Older Sophists*, edited and translated by Rosamond Kent Sprague, 50–54. Indianapolis: Hackett, 2001.

Plato. *Lysis, Symposium, Gorgias*. Translated by W. R. M. Lamb. Loeb Classical Library. Cambridge, MA: Harvard University Press, 1925.

———. *Phaedrus*. Translated by Alexander Nehamas and Paul Woodruff. Indianapolis: Hackett, 1995.

———. *Plato: Complete Works*. Edited by John M. Cooper. Indianapolis: Hackett, 1997.

———. *Plato on Poetry: Ion; Republic 376e–398b9; Republic 595–608b10*. Edited with commentary by Penelope Murray. Cambridge: Cambridge University Press, 1996.

———. *The Republic*. Edited by G. R. F. Ferrari and translated by Tom Griffith. Cambridge: Cambridge University Press, 2000.

———. *The Republic*. In *Plato: Complete Works*, edited by John M. Cooper and translated by G. M. A. Grube with revisions by C. D. C. Reeve, 971–1223. Indianapolis: Hackett, 1997.

———. *Republic, Books 1–5*. Translated by Paul Shorey. Loeb Classical Library. Cambridge, MA: Harvard University Press, 1930.

———. *Republic, Books 6–10*. Translated by Paul Shorey. Loeb Classical Library. Cambridge, MA: Harvard University Press, 1935.

———. *The Republic of Plato: Volume 1, Books 1-5*. Edited with commentary by James Adam. 2nd ed. Cambridge: Cambridge University Press, 1963 [digital ed. 2009].

———. *The Republic of Plato: Volume 2, Books 6-10*. Edited with commentary by James Adam. 2nd ed. Cambridge: Cambridge University Press, 1963 [digital ed. 2009].

———. *The Republic of Plato*. Translated by Allan Bloom. 2nd ed. New York: Basic Books, 1991.

———. *Plato: Republic 5*. Edited with commentary by Stephen Halliwell. Warminster, Eng.: Aris & Phillips, 1993.

———. *Plato: Republic 10*. Edited with commentary by Stephen Halliwell. Warminster, Eng.: Aris & Phillips, 1988.

———. *Statesman*. Translated by Chistopher J. Rowe. Indianapolis: Hackett, 1999.

———. *Symposium*. Translated by Alexander Nehamas and Paul Woodruff. Indianapolis: Hackett, 1989.

———. *The Symposium of Plato*. Edited with introduction and commentary by Robert Gregg Bury. Cambridge: W. Heffer and Sons, 1932.

———. *The Theaetetus of Plato*. Edited by Myles Burnyeat and translated by M. J. Levett. Indianapolis: Hackett, 1990.

Plato and Aristotle. *Plato: "Gorgias" and Aristotle: "Rhetoric."* Edited and translated by Joe Sachs. Newburyport, MA: Focus, 2009.

Thucydides. *The Landmark Thucydides: A Comprehensive Guide to the Peloponnesian War*. Translated by Richard Crawley and edited by Robert B. Strassler. New York: Touchstone, 1996.

OTHER WORKS

Agamben, Giorgio. "What Is a Destituent Power?" Translated by Stephanie Wakefield. *Environment and Planning D: Society and Space* 32 (2014): 65–74.

Allen, Danielle. *Why Plato Wrote*. Chichester and Malden: Wiley-Blackwell, 2010.

Anderson, Daniel E. *The Masks of Dionysos: A Commentary on Plato's "Symposium."* Albany: SUNY Press, 1993.

Annas, Julia. *An Introduction to Plato's "Republic."* Oxford: Oxford University Press, 1981.

———. *Plato: A Brief Insight*. New York: Sterling, 2003.

———. "Understanding and the Good: Sun, Line, and Cave." In *Plato's "Republic": Critical Essays*, edited by Richard Kraut, 143–69. Lanham, MD: Rowman & Littlefield, 1997.

Annas, Julia, and Christopher Rowe, eds. *New Perspectives on Plato, Modern and Ancient*. Center for Hellenic Studies Colloquia 6. Washington, DC: Center for Hellenic Studies, 2003.

Arendt, Hannah. *The Human Condition*. Chicago: University of Chicago Press, 1958.

———. "Philosophy and Politics." *Social Research* 57 (1990): 73–103.

———. "The Pursuit of Happiness." In *On Revolution*, 115–40. New York: Viking, 1963.

———. "Socrates." In *The Promise of Politics*, edited by Jerome Kohn, 5–39. New York: Schocken, 2005.
———. "Truth and Politics." In *Between Past and Future: Eight Exercises in Political Thought*, 227–64. New York: Viking, 1961.
———. "What Is Authority?" In *Between Past and Future: Eight Exercises in Political Thought*, 91–141. New York: Viking, 1961.
Badiou, Alain. *Plato's "Republic": A Dialogue in 16 Chapters*. New York: Columbia University Press, 2012.
———. "Pour aujourd'hui: Platon!" http://www.entretemps.asso.fr/Badiou/09-10.htm.
Balot, Ryan. *Courage in the Democratic Polis: Ideology and Critique in Classical Athens*. New York: Oxford University Press, 2014.
———. *Greed and Injustice in Classical Athens.* Princeton, NJ: Princeton University Press, 2001.
Baracchi, Claudia. "Another Apology." In *Retracing the Platonic Text*, edited by John Russon and John Sallis, 3–18. Evanston, IL: Northwestern University Press, 2000.
Beck, Frederick A. G. *Album of Greek Education: The Greeks at School and at Play*. Sydney: Cheiron Press, 1975.
Belfiore, Elizabeth. "Plato's Greatest Accusation against Poetry." In *New Essays on Plato*, edited by Francis Jeffry Pelletier and John King-Farlow, 39–62. Calgary: University of Calgary Press, 1983.
———. *Socrates' Daimonic Art: Love for Wisdom in Four Platonic Dialogues*. Cambridge: Cambridge University Press, 2012.
Benardete, Seth. *The Rhetoric of Morality and Philosophy: Plato's Gorgias and Phaedrus*. Chicago: University of Chicago Press, 1991.
Berger, Harry, Jr. "Facing Sophists: Charismatic Bondage in *Protagoras*." *Representations* 5 (1984): 66–91.
———. *Perils of Uglytown: Studies in Structural Misanthropology from Plato to Rembrandt*. New York: Fordham University Press, 2015.
———. "*Phaedrus* and the Politics of Inscription." In *Situated Utterances: Texts, Bodies, and Cultural Representations*, 415–54. New York: Fordham University Press, 2005.
———. "Plato's *Cratylus*: Dialogue as Revision." *Philosophical Forum* 2 (1970): 213–33.
———. "Plato's Flying Philosopher." *Philosophical Forum* 13.4 (1982): 385–407.
Beversluis, John. *Cross-Examining Socrates: A Defense of the Interlocutors in Plato's Early Dialogues*. Cambridge: Cambridge University Press, 2000.
Bickford, Susan. *The Dissonance of Democracy: Listening, Conflict, and Citizenship*. Ithaca, NY: Cornell University Press, 1996.
Blondell, Ruby. *The Play of Character in Plato's Dialogues*. Cambridge: Cambridge University Press, 2002.
Blundell, Mary Whitlock. *Helping Friends and Harming Enemies: A Study in Sophocles and Greek Ethics*. Cambridge: Cambridge University Press, 1989.
Bobonich, Christopher. "Persuasion, Compulsion, and Freedom in Plato's *Laws*." *Classical Quarterly* 41 (1991): 365–88.
———. *Plato's Utopia Recast: His Later Ethics and Politics*. Oxford: Oxford University Press, 2002.
Booth, Wayne C. *The Rhetoric of Fiction*. Chicago: University of Chicago Press, 1961.

Boyarin, Daniel. *Socrates and the Fat Rabbis*. Chicago: University of Chicago Press, 2009.
Brann, Eva. *The Logos of Heraclitus: The First Philosopher of the West on Its Most Interesting Term*. Philadelphia: Paul Dry Books, 2011.
———. *The Music of the Republic: Essays on Socrates' Conversations and Plato's Writings*. Philadelphia: Paul Dry Books, 2011.
Brisson, Luc. "Agathon, Pausanias, and Diotima in Plato's *Symposium: Paiderastia* and *Philosophia*." Translated by Michael Chase. In *Plato's "Symposium": Issues in Interpretation and Reception*, Hellenic Studies Series 22, edited by James Lesher, Debra Nails, and Frisbee Sheffield, 229–51. Washington, DC: Center for Hellenic Studies, 2007.
———. *Plato the Myth Maker*. Translated by Gerard Naddaf. Chicago: University of Chicago Press, 1998.
Brogan, Walter. "Socrates' Tragic Speech: Divine Madness and the Place of Rhetoric in Philosophy." In *Retracing the Platonic Text*, edited by John Russon and John Sallis, 32–40. Evanston, IL: Northwestern University Press, 2000.
Brumbaugh, Robert S. *Platonic Studies of Greek Philosophy: Form, Arts, Gadgets, and Hemlock*. Albany: SUNY Press, 1989.
Burnyeat, Myles. "Culture and Society in Plato's *Republic*." In *Tanner Lectures on Human Values*, 20:217–324. Salt Lake City: University of Utah Press, 1999.
———. "Introduction." In *The Theaetetus of Plato*, edited by Myles Burnyeat and translated by M. J. Levett, 1–241. Indianapolis: Hackett, 1990.
———. "Postscript on Silent Reading." *Classical Quarterly*, n.s., 47 (1997): 74–76.
Buxton, R. G. A. *Persuasion in Greek Tragedy: A Study of* Peitho. Cambridge: Cambridge University Press, 1982.
Cammack, Daniela. "Plato and Athenian Justice." *History of Political Thought* 36.4 (2015): 611–42.
Carmola, Katerie. "Noble Lying: Justice and Intergenerational Tension in Plato's *Republic*." *Political Theory* 31 (2003): 39–62.
Carson, Anne. *Economy of the Unlost: Reading Simonides of Keos with Paul Celan*. Princeton, NJ: Princeton University Press, 1999.
———. *Eros: The Bittersweet*. Princeton, NJ: Princeton University Press, 1986.
Cavarero, Adriana. *For More Than One Voice: Toward a Philosophy of Vocal Expression*. Translated by Paul Kottman. Stanford, CA: Stanford University Press, 2005.
———. *In Spite of Plato: A Feminist Rewriting of Ancient Philosophy*. Translated by Serena Anderlini-D'Onofrio and Aine O'Healy. New York: Routledge, 1995.
Cohen, Ted. *Thinking of Others: On the Talent for Metaphor*. Princeton, NJ: Princeton University Press, 2008.
Condren, Conal. *The Status and Appraisal of Classical Texts*. Princeton, NJ: Princeton University Press, 1985.
Cooper, John. "Plato's Theory of Human Motivation." *History of Philosophy Quarterly* 1 (1984): 3–21.
Cotton, A. K. *Platonic Dialogue and the Education of the Reader*. Oxford: Oxford University Press, 2014.
Creed, J. L. "Is It Wrong to Call Plato a Utilitarian?" *Classical Quarterly* 28.2 (1978): 349–65.

Crotty, Kevin. *The Philosopher's Song: The Poets' Influence on Plato*. Lanham, MD: Lexington Books, 2009.
D'Angour, Armand. "The Sound of *Mousikē*: Reflections on Aural Change in Ancient Greece." In *Debating the Athenian Cultural Revolution: Art, Literature, Philosophy, and Politics, 430–380 BC*, edited by Robin Osborne, 288–300. Cambridge: Cambridge University Press, 2007.
Deleuze, Gilles. "The Simulacrum and Ancient Philosophy." In *The Logic of Sense*, translated by Charles Stivale and edited by Constain V. Boundas and Mark Lester, 253–79. New York: Columbia University Press, 1990.
Demos, Marian. *Lyric Quotation in Plato*. Lanham, MD: Rowman and Littlefield, 1999.
Derrida, Jacques. *Dissemination*. Translated by Barbara Johnson. Chicago: University of Chicago Press, 1981.
Desjardins, Rosemary. *The Rational Enterprise: Logos in Plato's "Theaetetus."* Albany: SUNY Press, 1990.
Detienne, Marcel. *The Masters of Truth in Archaic Greece*. Translated by Janet Lloyd. New York: Zone, 1996.
Dobbs, Darrell. "Choosing Justice: Socrates' Model City and the Practice of Dialectic." *American Political Science Review* 88 (1994): 263–77.
Dover, K. J. *Greek Homosexuality*. Updated and with a new postscript. Cambridge, MA: Harvard University Press, 1989.
———. *Greek Popular Morality in the Time of Plato and Aristotle*. Indianapolis: Hackett, 1994.
Edelstein, Ludwig. "Platonic Anonymity." *American Journal of Philology* 83 (1962): 1–22.
Euben, Peter. *Corrupting Youth: Political Education, Democratic Culture, and Political Theory*. Princeton, NJ: Princeton University Press, 1997.
———. *The Tragedy of Political Theory: The Road Not Taken*. Princeton, NJ: Princeton University Press, 1990.
Farenga, Victor. "The Paradigmatic Tyrant: Greek Tyranny and the Ideology of the Proper." *Helios* 8 (1981): 1–31.
Farness, Jay. *Missing Socrates: Problems of Plato's Writing*. University Park: Pennsylvania State University Press, 1991.
Farrar, Cynthia. *The Origins of Democratic Thinking: The Invention of Politics in Classical Athens*. Cambridge: Cambridge University Press, 1989.
Ferrari, G. R. F. *City and Soul in Plato's "Republic."* Chicago: University of Chicago Press, 2003.
———. *Listening to the Cicadas: A Study of Plato's "Phaedrus."* Cambridge: Cambridge University Press, 1987.
———. "Plato and Poetry." In *The Cambridge History of Literary Criticism*, vol. 1, *Classical Criticism*, edited by G. A. Kennedy, 92–149. Cambridge: Cambridge University Press, 1989.
———. "Socrates in the *Republic*." In *Plato's "Republic": A Critical Guide*, edited by Mark L. McPherran, 11–31. Cambridge: Cambridge University Press, 2010.
Folch, Marcus. *The City and the Stage: Performance, Genre, and Gender in Plato's "Laws."* Oxford: Oxford University Press, 2015.
Ford, Andrew. *Homer: The Poetry of the Past*. Ithaca, NY: Cornell University Press, 1992.

———. *The Origins of Criticism: Literary Culture and Poetic Theory in Classical Greece*. Princeton, NJ: Princeton University Press, 2002.
Foster, M. B. "A Mistake of Plato's in the *Republic*." *Mind* 46 (1937): 386–93.
Foucault, Michel. *Discipline and Punish*. Translated by Alan Sheridan. New York: Vintage Books, 1977.
Frank, Jill. "By Nature and by Design." *Review of Politics* 75 (2013): 685–87.
———. "Circulating Authority: Plato, Politics, and Political Theory." In *Radical Future Pasts: Untimely Political Theory*, edited by Romand Coles, Mark Reinhardt, and George Shulman, 333–50. Lexington: University Press of Kentucky, 2014.
———. "Constitution." In *A Cultural History of Law in Antiquity*, edited by Julen Etxabe. New York: Bloomsbury, forthcoming.
———. *A Democracy of Distinction: Aristotle and the Work of Politics*. Chicago: University of Chicago Press, 2005.
———. "How Oligarchy Breeds Tyranny." *Public Books*, 3.7.2017. http://www.publicbooks.org/how-oligarchy-breeds-tyranny/.
———. "On *Logos* and Politics in Aristotle." In *Aristotle's Politics: A Critical Guide*, edited by Thornton Lockwood and Thanassis Samaras, 1–26. Cambridge: Cambridge University Press, 2015.
———. "The Political Theory of Classical Greece." In *The Oxford Handbook of Political Theory*, edited by John Dryzek, Bonnie Honig, and Anne Phillips, 175–92. Oxford: Oxford University Press, 2006.
———. "Wages of War: On Judgment in Plato's *Republic*." *Political Theory* 35 (2007): 443–67.
Freydberg, Bernard. *The Play of the Platonic Dialogues*. New York: Peter Lang Publishing, 1997.
———. "Retracing Homer and Aristophanes in the Platonic Text." In *Retracing the Platonic Text*, edited by John Russon and John Sallis, 99–113. Evanston, IL: Northwestern University Press, 2000.
Gadamer, Hans-Georg. "Plato and the Poets." In *Dialogue and Dialectic: Eight Hermeneutical Studies on Plato*, translated and with an introduction by P. Christopher Smith, 39–72. New Haven, CT: Yale University Press, 1980.
Garsten, Bryan. *Saving Persuasion: A Defense of Rhetoric and Judgment*. Cambridge, MA: Harvard University Press, 2006.
Gerson, Lloyd P. *From Plato to Platonism*. Ithaca, NY: Cornell University Press, 2013.
Gill, Christopher. "Dialectic and the Dialogue Form." In *New Perspectives on Plato, Modern and Ancient*, Center for Hellenic Studies Colloquia 6, edited by Julia Annas and Christopher Rowe, 144–71. Washington, DC: Center for Hellenic Studies, 2003.
———. "Plato on Falsehood—Not Fiction." In *Lies and Fiction in the Ancient World*, edited by Christopher Gill and Timothy Wiseman, 38–87. Liverpool: Liverpool University Press, 1993.
Gill, Mary Louise. "Method and Metaphysics in Plato's *Sophist* and *Statesman*." In *The Stanford Encyclopedia of Philosophy*, edited by Edward N. Zalta. Spring 2015 edition. http://plato.stanford.edu/archives/spr2015/entries/plato-sophstate/.
———. *Philosophos: Plato's Missing Dialogue*. Oxford: Oxford University Press, 2012.

Gonzalez, Francisco J., ed. *The Third Way: New Directions in Platonic Studies*. Lanham, MD: Rowman & Littlefield, 1995.
Gordon, Jill. *Turning toward Philosophy: Literary Device and Dramatic Structure in Plato's Dialogues*. University Park: Penn State University Press, 1999.
Gordon, Peter. "Self-Authorizing Modernity: Problems of Interpretation in the History of German Idealism," *History and Theory* 44 (2005): 121–37.
Griswold, Charles. "The Ideas and the Criticism of Poetry in Plato's *Republic*, Book 10." *Journal of the History of Philosophy* 19.2 (1981): 135–50.
———. "Relying on Your Own Voice: An Unsettled Rivalry of Moral Ideals in Plato's *Protagoras*." *Review of Metaphysics* 53 (1999): 283–307.
Hall, Edith. "Female Figures and Metapoetry in Old Comedy." In *The Rivals of Aristophanes: Studies in Athenian Old Comedy*, edited by David Harvey and John Wilkins, 407–18. London: Duckworth and the Classical Press of Wales, 2000.
Halliwell, Stephen. *The Aesthetics of Mimesis: Ancient Texts and Modern Problems*. Princeton, NJ: Princeton University Press, 2002.
———. "Antidotes and Incantations: Is There a Cure for Poetry in Plato's *Republic*?" In *Plato and the Poets*, edited by Pierre Destreé and Fritz-Gregor Herrmann, 241–66. Leiden: Brill, 2011.
———. "The Life-and-Death Journey of the Soul: Interpreting the Myth of Er." In *The Cambridge Companion to Plato's "Republic,"* edited by G. R. F. Ferrari, 445–73. Cambridge: Cambridge University Press, 2007.
———. "The Subjection of Muthos to Logos: Plato's Citations of the Poets." *Classical Quarterly* 50 (2000): 94–112.
———. Review of Nightingale. *Ancient Philosophy* 17 (1997): 452–57.
———. "The Theory and Practice of Narrative in Plato." In *Narratology and Interpretation: The Content of Narrative Form in Ancient Literature*, edited by Jonas Grethlein and Antonios Rengakos, 15–41. Berlin: Walter De Gruyter, 2009.
Halperin, David. *One Hundred Years of Homosexuality and Other Essays on Greek Love*. New York: Routledge, 1990.
———. "Plato and Erotic Reciprocity." *Classical Antiquity* 5 (1986): 60–80.
———. "Plato and the Erotics of Narrativity." In *Methods of Interpreting Plato and His Dialogues*, edited by James C. Klagge and Nicholas D. Smith, 93–129. Oxford Studies in Ancient Philosophy, Suppl. vol. 2. Oxford: Oxford University Press, 1992.
———. "Why Is Diotima a Woman?" In *One Hundred Years of Homosexuality*, 113–51. New York: Routledge, 1990.
Harris, William V. *Ancient Literacy*. Cambridge, MA: Harvard University Press, 1991.
Harvey, F. D. "Literacy in the Athenian Democracy." *Revue des Études Grecques* 79 (1966): 585–635.
Havelock, Eric. *Preface to Plato*. History of the Greek Mind 1. Cambridge, MA: The Belknap Press of Harvard University Press, 1963.
Heidegger, Martin. "The Age of the World Picture." In *The Question Concerning Technology and Other Essays*, translated by William Levitt, 115–54. New York: Harper and Row, 1977.
———. *What Is Called Thinking?* Translated by J. Glenn Gray. New York: Harper and Row, 1968.

Heller-Roazen, Daniel. *The Inner Touch: Archaeology of a Sensation*. New York: Zone Books, 2007.
Hobbes, Thomas. *Leviathan*. Edited by Richard Tuck. Cambridge: Cambridge University Press, 1991.
Hobbs, Angela. "Female Imagery in Plato." In *Plato's "Symposium": Issues in Interpretation and Reception*, Hellenic Studies Series 22, edited by James Lesher, Debra Nails, and Frisbee Sheffield, 252–71. Washington, DC: Center for Hellenic Studies, 2007.
———. "Plato and the England Riots." *Angie Hobbs' Blog*, August 15, 2011. https://blogs.warwick.ac.uk/drangiehobbs/entry/plato_and_the/.
———. *Plato and the Hero: Courage, Manliness, and the Personal Good*. Cambridge: Cambridge University Press, 2000.
Howes, George Edwin. "Homeric Quotations in Plato and Aristotle," *Harvard Studies in Classical Philology* 6 (1895): 153–237.
Hughes, Bettany. *The Hemlock Cup: Socrates, Athens, and the Search for the Good Life*. New York: Vintage, 2010.
Hyland, Drew. "*Eros, Epithumia*, and *Philia* in Plato." *Phronesis* 13 (1968): 32–46.
———. *The Virtue of Philosophy: An Interpretation of Plato's "Charmides."* Athens, OH: Ohio University Press, 1981.
Irwin, Terence. *Plato's Moral Theory: The Early and Middle Dialogues*. Oxford: Oxford University Press, 1979.
Iser, Wolfgang. *The Act of Reading: A Theory of Aesthetic Response*. Baltimore: Johns Hopkins University Press, 1980.
Isherwood, Charles. "Checking in with Glimmer Twins, Plato and Aristotle." *New York Times*, June 18, 2007. http://mobile.nytimes.com/2007/06/18/theater/reviews/18targ.html.
Jacobs, Carol. *Skirting the Ethical*. Stanford, CA: Stanford University Press, 2007.
Janaway, Christopher. *Images of Excellence: Plato's Critique of the Arts*. Oxford: Clarendon Press, 1998.
Kahn, Charles H. *Plato and the Socratic Dialogue: The Philosophical Use of a Literary Form*. Cambridge: Cambridge University Press, 1998.
———. "Plato's Theory of Desire." *Review of Metaphysics* 41 (1987): 77–103.
Kamtekar, Rachana. "Social Justice and Happiness in the *Republic*: Plato's Two Principles." *History of Political Thought* 22 (2001): 189–220.
Kastley, James L. *The Rhetoric of Plato's "Republic": Democracy and the Philosophical Problem of Persuasion*. Chicago: University of Chicago Press, 2015.
Kateb, George. "Courage as a Virtue." *Social Research* 71 (2004): 39–72.
———. "Socratic Integrity." NOMOS 40 (1998): 77–112.
Kennedy, George. *A New History of Classical Rhetoric*. Princeton, NJ: Princeton University Press, 1994.
Kierkegaard, Soren. *The Concept of Irony with Continual Reference to Socrates; Notes of Schelling's Berlin Lectures*. Translated by H. V. Hong and E. H. Hong. Princeton, NJ: Princeton University Press, 1990.
Klosko, George. *The Development of Plato's Political Theory*. 2nd ed. Oxford: Oxford University Press, 2007.

———. *History of Political Theory: An Introduction.* Vol. 1, *Ancient and Medieval.* 2nd ed. Oxford: Oxford University Press, 2012.
Knox, Bernard. "Silent Reading in Antiquity." *Greek, Roman, and Byzantine Studies* 9 (1968): 421–35.
Kochin, Michael. "War, Class, and Justice in Plato's *Republic.*" *Review of Metaphysics* 53.2 (1999): 403–23.
Korsgaard, Christine. "Self-Constitution in the Ethics of Plato and Kant." *Journal of Ethics* 3 (1999): 1–29.
Kottman, Paul A. *A Politics of the Scene.* Stanford, CA: Stanford University Press, 2007.
Kurke, Leslie. *Aesopic Conversations: Popular Tradition, Cultural Dialogue, and the Invention of Greek Prose.* Princeton, NJ: Princeton University Press, 2010.
Landauer, Matthew. "The *Idiōtēs* and the Tyrant: Two Faces of Unaccountability in Democratic Athens." *Political Theory* 42 (2014): 139–66.
———. "*Parrhesia* and the *Demos Tyrannos*: Frank Speech, Flattery, and Accountability in Democratic Athens." *History of Political Thought* 33 (2012): 185–208.
Lane, Melissa. "Founding as Legislating: The Figure of the Lawgiver in Plato's *Republic.*" In *Dialogues on Plato's "Politeia" (Republic): Selected Papers from the Ninth Symposium Platonicum,* edited by Luc Brisson and Noboru Notomi, 104–14. Sankt Augustin: Akademia Verlag, 2013.
———. *Method and Politics in Plato's "Statesman."* Cambridge: Cambridge University Press, 1998.
———. "Persuasion and Force in Platonic Politics," as "Persuasion et force dans la politique platonicienne." Translated into French by Dimitri El Murr. In *Aglaïa: Autour de Platon; Mélanges offerts à Monique Dixsaut,* edited by A. Brancacci, D. El Murr, and D. P. Taormina, 165–98. Paris: Vrin, 2010.
———. "Virtue as the Love of Knowledge in Plato's *Symposium* and *Republic.*" In *Maieusis: Essays in Ancient Philosophy in Honour of Myles Burnyeat,* edited by Dominic Scott, 44–67. Oxford: Oxford University Press, 2007.
Lear, Jonathan. "Allegory and Myth in Plato's *Republic.*" In *The Blackwell Guide to Plato's "Republic,"* edited by Gerasimos Santas, 25–43. Malden, MA: John Wiley and Sons, 2008.
Ledbetter, Grace M. *Poetics before Plato: Interpretation and Authority in Early Greek Theories of Poetry.* Princeton, NJ: Princeton University Press, 2003.
Levin, Susan B. *The Ancient Quarrel between Philosophy and Poetry Revisited: Plato and the Greek Literary Tradition.* Oxford: Oxford University Press, 2000.
Liddell, Henry George, and Robert Scott. *Greek English Lexicon.* 9th ed. Edited by Henry Stuart Jones. Oxford: Clarendon Press, 1996.
Lloyd, G. E. R. *Polarity and Analogy: Two Types of Argumentation in Early Greek Thought.* Indianapolis: Hackett, 1992.
Long, A. A. *Greek Models of Mind and Self.* Cambridge, MA: Harvard University Press, 2015.
Long, Christopher. *Socratic and Platonic Political Philosophy: Practicing a Politics of Reading.* Cambridge: Cambridge University Press, 2014.
———. "Who Let the Dogs Out? Tracking the Philosophic Life among the Wolves and Dogs of the *Republic.*" In *Plato's Animals: Gadflies, Horses, Swans, and Other Philosophical*

Beasts, edited by Jeremy Bell and Michael Naas, 131–45. Bloomington: Indiana University Press, 2015.

Lorenz, Katharina. "The Anatomy of Metalepsis: Visuality Turns Around on Late Fifth-Century Pots." In *Debating the Athenian Cultural Revolution: Art, Literature, Philosophy, and Politics, 430–380 BC*, edited by Robin Osborne, 116–43. Cambridge: Cambridge University Press, 2007.

Ludwig, Paul. "Eros in the *Republic*." In *The Cambridge Companion to Plato's "Republic,"* edited by G. R. F. Ferrari, 202–31. Cambridge: Cambridge University Press, 2007.

Mabbott, J. D. "Is Plato's *Republic* Utilitarian?" *Mind* 46.184 (1937): 468–74.

Manning, Erin. *Politics of Touch: Sense, Movement, Sovereignty*. Minneapolis: University of Minnesota Press, 2007.

Mara, Gerald. *The Civic Conversations of Thucydides and Plato: Classical Political Philosophy and the Limits of Democracy*. Albany: SUNY Press, 2008.

———. *Socrates' Discursive Democracy:* Logos *and* Ergon *in Platonic Political Philosophy*. Albany: SUNY Press, 1997.

Marrou, Henri Irénée. *A History of Education in Antiquity*. New York: Sheed and Ward, 1956.

McCabe, Mary Margaret. "Plato's Ways of Writing." In *The Oxford Handbook to Plato*, edited by Gail Fine, 88–113. Oxford: Oxford University Press, 2008.

McCoy, Marina. "The City of Sows and Sexual Differentiation in the *Republic*." In *Plato's Animals: Gadflies, Horses, Swans, and Other Philosophical Beasts*, edited by Jeremy Bell and Michael Naas, 149–60. Bloomington: Indiana University Press, 2015.

———. *Plato on the Rhetoric of Philosophers and Sophists*. Cambridge: Cambridge University Press, 2011.

McWilliams, Susan Jane. *Traveling Back: Toward a Global Political Theory*. Oxford: Oxford University Press, 2014.

Miller, Paul Allen. *Diotima at the Barricades: French Feminists Read Plato*. Oxford: Oxford University Press, 2016.

———. "Dreams and Other Fictions: The Representation of Representation in *Republic* 5 and 6." *American Journal of Philology* 136 (2015): 37–62.

———. *Postmodern Spiritual Practices: The Construction of the Subject and the Reception of Plato in Lacan, Derrida, and Foucault*. Columbus: Ohio State University Press, 2007.

Missiou, Anna. *Literacy and Democracy in Fifth-Century Athens*. Cambridge: Cambridge University Press, 2011.

Monoson, S. Sara. *Plato's Democratic Entanglements: Athenian Politics and the Practice of Philosophy*. Princeton, NJ: Princeton University Press, 2000.

Moravcsik, Julius. "Noetic Aspiration and Artistic Inspiration." In *Plato on Beauty, Wisdom, and the Arts*, edited by Julius Moravcsik and Philip Temko, 29–46. Totowa, NJ: Rowman & Littlefield, 1982.

Morgan, Kathryn A. *Myth and Philosophy from the Presocratics to Plato*. Cambridge: Cambridge University Press, 2000.

———. "Plato." In *Narrators, Narratees, and Narratives in Ancient Greek Literature: Studies in Ancient Greek Narrative*, vol. 1, edited by Irene J. F. de Jong, René Nünlist, and Angus Bowie, 357–76. Leiden: Brill, 2004.

———, ed. *Popular Tyranny: Sovereignty and Its Discontents in Ancient Greece*. Austin: University of Texas Press, 2003.

———. "The Tyranny of the Audience in Plato and Isocrates." In *Popular Tyranny: Sovereignty and Its Discontents in Ancient Greece*, edited by Kathryn A. Morgan, 181–214. Austin: University of Texas Press, 2003.

Morgan, Michael. "Belief, Knowledge, and Learning in Plato's Middle Dialogues." In *New Essays on Plato*, edited by Francis Jeffry Pelletier and John King-Farlow, 63–100. Calgary: University of Calgary Press, 1983.

Moss, Jessica. "What Is Imitative Poetry and Why Is It Bad?" In *The Cambridge Companion to Plato's "Republic,"* edited by G. R. F. Ferrari, 415–44. Cambridge: Cambridge University Press, 2007.

Munn, Mark. *The School of History: Athens in the Age of Socrates*. Berkeley: University of California Press, 2003.

Naddaff, Ramona. *Exiling the Poets: The Production of Censorship in Plato's "Republic."* Chicago: University of Chicago Press, 2002.

Nails, Debra. "Mouthpiece Schmouthpiece." In *Who Speaks for Plato*, edited by Gerald A. Press, 15–26. Lanham, MD: Rowman and Littlefield, 1999.

———. *The People of Plato: A Prosopography of Plato and Other Socratics*. Indianapolis: Hackett, 2002.

———. "Tragedy Off-Stage." In *Plato's "Symposium": Issues in Interpretation and Reception*, Hellenic Studies Series 22, edited by James Lesher, Debra Nails, and Frisbee Sheffield, 179–207. Washington, DC: Center for Hellenic Studies, 2007.

Narcy, Michel. "Why Was the *Theaetetus* Written by Euclides?" In *The Platonic Art of Philosophy*, edited by George Boys-Stones, Dimitri El Murr, and Christopher Gill, 150–66. New York: Cambridge University Press, 2013.

Nehamas, Alexander. *Only a Promise of Happiness: The Place of Beauty in a World of Art*. Princeton, NJ: Princeton University Press, 2007.

———. "Plato on Imitation and Poetry in *Republic* 10." In *Plato on Beauty, Wisdom, and the Arts*, edited by Julius Moravcsik and Philip Temko, 47–78. Totowa, NJ: Rowman & Littlefield, 1982.

———. *Virtues of Authenticity: Essays on Plato and Socrates*. Princeton, NJ: Princeton University Press, 1999.

Neumann, Harry. "Diotima's Concept of Love." *American Journal of Philology* 86 (1965): 33–59.

Nichols, Mary. "The *Republic*'s Two Alternatives: Philosopher-Kings and Socrates." *Political Theory* 12 (1984): 252–74.

———. *Socrates on Friendship and Community: Reflections on Plato's "Symposium," "Phaedrus," and "Lysis."* Cambridge: Cambridge University Press, 2009.

Nietzsche, Friedrich. *Thus Spoke Zarathustra: A Book for None and All*. Translated by Walter Kaufmann. New York: Penguin Press, 1966.

———. *Twilight of the Idols* and *The Anti-Christ*. Translated by R. J. Hollingdale. New York: Penguin, 1968.

Nightingale, Andrea Wilson. *Genres in Dialogue: Plato and the Construct of Philosophy*. Cambridge: Cambridge University Press, 1995.

———. *Spectacles of Truth in Ancient Greek Philosophy: Theoria in Its Cultural Context*. Cambridge: Cambridge University Press, 2004.
Notomi, Noburu. *The Unity of Plato's "Sophist": Between the Sophist and the Philosopher*. Cambridge: Cambridge University Press, 2007.
Nussbaum, Martha Craven. *The Fragility of Goodness: Luck and Ethics in Greek Tragedy and Philosophy*. Rev. ed. Cambridge: Cambridge University Press, 2001.
Ober, Josiah. *Political Dissent in Democratic Athens: Intellectual Critics of Popular Rule*. Princeton, NJ: Princeton University Press, 1998.
———. "Tyrant Killing as Therapeutic Stasis: A Political Debate in Images and Texts." In *Popular Tyranny: Sovereignty and Its Discontents*, edited by Kathryn A. Morgan, 215–50. Austin: University of Texas Press, 2003.
Ophir, Adi. *Plato's Invisible Cities: Discourse and Power in the "Republic."* New York: Routledge, 1991.
Osborne, Robin, ed. *Debating the Athenian Cultural Revolution: Art, Literature, Philosophy, and Politics, 430–380 BC*. Cambridge: Cambridge University Press, 2007.
Panagia, Davide. *The Political Life of Sensation*. Durham, NC: Duke University Press, 2009.
Parry, Richard D. "The Craft of Justice." In *New Essays on Plato*, edited by Francis Jeffry Pelletier and John King-Farlow, 19–38. Calgary: University of Calgary Press, 1983.
Partenie, Catalin, ed. *Plato's Myths*. Cambridge: Cambridge University Press, 2009.
Pébarthe, Christophe. *Cité, démocratie et écriture: Histoire de l'alphabétisation d'Athènes à l'époque classique*. Paris: De Boccard, 2006.
Penner, Terry. "The Wax Tablet, Logic, and Protagoreanism." In *The Platonic Art of Philosophy*, edited by G. Boys-Stones, D. El-Murr, and Christopher Gill, 186–220. Cambridge: Cambridge University Press, 2013.
Peterson, Sandra. *Socrates and Philosophy in the Dialogues of Plato*. Cambridge: Cambridge University Press, 2011.
Platt, Verity. "Likeness and Likelihood in Classical Greek Art." In *Probabilities, Hypotheticals, and Counterfactuals in Ancient Greek Thought*, edited by Victoria Wohl, 185–207. Cambridge: Cambridge University Press, 2014.
Polansky, Ronald M. *Philosophy and Knowledge: A Commentary on Plato's "Theaetetus."* Lewisburg, PA: Bucknell University Press, 1992.
Popper, Karl R. *The Open Society and Its Enemies*. Vol. 1, *The Spell of Plato*. 1944. Princeton, NJ: Princeton University Press, 2013.
Porter, James. *The Origins of Aesthetic Thought in Ancient Greece: Matter, Sensation, and Experience*. Cambridge: Cambridge University Press, 2016.
Press, Gerald. *Plato: A Guide for the Perplexed*. New York: Continuum, 2007.
———, ed. *Who Speaks for Plato? Studies in Platonic Anonymity*. Lanham, MD: Rowman & Littlefield, 2000.
Puchner, Martin. *The Drama of Ideas: Platonic Provocations in Theater and Philosophy*. Oxford: Oxford University Press, 2010.
Rancière, Jacques. *The Ignorant Schoolmaster: Five Lessons in Intellectual Emancipation*. Translated by Kristin Ross. Stanford, CA: Stanford University Press, 1991.

Recco, Greg. *Athens Victorious: Democracy in Plato's "Republic."* Lanham, MD: Lexington Books, 2007.
Reeve, C. D. C. *Philosopher-Kings: The Argument of Plato's "Republic."* Indianapolis: Hackett, 2006.
———. "Plato on Friendship and Eros." In *The Stanford Encyclopedia of Philosophy*, Summer 2016, edited by Edward N. Zalta. https://plato.stanford.edu/archives/sum2016/entries/plato-friendship/.
———. ed. *Plato on Love: Lysis, Symposium, Phaedrus, Alcibiades, with Selections from Republic, Laws.* Indianapolis: Hackett, 2006.
———. "Telling the Truth about Love: Plato's *Symposium.*" *Proceedings of the Boston Area Colloquium in Ancient Philosophy* 8 (1992): 89–114.
Robb, Kevin. *Literacy and Paideia in Ancient Greece*. Oxford: Oxford University Press, 1994.
Rokem, Freddie. *Philosophers and Thespians: Thinking Performance*. Stanford, CA: Stanford University Press, 2009.
Roochnik, David. *Beautiful City: The Dialectical Character of Plato's "Republic."* Ithaca, NY: Cornell University Press, 2003.
———. "The Political Drama of Plato's *Republic.*" In *The Cambridge Companion to Ancient Greek Political Thought*, edited by Stephen Salkever, 156–77. Cambridge: Cambridge University Press, 2009.
———. "The Political Pessimism of Plato's *Republic.*" *American Dialectic* 2 (2012): 92–116.
Rosen, Stanley. *Plato's "Republic": A Study*. New Haven, CT: Yale University Press, 2005.
———. *Plato's "Symposium."* 2nd ed. New Haven, CT: Yale University Press, 1987.
Rowe, Christopher. *Plato and the Art of Philosophical Writing*. Cambridge: Cambridge University Press, 2007.
Russon, John. "Just Reading: The Nature of the Platonic Text." In *Retracing the Platonic Text*, edited by John Russon and John Sallis, ix-xix. Evanston, IL: Northwestern University Press, 2000.
Rutherford, R. B. "Comments on Nightingale." In *New Perspectives on Plato, Modern and Ancient*, Center for Hellenic Studies Colloquia 6, edited by Julia Annas and Christopher Rowe, 249–62. Washington, DC: Center for Hellenic Studies, 2003.
Satkunanandan, Shalini. *Extraordinary Responsibility: Politics beyond the Moral Calculus*. Cambridge: Cambridge University Press, 2015.
Saxonhouse, Arlene W. "Democracy, Equality, and *Eidê*: A Radical View from Book 8 of Plato's *Republic.*" *American Political Science Review* 92 (1998): 273–83.
———. "Eros and the Female in Greek Political Thought: An Interpretation of Plato's *Symposium.*" *Political Theory* 12 (1984): 5–27.
———. *Fear of Diversity: The Birth of Political Science in Ancient Greek Thought*. Chicago: University of Chicago Press, 1992.
———. *Free Speech and Democracy in Ancient Athens*. Cambridge: Cambridge University Press, 2008.
———. "The Socratic Narrative: A Democratic Reading of Plato's Dialogues." *Political Theory* 37 (2009): 728–53.

Sayre, Kenneth. *Plato's Literary Garden: How to Read a Platonic Dialogue*. Notre Dame: University of Notre Dame Press, 1995.

Schiappa, Edward. *Protagoras and* Logos: *A Study in Greek Philosophy and Rhetoric*. Columbia: University of South Carolina Press, 2003.

Schiller, F. C. S. *Plato or Protagoras? Being a Critical Examination of the Protagoras Speech in the "Theaetetus" with Some Remarks upon Error*. Oxford: Blackwell, 1908.

Schlosser, Joel Alden. Review of *Philosophers in the "Republic": Plato's Two Paradigms*, by Roslyn Weiss. *Bryn Mawr Classical Review*, March 3, 2013. http://bmcr.brynmawr.edu/2013/2013-03-33.html.

———. *What Would Socrates Do? Self-Examination, Civic Engagement, and the Politics of Philosophy*. Cambridge: Cambridge University Press, 2016.

Schoener, Abraham. "Not the Sophist." In *Retracing the Platonic Text*, edited by John Russon and John Sallis, 41–56. Evanston, IL: Northwestern University Press, 2000.

Schofield, Malcolm. "*Fraternité, inégalité, la parole de dieu*: Plato's Authoritarian Myth of Political Legitimation." In *Plato's Myths*, edited by Catalin Partenie, 101–16. Cambridge: Cambridge University Press, 2011.

———. *Plato: Political Philosophy*. Oxford: Oxford University Press, 2006.

———. *Saving the City: Philosopher-Kings and Other Classical Paradigms*. London: Routledge, 1999.

———. "Sharing in the Constitution." *Review of Metaphysics* 49 (1996): 831–58.

Schultz, Peter. "Style and Agency in an Age of Transition." In *Debating the Athenian Cultural Revolution: Art, Literature, Philosophy, and Politics, 430–380 BC*, edited by Robin Osborne, 144–87. Cambridge: Cambridge University Press, 2007.

Sprague, Rosamond Kent. *Plato's Philosopher-King: A Study of the Theoretical Background*. Columbia: University of South Carolina Press, 1976.

Steinberger, Peter. "Who Is Cephalus?" *Political Theory* 24 (1996): 172–99.

Stern, Paul. *Knowledge and Politics in Plato's "Theaetetus."* Cambridge: Cambridge University Press, 2008.

Strauss, Leo. *The City and Man*. Chicago: University of Chicago Press, 1978.

———. *On Plato's "Symposium."* Chicago: University of Chicago Press, 2001.

Svenbro, Jesper. *Phrasikleia: An Anthropology of Reading in Ancient Greece*. Ithaca, NY: Cornell University Press, 1993.

Szlezak, Thomas A. *Reading Plato*. Translated by Graham Zanker. New York: Routledge, 2005.

Tarnopolsky, Christina. "Plato's Politics of Distributing and Disrupting the Sensible." *Theory & Event* 13.4 (2010). muse.jhu.edu/article/407146.

———. *Prudes, Perverts, and Tyrants: Plato's "Gorgias" and the Politics of Shame*. Princeton, NJ: Princeton University Press, 2010.

Tecusan, Manuela. "*Logos Sympotikos*: Patterns of the Irrational in Philosophical Drinking; Plato Outside the *Symposium*." In *Sympotica: A Symposium on the "Symposion,"* edited by Oswyn Murray, 238–60. Oxford: Clarendon Press, 1990.

Tell, Håkan. *Plato's Counterfeit Sophists*. Hellenic Studies Series 44. Washington, DC: Center for Hellenic Studies, 2011.

Thayer, H. S. "Plato's Quarrel with Poetry: Simonides." *Journal of the History of Ideas* 36 (1975): 3–26.

Thomas, Rosalind. "The Origins of Western Literacy: Literacy in Ancient Greece and Rome." In *The Cambridge Handbook of Literacy*, edited by David R. Olson and Nancy Torrance, 346–61. Cambridge: Cambridge University Press 2009.

Trivigno, Franco V. "Childish Nonsense? The Value of Interpretation in Plato's *Protagoras*." *Journal of the History of Philosophy* 51 (2013): 509–43.

Valiquette Moreau, Nina. "Musical Judgment: Aesthetics and Jurisprudence in Plato." Ph.D. diss., McGill University, 2013.

———. "Musical Mimesis and Political Ethos in Plato's *Republic*." *Political Theory* 45 (2017): 192–215.

Vegetti, Mario. "How and Why Did the *Republic* Become Unpolitical?" In *Dialogues on Plato's "Politeia" ("Republic"): Selected Papers from the Ninth Symposium Platonicum*, edited by Noburu Notomi and Luc Brisson, 3–15. Sankt Augustin: Akademia Verlag, 2013.

Villa, Dana. *Socratic Citizenship*. Princeton, NJ: Princeton University Press, 2001.

Vlastos, Gregory. "Slavery in Plato's Thought." In *Platonic Studies*, 147–63. 2nd ed. Princeton, NJ: Princeton University Press, 1981.

Von Reden, Sitta, and Simon Goldhill. "Plato and the Performance of Dialogue." In *Performance Culture and Athenian Democracy*, edited by Simon Goldhill and Robin Osborne, 257–92. Cambridge: Cambridge University Press, 1999.

Wallace, Robert. "Plato, *Poikilia*, and New Music in Athens." In *Poikilia: Variazioni sul tema*, edited by Elisabetta Berardi, Francisco L. Lisa, and D. Micalella, 201–13. Acireale: Bonanno, 2009.

Wallach, John R. *Platonic Political Art: A Study of Critical Reason and Democracy*. University Park: University of Pennsylvania State Press, 2010.

Walton, Jo. *The Just City*. New York: Tor Books, 2015.

Warman, M. S. "Plato and Persuasion." *Greece & Rome*, Second Series, 30 (April 1983): 48–54.

Weiss, Roslyn. *Philosophers in the "Republic": Plato's Two Paradigms*. Ithaca, NY: Cornell University Press, 2012.

———. *The Socratic Paradox and Its Enemies*. Chicago: University of Chicago Press, 2006.

———. "When Winning Is Everything: Socrates' Elenchus and Euthydemian Eristic." In *Plato: Euthydemus, Lysis, Charmides*, edited by Thomas Robinson and Luc Brisson, 68–75. Sankt Augustin: Akademia Verlag, 2000.

———. "Wise Guys and Smart Alecks in *Republic* 1 and 2." In *The Cambridge Companion to Plato's "Republic,"* edited by G. R. F. Ferrari, 90–115. Cambridge: Cambridge University Press, 2007.

West, Elinor J. M. "Plato's Audiences, or How Plato Replies to Fifth-Century Intellectual Mistrust of Letters." In *The Third Way: New Directions in Platonic Studies*, edited by Francisco J. Gonzalez, 41–60. Lanham, MD: Rowman and Littlefield, 1995.

White, James Boyd. *Acts of Hope: Creating Authority in Literature, Law, and Politics*. Chicago: University of Chicago Press, 1995.

White, Stephen A. "Thrasymachus the Diplomat." *Classical Philology* 90 (1995): 307–27.

Whitehead, Alfred North. *Process and Reality*. New York: Free Press, 1979.

Winkler, John J. *The Constraints of Desire: The Anthropology of Sex and Gender in Ancient Greece*. New York: Routledge, 1990.

Wohl, Victoria. *Love among the Ruins: The Erotics of Democracy in Classical Athens*. Princeton, NJ: Princeton University Press, 2002.

Yunis, Harvey. "The Protreptic Rhetoric of the *Republic*." In *The Cambridge Companion to Plato's "Republic,"* edited by G. R. F. Ferrari, 1–26. Cambridge: Cambridge University Press, 2007.

———. *Taming Democracy: Models of Political Rhetoric in Ancient Athens*. Ithaca, NY: Cornell University Press, 1996.

Zilioli, Ugo. "The Wooden Horse: The Cyrenaics in the *Theaetetus*." In *The Platonic Art of Philosophy*, edited by G. Boys-Stones, D. El-Murr, and Christopher Gill, 167–85. Cambridge: Cambridge University Press, 2013.

Zuckert, Catherine. *Plato's Philosophers: The Coherence of the Dialogues*. Chicago: University of Chicago Press, 2009.

INDEX

accountability, 16, 49, 128
acquiescence, 13, 61, 84, 85, 106, 109, 130, 131, 148, 149
actuality, 187, 215, 220
Adam, James, 2n4, 49nn105–6, 83n4, 93n23, 109n48, 176n16, 219n7
advantage, 60, 94, 128, 212, 214, 215, 224; and disadvantage, 92, 95; of the stronger, 8, 60, 73, 112, 214, 221. *See also* justice
aesthetics, 30n41, 37, 38–40. *See also* art
Agathon, 8, 25, 152–55, 157, 159–68
agency, 5, 46n94, 97, 98, 118, 127, 129, 130
aischropolis. *See* Uglytown
aisthēsis. *See* sense perception
Alcibiades, 42, 143, 160–62, 164, 168, 169
Alcibiades I, 167
alienation, of authority, 28, 51, 55–60, 77
Allen, Danielle, 2n3, 4n13, 5nn14–15, 9n25, 15n42, 21n10, 22n13, 30, 45, 50n3, 97n26, 133n57
analogy, 39, 43n83, 53–54, 62n41, 70–71, 99, 108–10, 131–35, 174–81, 188n40, 206–7; between learning to read and coming to know, 4, 6, 10, 173; between soul and city, 75–77, 86, 101, 218–20; between sun and good, 19, 21, 133–35, 172, 181–83, 192, 206–7

anangkē. *See* compulsion; necessity
Annas, Julia, 7n19, 22n11, 28n30, 63n43, 180n22, 181, 182
antidote, 62, 64, 71, 77. *See also pharmakon*
anxiety, 12, 85, 94
Apollodorus, 25, 41, 163–67, 197
Apology, 27, 47, 52, 61n36, 77n72, 100, 120, 112n2, 127, 167, 168
aporia, 16, 43, 126, 162, 166, 167, 176–80, 189, 226; as lacking resources, 104, 167
appearances, 10, 11, 20, 21, 36–47, 62–75, 79, 83, 176–83, 215, 217–21
appetites, 73, 86, 101, 102, 143
Arendt, Hannah, 5n15, 9, 12, 19–22, 25, 40, 49, 191n46, 192n51, 192n54, 221n10, 222n13
Aristodemus, 25, 41, 163–67, 197
Aristophanes, 8, 143, 151, 156n38, 160, 166, 168
Aristotle, 1, 40n74, 103, 123n33, 131, 133n58, 186, 187n35, 208, 224n16
art, xi, 17n49, 26, 30–32, 36–37, 40n74, 44, 63–64, 93, 155n37, 172, 175, 179; and artistry, xi, 18, 30, 39, 45, 67, 73, 150, 178, 209; as *technē*, 2–3, 6, 55–59, 82, 112–13, 124, 131, 133, 175, 179, 200–201, 208. *See also* aesthetics

244 *Index*

artifact, 20, 63, 66–67, 70–71
Athenian visitor, 7, 13n36, 28, 113, 115, 117n23
attention, 3, 4, 6, 18, 39, 43–44, 65–66, 79, 114, 167n63, 182, 202–6, 216, 219, 224
audience, 7, 29, 32n51, 35, 41–48, 51–52, 58, 64, 73, 84–85, 137–39, 158, 185, 202–6, 219. *See also* reading
authoritarian, 5, 20–22, 26, 29, 35
authority, 1–5, 7–9, 11–29, 33–34, 41–49, 51–62, 77, 82, 91–92, 113–14, 128–35, 150, 156–57, 196, 224. See also *exousia*
auxiliaries, 12, 95, 99–100, 105, 118. *See also* warriors

Badiou, Alain, 20n8, 29n34, 65n48
Balot, Ryan, ix, 100n34, 143n11
beautiful, 86, 89, 94, 95, 97, 134, 146, 152–61, 166–69, 179, 181; describing gods, 90; describing justice, 83, 86, 210–23; describing minds, 92, 93; describing philosophical discussions, 128, 134, 135–40, 174, 209; describing Socrates, 42, 163n51
beauty, 9, 11, 19, 38–39, 68, 71, 89–90, 93n24, 97, 134, 136, 138, 141, 152, 154, 161, 167–70, 178, 182. See also *poikilia*
Belfiore, Elizabeth, 51n8, 70n61, 71n63, 155n37, 157n41
belief, 3–5, 19, 22n15, 99–100, 120–23, 127–31, 180–81, 202. *See also* opinion
Berger, Jr., Harry, ix, x, 4n11, 13n36, 20n8, 21n10, 22n12, 22nn14–15, 24, 28n29, 38, 39n71, 40, 53n17, 55n19, 62n40, 85nn7–8, 86n9, 92n20, 99nn31–32, 102n36, 103, 106n41, 108n47, 113n4, 136n65
bia. *See* force; violence
Bickford, Susan, 114n9, 139
Blondell, Ruby, 6n18, 29n34, 35, 41n78, 44n85, 63n45, 98n30, 114n10, 124n34, 125n37, 125n39, 126nn43–44, 149n24
Bloom, Allan, 2n4, 6n18, 31n48, 36n62, 49n105, 69n59, 77n73, 112n2, 118n24, 128n46, 141n2, 142n4, 173n4, 219n7
Boyarin, Daniel, 154

Brann, Eva, 98n30, 184n30, 191
Burnyeat, Myles, 30n35, 47n98, 62nn40–41, 67n55, 118n24, 138n69, 173, 183n28, 188, 190, 197n64, 202, 203n72

calculation, 73, 76, 176–78, 206
calculative rationality, 71–80, 86, 98–109, 117, 144, 191, 206–9, 222, 226
Callicles, 8, 126, 140n72
capacity, 27n23, 43, 44, 48–49, 68, 74, 95, 100, 102, 105, 121, 140, 150, 178, 187–89, 195–96, 202–3, 207, 213, 217, 226; and incapacity, 3, 72, 77, 85, 86, 97. See also *dunamis*; *exousia*; possibility; potentiality
Carson, Anne, 39n72, 55n20, 57n28, 58n31, 62n41, 63n45, 67, 143n9
cave allegory, 19, 20–21, 136, 147, 172, 174, 181n24, 206–7
Cephalus, 50, 52–55, 58, 59, 101, 102, 112, 172
children, 2, 53, 64, 97–98, 106–10
citizens, 5, 7, 14–16, 18, 44–49, 75, 97, 103–5, 115–18, 223–24; and citizenship, 15, 49, 151
city: beautiful, *kallipolis*, 136, 173, 206–9, 222; fevered, 62, 86–87, 93, 141; healthy, ix, 62, 86–87, 222–23; ideal, 11, 12, 18, 19–21, 26, 31, 33, 37–39, 50, 64, 75–77, 81–86, 95–96, 100, 101–10, 118–21, 136–37, 142, 147; in speech, 62, 77, 173, 175, 206–9, 212
coercion. *See* compulsion; force
complexity, 30, 38–43, 68, 93, 94–98, 122, 178–80, 211. *See also* beauty; intricacy; *poikilia*
compulsion, 3, 9, 13, 33–34, 49, 61, 78, 105, 115–20, 125n40, 136, 138, 139, 145, 147–50, 153, 169, 171, 176–80, 203, 207–9. *See also* force; necessity
consequentialism, 82–83, 86, 110, 112, 139, 210–17, 226. *See also* instrumentalism; utilitarianism
constitution, 9, 11, 14–16, 31, 38–39, 75–80, 105–10, 149–50, 171, 206–9, 222–24. *See also* self-constitution

contradiction, 17, 33–36, 41–47, 71–75, 94–98, 137–38, 176–80, 189
contrivance. See *mēchanē*
convention: as law, 60–62; as morality, 57–60, 62, 109–10, 216
Cooper, John, 2n4, 144n14, 155, 156, 165, 198
copy, xi, 17, 34–41, 65–66, 165, 170. *See also* imitation; impersonation; mirror
couch, 62–67
courage, 87, 98–109, 117, 151, 190
Crotty, Kevin, 9n26, 17, 39n73, 44n86, 46n94, 84n6, 89n16, 97n28
curriculum. *See* education

deception, 12, 14, 17–18, 51–52, 63–69, 72–73, 82–86, 88–92, 94–97, 106–8, 113, 118–23, 126–27, 134, 138–40, 158, 182, 200, 205, 211, 212, 220. *See also* imposture; lies; *mēchanē*; misrepresentation
Deleuze, Gilles, 66
democracy, 9, 11, 13–18, 21, 38, 45–49, 93, 128, 139, 169–71; Athenian imperial, 15, 18, 48, 96, 114n11, 142–45, 150–51, 163, 168–71
dēmos, 11, 13–16, 34–35, 47–48, 54, 69–70, 77–79, 83, 86, 101–2, 105, 112, 130, 134–35, 145–46, 150–51, 195, 210–12, 218
desire, 4, 18, 20–21, 46n94, 49, 51, 72–75, 79–80, 82–86, 87–88, 99–102, 110, 140, 141–71, 173, 210–15, 220–21
device. *See mēchanē*
dialectics, 5, 7n19, 18, 71, 109, 172–83, 191, 203, 206–9
dianoia, 62, 68–69, 74–75, 92–95, 177–78, 180, 199
Diogenes Laertius, 5, 60n32
Diotima, 153–71
disidentification, 16–17, 44–48, 79, 137–39
disputation, 17, 126, 197–98
divided line, 19, 23, 51, 68–69, 131, 180–81
doxa. *See* belief; opinion
dunamis, 48–49, 181, 183–89, 192–93, 195–96, 202–3, 207. *See also* capacity; *exousia*; possibility; potentiality

education, 3–14, 22n15, 34–49, 52–55, 64n46, 77–80, 81, 119–21, 175, 224–26; of *Republic* 2–3, 18, 77, 84, 87–110, 117–18, 121–23, 141–42, 147, 169, 204–5; of *Republic* 7, 142, 175–82
eidē. *See* forms; ideas; looking: and looks
eidola. *See* images
Eleatic: monism, 198; visitor, 2, 3, 7, 13n36, 28, 113, 115, 124–25, 132–33
elenchos, 114–15, 123–27, 130–31
elites, Athenian, 14–15, 22n15, 46–48, 52–54, 77
encomium, 83–85, 110, 158, 225
equality, 11, 13, 128
Er, myth of, 6n17, 30n39, 66, 105, 223, 225
eristic. *See* disputation
erōs. *See* desire
Eros, 152–53, 157, 159–63, 171
Euben, Peter, ix, x, 5n16, 9n25, 16n45, 27n24, 49, 52n12, 53n14, 53n16, 55n19, 58n29
Euclides, 196–99
euētheia: as good disposition, 50, 89, 92–98; as simpleminded, 50, 92–98, 105, 109. *See also* simplicity
Euripides, 25, 38n68, 165
Euthyphro, 91, 140n72
Euthyphro, 73
exousia, 48–49, 140
experience, 2–9, 24, 30, 32n51, 46n94, 47, 123, 128, 133, 135, 139, 161, 167–69, 175, 189–92, 202–6, 217–21, 224–26
expertise, 3, 5, 51–52, 77, 155; and expert knowledge, 15, 113–15, 136, 222. *See also* calculative rationality

failure, 12–13, 16–17, 28n29, 34, 46–49, 76, 98, 102–3, 126–27, 131, 137–38, 164–65, 204–5, 207, 220
fallibility, 9–11, 13, 18, 24, 44n86, 198, 207, 216, 224–25; and infallibility, 190–93
falsity, 3–4, 17–18, 62–70, 88–92, 119–20, 158, 196, 199–200, 211–12; and falsifiability, 189–93, 198–99, 209

Farrar, Cynthia, 8n20, 184n31, 190, 194n58, 195
fathers, 19, 21–27, 40n74, 53–60, 107, 152, 159–60, 194, 199–200
Ferrari, G. R. F., 12n33, 13n35, 27n24, 28, 29, 30n39, 30n41, 32n50, 45, 50n3, 63n44, 86n11, 101n35, 114, 115n12, 131n51, 176n17, 222n15
force, 12, 14, 18, 20, 33, 45n94, 58n29, 61, 78, 94, 113n5, 115–31, 137–40, 147–48, 218, 226. *See also* compulsion; necessity; violence
forms, 19–20, 62–69, 156–57, 169–70, 175–79, 226. *See also* ideas
founders, 54, 86, 89–92, 95, 100, 105–6, 118, 147, 206–9. *See also* law: and lawgivers
free and beautiful discussions, 135–40
freedom, 11, 13, 48–49, 115–18, 138–40, 170–71
free speech, 16n45, 140, 161
Freydberg, Bernard, 54, 69n60, 150n25, 180n21

Gadamer, Hans-Georg, 88
Garsten, Bryan, 122
geometry, 39, 176–80, 188
Gerson, Lloyd, 2n3, 16, 17n47
Gill, Mary Louise, 1n2, 30n35, 30n39, 52n11, 183n28, 184n32, 190n44, 203–4
glutton, 169–70
gods, 34–37, 89–92, 130, 203–6
good, 21–22, 38, 44, 73–74, 78–80, 85–86, 89–98, 103–5, 107–9, 127, 151–53, 156–57, 161, 167–69, 179–83, 203–5, 210–17. *See also* analogy: between sun and good
Gorgias, 120, 125n40, 140
Gorgias, 8, 69, 112–15, 120, 125n40, 126, 127, 140
grammar, 3, 22, 122–23, 133. *See also* voice
guardians, 12n33, 86–109, 118, 120–23, 174. *See also* philosophers: philosopher-kings; warriors
Gyges, 49, 65, 66, 83, 112, 211

Halliwell, Stephen, x, 1n2, 26n22, 27, 28, 29n32, 30n39, 30n41, 31n47, 32n50, 32n51, 33n56, 34n57, 34n58, 36n61, 37, 38n69, 41n77, 42n81, 45n94, 47, 50n2, 63n43, 65nn49–50, 67n56, 106n44, 107n45, 147n22, 157n40, 199n70
Halperin, David, 9n25, 22n15, 151n27, 163, 164, 165, 166n60
happiness, 12–13, 92, 107–8, 151–52, 156, 217–20
harm, do no. *See* justice
hearing, 23–24, 45, 135, 137, 174, 190, 192n52, 202. *See also* listening
Heidegger, Martin, 20n8, 28n30, 193–94
helping friends, harming enemies. *See* justice
Heraclitus, 34n57, 183, 184, 193
Hesiod, 50, 76, 79, 89
Hippias, 93n24, 154
Hippias Major, 93n24, 71
Hippias Minor, 42, 52, 57n27, 126n44
Hobbes, Thomas, 1, 26n23, 65
Homer, 25n21, 50–52, 54–55, 57–58, 65, 69–71, 76–77, 89, 183
hubris, 141, 162

idealism, 26n23, 27, 43n83, 61, 215
ideas, 19–21, 26–27n23, 39–40, 67–71, 143–44, 158, 162, 168, 182–83, 202, 206, 208, 216–17, 226
images, 6–13, 17–20, 22–23, 30, 65–69, 70–73, 76, 88, 90–91, 130, 140, 161, 165, 175, 178, 180–81, 199–202, 207, 220, 222
imagination, 18–19, 40–41, 44–45, 51, 68–69, 139–40, 180–81, 217–24
imitation, 3–4, 27–28, 32–33, 35–46, 64–68, 79, 88, 90–92, 95, 138, 163–65, 170, 179–80, 200. *See also* copy; impersonation; mirror
immortality, 154–58, 160, 164, 168
impersonation, 8, 32, 199–200. *See also* copy; imitation; mirror
imposture, 199–202. *See also* deception; lies; misrepresentation
innovation, 30–32, 42, 63
instrumentalism, 27, 71, 83, 86, 151–58, 213–15, 226. *See also* use; utilitarianism
intricacy, 9, 38–40, 68, 93, 178, 199. *See also* beauty; complexity; *poikilia*

Ion, 70, 71
Ion, 52, 65, 68, 70
Iser, Wolfgang, 30nn37–38, 30n41, 45n89, 45n92

judges, 127–31, 133–34, 159–60, 217–21
judgment, 76–77, 87–88, 97–99, 107, 121, 127–29, 136, 173, 177, 180, 183, 190, 202, 216–21, 224–26
justice: as advantage of the stronger, 8, 60, 73, 112, 214, 221; as do no harm, 59, 205, 216, 221–24; as good by itself and for its consequences, 82–86, 210–26; as good for its consequences, 82–83, 210–15; as good in and by itself, 82–86, 109–10, 210–15; as helping friends and harming enemies, 56–60, 110, 112, 215–16; as Justice, 83–86, 109–10, 204, 210–15, 225; as one man:one art, 42, 75, 87, 221–23; as poetic, 210–26; as what is owed, 55–61, 215–17, 221–23

kallipolis, 54, 76, 82, 103, 105, 106n41, 106n43, 108–9, 115–18, 134, 136, 142, 144, 147, 157n40, 169, 170, 173, 191, 208, 209, 212, 213, 222, 223
Kastley, James, 16n44, 69n59, 113n5, 115n14, 137, 139n70, 147n19
Kateb, George, 16n46, 100n34

Lane, Melissa, x, 2n5, 16n46, 89n17, 113n4, 113n6, 116, 117, 132n53, 132n55, 144n15, 207, 208
lanthanō, 83–84, 93–94, 106, 120, 204–5, 220. *See also* deception; *mēchanē*; tyranny
law, 47, 49, 61, 72–75, 81, 84, 89, 90, 95–96, 98–106, 109–10, 112, 115–18, 130, 137, 146–48, 154, 170–71, 179, 207–9; and lawgivers, 7, 69, 179, 207–9; and lawlessness, 25, 109. *See also* founders
Laws, 7, 9nn25–26, 13n36, 41n80, 69, 77n73, 113, 115, 117n23
lies, 85, 88; founding or noble, 64, 76n71, 96, 108, 118–23, 129, 212; true, 65–66, 88,
90–91, 100, 109, 119, 121, 199–200; verbal, 65–66, 88, 90–91, 119, 121, 158, 198–200, 222. *See also* deception; falsity; imposture; *mēchanē*
light, 173–74, 182–83
listening, 111–15, 140, 174, 192n52, 226; and listeners, 70, 127–31, 133–140. *See also* hearing
literacy. *See* reading
Lloyd, G. E. R., 131n51, 132, 133
logistikon. *See* calculative rationality
logos, 21–26, 28, 33, 71–75, 123–31, 135–38, 172–76, 189–92, 196–209
Long, A. A., 72
looking, 6–9, 10–11, 24, 29–30, 40, 43–44, 178–79, 219–20; and looks, 62–69, 79, 182–83, 206–7. *See also* seeing; spectators
love. *See* desire
love, ladder of, 153–63, 167–70
lovers, 160–61, 168–69, 171; of money, 146–49; of poetry, 34, 79–80; of sights and sounds, 10–11, 129–30, 172–74, 220–21; of wisdom, 10–11, 145, 159, 172–74, 220–21. See also *paiderastia*
Ludwig, Paul, 143

Mara, Gerald, x, 5n16, 9n27, 16n45, 49n106, 60n34, 108n47, 140n73, 198, 224n17
Markell, Patchen, x, 169n65
mastery, 3–4, 69–70, 96–97, 100–103, 105, 109, 128, 141–42, 147, 156–58, 170–71
measurement, 72–74, 192–96, 199–200, 206, 214, 216–17
mēchanē, 63–69, 73, 85, 88, 91, 100, 107–8, 119–23, 134, 154–58, 165, 182
Meno, 14n38, 42, 57, 102n36
metals, myth of. *See* lies: founding or noble
midwifery, 162–63, 183, 199–202, 224
Miller, Paul Allen, x, 162
mimēsis, xi, 17–18, 25–27, 32–47, 62–78, 88–89, 105, 149–50, 164–66, 226; and mimetic knowledge, 79–80, 95, 150–51, 178, 217, 220–21; and mimetic pedagogy, 35–47

mirror, 12-13, 34-37, 41, 64, 68, 85, 95, 109, 141, 149, 155. *See also* copy; imitation
misrepresentation, 90-92. *See also* deception; imposture; lies; *mēchanē*
moderation, 87, 98-99, 100-104, 117, 213-14
money, 53-54, 101-2, 216. *See also* wealth
Monoson, S. Sara, 5n16, 9n27, 10n29, 16n45, 29n34, 151n27, 219
mothers, 25-26, 159-60, 165-66
motion, 23-24, 42-44, 183-92, 198-99
Munn, Mark, 143
music, 31, 77, 84, 174-75, 179-80

Naddaff, Ramona, 32n52, 41n80, 55n21, 56n22, 62n41, 63, 71n63, 74, 75n69, 90n19, 97n27
Nails, Debra, 8, 27n27, 61n37, 162, 165n58, 198n67
narration, 7-8, 27-33, 84, 196-99
necessity, 49, 78, 106, 147, 152-53, 159-60, 169-71, 194. *See also* compulsion; force
need. *See* Penia
negation, 16-18, 153, 159
Nehamas, Alexander, 23n16, 31n47, 63n43
Nichols, Mary, 84n6, 152, 160n44, 176n17
Nightingale, Andrea, 8n23, 10n29, 11n31, 34n57, 51n5, 113n3, 113n7, 114n8
nous, 19-20, 68, 172
nuptial number, 76-77
Nussbaum, Martha, 8n23, 50n3, 143n9, 144n16, 161n46, 165n58

obedience, 23-24, 73-74, 98-105, 122-23, 126-27, 129-31
one man:one art. *See* justice
Ophir, Adi, 24n18, 29n32, 181n23, 208n83
opinion, 2-3, 9-11, 20, 24-25, 51, 56, 72-75, 83, 99, 102, 109, 132-33, 178, 183, 189-94, 202, 206-9, 217, 224-26. *See also* belief
order, 100-105, 117-18, 191, 207-9; and orderliness, 101-3, 146, 149
original, 41, 66, 160, 163-66, 170, 180, 195
overreaching, 15, 18, 87, 141, 142-44, 167-71, 225

paideia. *See* education
paiderastia, 151-52, 160, 168
painting, 22, 30-31, 62-69, 92-93, 208
Parmenides, 8, 183, 184, 198, 203
Parmenides, 30n39
partiality, 9, 40, 66-68, 79, 173, 179, 202, 216-17, 221, 224
passion, 141, 144-50, 162. *See also* desire
passivity, 22, 24, 99
pedagogy. *See* education
Peloponnesian War, 8, 15, 31, 47, 143
Penia, 153, 159, 160, 162, 166, 171
people, the. *See dēmos*
perception. *See* sense perception
perspective, 30-31, 66-69, 79, 201-2, 218-20
persuasion, 18, 21, 48, 111-40, 157-58; distinguished from compulsion, 115-18; distinguished from deception, 118-21; middle voice, 122-23, 127-31; and obedience, 122-23
Phaedo, 44n86, 86n9, 173n6, 206, 207
Phaedrus, 22, 23, 25, 26, 151, 152, 154, 155, 158, 159, 165
Phaedrus, 8, 17, 22-26, 28, 30n39, 33n53, 42, 45, 47, 50, 52, 54, 57, 62n38, 113-14, 145n17, 153, 167, 168, 173, 177n18, 195, 196
pharmakon, 23, 26, 62, 64, 107, 225
philosophers: erotic, 145-51, 166-71; philosopher-kings, 5, 11-13, 19-26, 31n48, 53-54, 76-77, 129-30, 134, 136-37, 141-51, 153, 169-71, 191, 203-5; by nature, 145-51, 171
phronēsis, 15, 68-69, 120, 159, 175, 202-6, 217-20. *See also* wisdom
Platonism, 20n8
Platt, Verity, x, xi, 31, 44n84
play, 6-9, 51, 70, 139-40, 149-50, 179-80
pleonexia. *See* overreaching
poetry: benefit of, 75-80; censorship of, 18, 33-35, 38, 42n83, 50, 62, 73, 75, 81-82, 89-98, 107, 110, 179; and exceptions to censorship, 34-36, 78; use of, 69-71, 78

poetry, mimetic, 32–42, 50–56, 62–82, 88, 93, 137–39, 149–50, 164–66, 198–99, 207–9, 226; of Plato, 17–18, 26–27, 31–33, 45; quarrel with philosophy, 26, 33–34, 50–51. See also *mimēsis*

poiēsis, 26–27, 45

poikilia, 9, 35, 38–44, 68, 73–74, 91–95, 178–80, 211. *See also* beautiful; complexity; intricacy; vexed

Polemarchus, 50, 52, 54–61, 105, 110–12, 114, 124, 126, 127, 139, 172, 174, 214–17, 225

politeia. *See* constitution

political philosophy, 10–11, 26–27, 175–77, 203–9, 224–26

Poros, 153, 159, 160, 161, 162, 171

Porter, James, 31nn43–44, 40n74, 92n20, 191

possession, 142–43, 151–56, 159–63, 167–71, 216–17. *See also* self-possession

possibility, 17, 26–27n23, 44, 79, 188–89. *See also* capacity; *dunamis*; *exousia*; potentiality

potentiality, 186–87. *See also* capacity; *dunamis*; *exousia*; possibility

pregnancy, 162–63, 183

Press, Gerald, 21n10, 28n27, 29nn33–34, 31n47, 32

Protagoras, 3, 8, 51n7, 51n9, 52, 56, 102n36, 126, 140n72, 183–85, 187, 189, 190, 192–96, 199–201

Protagoras, 2, 3, 4n9, 22, 24, 52, 56, 79, 102n36, 114n9, 115n15, 154

provocatives, 43, 176–83, 189

pseudos. *See* deception; imposture; lies; *mēchanē*; misrepresentation

puzzle. See *aporia*

Rancière, Jacques, 3, 4, 20n8, 45n88

reading, 9, 18, 21–27, 198–99, 219–20; dramatically, 29–30; learning to, 1–8, 15–16, 24, 46–48, 95, 132–33, 173, 202–3, 224; negatively, 16–17; poetically, 30–33, 41–49, 137–39. *See also* audience

Reeve, C. D. C., 2n4, 49n105, 126n44, 166n62, 170, 172n2, 175nn12–13, 177n18, 180n22

representation, xi, 17–18, 32–48, 61–62, 64–71, 76–82, 88, 91–92, 137–40, 164–66, 177–78, 195, 198–200, 219–20. *See also* misrepresentation

reproduction, 106–9, 159–64; and self-reproduction, 163, 167–68

resistance, 14–18, 41–49, 100, 117–18, 127, 130, 137–40, 221

resourcefulness, 113, 153, 154, 159, 160–63, 166, 167, 171, 225. *See also* Poros

rhetoric, 112–15, 140

Robb, Kevin, 22n15, 47n97, 51, 65n49, 70n62, 96n25

Rokem, Freddie, 165

Roochnik, David, 6n18, 106n42, 222n14

Rosen, Stanley, 15n42, 50n3, 113n5, 142n5, 151, 153, 155n37, 159n42, 160n43, 162, 166n62

Rowe, Christopher, 7n19, 21n10, 48n103, 113n4, 137

Satkunanandan, Shalini, x, 73n65, 221n11

Saxonhouse, Arlene, x, 5n16, 11n30, 16n45, 27n24, 39n71, 42n81–83, 90n18, 106, 140n72, 142n6, 147n22, 157n40

Schiappa, Edward, 51n9, 194

Schlosser, Joel, x, 3n7, 5n16, 14n38, 16n45, 41n79, 146n18

Schofield, Malcolm, 15, 28n28, 41n80, 48n104, 98n30, 118n24, 121n27, 176n14

seeing, 3–4, 6, 10–11, 14, 18, 23–24, 35–45, 64–69, 94–95, 109, 111–12, 130, 133–35, 137–39, 172–74, 177–90, 192–93, 203–5, 207, 210, 217–21, 225. *See also* looking; spectators

self-authorization, 5, 26–27, 41–49, 81, 138–39, 224. *See also* self-constitution; self-governance

self-constitution, 45, 150, 222–24. *See also* self-authorization; self-governance

self-governance, 5, 9, 11, 14–15, 18, 26–27, 224–26

self-knowledge, 18, 57–58, 167–68, 170, 205–6

self-possession, 45–46n94, 170–71

sense perception, 6, 18, 21, 24, 39–40, 43, 93–95, 134–35, 139–40, 172–96, 199–209
Shorey, Paul, 2n4, 49n105, 55n21, 70n61, 119, 136, 173n4, 214
Simonides, 8, 39n72, 50, 52, 55–60, 67, 70, 79, 215, 216
simplicity, 28, 38–39, 84–86, 89–93, 95–96, 101, 105, 110, 176–77, 179, 213; of mind, 92–98
sophia, 15, 31–32, 98, 205–6. *See also* wisdom
Sophist, x, 2, 3, 4n10, 7, 9n26, 13n36, 17, 22, 24, 51, 113, 124, 125nn41–42, 133
sophists, 7–8, 51–52, 62–63, 69–70, 84–85, 136, 145–46, 154
Sophocles, 50, 101
soul writing, 5, 21–25
spectacle, 139–40, 208, 218–21. *See also* theater
spectators, 8–11, 39, 220. *See also* looking; seeing
speech: oral, 1–2, 22–25; written, 8–9, 21–33, 47, 196–99
stars, 38–41, 68, 92–93, 178–79
Statesman, 2, 3, 4, 7, 9n26, 13n36, 22, 24, 113, 115, 132, 133, 191
Stern, Paul, 6n18, 133n61, 183n28, 188, 189, 206n78
Strauss, Leo, 9n25, 29n34, 118n24, 153
sun, 206–7. *See also* analogy: between sun and good
sun-good analogy. *See* analogy: between sun and good
Svenbro, Jesper, 2n3, 21n10, 29, 30n35, 45n90, 47n98, 219
Symposium, 1, 7, 8, 9, 13n36, 17, 18, 25–27, 41, 42, 85, 141, 142n6, 143, 145n17, 150–51, 156n38, 157–58, 160, 162–70, 195, 197, 213, 217

taming, 78, 100–101, 148
Tarnopolsky, Christina, x, 5n16, 85n8, 114n11, 115, 124n34, 125n37, 125n40, 131n51, 173n7, 174n10
technē. *See* art
Thamus, 23–26

Theaetetus, 4, 6, 124, 133, 177, 178n19, 180, 183–85, 188–90, 194, 196, 197, 199, 201–3
Theaetetus, 2, 4–6, 8, 9, 17, 18, 24, 27, 28, 34, 47, 48, 51n7, 51n9, 87n13, 133, 138n69, 156, 162, 177–80, 183, 184, 187–89, 191, 193n57, 195, 196, 198, 200–203, 205–7, 217
theater, 1, 8–9, 13, 16, 26, 29–30, 39, 46–47, 64n47, 77–78, 166, 198, 218–20. *See also* spectacle
theōros. *See* spectators
Theuth, 23–26, 45, 54
Thrasymachus, 44n84, 48, 60–62, 71, 73, 81–84, 86, 92–94, 105, 110, 112, 124–29, 131, 137, 139, 148, 169, 211–14, 223–25
touch, 192–93
transmission, 22, 52–54
tyranny, 11–15, 20, 25, 49, 61–62, 77–78, 83–84, 94–95, 104–6, 108–9, 117–18, 141–44, 148–50, 168–71, 205, 211, 217–20, 225–26

ugly, 89, 94–95, 97, 134, 154–59, 168
Uglytown, 38, 39n71, 105–9, 136–37, 206–9
unity, 17, 31–32, 45n94, 96, 107–8, 159–60, 168, 173, 176–77, 180, 188–89, 193–94, 198, 203–4, 207, 226
use, 54, 187–88, 225; of *erōs*, 151–57; of justice, 214–17; of poetry, 69–71, 78; and uselessness, 69–70, 79–80, 130, 145–47, 171, 214–17; and utility, 26–27, 70–71
utilitarianism, 78–79, 83, 213–15

verisimilitude. *See* copy; imitation; mirror
Vernant, Jean-Pierre, 39
vexed, 35–36, 42–47, 91, 210–11. *See also poikilia*
violence, 67–68, 89, 125. *See also* compulsion; force
Vlastos, Gregory, 116
voice, 24–25, 27–29, 56–60, 76, 84, 113–14, 125, 174; active, 122–23, 124–25, 127–31, 157–59; middle, 115, 122–23, 127–31, 133–35, 157–59, 191; passive, 122–23, 125–26, 127–31, 157–59

war, 69–71, 86–87, 107, 151, 225–26; as civil war, 76–77. *See also* Peloponnesian War
warriors, 86–109, 121
wealth, 53–54, 103, 159–60. *See also* money
Weiss, Roslyn, 60n33, 61n35, 85n8, 105, 125n37, 136n64, 146n18, 147, 148, 176n17, 216n5
White, James Boyd, 49, 122, 124
White, Stephen, 8n21, 61
wind-egg, 189, 199–202, 224
wisdom, 10–11, 15, 18, 23–27, 51–52, 87–88, 167–71, 202–6, 220–21. See also *phronēsis*, *sophia*
wizardry, 63

wonder, 1, 12–13, 16, 33–34, 40–44, 72–73, 87–88, 94–95, 106–7, 137–38, 156–61, 166–67, 176–77, 197–98, 211–12
work: by-work, 135, 138; of calculative rationality, 71–72; of *erōs*, 161–64, 166–69; of philosophy, 6–7, 34, 37, 150, 212–13, 216, 225–26; workmate, 158, 161–63
writing, 8–9, 21–33, 42–47, 54, 194–99. *See also* soul writing

Yunis, Harvey, 15n42, 48n103, 113n7, 116, 136n66

Zuckert, Catherine, 6n18, 31n48, 124, 142n7, 144n15, 167, 168n64, 178n19, 197n65, 198n67

www.ingramcontent.com/pod-product-compliance
Lightning Source LLC
Chambersburg PA
CBHW021940290426
44108CB00012B/912